THE JOURNEY FROM MUSIC STUDENT TO TEACHER

The Journey from Music Student to Teacher: A Professional Approach helps prospective music educators begin their transition from music student to professional music teacher. This textbook acknowledges that students must first recognize personal perspectives through which they understand the profession, and uncover their assumptions concerning learning and teaching. Only then can they make mindful informed decisions about their professional education. The text uniquely works to build upon the individual's personal experience to enhance their approach to the profession.

The topics and activities are deliberately organized to help the reader think as a professional rather than a student. Divided into three parts: (a) discovery of self, (b) discovery of teaching, and (c) discovery of learners; the three parts address the primary stages of teacher development. Within each part, readers are connected to the theoretical foundations of the text and the process of becoming an insider to the profession.

The Journey from Music Student to Teacher: A Professional Approach incorporates online resources and tools that are already familiar to students in their world of networking through social media

Features include:

- social networking activities to aid self-reflection and discussion

- 'Connecting to the Profession' sections that provide resources which help to bridge the gap between theory and practice

- glossary terms to provide a solid base in professional terminology

- an integrated companion website, including videos of teaching practice and further activities for self-reflection, plus instructor material.

"I like this better than anything else I have used."
—Dr. Diana M. Hollinger, San José State University

Michael A. Raiber is Professor of Music Education at Oklahoma City University.

David J. Teachout is Associate Professor and Department Head of Music Education at the University of North Carolina at Greensboro.

THE JOURNEY FROM MUSIC STUDENT TO TEACHER

A PROFESSIONAL APPROACH

Michael Raiber and David Teachout

Routledge
Taylor & Francis Group

NEW YORK AND LONDON

First published 2014
by Routledge
711 Third Avenue, New York, NY 10017

and by Routledge
2 Park Square, Milton Park, Abingdon, Oxon OX14 4RN

Routledge is an imprint of the Taylor & Francis Group, an informa business

Library of Congress Cataloging-in-Publication Data

Raiber, Michael.
The journey from music student to teacher: a professional approach / Michael Raiber and David Teachout.
       pages cm
    1. Music teachers—Training of.   2. Music—Instruction and study.   I. Teachout, David.   II. Title.
MT1.R23   2013
780.71—dc23
2013013858

ISBN: 978-0-415-80684-8 (hbk)
ISBN: 978-0-415-80685-5 (pbk)
ISBN: 978-1-315-88519-3 (ebk)

Typeset in Mixage
by Apex CoVantage, LLC

CONTENTS

TABLES, FIGURES, AND CLASS ACTIVITIES

TABLES

FIGURES

CLASS ACTIVITIES

PREFACE–BEGINNING YOUR JOURNEY

After more than 25 combined years of successful teaching in secondary music classrooms, we were attracted to music teacher education at similar points and times in our careers. As we began to work with preservice music teachers, it became evident that the initial introduction to music teaching is a crucial time in a music educator's professional development. Music education majors do not enjoy the same benefits as do students in other professional programs or degrees. For example, an engineering major will likely have occasions to apprentice within a new environment such as an engineering firm. During this time in a new professional environment, he or she will have the opportunity to take on a new role as a professional engineer and begin to think, act, and even look in ways that the role requires. The newness allows the individual to 'move forward' as a professional. Music educators, on the other hand, reenter environments that are very similar to those where they were once students. Without the reinforcement that a new professional environment provides, preservice music teachers must have other opportunities to help them consider how to think, act, and look like professional music educators if they are to make a successful transition into the field. For this reason, we have decided to write *The Journey from Music Student to Teacher: A Professional Approach* providing a framework for establishing professional role identity among preservice music educators during their introduction to the field. This book is intended for the Foundations in Education, or Introduction to Music Education course, required of most students as they start their undergraduate study in music education. It is intended for the student, and our communication now turns to YOU, the student on the journey, along with your coach, your teacher.

BEGINNING THE JOURNEY

As the title of this text indicates, you are about to embark on a journey, a professional excursion to help you evolve from your role as a music student to your role as a music teacher. Since grade school and throughout your schooling, you have learned to operate successfully as a *student*. This process has likely become so ingrained that you are not consciously aware of its occurrence (Froehlich, 2007). However, each of you has taken part in defining your role as a music student. No two individuals have developed an identical definition because each of you brings a unique background that has influenced your identity as a student. Nonetheless, there are many commonalities among your experiences and these shared understandings have served to 'socialize' you to the expectations of your student roles (Kelly, 2009). As the socialization process unfolded, you acquired a personal identity as a student and learned the norms, values, behaviors, and social skills appropriate to the social position your student role held within each environment you were in, including the music room or rehearsal hall. Looking forward, *The Journey from Music Student to Teacher: A Professional Approach* will help as you engage this same process while defining your *teacher* role.

We have chosen to start from your understanding as a music student because novice teachers often use this perspective as the lens through which to view their roles as music teachers (Froehlich, 2007). As you began to contemplate becoming a music teacher, you likely started to explore what it would be like. You looked to music teachers in your life to help you. You observed what they were doing and talked to them to get advice and gain their perspective as a music teacher. While this is an admirable process, it is important to remember that your understanding of the music teacher role is as an observer of the role. In sociological terms, you are an 'outsider.' You have likely had other experiences where you observed phenomena from the outside and developed expectations of what it must be like on the inside only to find as an 'insider' that your initial perspectives were not entirely accurate. *The Journey from Music Student to Teacher: A Professional Approach* will help you begin to define your unique teacher role(s) from the inside perspectives of professional music educators.

ORGANIZING THE JOURNEY

We organize the text into three parts. In Part I we address self concerns. At this stage, teachers' primary thoughts are about their abilities to do what is asked of them. There may be moments of role conflict during this stage as teachers negotiate their preconceived ideas about teaching music with the reality of the actual process. To help resolve these conflicts, teachers should critically examine their initial ideas about music teaching. So, in Chapter 1 we help you investigate your various concepts of the music teacher role. In Chapter 2, we explore your beliefs about how music should be taught and learned. We close Part I in Chapter 3 by helping you develop an informed understanding of what you may need to know and be able to do as a professional music educator.

As teachers begin to alleviate their self concerns, primary thoughts move from themselves to *teaching concerns,* which is the focus of Part II. At this level, developing music teachers become concerned with questions about designing and delivering instruction. To address these concerns, in Chapter 4 we investigate the various ways music has been taught in the past, how it is being taught currently, and how it may be taught differently in the future. In Chapter 5, we address the responsibilities of music teachers to deliver engaging and motivating instruction and help you take a personal inventory of the tools you have or need to develop as you meet these responsibilities. Chapter 6 addresses concerns about designing instruction as you investigate the various ways that music teachers develop everything from individual lesson plans to an entire curriculum. This part concludes in Chapter 7 with a brief investigation of several established methods and approaches for teaching music. You will have the opportunity to compare the foundations of these approaches and use this information to help you address your current and future teaching concerns.

Part III explores the third stage of teacher development, which is marked by teachers moving beyond a primary concern for one's self or for the teaching task, and becoming most aware of the impact they have on *student learning*. Chapter 8 focuses on student diversity and the role music teachers play in facilitating effective learning among all their students. Addressing concerns about what music students should learn, Chapter 9 provides a framework for your investigation of this important issue. Perhaps one of the fastest-growing bodies of research is in human learning. Chapter 10 presents an overview of this research in the context of music learning. Part III closes with Chapter 11 addressing concerns about how you might measure what and if your students are or are not learning.

There are two important issues to consider as you work your way through this text. First, even though the teacher-concerns model appears to be a linear hierarchical process, it is also a dynamic process. This means there is often no clear delineation between stages and there can be times when a mixture of concerns are driving teacher thinking. Additionally, it is not uncommon for teachers in new contexts or environments to revert to self concerns or teaching concerns even if they had progressed to student-learning concerns in more familiar environments. Second, we do not want to give the impression that you will make the journey from music student to music teacher in the time it takes to finish this course or this text. The information in this text is intended to help you start this journey. Many highly effective music teachers consider themselves to still be on their journeys even after many years of successful music teaching. We believe your journey will last as long as you are passionate about being the most effective music teacher you can become. It can last a lifetime. So, while the destination may be elusive, the trip alone is worth the efforts you will make along the way. Enjoy!

FEATURES

Each chapter includes special features to help you along your journey.

- **Sidebars**—These contain questions for you to consider at certain points throughout the text. Each is correlated with a specific activity that is listed at the end of each chapter. Engagement in these activities is optional, but we believe they can help increase understanding of key concepts in the text.

- **Discussion Boards**—These are suggested topics for use on a class discussion board. Many colleges and universities use course management software that contains this feature. These discussions will allow you to share your ideas, thoughts, and opinions with others in a different forum from in-class discussions. For those who like more time to think about their responses, you will have a place for your voice to be heard.

- **Blog on**—These are prompts for use in your personal teaching blog or journal. These prompts allow you to take time and reflect on your personal perspectives as you consider the issues being discussed in the text and in your course.

- **144 Social Place**—These are prompts that can be used with social media that limits the number of characters (144) you can use to express your ideas. As many of you communicate with others in this manner on a regular basis, we have chosen to use this form of communication to help you address key points in the text.

- **Individual Activities**—These are instructions for activities that we believe to enhance your understandings of more complex concepts in the text. They are optional and can be assigned at the discretion of your instructor. Artifacts developed from these activities are referred to in parts of the text.

- **Connecting to the Profession**—At the end of each part of the text you will find additional resources for you to use while further investigating certain concepts presented throughout the chapters in the part. You will find connections to additional research, professional journals, web resources, and materials to use during classroom observations.

COMPANION WEBSITE

The companion website **www.routledge.com/cw/raiber** contains several features. There are two sides to the site. The open side contains features for both class members and instructors to use. These include:

- videos of K-12 music teaching episodes that can be used during class for group observations or outside of class for individual observations

- videos of teacher being interviewed about their perspectives of the concepts we address in the text

- videos of other preservice teachers talking about their experiences with the concepts discussed in the text

- a brief section on the responsibilities and ethics required of preservice teachers who choose to enter K-12 classrooms for observations.

- links to a number of music education organization websites

- annotated web links to on-line resources.

The closed side of the site is intended for course instructors only and requires a password for access. Instructors can obtain a password by following instructions on the website to contact our sales office. Features on this side of the site include:

- An overview of the theoretical foundations pertaining to social role development theory on which the text is founded.

- Instructor insights for each chapter of the book further explaining the intent of activities and their connections to the content of the text.

- The link to an instructor forum where instructors who are using this text can post questions or share ideas they have developed. The authors will take part in this forum to help clarify concepts and gain additional perspectives on the material.

- PowerPoint® slides that the authors have used in teaching the content of this text to university classes.

- Sample forms for observations.

ACKNOWLEDGMENTS

We begin by thanking a mentor who inspired both of us to become music teacher educators. Dr. Stephen Paul was a faculty member at the University of Oklahoma School of Music during the time we were both teaching in public schools within the state. Steve's calm and engaging demeanor was what first attracted anyone to listen to his ideas. However, in a very short time, his passion for helping young teachers to become empowered music educators became evident. This book started in Steve's hands and was initially his dream. The foundations upon which this book is built were conveyed during many hours of exhilarating conversation with Steve, often involving a "Coke and a cookie." Unfortunately, Steve left this world much too quickly and we both lost a dear friend and mentor. It is in his spirit and, we hope, with his posthumous approval that this book has been completed. We have endeavored to hold true to the ideals that Steve professed so eloquently. It has been a labor of love to honor one of the great thinkers in music teacher education.

We would also like to thank all the music teachers that have allowed us in their classrooms with video equipment. Cristi Miller opened her classroom at Ralph Downs Elementary School in Oklahoma City for an entire semester and taught constantly with two cameras running in her room. Tony Gonzales and Brenda Wagner from Norman North High School in Norman, Oklahoma, Marty Ortega from Brink Jr. High School in Moore, Oklahoma, and Sandy Knudson and Bev Anyon from Adams Elementary School in Norman, Oklahoma have all allowed us to video a day in their classroom while students from the University of Oklahoma were visiting. Their willingness to invest in young music teachers and to 'put it on the line' for all to see is most appreciated.

On a personal note, I (Mike) would like to thank my colleagues at both Oklahoma State University and Oklahoma University for their guidance and patience as I continued to work on this book. I also need to thank the many students at both universities who have read various versions of the materials within this book and provided their insights and suggestions. In addition, the members of the Society for Music Teacher Education (SMTE) Executive Committee have been a great help with ideas and challenges. In particular, Susan Conkling and Doug Orzolek have been good friends who have provided great insight to understanding music teacher development. David, my co-author, has been an inspiration to me since I first met him while he was teaching a brass sectional in my band room in Broken Arrow, Oklahoma. Watching him teach, I knew very quickly what quality he brought to the profession and that we shared many similar ideas. Finally, I want to thank my family. My daughters Erin and Olivia have supported my work even when it meant missing something in their lives, and my wife Lisa, also an educator, who has supported my work throughout this process and challenged me to keep thinking about what is best for young music teachers.

On a similar personal note, I (David) would like to thank first my students and colleagues from my public school teaching career at Highland East Junior High in Moore, Oklahoma. They all shared lessons about teaching and learning that continue to serve me well. Likewise, the students I have encountered during my time in higher education have helped to substantiate many of the ideas presented in this text. Having served on the SMTE Executive Committee in one capacity or another since 2000, I feel privileged to witness the great ideas being developed in music teacher education. This is particularly true of the work in music teacher socialization, which is at the heart of this text. I am grateful to have Michael as a coauthor, and more importantly as a friend and confidant. His calm, caring, but always honest way of moving through life continues to be an inspiration. Most importantly, I thank my wife Ginny and our children, Sophie, Ben, and Ella, for their love, support, and understanding throughout this project.

Michael Raiber and David Teachout

May 2013

VISUAL TOUR: A GUIDE TO THE FEATURES IN *THE JOURNEY FROM MUSIC STUDENT TO TEACHER*

'SIDEBARS'

In the margins of the text you will find these boxes with questions and points to consider.

> **1.1 TEACHING AND LEARNING**
>
> 1. Are you a teacher? Why or why not?
>
> 2. What does it mean to teach?
>
> 3. What does it mean to learn?
>
> 4. Are there differences between a teacher and a professional educator? If so, what are they? (see Class Activity 1.1, p. 20)

These boxes contain questions that explore specific ideas in the text. There are class activities associated with each of these boxes, which can be found at the end of the chapter. These associated activities are intended to enhance your understanding of the concepts or ideas that are presented in the text at that time. The activities may be explored during class time or, in some cases be completed on your own time.

'DISCUSSION BOARD'

DISCUSSION BOARD
My Most Influential Teacher

Log on to the class discussion board and post your response to the following: *Without using names, please describe your favorite teacher. What made this teacher special? What traits did this teacher exemplify that made him/her stand out from others? What impact did this teacher have on your schooling and life in general?* Feel free to read the responses of your colleagues and add your comments to their responses.

These activities encourage you and your colleagues to participate in an on-line discussion and/or debate about an issue presented in the text, creating a collaborative atmosphere for your learning.

'144 SOCIAL PLACE'

144 SOCIAL PLACE . . .
How Do You Learn Best?

As you think back over your formal schooling, were there any times that learning was particularly meaningful to you? When was a time you learned something that you did not know previously, and this new information has stuck with you ever since? Is there a particular event or moment in your life when you really learned something well? In 144 characters or fewer, describe one of those times and why you believe it was particularly meaningful.

Inspired by social networking, these activities encourage you to share ideas with your classmates in 144 characters or fewer, keeping it quick, clear and concise.

'BLOG ON'

BLOG ON . . .
Teacher Introduction

Take turns in class getting up in front and announcing the following:

Hello class, my name is Mr. or Ms. [use your last name] and I will be your teacher today. I look forward to helping you learn more about [choose any topic you wish].

As a method of self-reflection, the authors encourage you to keep a blog or journal as you work your way through your journey to becoming a music teacher. The 'Blog on' activities are intended to stimulate this development by prompting ideas for entries throughout the text.

'INDIVIDUAL ACTIVITIES'

INDIVIDUAL ACTIVITY
Develop Your Own Metaphor

Create your own school metaphor. Write a short paper (1-2 pages) describing your metaphor. Try to think of how the metaphorical characters that exist in these images equate or relate to various parts of the schooling process (e.g. administration, teachers, students, curriculum, etc.). You might begin with listing the characters in the metaphorical image like those in the two examples above (factory and museum). Assign each of these characters to roles within the school: teachers, students, administrators, librarians, etc.

These activities build upon theories within certain chapters to enhance your understanding of issues that can affect or become part of your teaching

'CONNECTING TO THE PROFESSION'

Where you see this icon:

Resources relating to that portion of text can be found at the end of each 'part' of the book in the 'Connecting to the Profession' section.

These resources include glossary terms, suggested research articles, journal articles, web resources and materials for classroom observations. For further individual study or to enhance your classroom discussions, these resources connect theories in the text to the practice of the classroom.

Where you see this icon next to the 'Connecting to the Classroom' section:

Here materials are described and can be found on the student resources section of the companion website **www.routledge.com/cw/raiber**.

Contemporary videos of k-12 music teaching episodes and teachers being interviewed, are hosted on the site, as well as a brief message about responsibilities and ethics associated with visiting k-12 classrooms for observation and field teaching. Annotated web links to on-line researches are included.

Introduction—Drawing Your First Map

As with most any journey, a map might prove helpful. Because we believe that each of you will be on similar but essentially different journeys, we cannot simply provide you with a common map. You will be exploring new territories and, like other explorers, will need to develop your own map as you travel. How can you begin to develop your map for this journey? One answer may be in developing a *concept map*. Daugherty, Custer, and Dixon (2012) state, "Concept maps demonstrate how people visualize relationships between various concepts. . . . a concept map is a graphical node–arc representation of concepts and their relationships with each other" (p. 10). Concept maps are often organized around a topic or theme generated by a central question. As an example, we pose the question, "What should all musicians know and be able to do with music?" Themes or concepts associated with the topic are presented in *nodes* on the map. Note in Figure P.1 there is a central node labeled *musician* and then four

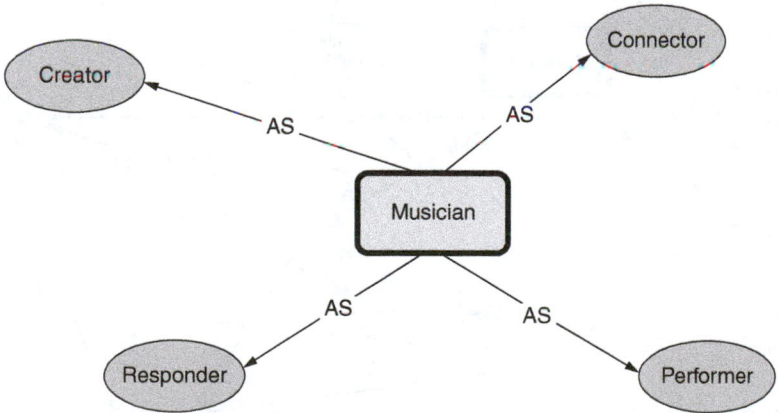

FIGURE P.1 Central topic and four nodes with linking lines. The linking lines represent Musician as Performer, Musician as Responder, Musician as Creator, and Musician as Connector.

other nodes labeled *Performer, Connector, Creator*, and *Responder* surrounding the central node.

The nodes in Figure P.1 are connected with *linking lines* and are marked with *linking phrases* to describe the relationships among the concepts listed in the nodes. This map suggests that our concept of a musician has four primary domains of engagement with music. From this point, other nodes can be added and linked with additional linking lines within each of the four domains and between them.

Figure P.2 is our completed concept map depicting our ideas addressing the central question. From the original five nodes in Figure P.1, additional nodes have been added to help illustrate the concepts more clearly. Linking lines have been used to connect the nodes within each of the four domains and then among nodes in all of the domains. The resulting map reveals a number of complex concepts concerning what we believe every musician should know and be able to do with music.

What if you were to develop a concept map to address the question, "What knowledge, skills, and dispositions are necessary for you to acquire and/or develop as

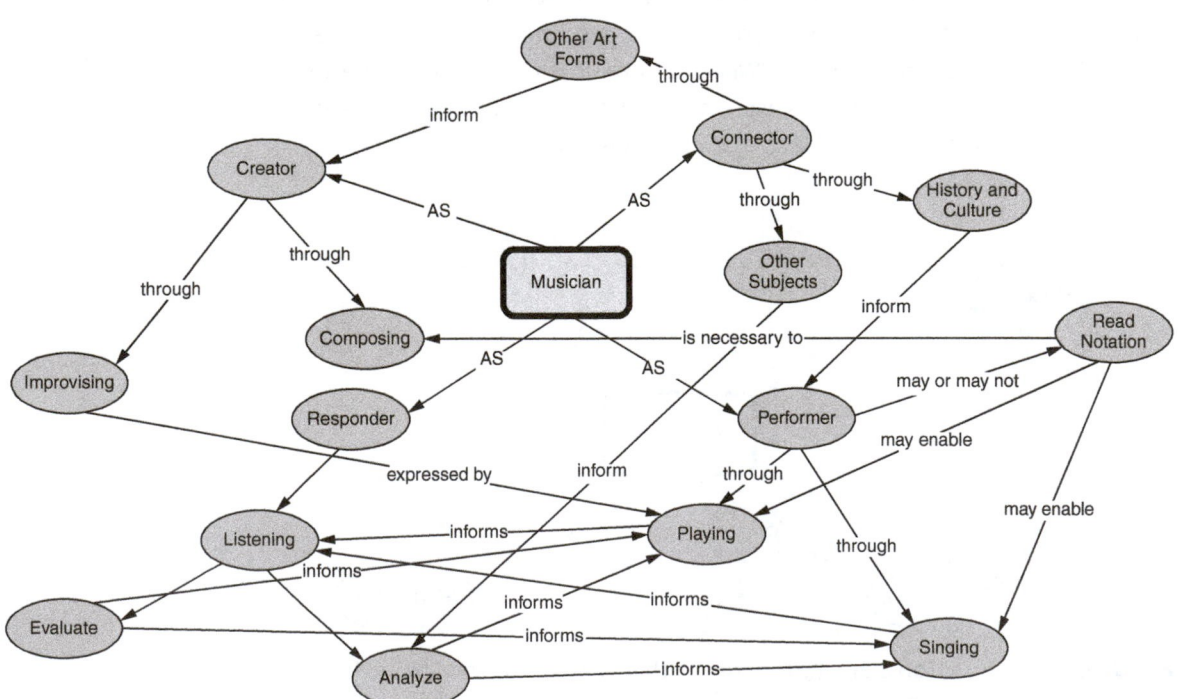

FIGURE P.2 Concept map of what a musician should know and be able to do with music.

you become a professional music educator?" Might it reveal a starting place for your journey? We think it will. To develop your map we suggest the following procedure:

- **Brainstorm**—Take time to make a list of all the facts, terms, ideas, or concepts that you think of to address the focus question. It may help to write these ideas on Post-it® notes and stick them on an open area like a poster board.

- **Organize**—Spread out all your Post-it® notes and begin to group them according to related ideas. You may find that some ideas relate easily to others and some tend to stand on their own. Within larger groups, you may be able to develop sub-groups. In the process of grouping, you may discover new items that you had not considered previously. Feel free to add or delete any concepts in this phase. Be sure to make note of concepts that may relate to more than one group.

- **Layout**—On your poster board, come up with an arrangement that best represents your understanding of the relationships and connections among the groups you have formed. We suggest you place the concepts most closely connected to the central topic in the center or at the top and then add others either further out from center or further down on the layout to show the hierarchical relationships you have developed among these concepts.

- **Linking**—Draw lines and arrows to connect your groups and show the relationships among the connected ideas. It is often helpful to add a word or short phrase to each line describing the nature of the relationship.

- **Finalize**—Once your map is arranged in such a way you believe it to represent your ideas accurately, you need to convert your map into a permanent form that

TABLE P.1 Sources for concept-mapping software.

Name of software	Web address
Inspiration	www.inspiration.com
Smartdraw	www.smartdraw.com
Decision Explorer	www.banxia.com/dexplore/demo.html
SemNet	www.biologylessons.sdsu.edu/about/semnetdown.html
Visual Mind	www.visual-mind.com
MindManager X5Pro	www.mindjet.com/US/ (21-day trial)
Cmap	http://cmap.ihmc.us/
VisiMap Professional	www.coco.co.uk/
Smart Ideas	www2.smarttech.com/st/en-US/Products/SMART+Ideas

others can read and understand. Be creative and use all means available to depict your understanding as clearly as possible. This can also be done using a number of computer programs that can help you create your final map. A simple web search will reveal many such programs that are available for free use. Table P.1 lists some software that provides 30-day free trials.

Study your map and note the concepts you believe to be important in your development as a music teacher. This is *your* starting place. Store this map so it will be easily found later in the semester or when you have completed this text. We will revisit it at that time. Until then, enjoy your journey!

DISCOVERY OF SELF

What Is Your Role as a Music Teacher?

1

As you begin your journey toward becoming a professional music educator, you possess a unique history of what brought you to this point. You undoubtedly possess a love of music and the desire to help others experience that connection. Perhaps you come from a family of musicians. Maybe you are the first in your family to attend college. You may have had one or more truly excellent teachers who inspired you to pursue a career in education. Many of you likely bring actual teaching experience—as section leaders, drum majors, summer camp counselors, etc.—and have felt first-hand the joy of helping others learn a new skill or discover a new idea. Each of these experiences, and many others unnamed, comprise the profile of perceptions that influence what you think regarding your role as a music teacher. This perception of teacher role is important because it will guide the decisions you make and the actions you take in your future classrooms. As you progress through your program, you will add experiences that will undoubtedly cause you to reconsider your role. This is good. When it happens, it means you are growing as a professional.

A powerful component of your development at this point is the community of future music educators who are sharing this journey with you, each of whom brings his or her unique history. As you get to know your colleagues in this class, you will discover many similarities and many differences between their histories and yours. As a result, there will be times when their perspective will affirm yours. There will be other times when what they say will challenge what you have come to believe and cause you to either dig deep to discover previously unacknowledged convictions for your beliefs or consider the possibility that other viable (or better) alternatives exist. These affirmations and challenges, particularly coming from a community of peers, will help to accelerate your growth as a music education professional.

How well do you know your colleagues? Maybe this is the first semester of your degree program and you are in a class with people who are mostly strangers. On the other hand, you may be further along in your program and recognize nearly everyone in the class. Even so, there are probably aspects about some of your colleagues that may surprise you.

DISCUSSION BOARD
Name, Hometown and Instrument

Log onto your class discussion board and list your name (use a nickname if that is what you prefer), your hometown, and your instrument. Then give a brief statement about why you want to teach music. After making your post, take some time to read other posts. This is a first step toward getting to know your colleagues. See if you can learn something new.

IDENTIFYING THE ROLE

1.1 TEACHING AND LEARNING

1. Are you a teacher? Why or why not?

2. What does it mean to teach?

3. What does it mean to learn?

4. Are there differences between a teacher and a professional educator? If so, what are they? (see Class Activity 1.1, p. 20)

Now that you are thinking about pursuing a music education degree, or are actually enrolled in a music education degree program, ask yourself the question: "Am I (now) a teacher?" You may be uncertain at this point, and that is quite normal and healthy. Consider all the possible ways there are to teach. Have you ever helped a little brother or sister with homework? Have you ever helped a friend learn a sport, such as tennis, golf, racquetball, or bowling? Have you ever shown anyone (like your parents) how to use the computer? Have you ever been in charge of people, such as being a section leader in a musical ensemble, or serving as a supervisor in a job? Have you ever taught summer camp or done any babysitting or worked in child care? Answers to these questions may lead you to answer, "Yes, I am (or have been) a teacher."

If you believe you have been a teacher at one time or another, it is logical to assume you taught something to someone else. So, what does it mean, to teach?' Merriam-Webster defines **teach** as a transitive verb meaning, "a) to cause to know something, b) to cause to know how, or c) to accustom to some action or attitude" ("Teach," n.d.). This definition suggests that to teach, one must share knowledge, a skill, or a disposition about something with someone else. On the surface, this proposition appears to be rather simple. If you know something, are able to do something, or have a position on something and share that with other people, by this definition, you have taught them. This definition also suggests that to teach you need to either have knowledge of a subject, be able to do something skillful, or have what you believe to be an informed opinion about something. If you possess one or more of these elements, this definition suggests you can teach.

Let's take the next logical step in this discussion. If you believe that you have taught something to someone, then it would be reasonable to assume that this other person 'learned' something from the encounter. What does it mean, 'to learn?' Again, Merriam-Webster defines **learn** as a transitive verb that means, "a) to gain knowledge or understanding of or skill in by study, instruction or experience, b) to come to be able, c) to come to realize" ("Learn," n.d.). You may gather from this definition that learning is not reliant on teaching. Learning by study or experience can be an individual endeavor and does not require a 'teacher.' This definition also suggests learning can be defined by acquiring a skill or knowledge. Learning can be a product of instruction, but is not solely dependent upon teaching. So, what does this mean for our original question, "Are you a teacher?"

144 SOCIAL PLACE
Varieties of Teaching

Using 144 characters or fewer, make a list of all the varieties of teaching that you can possibly imagine and send them to class members. As you get thoughts from your colleagues, start a list of all the possibilities in a course notebook.

Much debate has surrounded the *professional* status of teaching (Larson, 1977). Early thought on this subject, from the 1930s to the 1960s, suggested that professions all exhibit the same traits or attributes (Carr-Saunders & Wilson, 1933; Pavalko, 1988). Five generally agreed-upon attributes include:

1. Possession of a specialized body of knowledge and techniques.
2. Establishment of a standardized course of training for imparting the specialized knowledge.
3. Testing of applicants for knowledge and competence upon completion of training, followed by the granting of licenses to practice.
4. Licensed practitioners hold a legal occupational status that guarantees them a monopoly over their sector of the market.
5. Autonomy from direct supervision and the substitution of collegial control in place of hierarchical control.

(Sumpter, 2008, p. 11)

As you peruse this list, many parts of this attribute model may appear to apply to professional teaching. Particularly in music education, a vast and very specific body of knowledge and technical information exists. Knowledge about music theory, music history, performance practice, and child psychology are only a few of the many content areas that music teachers work to understand. Music teachers also must acquire techniques in instrumental performance and in vocal performance. Standardized courses of training are also evident for music teachers. You are likely enrolled in a degree program that leads toward teacher certification. The standards for the certification process are usually maintained by the state in which you wish to earn licensure, and colleges/universities with degree programs in education align their courses of study to meet at least the minimal standards of these requirements. Certification testing may vary from state to state, but nearly every state requires that teachers pass a set of exams to be certified to teach.

Whether or not teachers hold a monopoly on any sector of the market is worth exploring. In most accredited public schools, teachers must hold state teacher certification to be eligible for employment. However, alternatives to the traditional public school offer a different story. Some charter schools and most private or parochial schools do not require state certification. Some require a different type of certification while some do not require certification at all. In addition, there are often means in each state for alternative certification that may allow individuals with little or no formal teacher education to apply and receive a teaching certificate, usually for a limited time period. Other programs like *Teach for America* place recent college graduates in teaching positions in high need urban settings. Training programs for *Teach for America* are five weeks in length and do not lead to certification (Teach for America, n.d.). That said, traditional public schools comprise 73 percent of all schools servicing the elementary and secondary school students in the U.S. (Keigher, 2009). Simply because there exist several well-recognized alternatives to the traditional public school does not negate the fact that teachers with certification hold a monopoly over a clearly strong majority of the market.

Teacher autonomy, as it is described in this attribute model, however, deserves further examination. Nearly every state has adopted the Common Core State Standards Initiative, mandating what students should know and be able to do in English language arts and in mathematics; meanwhile parallel efforts have resulted in national standards being developed for world languages, science, and the Arts (NGA Center–CCSSO, 2010). Although the National Standards for Arts Education are voluntary, they have been "adopted or adapted by forty-nine state departments of education, and have become the benchmark document by which K-12 arts learning is measured in dance, music, theatre, and visual arts" (National Arts Education Association, 2012). The idea of having education standards can be a helpful proposition, providing essential guidance to newer teachers and offering those with experience some needed creative challenges (see Chapter 9).

Yet problems occur when such well-meant guidelines are administered and monitored in ways that ignore how students and their needs may differ from classroom to classroom, from neighborhood to neighborhood, and among varying demographic areas (inner city, suburban, rural). Often times, teachers are required to structure their lessons to meet particular curricular demands. In some cases, teachers are required to use specified materials and meet designated time lines that prescribe when each element should be addressed. These curricula are often products of state agencies that debate at the legislative level issues concerning what should or should not be included. When such 'across the board' approaches to education standards are implemented, teachers lose their autonomy to be creative in their efforts to improve student learning by addressing the unique challenges posed by each learning situation.

Most professional educators work under direct authority of a supervisor who oversees what teachers do in their classrooms. These supervisors are usually principals, assistant principals, curriculum supervisors, assistant superintendents and even superintendents in some smaller districts. They are often charged with responsibilities to observe and assess teachers' performances in the classroom, with the prospect of merit pay or continued employment being based upon these assessments (Jacob & Lefgren, 2006). Determining and nurturing teacher quality is important. However, when the teacher evaluation process is pursued as a 'top-down' endeavor, it is plagued by (a) infrequent evaluations, (b) lack of evaluator knowledge about the content areas in which they evaluate teachers, and (c) the absence of high-quality feedback for teachers (Donaldson, 2010; New Teacher Project, 2009). Alternatives to typical administrative assessment procedures, such as peer evaluation and follow-up mentoring, are effective at addressing teachers' developmental needs, but these are rare and often are implemented in addition to official assessments, which are completed by supervisors (Goldstein & Noguera, 2006; Humphrey et al., 2011). Consequently, there is much more hierarchical control than collegial control over both curricular content and teacher development.

So, if we ascribe to the attribute model, we see that the first four attributes (specialized content, standardized training, testing for licensure, and legal status ensuring a monopoly) occur regularly. The last attribute (autonomy), however, is becoming increasingly less common in the education profession. Unfortunately, it is the absence of autonomy that limits the creative vision for what could be accomplished in the classroom. When teachers are strictly mandated about what and how to teach, they become hyper-attentive to the dictates of those in authority at the expense of their sensitivity toward the genuine needs of the students in their classrooms (Katzenmeyer & Moller, 2009). However, such authority does not materialize only as state- or district-mandated curriculum guides. In secondary school music, for example, the tradition of preparing for recurring concert and contest performances often dictates the activities and type of literature that, in essence, comprise the curriculum. Have you ever thought of what students in music might be able to explore if each performance could be followed by something other than preparation for the next performance?

When autonomy is limited, a natural response is to focus on parameters being imposed. Teachers who focus on such restrictions tend to become technically proficient at adhering to the 'letter' of the policies given to them. They look to artifacts of authority (end-of-grade tests, textbooks, curriculum guides, music contest ratings, etc.) to set goals and determine whether or not those goals have been met. They work to develop their skill sets and to implement 'tried and true' techniques aimed at ensuring the highest numbers of students meet externally imposed guidelines. Throughout the teacher education literature, this description of 'teacher as **technician**' has been contrasted with the role of 'teacher as **professional**' (Halliday, 1998; Katzenmeyer & Moller, 2009; Kellaghan, 1971; Wood & Whitford, 2010; Zeichner & Liston, 1987).

Teachers who envision themselves as professionals understand that their primary responsibility is to their students. While those in either role (professional or technician) understand the craft of teaching, teachers who view their role as professionals acknowledge the realities of mandated standards and traditions of the profession, yet they see beyond such parameters to find creative and effective ways to meet students' learning needs. Professional educators work constantly to develop the knowledge, skills, and dispositions necessary to promote in students meaningful lifelong learning that has the potential to improve their quality of life. These educators see this goal as their mission and view the craft of teaching as a means to reaching this end. Table 1.1 presents some of the differences in how teachers in these two roles address (a) what they teach (subject

TABLE 1.1 Teachers as technicians vs. teachers as professionals.

GENERAL CONCERN	TEACHING	LEARNING
Issue	*Teachers as Technicians*	*Teachers as Professionals*
Subject Matter (the content of the lesson)	Decisions about what to teach are solely driven by outside sources such as a text or curriculum guide. These teachers seldom question either the scope or sequence of what is being presented.	Decisions about what to teach are based on ways the lesson acknowledges and extends students' current understandings. These teachers consider the child's overall cognitive, emotional and moral development as they make decisions.

(Continued)

TABLE 1.1 (*Continued*)

GENERAL CONCERN	TEACHING	LEARNING
Issue	*Teachers as Technicians*	*Teachers as Professionals*
Pedagogy (how the content is shared with the student)	These teachers rely strongly on 'recipes' intended for any situation. Many taken-for-granted assumptions drive the decision-making process. Most prevalent is the idea that one should teach as he or she was taught, without critically examining the process.	These teachers recognize that children learn differently. They address these unique needs as they plan instruction. Similarly, they work past the day-to-day activities to identify the particular needs of their students and provide environments in which education is relevant to students' lives.
Assessment (how we know what has or has not been learned)	Assessment is an event that occurs almost exclusively at the end of instruction. A steadfast reliance on external sources elevates standardized tests to being the prime measure of student learning. Instruction is often solely aimed at the assessment. Follow-up on content rarely occurs after assessment has been administered.	Multiple forms of assessment are used before, during, and after instruction. Assessment is used during instruction to inform both the student and educator about learning. These educators help students realize their full potential and recognize that children are more complex than any single test can assess.
Social Impact (who is involved in the process of schooling, where it is taking place, and why)	These teachers tend to focus entirely on the classroom alone and do not consider outside influences on the students. They tend to view themselves acting alone, as the sole influence on student learning. Little consideration is given to altering parts of a lesson. They believe that in 'covering' the material, their job is done. It is the child's job to learn.	These teachers are well informed and consider current thinking about education and youth culture when engaging children in learning. They recognize that parents and society at large impact student learning significantly. They understand that learning is often a collaborative process and that their professional responsibilities to a child are focused on the whole of his/her life and not just isolated to a classroom for a finite period of time.

Source: Runte, 1995.

matter), (b) how they teach (pedagogy), (c) how they know learning is or is not taking place (assessment), and (d) the impact of forces outside the classroom on student learning (social impact).

QUALITIES OF THE EXCELLENT PROFESSIONAL EDUCATOR

1.2 INNATE OR LEARNED

Think of the most excellent teacher you can imagine and make a list of all of that person's qualities. Which ones do you think are innate (born with) and which qualities can be learned? (see Class Activity 1.2, p. 20)

We have all probably heard the expression: "Good teachers are not made, they are born." This statement implies some interesting presuppositions, or prejudices. First it assumes that individual teaching qualities cannot be learned; they are somehow an inherent part of one's personality that are genetic—fixed and unchangeable. Because these qualities cannot be learned, teachers cannot change over time; they are either good teachers or they always will be bad teachers. The inevitable conclusion of this line of argumentation is that teacher education is futile; either you can do it already, or you might as well give up. Obviously, because this is a book designed to help people learn to become fine teachers, we disagree.

Let us examine teaching qualities: are they inherited or learned? Consider some of the most common 'good teacher qualities,' such as mastery of the subject, ability to inspire students, and a good sense of humor. Which of these qualities can be learned or improved upon, and which, if any, are we just born with? This discussion can quickly dissolve into a debate about **talent** versus effort, or of ability versus work ethic, or of inspiration versus perspiration. Take 'mastery of the subject' as an example, with musical performance as the specific case. Are we born being able to perform masterfully? Obviously, no. Do different people achieve differing levels of mastery of music performance? Obviously, yes. Are some people barred by some mystical 'lack of talent' from ever making music in a meaningful way, while others just naturally sing or play beautifully from childhood? Good question.

We follow the argument that 'talent' is something that represents a speed limit for learning, rather than an absolute barrier to learning (Ericsson, Charness, Hoffman, & Feltovich, 2006; Gardner, 1993; Sternberg & Grigorenko, 1997). We believe that people with a particular 'talent' may acquire knowledge and skills within a specific subject area very quickly—the speed limit of their learning is somewhere near freeway speed. No doubt, you can make a list of those you know who seem to be 'born' to do something. For many of these people, their speed limit for acquiring knowledge and skills in a specific subject—like music or sports—is so fast it may not be easily observable. Others without the same talent may proceed down the street at the speed more appropriate for a school zone.

Other parts of the 'talent' equation are effort and guidance. If the speed limit varies, so does driving time and driving skill. A person who works hard at performing while moving at school zone speed, say at 25 miles per hour, but spends four hours a day at work, may go a hundred miles that day. The person zipping along at freeway speed, 70 miles per hour, for only 30 minutes a day, only covers 35 miles. A driver who is constantly running off the road due to lack of guidance, no matter what the speed, can end up crashed in the ditch. Talent alone does not determine achievement. The entire equation of talent plus effort, opportunity and guidance has an impact on what can be achieved.

To explore this metaphor further, remember that the learner *must be* the driver. A teacher functions much as a driver's education instructor would. He or she sits beside the student (if the instructor sits in front of the student, it tends to block the view), gives useful advice ("watch out for that pothole" or "don't get so close to that truck") and has an emergency brake pedal handy in case of danger.

If mastery of the subject, whether discussing musical performance or nuclear physics, is limited somewhat by a natural 'speed limit' or talent, is the same true of other teaching abilities? Herein lies one of the most important questions to be discussed in this course—can people actually improve as teachers, and if so, how do they make the necessary improvements? We believe there are specific concrete activities in which one can engage to help him or her to grow in every important facet of teaching. This growth will take time, but much like any lengthy journey, there are steps to take along the way and the goal of this book is to help a young teacher plot out a map for this journey. The journey will be filled with unexpected bumps and detours, and sometimes even washed out bridges, but a determined person will find a way to make it through to the desired destination, and, with luck, even on time.

DISCUSSION BOARD
My Most Influential Teacher

Log on to the class discussion board and post your response to the following: *Without using names, please describe your favorite teacher. What made this teacher special? What traits did this teacher exemplify that made him/her stand out from others? What impact did this teacher have on your schooling and life in general?* Feel free to read the responses of your colleagues and add your comments to their responses.

A FIRST LOOK AT PRINCIPLES OF TEACHING: ACTIVE LEARNING

1.3 A TALE OF TWO CLASSES

Classrooms can often be classified by the roles the students play as active or passive learners. After reading Scene I and Scene II in the text, which classroom would you prefer to be in (a) as a student, and (b) as a teacher? Why? (see Class Activity 1.3, pp. 20–21)

Scene I: in this fourth-grade classroom . . . students are sitting in neat rows, facing the front of the room. They are listening to an excellent recording of Beethoven's 5th Symphony, section by section. The teacher has handed out worksheets that help the students to see the various themes from each section and how they fit together. Student behavior is subdued, but fairly attentive—when the teacher asks questions, the same three students always seem to have a correct answer. Others just sit and watch.

Scene II: in this fourth-grade classroom . . . students are seated on carpet squares arranged in an open space in the room. They are echoing the teacher, singing descending major thirds in response as she sings them using Solfège syllables. The teacher frequently asks one student at random to sing alone, and each student seems eager to be a soloist. On the board is a graphic representation of the Solfège syllables "mi" and "do" . . . after a period of echoing, the teacher merely goes to the board, points at the two symbols on the board, and the class sings "mi, do" . . . As the students begin to gather their things to leave the room for their next class, a recording of Beethoven's 5th Symphony comes on and as they leave the room one can hear . . . "mi - mi - mi - do" . . .drifting down the hallway . . .(this teacher is using "la" based minor).

As we can see from the examples above, many fine music educators use activity-based instruction. These activities vary in the levels of engagement required by the students. Even when students seem to be **passive**, they can be actively engaged in listening to and thinking about music. All **active learning** is not visible. We believe that educational activities should, however, meet three requirements: (a) there must be a pre-planned, specific learning goal in mind to be achieved through participation in the activity, (b) students must *do* something while actively participating in their own leaning, and (c) the teacher must explain, guide, and facilitate the students as they act out the learning task.

TEACHING AS A PERFORMING ART

The concept of active learning can certainly be applied to music teacher education. When learning to teach, active learning theory would dictate that the most important part of the curriculum would be the practice of teaching. In this sense, this statement is easily supported by a reverse argument. As musicians, we of all people should be aware of the importance of practicing to the development of performing skills. Imagine, for a minute, what the study of musical performance would be like, if we tried to teach performers the way that traditional music education programs have taught teachers:

THE STORY OF HANS

Hans enters music school to study violin. We give him courses in music theory and history so that he will understand the music to be played. We give him courses in kinesthetics of playing the violin, the theory of violin playing, great violinists, violin literature, and history of the violin. But we do not give him a violin. He does all the studying in his head. He memorizes fingerings for major scales, chromatic scales, and studies how to play harmonics. He studies the psychology and sociology of violin playing. He makes all "A's" and "B's." In his senior year, he has a seminar/discussion course on the philosophy of violin playing. He is truly well educated on the subject of playing the violin. But, he has not played a note.

Then, during the last semester of his senior year, we hand him a violin and ask him to play a senior recital at the end of the term. He muddles through, showing some promise, and the next year, in his first professional playing job, the conductor excuses his poor playing by stating, "Oh well, the first year is usually terrible anyway" (adapted from Paul, 1994).

TEACHING IS PERFORMING. Just as musicians get in front of people and express their feelings and thoughts in musical language, music teachers get in front of people and express their feelings and thoughts in spoken, written, graphic, gestural, musical, and other verbal and non-verbal languages. This complexity points out the difficulties as well as the excitement and rewards of teaching. Teachers must become fluent in many different modes of communication; they must become performers in many different media. It should go without saying that performance is only learned through intelligent practice. We are reminded of the adage "practice does not make perfect, practice makes permanent." Possibly the most important statement in this book is:

> ### You only learn to teach by teaching

A word of caution, however: you should always keep in mind the intelligent or reflective aspect of practice. Simply doing something (teaching) will not lead to effective practice. Intelligent or reflective practice is not mindless repetition. The schematic for reflective practice is simple: You do something. You look to see how you did. If you were successful, you note why you were successful so that you can do it again. Without the reflective component, your first success may not lead to future successes. If you were unsuccessful, you correct or choose a new course, and you try again (see Figure 1.1).

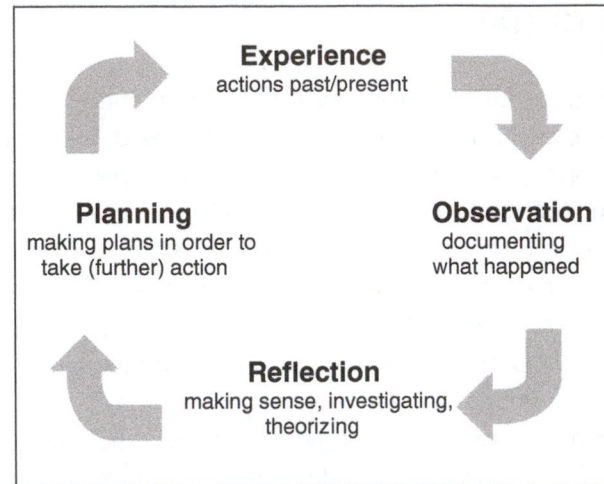

FIGURE 1.1 Model of reflective practice.
Source: Kolb, 1984.

1.4 THE REFLECTIVE PRACTITIONER

How does reflection serve as a distinguishing characteristic differentiating a *teacher as profess-ional* from a *teacher as technician*? (see Class Activity 1.4, p. 21)

If you engage in activities without taking the time to think about what has happened, you would be engaged in what is called 'mindless practice.' The activities themselves do not guarantee that anyone will learn simply by doing them. Because of this, we have built in ways for you to reflect on many of the activities in this book. One of the primary ways we suggest you do this is by keeping a teaching blog. Your instructor will give you specific instructions for how he or she would like you to get this going. The important aspect in this is not the form you use for your blog, but that you use it to explore your reflections about teaching. There are prompts in this book that will ask you to reflect in your blog on certain thoughts or ideas. You may also wish to maintain reflections about what you observe in others' teaching. We hope this will be the first step in developing a habit of **reflection** that will serve you well as you take on the role of a professional music educator.

BLOG ON . . .
Teacher Introduction

Take turns in class getting up in front and announcing the following:

Hello class, my name is Mr. or Ms. [use your last name] and I will be your teacher today. I look forward to helping you learn more about [choose any topic you wish].

After you have had an opportunity to publicly announce the statement above to the class, take time to blog about your thoughts. Here are some questions that may help you get started. Feel free to address other ideas as well.

- How did it feel to claim the teacher role out loud?
- What were you thinking about most when you made this claim?
- What surprised you most as you stood and made this statement?

CLASS ACTIVITIES

Class Activity 1.1: Teaching and Learning (Cluster!)

Your instructor will call out a category by which you should sort yourselves into groups (eye color, shirt color, birth month, etc.). Once you find all the other class members that share this attribute, introduce yourself to your group with your name, your hometown and your primary performance instrument (yes, voice is an instrument). Work to learn this information about your colleagues. You will do this several times and be in several different groups. Each time you cluster and after everyone has been introduced, address one of the following questions:

- Cluster 1—*Are you a teacher? Why or why not?*
- Cluster 2—*What does it mean, "to teach"?*
- Cluster 3—*What does it mean, "to learn"?*
- Cluster 4—*Are there differences between a teacher and a professional educator? If so, what are they?*

After you have had an opportunity to discuss these questions in your clusters, your instructor may ask you to share your thoughts with the full class. It is important that as many ideas as possible are shared. Make sure you speak up and share your thoughts with the class.

Class Activity 1.2: Innate or Learned

In small groups of four to five people, start a list of the qualities of the most excellent teacher ever. You may have a particular teacher in mind as you make this list or you may combine qualities from several teachers you have had in the past. This could be an entirely fictitious teacher who embodies the qualities you would like to see in such a teacher. Once you have a list, begin to classify these qualities as (a) those that are simply **innate**—a person must be born with these qualities in order to possess them or (b) those that can be **learned**—it may take serious work, but one can acquire these qualities through education or training.

Class Activity 1.3: A Tale of Two Classes

Take several minutes to read the examples in the 'Active Learning' section (p. 16). Try, by yourself, to write down the differences between the two classes. Which classroom would you prefer to be in (a) as a student, and (b) as the teacher? Once you have written your thoughts, pair up with one other person and discuss your results for several minutes. Then, come back together as a full class and have one member of each pair summarize their findings, leading to a full class discussion.

Class Activity 1.4: The Reflective Practitioner (Hoop Reflections)

For this activity you will need a flying disk or paper plate and a hoop. This activity needs two volunteers, one to throw or fly the disk or plate and the other to hold the hoop. Set the thrower about 10 to 15 feet from the hoop. When both are ready, the thrower should attempt to fly the disk through the hoop. After the first attempt stop and address the questions below:

1. Did the disk go through the hoop?
2. If so, how can we ensure that this can be done again? What does the thrower need to replicate from his/her first attempt?
3. If not, what does the thrower need to change to be successful on his/her second attempt?

Make a second attempt and note if this was successful or not. If necessary you can go back to the questions above and continue to make adjustments until the thrower successfully gets the disk through the hoop.

2

What Do You Believe about Learning and Teaching?

Perhaps the most important single cause of a person's success or failure educationally has to do with the question of what he believes about himself.

(Arthur Combs)

There are two vignettes below that describe two different teachers in the process of teaching/rehearsing their eighth-grade bands. As you read each of them, ask yourself what you think they believe about how students learn best and what they need to do as teachers to ensure that students learn.

Mountain Boomer Jr. High School

8th-Grade Advanced Band

Mr. Smith

As students enter the classroom, Mr. Smith greets them with a reminder to get their instruments quickly and be seated, ready to warm up when the bell rings. Most students hustle to the storage room and get their instruments, but John and Blake hang out in the corner of the storage room so they can send a text without getting in trouble. Texting is not allowed during school hours. Consequently, John and Blake are late to their seats.

Mr. Smith addresses their arrival with, "Gentlemen your tardiness to rehearsal will cost each of you two demerits. John, that puts you over the limit. Please see me after class about your detention."

Mr. Smith goes on to start rehearsal with a breathing drill for the winds and brass while the percussion gets set for the full ensemble warm-up. After leading the students through their daily set of ensemble drills addressing ensemble pulse, articulation, note length, and tonal energy, Mr. Smith asks the students to put *Courtly Airs and Dances* on their stands and to prepare to start the fifth movement. The percussion section scrambles to get their equipment for this movement.

Mr. Smith begins this part of the rehearsal by addressing the clarinet section. "Clarinets, you need to play this movement with a firm articulation and a long-lifted note length. Let's hear you at letter B please."

After the clarinets play the first two measures Mr. Smith stops them. "You are not all playing with a firm articulation and note lengths are not matching. Please, listen and match." The clarinets play again and are stopped after four measures. Mr. Smith says, "I am sorry folks, but you are still not matching, Can I hear you one at a time please?" Mr. Smith goes to the metronome and says, "We will start with four beats from the metronome and then James will play the first two measures. Jamie you will wait for four beats and then you will play. Each of you will follow around the section that way." Mr. Smith offers feedback to each player during the rests. After all the players have played, Mr. Smith comments, "I am sure you hear that very few of you are matching. You need to listen more closely and make adjustments to your articulation and note length. Let's take everyone at letter B please" and the rehearsal continues. . .

CHANGE OF SCENE

Rose Rock Middle School

8th-Grade Advanced Band

Ms. Jones

The bell rings for fourth period and Ms. Jones moves into the hallway to greet students as they enter for band rehearsal. She sees James and asks, "How did you guys do last night?" referring to his basketball team. "Okay," says James, "we lost, but not by as much as last week. I think we are getting better." "Well, that's what is most important. Keep that up and the wins will come. You'd better get your trombone and get ready," Ms. Jones says as she motions for him to move on into the room.

James looks at the white board as he enters the room to see what today's rehearsal order will be. He notes four rhythms that are written on the board followed by *Courtly Airs and Dances Mvt. V* and *Roughriders March*. James retrieves his trombone case from the shelf and gets ready for rehearsal. He sees Amy and Jennifer huddled in the corner of the storage room with Amy's phone as they send a text to a friend.

Ms. Jones steps up on the podium as Amy and Jennifer come into the room with their instruments. Ms. Jones comments on their late arrival by saying, "Ladies, I am sorry that you have chosen to be late for rehearsal. Because you have delayed everyone's ability to start on time, we need find a way to keep this from happening again. Please, see me after class." Amy and Jennifer sit down quickly.

Ms. Jones starts rehearsal with some breathing exercises for the winds and brass. She notes that the percussion section is setting the equipment necessary for *Courtly Airs and Dances*. As the winds and brass are working on a breathing exercise requiring them to inhale for 4 and exhale for 8, Ms. Jones begins to play a concert F on her clarinet as students exhale for 8. She then motions for the students to get their instruments in playing position and match her on this pitch. She motions for the percussionists to join the ensemble on a keyboard instrument. After a couple of attempts, the students begin to match her. She then points to herself indicating that she will play without them and she models a rhythm. She points to the students, gives them four beats and they attempt to echo the rhythm. Again, after a couple of attempts they reproduce her rhythm. She points to herself again and plays the rhythm with stronger articulations and shorter note lengths than her first model. The students echo the pattern with these added elements. Ms. Jones asks, "Which of the four examples written on the board is the proper notation for what we are playing? Pick one, and when I tell you, close your eyes and hold up 1, 2, 3 or 4 fingers to let me know what you think. Ready . . . go." The students follow directions. "Now," says Ms. Jones. "open your eyes. It looks like we have a difference of opinions. Some think it is number 1, some think it is number 4. I will play it again. Follow your answer on the board and see if it matches what I play." Ms. Jones plays the rhythm with the same articulation and note lengths as before. "Now," she says, "tell your neighbor on your right what number you think it is." The students share quickly. "How many of your neighbors told you that it was rhythm 1?" All hands go up. "Excellent! That is correct."

Ms. Jones looks to the clarinet players and says, "Clarinets, would you play that rhythm for us please?" The clarinetists get ready, Ms. Jones gives them a four beat count in, and they play. "Trumpets, did the clarinets all match their articulations?" The trumpets all look at each other and no one responds. "Hmmm," says Ms. Jones. "Maybe you need to hear it again. Please, listen closely this time." She counts the clarinets in again and they play. Looking back at the trumpets, she asks, "What do you think, did they match?" Brian speaks up this time and says, "I think some are playing with a heavier articulation than others." Ms. Jones looks to the clarinets and says, "Let's say that some of you are playing with the weight of a basketball bouncing and others with the weight of the tennis ball bouncing. Can you get all of your articulations to be the weight of a tennis ball?" Ms. Jones models on her instrument one more time and the students echo back. "Brian, is that matching better?" asks Ms. Jones. Brian nods to indicate that it does.

Ms. Jones looks to the clarinetists and asks, "Clarinets, where do you find this rhythm in the fifth movement of *Courtly Airs and Dances*?" Amy raises her hand and says, "At letter B." "You bet," says Ms. Jones. "Can you all look at that rhythm on your parts and play it on a concert F one more time?" The clarinet players do as instructed. "What do you think, clarinets? Did that match articulation weight?" Jennifer says, "I heard more basketballs that time." Ms. Jones nods and says, "Let's do that one more time and match those tennis ball weights." The clarinets play it one more time. "What do you think, Jennifer?" "That is much better," says Jennifer. "Great," says Ms. Jones. "Would you play that rhythm with the pitches that are indicated." And the rehearsal goes on . . .

DISCUSSION BOARD
Two Different Rehearsals

If you are not a wind player, brass player, or percussionist, you will need to translate these rehearsals to a setting that is familiar to you, like a choral or orchestral rehearsal at the middle school/junior high school level. Once you have done this, address the questions below.

Which of these rehearsals is most like the ones in which you have taken part? What might students learn in Mr. Smith's rehearsal? What about Ms. Jones' rehearsal? In which rehearsal would you feel most comfortable? Why?

TEACHING HOW WE BELIEVE

Mr. Smith and Ms. Jones have different approaches to teaching an eighth-grade band class. They both have invested time, thought, and energy in preparing for their rehearsals. They both believe they are doing what is best for their students, helping them learn in the most effective ways. The students, however, are going to have very different experiences in these two classrooms. Why might these two teachers choose to approach these classes differently?

One explanation is that these two teachers subscribe to different belief systems about how students learn, which affects how each teacher chooses to teach. Teachers

2.1 DRAWING A CLASSROOM

If you were to draw a picture of a typical classroom, what might that picture tell you and others about your beliefs concerning teaching and learning? (see Class Activity 2.1, p. 38)

make decisions based on what they believe should take place in their classrooms (Tatto, 1998). "All teachers hold beliefs, however defined and labeled, about their work, their students, their subject matter, and their roles and responsibilities" (Pajares, 1992, p. 314). From these beliefs teachers make decisions concerning who to teach, what to teach, and how to teach. Even with mandated curricula, two teachers rarely emphasize the exact same points in the subject matter. It is even more rare that two teachers will present the material in exactly the same way.

Why are these differences present? What drives a teacher to teach as he or she does? Are these differences limited only to instruction or do such differences impact other interactions in the classroom as well? These are questions that all teachers, including music educators, should consider. As we explore these questions in this chapter, some of the concepts presented will likely be easy to observe and understand. Other concepts, however, may not be so easily observed. They may not be as obvious, because they may be what some call *taken-for-granted assumptions* (Rokeach, 1968) that you and others hold about learning and teaching. Often, these assumptions are never examined because they are believed to be 'truth.' Rokeach terms these "existential presumptions" because they "are perceived as immutable entities that exist beyond individual control or knowledge. People believe them because, like Mount Everest, they are there" (as cited in Pajares, 1992, p. 309). Uncovering these assumptions may not be easy or pleasant. You may become uneasy when you find that some of the basic assumptions you have made about learning and teaching may not be the well-examined facts you believed them to be.

144 SOCIAL PLACE
How Do You Learn Best?

As you think back over your formal schooling, were there any times that learning was particularly meaningful to you? When was a time you learned something that you did not know previously, and this new information has stuck with you ever since? Is there a particular event or moment in your life when you really learned something well? In 144 characters or fewer, describe one of those times and why you believe it was particularly meaningful.

UNCOVERING YOUR BELIEFS

Identifying and understanding **teacher beliefs** is not easy, partly due to an inability to define them. Pajares (1992) states that a definition of 'beliefs' is complicated because:

> [Beliefs] travel in disguise and often under alias—attitudes, values, judgments, axioms, opinions, ideology, perceptions, conceptions, conceptual systems, preconceptions, dispositions, implicit theories, explicit theories, personal theories, internal mental processes, action strategies, rules of practice, practical principles, perspectives, repertories of understanding, and social strategy, to name but a few that can be found in the literature.
>
> (p. 309)

In addition, these beliefs are products of many things. Family backgrounds, school experiences, religious convictions, cultural experiences, and professional education all influence the formations of beliefs.

Because beliefs are complicated products of personal experience, they should not be judged to be 'good' or 'bad' based upon some arbitrary set of criteria. As we discussed in the first chapter, what takes place in the processes of teaching and learning is contextual. What may be effective and appropriate in one setting may not be in another. Therefore, you will not find a list of acceptable beliefs listed in this chapter. What is of concern is that *you* examine *your* beliefs. Music educators who do not examine their beliefs are most likely those who reinforce the age-old archetype of simply teaching as they were taught (Thompson, 2007). Should we, as teachers, continue on this path of inadvertently recreating the past in our classrooms, it will not take long for what we do to become irrelevant to our students, our schools, and our society.

Examining beliefs is not a simple task, because some beliefs are hidden or implicit. How might one go about examining those beliefs? It seems we need a tool to help us do two things. First, we need a tool to make our conceptions of teaching and learning *visible* and therefore available for examination (Thomas, 2006). We need something to help us uncover what we believe, even if those beliefs are not immediately clear and obvious to us. Second, we need some means to talk about these beliefs so that we might assess their potential impact, viability, and value in the contexts of our own teaching (Thomas, 2006). **Metaphors** can be an effective tool to accomplish both of these tasks (Cameron, 2008; Cienki, 2008; Cooper, 1986; Cormac, 1985; East, 2009).

The use of metaphors and their impact on our thinking has been a well-studied phenomenon. Since the publication of *Metaphors We Live By* (Lakoff & Johnson, 2003), many have examined the pervasiveness of metaphorical thought in the varied facets of life. Aubusson, Allan, and Ritchie (2006), state that, "Since the mid-twentieth century, philosophers have accepted that metaphor and analogy permeate all discourse, are fundamental to human thought, and provide a basis for mental leaps" (p. 1). These 'mental leaps' are of particular interest as you examine your beliefs. If much of what you have come to believe about learning and teaching is a product of the experiences you have had in your formal schooling, it is little wonder why you would conceive of teaching in the same ways as you have been taught (Pajares, 1992). However, in the process of your professional education you may encounter ideas or beliefs about teaching and learning that do not 'feel right' to you. Rather than simply ignoring these issues or labeling them as 'weird,' 'uninformed,' or 'unworkable,' it is best to examine why you feel certain ways about these ideas and beliefs. This exploration may help you make some 'mental leaps' to new ideas that could inform your teaching decisions in the future. Metaphorical examination can help with this exploration, particularly when ideas are founded on beliefs that are hidden or implicit (Harrison & Treagust, 2006).

Understanding metaphorical structure may help you know how using metaphor can create new meanings for you as a music educator. The first part to consider is the **target** (Thomas, 2006, p. 108). The target is the particular concept being clarified or amplified by the metaphor or analogy. In this case, let's consider the student as the target. What you believe about your students' prior knowledge will affect how you approach instruction. The **source** (p. 108) is that which is known and is used to clarify or amplify the target. A source sometimes used to amplify beliefs about students' prior knowledge is a blank slate waiting to be written upon or an empty vessel waiting to be filled, meaning that the students have no prior knowledge before entering your classroom or studio. This metaphorical idea is often referred to as *tabula rasa*. The **ground** (p. 108) is comprised of shared elements between the target and source. This is the point where we compare the student with an empty vessel to find what they share in common. As you examine the *tabula rasa* metaphor in terms of a music-learning environment, the ground reveals some concerns. While students may enter the classroom with limited subject matter knowledge and skills, they bring with them a myriad of ideas, feelings, and prior experiences with music that will certainly influence their learning. If a teacher operates with an unconscious *tabula rasa* assumption and does not take the opportunity to examine the ground objectively, instruction is not likely to meet the students' needs.

Using metaphors, you can examine your beliefs about learning and teaching music, compare your actions with your beliefs, and determine if the two are congruent. If they are not, this may be a time for a 'mental leap' to alter either your beliefs or your practice. This type of professional reflection is what helps teachers (re)conceptualize their role(s) in the educational environment in which they work.

There are, however, limitations to what we can know and understand from metaphorical thinking. Consider the following conversations:

MOM: How was your new teacher?

STUDENT: She was great. She helped me learn my math! I am so excited, I feel I have a Fairy Godmother!

Another student might react to the same teacher differently:

STUDENT: She was the Wicked Witch of the West, and I spent all day looking for a bucket of water.

Obviously, neither comparison is complete or totally fair; humans resist categorization. Both descriptions, however, convey a powerful impression in very few words—an impression that paints a picture implying many more qualities that do not need to be spelled out. In this way, metaphors make thinking efficient. But, they can also make thinking narrow. The Fairy Godmother above is a clear and concise image, but no teacher with normal human shortcomings will fit the metaphor exactly. Each person, teacher or student, is more complex than, and therefore not completely described by, a metaphor or an analogy. It is important to keep these two opposite tendencies of efficiency and narrowness in mind as we begin looking at metaphors for schools, teachers, and students.

> **2.2 METAPHORS FOR MR. SMITH AND MS. JONES**
>
> What metaphor(s) might describe Mr. Smith's role in his classroom? What about Ms. Jones?
>
> What metaphor(s) might amplify our understanding of Ms. Jones, belief concerning how students learn best? What about Mr. Smith? (see Class Activity 2.2, p. 38)

METAPHORS FOR SCHOOLS

There are a number of common metaphors for schools. A garden (the word *kindergarten* is literally the German word for 'child-garden'), a hospital, and a factory are common images. The garden is a place where young plants (students) are nurtured, given the right amounts of food and water and light, and protected while they become mature and flower. The hospital is a place where doctors (teachers) diagnose patients (students) and prescribe treatments (programs, textbooks, activities) that will help them to heal and become complete (as scholars and people). The factory is an environment where managers (administrators) ensure that workers (teachers) process the proper components (knowledge) to fit into the product (the students). For the sake of discussion, as well as to explore the use of metaphor as an aid to thinking, we will consider a school as a factory and then as a museum.

The factory. In the early twentieth century, as public schools became larger and the American population grew, schools began to take on particular qualities similar to factories. Buildings were built with many identical rooms, connected by long, straight hallways. 'Information' or 'knowledge' became the 'value-added' component to the product manufactured by the factory. The students were the 'raw materials' from which 'responsible, educated citizens' were to be created, placing them in the role as the product. Students' minds were thought of as 'blank slates' upon which would be written the collected knowledge and wisdom of the culture.

In this factory metaphor, the teacher is the giver of information, or the transmitter of knowledge. The curriculum is highly structured so that all students will receive the exact same and equal experience. This 'teacher-proof' curriculum is used to designate teaching methods that will work for all classrooms. Scientific study of these methods attempts to ensure that the proper learning takes place. 'Quality control' is determined by student achievement that can be measured and reported easily.

Administrators become 'managers,' part of the team of 'bosses' as opposed to the teachers, who are 'workers.' These 'managers' are ultimately responsible for the 'product' that is produced in their school. Many administrators are evaluated by a report on how the school faired in the latest round of testing. If the product is below standard, those for whom the product is being manufactured hold management responsible (parents, community members, college admissions). Management also distinguishes between high value and low value products and passes those distinctions on to workers assembling the product. Those workers who, according to societal consensus and testing practice, work in low value areas (e.g. visual art, music, dance, drama, etc.) are often marginalized.

The 'assembly line' is an apt metaphor for this type of school, where students move through in homogenous groups often determined by age alone. As products, they are expected to passively accept the education that is 'being done to them.' Moving through the school as products, students travel from classroom to classroom and are treated with standard pedagogical methods imbedded in prescribed textbooks. They are expected to perform up to 'standards' that are set by the school, the society, and the textbook manufacturers. Should standards not be met, the 'product' is deemed faulty and either retooled or rejected. Teachers have little or no autonomy to make decisions about what and how they teach and are judged entirely by the product they generate. The product is evaluated via standardized methods that ensure each is the same. The ultimate goal for the school operating as an assembly line is to get the best product to the end of the line where it can be consumed by society. There is little concern for the products' wellbeing after leaving the factory.

The museum. Another metaphor for a school might be as a museum. Within the museum there are artifacts that represent the collected knowledge and culture of a given society. The curator (administrator) works with the museum board (school board and other community influences) in determining what artifacts (the curriculum) are necessary to meet the needs and mission of the museum. Once artifacts are in hand, the museum staff (teachers and administrators) designs displays (instruction) for presenting the artifacts in the most striking manner possible. The design team's goal is to draw viewers (students) to the artifacts so they can study them and know them more completely. The buildings are open, filled with natural light and large areas where viewers can gather and share thoughts or ideas. Some exhibits are even outside.

As viewers enter the museum, they are given a layout of the available displays and information about an application they can download to their phone that will provide additional information about the artifacts. The design team realizes that young viewers in particular have come to understand and connect with their world through technology and they wish to be responsive to this possible learning avenue. Docents (teachers) meet groups of viewers and guide them through the museum. They describe each exhibit in hopes that their information will enlighten the viewers and entice them to know more. The viewers are allowed to linger at exhibits that pique their curiosity. For those who are interested, details are available on where to find information and how to go about researching these artifacts.

In a school that operates as a museum, students move through the curriculum as teachers help them make connections among all the subjects they are studying. Teachers help students appreciate the knowledge and skills that are represented in each subject and invite them to explore each subject in new and different ways. Some students may be initially attracted to the science and/or math knowledge contained within the subject matter being studied. Others may more enticed by the design and aesthetics represented in the subject. In this approach to education, teachers have autonomy to explore ideas as presented by the students and to do so in ways they believe will be most effective. The students have a responsibility to be active and equal partners in their education. Because of this, teachers challenge students to express what they are thinking and allow the instruction to move in directions that are not preconceived. This approach often allows learners from multiple viewpoints to find that they have much in common with each other. Because of this approach, all ways of knowing and doing are considered essential to truly understanding the subject matter. Teachers are still held accountable for student learning, but student learning is assessed in authentic manners allowing students to demonstrate their understandings in ways that are relevant to them.

TEACHER AND STUDENT ROLES

As you investigate the factory model and the museum model, you may have wondered about the teacher's role within these models and if that role fits with the type of teacher you see yourself becoming. Perhaps the teacher's role could be best described as the *sage-on-the-stage*, where the focus is on a wise and knowing teacher who passes on the knowledge she has acquired over years of study to wanting learners who are eager to gather all they can. Maybe the teacher's role is more the *guide-on-the-side* who was not the focus of the classroom, but a mentor who helped learners understand and meet their learning needs and desires. In many classrooms the teacher's role lies somewhere between these two extremes.

Some metaphors for examining teacher's roles might include thinking of a teacher as a dictator, an architect, a traffic cop or a dance instructor. Thinking of a teacher as a dictator you might want to consider questions about the ways in which teachers have absolute control over learners in matters of teaching and learning such as subject matter, student behavior, parental rights, school policies, students' rights, class objectives, protecting the learning environment, and helping special learners. Architects design environments that encourage people to behave in certain ways. Thinking of teachers in this manner requires you to examine their role in designing learning activities as intellectual environments that help students navigate the hallways of curiosity and knowledge. In the role of teacher as traffic cop you might consider how teachers supervise the flow of information—how they might guide the movement of students either physically through the building or intellectually through the subjects. Perhaps this role places the teacher's primary focus on enforcing rules. Acting as dance instructors, the student and teacher move together through the subject, with the teacher leading. Leading in dance is a very subtle kind of leading and often the lead is exchanged between the two partners. In this metaphor, teachers and students are partners, often exchanging the lead, but always immersed in the subject. As you examine each of these roles you are likely to note there are times when a teacher must act as a dictator and other times she must act as a dance instructor. So, teachers' roles are not fixed, but are dependent upon the context in which they are working.

The learners also play a role in each metaphor. Essentially the learner's role in the metaphor is either active or passive. Many implicit beliefs about learners place them in passive roles. A commonly held tacit belief is that education is something that is done *to* the learner. Because of the interaction between the teacher and the learner, as the learner's role is defined, the teacher's role is also modified and vice versa. Such may be the case when the teacher's role is to shape or mold the learner, which places the learner in the role of absorber of behavior and knowledge. While some could argue that the act of absorbing does require action on the part of the learner, descriptions that outline these roles require minimal action on the part of the learner.

Some believe that it is essential for learners to interact with others and, therefore, place great emphasis on social learning. Teachers holding this belief often model for learners who observe and imitate. Some believe that learners achieve best when they

2.3 COMPARING TEACHER METAPHORS

What might encourage a music teacher to approach her teaching as a Dictator, Traffic Cop, Architect, or Dance Instructor? (see Class Activity 2.3, p. 38)

(learners) act as problem solvers and critical thinkers. Teachers with this belief often map out appropriate problems and challenges to be considered by the learners who work to find solutions. These teachers must be keenly aware of the learners' development so the challenges presented are appropriate. Others may conceive of the learner like a computer where information is taken in and processed. The teacher, in the role of programmer, must make sure that correct information is going in at all times so that the learner can process it and produce new information based upon this input. Some teachers place the student in a role as regulator of their own learning. In this case, the teacher helps learners understand how they learn and then encourages them to develop strategies for future learning. Still others believe learning does not take place until the learner is honestly bothered by not knowing something. This view places the teacher in the role of 'resource' for the learner who is experiencing **cognitive dissonance**. The teacher steers the process of discovering meanings to resolve this dissonance through active engagement with the subject matter being studied. Teachers expressing this belief are often focused on the context for learning and place learners in authentic circumstances so that learning can be situated in a time and place (Ireson, 2008).

An honest assessment of teacher and students' roles within the metaphors with which you identify most may help you to uncover some of the embedded or implicit beliefs that you hold about learning and teaching. We would reiterate that one set of beliefs is not necessarily better than another set. However, if you go on to become a professional music educator and never examine your beliefs about learning and teaching, you are more likely to simply teach as you were taught without examining the process. The way you were taught might be very effective and appropriate for the learners with whom you work, but professional educators make mindful decisions about their practices and do not simply puppet what has come before without examination.

INDIVIDUAL ACTIVITY
Develop Your Own Metaphor

Create your own school metaphor. Write a short paper (1–2 pages) describing your metaphor. Try to think of how the metaphorical characters that exist in these images equate or relate to various parts of the schooling process (e.g. administration, teachers, students, curriculum, etc.). You might begin with listing the characters in the metaphorical image like those in the two examples above (factory and museum). Assign each of these characters to roles within the school: teachers, students, administrators, librarians, etc.

How many parallels work and how many stretch the comparison too far? How does your metaphor 'create' a positive school environment? What are its strengths? Weaknesses? What role(s) does the teacher assume? What role(s) do the students assume?

At some point in the process of designing your metaphor, you need to draw a picture of a typical learning environment within a school that is operating according to these beliefs. Include all the detail you can in your drawing. (Yes . . . stick figures are acceptable!) For some, you will want to write first and then draw. For others it may be more helpful to draw first and then write about what you drew. Do both in whatever order works best for you.

Until now, we have asked you to consider one metaphor that might encompass everything in an educational environment. This was necessary in learning to use metaphors as a tool for uncovering some of your embedded beliefs. However, one metaphor will not adequately explain all the ways a school operates, address the multiple roles a teacher must take on, nor describe all the complexities involved in student learning. As you continue to consider what you believe about learning and teaching music, you will build a belief system that is multifaceted and complex. Teaching and learning are 'messy,' meaning they will not follow textbook descriptions of the processes at work.

To understand this point, let's go back to the opening scenario in this chapter and use metaphorical tools to help us understand some of the teacher decision-making. Mr. Smith appears to be a well-prepared teacher who takes on many of the responsibilities of a traffic cop. He directs his students physically through the classroom and enforces rules clearly. He also directs students' learning with very specific instructions. He takes on the responsibility for what the students will learn and how they will learn it. As an architect, he designs the learning activities in very specific sequential steps. He is responsible to ensure that students are building their understandings according to his design. As a dictator he controls the focus of the rehearsal and what information is shared. He alone decides when students have achieved objectives and when they have not. The students, though participants in the rehearsal, appear to be operating in a passive role as recipients of information. Their role is to do what Mr. Smith instructs them to do. They have no hand in deciding how things will be done, or in evaluating the outcomes of their efforts. Mr. Smith's view of his students may include seeing them as information processors where he is responsible to make sure all the information going in is very detailed and accurate. Having given his students these bits of input, he believes they will process the information and give it back to him correctly.

Ms. Jones is also a very organized teacher. She appears to share some of the same beliefs as Mr. Smith; but some other beliefs about her role and her students' roles in her classroom appear to be different. Similar to Mr. Smith, Ms. Jones also appears to act like a traffic cop. She physically directs students in the classroom and, to a certain degree, directs their learning while maintaining the structure of the classroom and upholding rules. She also takes on the role of architect in designing instruction. She, however, makes sure that students see the structure of this design by listing the rehearsal and instructional materials on the board. From this perspective, it appears Ms. Jones believes her students can become self-regulated learners and, if given the structure, can prepare for rehearsal on their own. Ms. Jones also takes on the role of dance instructor in her teaching, carefully leading the students through the process of discovering necessary knowledge and skills so they can perform successfully. There was very little 'telling' in her teaching as she worked to help students uncover what they needed to know. She placed the students in the role of problem solvers as she allowed them to experiment with ways to match her models. She also exercised a belief that her students were social learners and crafted multiple ways students could interact with each other to enhance both their own learning and that of another person. Without relinquishing control of the classroom or abdicating her responsibilities as a professional music educator, she allowed students autonomy in evaluation and feedback. Ms. Jones demonstrates instruction that leads students to a point where they can construct their own understandings of the material being studied.

CONNECTING BELIEFS WITH PHILOSOPHY

As you can see from the examples above, teachers' belief systems impact their instructional choices (Cheng, Chan, Tang, & Chen, 2009). As these belief systems become formalized, they align with particular teaching philosophies (Korn, 2012). It may seem very early in your exploration of music teaching to think about your teaching philosophy, but as you have seen in this chapter, your philosophical position (as defined by your beliefs) impacts how you think about many aspects of teaching and learning. Even if you cannot articulate your philosophy, you operate from beliefs that construct the foundation of your philosophy in your decision-making. While it is not in the aim of this text to provide a thorough exploration of teaching philosophies, you can gain a basic understanding of philosophies that can be categorized in the differing perspectives of *teacher-centered* philosophies and *student-centered* philosophies.

Teacher-centered philosophies support practices that clearly put the teacher in a leadership role. Schug (2003) defines this instruction as including:

> . . . a high degree of teacher direction and a focus of students on academic tasks. And it vividly contrasts with student-centered or constructivist approaches in establishing a leadership role for the teacher. Teacher presentation, demonstration, drill and practice, posing of numerous factual questions, and immediate feedback and correction are all key elements. Teacher-centered instruction has again and again proven its value in studies that show it to be an especially effective instructional method.
>
> (p. 94)

Some specific teacher-centered philosophies include **Perennialism**, **Essentialism**, and **Positivism**. Those teaching from a perennialist perspective contend that ideas are universal and, therefore, relevant and meaningful throughout time to everyone. For this reason, little importance is placed on student interest; however, there is a strong focus on scientific reasoning and mathematics because they never change. Essentialism supports teachers who believe there is common core of information and skills for all individuals in a given culture. Teachers with this philosophy put more focus on basic core information that will help students survive today. Content includes fewer past ideas, as these teachers accept that core information will change as time goes on. These teachers use a variety of methods including required reading, lectures, memorization, and repetition. Positivism rejects any information that cannot be formally measured, as it "limits knowledge to statements of observable fact based on sense perceptions and the investigation of objective reality" (Johnson, Dupuis, Musial, Hall, & Gollick, 2010, pp. 111–112). Teachers with these beliefs focus on clear directions so students understand what and how they will be learning. Instruction includes repetition and practice with different media, so students obtain clear understandings of the topics studied. A sizeable amount of instructional time is dedicated to testing with the hopes of ensuring student learning.

Student-centered (also known as learner-centered) teaching philosophies encourage teachers to approach instruction from the students' perspective, and are focused on meeting students' needs. Student-centered teachers believe that students must have autonomy in the classroom to make their own decisions about their own learning. These teachers recognize, however, that their job is to guide students through their learning experiences. Brown (2008) states, "Students are given choices and are included in the decision-making processes of the classroom. . . . Ultimately, the students are treated as co-creators within the learning process and as individuals with relevant ideas about how learning takes place" (p. 30). Some specific student-centered philosophies include

Progressivism, **Humanism**, and **Constructivism**. Those who ascribe to progressive teaching philosophies teach with the belief that "ideas should be tested by experimentation and that learning is rooted in questions developed by learners" (Johnson et al., 2010, p. 114). They believe that human experience is more instructive than authoritative and that change should be embraced rather than ignored. These teachers believe that organized freedom allows students to take responsibility for their learning. Teachers working from a humanist perspective are "concerned with enhancing the innate goodness of the individual" (Johnson et al., 2010, p. 115). They focus on individuals through a process of developing a free, self-actualizing person, and they believe education should start with the choices made by the individual. Humanistic teachers work to ensure their classrooms are welcoming and that students feel comfortable in sharing their thoughts, feelings, beliefs, fears, and aspirations with each other. Constructivism "emphasizes developing personal meaning through hands-on, activity-based teaching and learning" (p. 117). Constructivist teachers are responsible for creating effective learning situations where students can have authentic experiences with the content. They believe personal meaning is the best way for students to connect to the content and that students will be more prepared for the ever-changing world if they learn how to develop critical thinking skills. The constructivist classroom focuses on the ways a learner internalizes, shapes, or transforms information.

In future coursework, you will likely explore each of these philosophical approaches to teaching in much more detail. For now, reflecting on these ideas will help you to consider which seem to resonate with what you believe about teaching and learning music. Again, we encourage you not to separate these into categorical 'good' and 'bad' approaches, because we believe that both teacher-centered and student-centered philosophies have their place in teaching music effectively. It is the professional music educator's responsibility to decide which approach will serve students best. As long as music educators are making informed decisions about how they approach their instruction, we believe they are acting as professionals.

BLOG ON . . .

My Beliefs

Which of these philosophical positions appeal most to you as a learner? What about as a teacher? Do you think that it is possible to have different beliefs as a teacher than as a learner? What impact might your understanding of your beliefs about teaching and learning have on your decision-making in both how you learn and in how you teach?

CLASS ACTIVITIES

Class Activity 2.1: Drawing a Classroom

In groups of 4–6, take a large sheet of paper (Post-it® charts work great) and draw a picture of a typical learning environment. Be sure to include all those who participate in this setting in your picture and all the detail you can provide. Be prepared to present this picture to the class and explain what your picture represents.

Class Activity 2.2: Metaphors for Mr. Smith and Ms. Jones

In groups of 4–6, go back and read the opening scenario in this chapter. As a group, discuss the following questions:

What metaphor(s) might describe Mr. Smith's role in his classroom? What about Ms. Jones? What metaphor(s) might amplify our understanding of Ms. Jones belief concerning how students learn best? What about Mr. Smith?

Each group member should keep notes on the answers to each of these questions. If the group cannot think of a metaphor that might work, make note of that as well and what you discussed while you were considering what might work. We will come back to this after the next section.

Class Activity 2.3: Comparing Teacher Metaphors

Divide your class into four groups. Each group should select one of the metaphors below and consider the questions listed with each. Be prepared to present your answers to the class.

Dictator:

A dictator is someone who assumes sole and absolute power. He or she is the only decision-maker in the setting and operates with absolute authority. Initially, the term 'Dictator' did not have the negative meaning it has later assumed. Rather, a Dictator was a person given sole power for a specific limited period, in order to deal with an emergency. At the end of his term, the Dictator was supposed to hand power over to the normal authorities. In what ways do teachers have absolute control over learners? In what ways do they *not* have absolute control? Consider the elements of teaching and learning: subject matter, student behavior, parental rights, school policies, students' rights, class objectives, protecting the learning environment, helping special learners, etc. In which of these areas do teachers exercise absolute control in their classes? In which areas do they have very little or no control? What might encourage a music teacher to take on the role of *Teacher as Dictator*?

Architect:

Architects design environments that encourage people to behave in certain ways. They plan spaces that help people to feel certain emotions or even to think in certain patterns. Frank Lloyd Wright designed entryways for buildings that were small and had low ceilings so that upon entering the main structure the higher ceilings and large open rooms would create a feeling of optimism, of arriving in an exciting place. Do teachers design learning environments for similar purposes? Starting with the classroom, do teachers arrange chairs and desks in certain ways to make different activities possible or to encourage or discourage discussion among students? Do they design learning activities as intellectual environments that help students to navigate the hallways of curiosity and knowledge? What might encourage a music teacher to take on the role of *Teacher as Architect?*

Traffic Cop:

A traffic cop is a policeman who controls the flow of automobile traffic. As such, he or she is charged with getting the flow of traffic to move as effectively and efficiently as possible. Traffic cops also act as crossing guards, helping pedestrians cross heavy traffic areas safely. What does a teacher do that is similar to what a traffic cop does? Does he or she supervise the flow of information? Does he or she guide the movement of students either physically through the building or intellectually through the subjects? Are subjects straight streets with clear-cut intersections presided over by traffic cops? Do teachers put their primary focus on enforcing rules? What might encourage a music teacher to take on the role of *Teacher as Traffic Cop*?

Dance Instructor:

Parker Palmer, in his book *The Courage To Teach* (2007), describes teaching and learning as a dance. The dance floor is the subject matter field, and together student and teacher move through the field of the subject, with the teacher leading. Leading in dance is a very subtle kind of leading, however, and often the lead is exchanged between the two partners. In this metaphor, teachers and students are partners, often exchanging the lead, but always immersed in the subject. In what ways could you envision the dance floor as the subject matter? How might a teacher lead the learner as though they were dancing? How is this type of leadership different than in the other metaphors? How might the learner engage with the subject matter in this metaphor? What might encourage a music teacher to take on the role of *Teacher as Dance Instructor*?

What Do You Need to Know and Do as a Music Teacher?

3

. . . classroom teaching . . . is perhaps the most complex, most challenging, and most demanding, subtle, nuanced, and frightening activity that our species has ever invented . . . The only time a physician could possibly encounter a situation of comparable complexity would be in the emergency room of a hospital during a natural disaster.

(Lee Shulman, *The Wisdom of Practice*)

Even before reading this text, you probably knew that music teachers needed to have special **knowledge**, **skills**, and **dispositions** to be effective in the classroom. In your education you have likely witnessed that some teachers seem to have greater knowledge and skills than others. Consider a teacher you believe to be highly influential in your life—this could be the same teacher you wrote about in the *Most Influential Teacher* activity in Chapter 1. Did this teacher know the subject well and know how to share that knowledge with you? Did this teacher have a collection of skills that helped him or her to be effective? Did this teacher demonstrate certain professional attitudes, values, and beliefs both verbally and non-verbally as he or she interacted with you in a learning environment? We would suggest the answer to all three of these questions is 'Yes.' Professional educators must possess the knowledge, skills, and dispositions necessary to accomplish their educational goals.

Knowledge, skills, and dispositions can be acquired through formal and informal means. Formal means might include schooling, textbooks (like this one), teaching materials, and workshops. Informal means would include teaching experience—what some call the wisdom of practice—and observations. Most likely, much of your degree program is focused on helping you develop knowledge, skills, and dispositions using both of these means. It is equally likely that your degree program alone will not provide you with *everything* you need in any of these areas. You should begin to take on the personal responsibility of developing each of these areas as early as you can in your professional education. Why must this be done individually in addition to what you do in class? Because

3.1 WHAT IF YOU WERE TO TEACH A SKILL?

If you were to teach your classmates how to accomplish some simple task like making a PB&J (peanut butter and jelly) sandwich, what might your approach to this lesson tell you about the knowledge, skills, and dispositions you believe necessary for teachers to be effective? (see Class Activity 3.1, p. 56) your needs are different from those of others. Your current needs are dependent upon your previous experiences. Your needs are also dependent upon your understandings and attitudes about music, learning, children, and schools. Your future needs will be affected by where you choose to teach, who your students are, current societal changes, the economy, and state or federal legislation. These disparate forces impact you to such a degree that **no single source can provide you with all you will need to know and be able to do to be an effective professional music educator.**

BLOG ON. . .
Knowledge, Skills, and Dispositions

Imagine a place where you would like to be teaching. Consider the make-up of the student population in your learning environment. Consider the community in which this environment resides. Consider what you are teaching (e.g. general music, band, orchestra, choir, mariachi, guitar, popular music ensemble class, etc.). What do you think you will need to know and be able to do so you are an effective music educator in this environment? What attitudes will help you become an effective teacher? Start a list in your blog of the knowledge, skills, and dispositions you believe you will need. Remember where this list is in your blog so you can refer to it often.

The knowledge, skills, and dispositions you need are, in part, unique to you. Consequently, we have chosen not to provide you with specific lists that suggest acquisition of those items on these lists would guarantee you to be an effective professional music educator. Such a process of developing a prescription for effective music teaching would be no different than to suggest a doctor diagnose an illness and prescribe medication without taking a complete medical history of the patient. While certain general considerations may apply to most medical cases, each case is unique and requires careful consideration of all contributing factors before an effective diagnosis can be made. Similarly, music teachers must consider all contributing factors that affect teaching and learning before educational decisions can made.

While these contributing factors require unique and specific attention, we can consider general collections of knowledge, skills, and dispositions that are most commonly required of all professional music educators. In-depth understanding of these larger categories may allow you to identify the specific elements you will need to acquire to be effective in your environment. Understandings in these categories may also provide you with a means to discuss what you observe as you watch yourself and others teach. Being able to isolate the knowledge, skills, and dispositions exemplified by effective teachers may help you understand their effectiveness and allow you to achieve the same in your teaching.

TEACHER KNOWLEDGE NECESSARY FOR MUSIC TEACHING

What knowledge do great music teachers use in the process of their music teaching? How do they transform what they know about music into forms of knowing that students can comprehend? How do they help students understand the subject when these students are initially confused about what they are attempting to learn? Answers to these questions suggest that music teachers have different knowledge than do music performers. While the music teacher and the music performer are both professionals and must know much about music, the music teacher must have different knowledge to facilitate student learning effectively. Millican (2012) illustrates this point by stating:

> We have all had the experience of taking a class led by a person who obviously has a great deal of knowledge on the subject but is unable to effectively communicate those concepts. These people seem to get frustrated easily and may even become exasperated when we cannot grasp what, to them, seem to be the most basic concepts or skills. Perhaps you have had a music teacher who was a brilliant performer but was less than capable in communicating his or her knowledge . . .
>
> (p. viii)

We must be clear that subject matter knowledge is critically important for music teachers and you should not fall into the trap of what Shulman (1986) terms the "missing paradigm" (p. 184). He claims that one cannot examine teaching and learning without considering the content of what is being taught. Yet, content alone is not sufficient to enable student learning.

Shulman (1987) suggests that the knowledge base for teachers is a fusion of several different forms of knowledge. Millican (2008) drew from Shulman's ideas and developed a modified knowledge base framework that includes **content knowledge**, **general pedagogical knowledge**, **curriculum knowledge**, **knowledge of learners and their characteristics**, **pedagogical content knowledge**, **knowledge of educational contexts**, and one category not mentioned by Shulman, **administrative knowledge** (see Figure 3.1).

<aside>

3.2 WHAT DO YOU NEED TO KNOW AND DO?

To be a highly effective professional educator, what must a teacher know and be able to do? (see Class Activity 3.2, p. 57)

</aside>

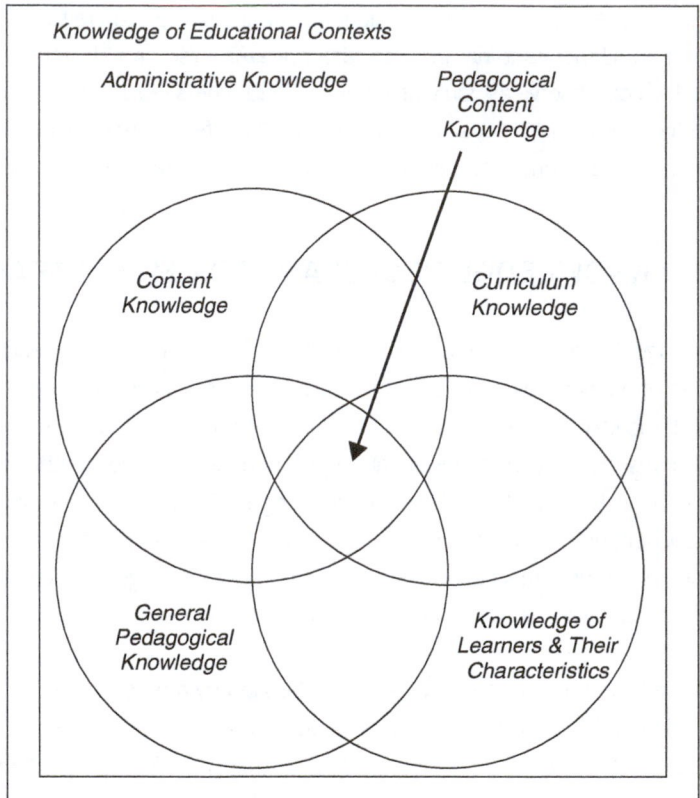

FIGURE 3.1 Pedagogical content knowledge model.
Note: This model is from Millican (2008, p. 69), which was modified from Shulman (1986, 1987), and is reprinted here with permission.

Ball, Thames, and Phelps (2008) affirmed that Shulman's ideas had immediate and long-lasting impact on educators and researchers, stating Shulman has been "cited in over 1200 refereed journal articles" and that "This interest has been sustained with no less than fifty citations to [Shulman's 1986 and 1987] articles in every year since 1990" (p. 390). In spite of all this attention, pedagogical content knowledge (PCK), the centerpiece of Shulman's work, continues to be an elusive concept lacking a precise definition and a long-standing research base (Ball, Thames, & Phelps, 2008). In an attempt to provide greater precision about PCK and the ways the other types of teacher knowledge contribute to PCK, Ball and colleagues (2008) examined the practice of teaching a particular set of concepts—in this case mathematics concepts—and the ways teachers needed to know that content to best support student learning. Below is an exploration of Shulman's ideas through the lens of Millican's (2008, 2012) modified framework, augmented with the findings of Ball et al. (2008).

Millican presents **content knowledge** as knowing the subject. In this sense, music teachers need to understand music as a topic of study. This way of knowing music is perhaps different from the ways you came to know music in your pre-collegiate years. Often, those who choose to major in music education have had many positive experiences performing music in large ensembles during their high-school years. You have likely been very successful in your performance experiences and may equate these to music study, when, in fact, you probably have limited experiences studying music as an academic subject. Studying a topic as an academic subject includes both substantive understanding (the principles used to organize the facts) and syntactic understanding (a set of rules that determine the appropriate use of these facts) (Shulman, 2004). Therefore, a music educator should not only understand how a dominant seventh chord is spelled in the key of C major (substantive understanding), but should also understand why a specific composer may choose to use this sonority in a particular work (syntactic understanding).

As we noted earlier, Ball, Thames, and Phelps (2008) studied teacher knowledge related to mathematics instruction. While their content is different from our focus on music, they suggest that the understandings we discussed above come under their heading of **common content knowledge**. They consider this as knowledge used in settings other than teaching. This includes such abilities as recognizing errors, pronouncing terms correctly, and understanding basic theoretical foundations as they apply to the subject. This knowledge is required for teaching, but is not exclusive to it.

Millican's (2008) model also includes both *general pedagogical knowledge* and *curriculum knowledge*. Shulman (2004) defines **general pedagogical knowledge** as "the ways of representing and formulating the subject that make it comprehensible to others" (p. 203). Because there is no single most powerful form for teaching every learner, professional music educators must possess many alternative forms of general pedagogical knowledge. Effective teachers acquire this knowledge in multiple ways. Some acquire their understanding from research, while others acquire it from the wisdom of practice (Shulman, 2004). General pedagogical knowledge also includes an understanding of what makes some topics easy to learn and others more difficult to understand. Your pedagogical knowledge may provide you with multiple ways to help a child sing on pitch, or help an adolescent boy manage his voice change.

Curriculum knowledge is closely aligned with general pedagogical knowledge, but beyond knowing how to teach the subject, it includes a teacher's understanding of

The full range of programs designed for the teaching of particular subjects and topics at a given level, the variety of instructional materials available in relation to those programs, and the set of characteristics that serve as both the indications and contraindications for the use of particular curriculum or program materials in particular circumstances.

(Shulman, 2004, p. 204)

Curriculum knowledge provides the teacher with a broad sense of knowing what concepts or skills to present, when to present them, and what materials would be most beneficial to students learning the concept or skill. For example, curriculum knowledge will inform your choice of appropriate materials for use in a vocal music classroom within a high poverty urban high school versus materials you might use in a similar class within an affluent suburban high school. This same collection of understandings will help an elementary music teacher decide when it is appropriate to introduce *la* after their kindergarten students have demonstrated understanding of several *so mi* tunes in their Kodály-based music classroom.

Ball, Thames, and Phelps (2008) suggest that **specialized content knowledge** (SCK) is the knowledge used for and exclusive to teaching. By this definition it appears they combine elements of general pedagogical knowledge and curriculum knowledge in Millican's model. This includes the ability to recognize errors students make and understand the nature of those errors so appropriate solutions can be prescribed. SCK goes beyond the procedural knowledge that a performer must possess, to include the ability to communicate understanding to students who may not comprehend the topic immediately.

Millican (2012) defines **knowledge of learners and their characteristics** as information that helps teachers understand "what students like, what they find challenging, [and/or] common misconceptions or misrepresentations they have about particular topics" (p. viii). In short, knowledge of learners means knowing their potential to learn the topic at hand. Similarly, Ball, Thames, and Phelps (2008) define *knowledge of content and students* as a combination of subject matter understanding with knowledge of the students. It includes anticipating student ideas and interprets student understanding as it evolves through student language. These understandings address who the learners are in terms of both the psychological and sociological influences on their learning. Psychological understanding, or knowing how a student might interpret or misinterpret a concept or idea, allows the teacher to contextualize content, materials, and activities so the topic may be more readily understood by specific learners. For example, this knowledge helps a band director know that her clarinet players might struggle with understanding how their parts relate rhythmically with the rest of the ensemble. Such information will help the teacher devise alternative means for teaching this content to the clarinet section. Sociological understanding considers the influence of elements such as ethnicity and culture on student behavior and learning. Knowledge of cultural factors may help you understand why some Native American students will not look an authority figure, such as a teacher, in the eye, as their culture views such action as a challenge to authority and as being disrespectful. Requiring such behavior from a Native American student could have detrimental effects on his learning in your classroom.[1]

Millican (2012) asserts that the point at which all four of the previous knowledge domains intersect represents what Shulman (1986, 1987) termed **pedagogical content knowledge** (PCK). As we noted before, PCK has been difficult to define (Haston & Leon-Guerrero, 2008). However, Magnusson, Krajcik, and Borko (1999) state:

> Pedagogical content knowledge is a teacher's understanding of how to help students understand specific subject matter. It includes knowledge of how particular subject matter topics, problems, and issues can be organized, represented and adapted to the diverse interests and abilities of learners, and then presented for instruction. . . . The defining feature of pedagogical content knowledge is its conceptualization as the result of a *transformation* of knowledge from other domains.
>
> (p. 96)

When defined this way, PCK seems to include everything a teacher knows and does when teaching a topic. It blurs distinctions between teacher beliefs, teacher knowledge, teaching skills, and professional dispositions. Because PCK is all-inclusive, using it to help teachers understand what they need to know and be able to do specifically is difficult. Millican's model does, however, help us understand how four distinct ways of knowing contribute to the complexity of teaching.

Table 3.1 suggests how this model might be used to deconstruct knowledge used by a middle-school band director. While this table may help us discuss these domains of teacher knowledge, we suggest you consider that teachers do not think in such

---

[1] There is much more to know and understand about the psychological and social influences that will affect student learning in your classroom. The last section of this text (Chapters 8–11) addresses these understandings in much greater detail.

TABLE 3.1 Instructional example of each knowledge domain's contribution to pedagogical content knowledge.

Example	Knowledge domain
• Selecting a piece of repertoire for the ensemble that introduces the students to tonality other than major or minor	Curricular knowledge
• Reading and analyzing the tonal content of the selected score	Subject matter knowledge
• Relating D dorian (the tonal content of the piece) to the key of C major using 're' as resting tone (rather than 'do')	Pedagogical knowledge
• Anticipating that the brass section (almost all male) may struggle with audiating 're' as resting tone	Knowledge of students and their characteristics
• All the above leading to a plan to have the woodwinds play dorian tonal patterns as the brass play a drone tone on 're'	Pedagogical content knowledge

compartmentalized fashions as is suggested by the linear nature of the table. As the earlier model seen in Figure 3.1 shows, there are areas where different domains overlap and inform each other. For example, a band director is not likely to select repertoire based solely on her curriculum knowledge, but is likely to also consider her students and their characteristics as she is making this selection.

SKILL SETS FOR EFFECTIVE MUSIC TEACHING

Skills refer to things teachers DO. Depending upon the subject, these skills can be general and broad or specific and focused. Before going on with this discussion, however, it may help if you understood how we think of skills. Many of the skills we have listed could be viewed as teaching giftedness or talent rather than as teacher skills. We have chosen to list these as skills because skills can be learned. Talents are often thought to be the product of genetic endowment or characteristics with which you are born. While there is obviously a predisposition for some people to possess greater abilities in any of the skill sets we have listed, we believe it is possible to learn and/or improve these skills over time. For example, you may not be a naturally organized person, but you can learn to be more organized with the right motivation.

Many have investigated what current and future teachers consider important skills for all music teachers to possess (Miksza, Roeder, & Biggs, 2010; Rohwer & Henry,

2004; Teachout, 1997; Welch, Purves, Hargreaves, & Marshall, 2010). These researchers found that effective music teachers needed to possess various sets of skills. These include **personal skills** such as enthusiasm, **pedagogical skills** like being able to motivate students, **administrative skills** necessary to manage classroom materials, and **musical skills** necessary to model musical behavior effectively. Researchers investigating the desired skills for all beginning teachers, regardless of subject, have found similar collections of skill sets (Chong & Cheah, 2009). In addition to personal and pedagogical skills, these findings also highlight the need to develop interpersonal skills, reflective skills, and administrative and management skills.

In addition to being enthusiastic, a teacher's personal skill set should include coping skills, time management skills, leadership skills, planning skills, and the ability to set priorities for the well-functioning classroom (Chong & Cheah, 2009). This list is not all-inclusive, but recent research cites many of these items as the personal skills most desired by young music educators (Miksza, Roeder, & Biggs, 2010). This skill set helps the teacher establish a learning environment within given parameters that best facilitates student achievement. For example, it is possible for some students to miss their music class unexpectedly for other endeavors such as mandated testing, athletic events, or school field trips. While we hope that such interruptions are minimal, they are not uncommon. A music teacher's ability to cope with the given situation and plan effective instruction for those who remain in the classroom will determine the effectiveness of the music learning for these remaining students. His leadership skills will likely help him work with others in the school to limit these interruptions.

Pedagogical skills include the abilities that help a music teacher operate her classroom while presenting instruction effectively. Within most music classrooms, a teacher's choice of teaching method, motivational skills, classroom management skills, delivery skills, and pacing skills are all interdependent. A music teacher who can deliver instruction in a manner that engages all students while maintaining an appropriate challenge level through effective pacing will often find her students to be motivated. Combined with the ability to monitor student behavior, this teacher's classroom management skills will focus on maximizing student learning rather than simply enforcing rules and regulations of the classroom. Effective music teachers also recognize that students, even those of the same age and similar backgrounds, differ in their ability to learn. Such teachers will adjust instruction to meet each student's needs, which requires specialized teaching skills.

All teachers, but especially music teachers, work as members of learning communities. These communities include parents, colleagues, administrators and others in the community (NBPTS, 2002). Often, due to the visibility of the music programs at many schools, music teachers find themselves and their students in the role of 'school ambassadors,' representing not just the music program, but also the overall nature of the school to others outside the building. The teacher's interpersonal skills allow him to "engage in meaningful communication and participate in collaborative efforts within the school as well as wider communities of learning for school-wide improvements" (Chong & Cheah, 2009, p. 6).

Administrative and management skills allow the music educator to meet demands both inside and outside the classroom.[2] The ability to organize music, paperwork, files, and equipment is essential to being effective in the music classroom. Music educators often have direct contact with more students than the average classroom teacher. With that volume comes additional student files, large amounts of music and other teaching materials, and specialized devices like instruments and sound equipment. These materials must be organized so instructional time is not consumed by trying to locate the necessary equipment for a particular activity. With the demands of many extra- and co-curricular activities, there may also be the need to account for money and legal forms such as medical releases. It is essential that a music teacher manage these responsibilities well.

In addition, music educators must have the ability to organize people. For instance, a choir director will need to be able to get his three choirs to a performance on time, with all the necessary equipment. To accomplish this, he must organize how the group will travel. He will need to be able to monitor the students while traveling and during the event. He will need to ensure student safety throughout the event. He will need to make sure students are prepared properly for their performance while meeting the community's expectations of the choral program on all accounts. His administrative and management skills will help him meet these demands.

Though seemingly obvious, excellent music educators need to possess superior musical skills. These include, but are not limited to, performance skills, which not only incorporates skill on one's primary instrument, but also includes piano skills and skills on many other secondary instruments. We contend that any genre of musical expression in which you choose to engage and possibly teach is acceptable as long as it is developmentally and culturally appropriate for the learners. One type of music or one way to express musical ideas is not necessarily superior to any other as long as the musicians involved perform

---

[2] Earlier we presented Millican's (2008) idea of 'administrative knowledge.' We distinguish administrative knowledge (knowing the administrative tasks required of a particular teaching situation) from administrative skills (the ability to *take action* effectively based on one's administrative knowledge).

with authenticity regarding the particular genre being presented. In addition to expressing yourself in the most musical manner possible, you need to have excellent tonal and rhythmic aural skills. You may need to develop conducting skills so you can communicate your musical ideas to students in ensemble settings. You will need to develop highly acute listening skills that will inform your understanding of music. You will need excellent notational reading skills that allow you to convert what you see to musical expression at sight. You should also be able to compose and arrange music as well as improvise at acceptable levels. Excellent professional music educators are highly skilled musicians.

DISCUSSION BOARD
Knowledge and Skills of Music Teaching

Within the descriptions of teacher knowledge and skills, were there aspects that surprised you? If so, what surprised you and why do think you may not have considered these before now? If not, how did you come to understand that these would be required of you as a professional music educator? Read your colleagues' posts and comment on how their perceptions are similar or dissimilar from yours.

DISPOSITIONS FOR EFFECTIVE MUSIC TEACHING

There is considerable debate about the presence and effectiveness of teaching dispositions (Jung & Rhodes, 2008; Shiveley & Misco, 2010; Villegas, 2007; Wasicsko, 2007). In fact, there is concern about how to simply define what a disposition is. Villegas (2007) defines dispositions as "tendencies for individuals to act in a particular manner under particular circumstances, based on their beliefs" (p. 373). The Council for the Accreditation of Educator Preparation (CAEP, formerly NCATE) uses a similar definition. They state that professional dispositions are "professional attitudes, values, and beliefs demonstrated through both verbal and non-verbal behaviors as educators interact with students, families, colleagues, and communities. These positive behaviors support student learning and development" (National Council for Accreditation of Teacher Education, 2010). The key debate point lies in the argument that dispositions are different from attitudes. Attitudes may provide motivation for behavior, but may not be an accurate predictor of actual practice. "For example, a teacher may have a positive attitude toward teaching struggling students to read but may fail in any attempts to accomplish that goal" (Schussler, Stooksbury, & Bercaw, 2010, p. 350). Thus, dispositions must be more than positive or negative ideas about teaching and learning. They must connect a teacher's knowledge and skills to the actual actions that must take place to facilitate effective learning. In this sense, effective teaching requires "more than ability. It involves an inclination to put one's ability to use and the sensitivity to know when a situation calls for specific skills" (Schussler et al., 2010, p. 351). Therefore, we have adopted the following definition: "Dispositions involve the inclination of a teacher to achieve particular purposes and the awareness of the self and the context of a given situation to employ appropriate knowledge and skills to achieve those purposes" (Schussler et al., 2010, p. 351).

Another part of the debate surrounding teacher dispositions focuses on teachers' abilities to learn dispositions. If we agree that there are certain dispositions or collections of dispositions that help teachers put their knowledge and skills into effective action, one may question whether it is necessary for a teacher candidate to exemplify these dispositions prior to her professional education or if it is possible to learn such dispositions. We take the position that dispositions can be learned. As Ruitenberg (2011) states,

> it is unclear whether teacher education programs should focus on selecting the right kind of person, or on educating the student for a profession. I suggest that a clearer distinction should be made between predispositions (value commitments that a person may or may not act upon) and professional dispositions (characteristics attributed to a person based on actually observed actions), and that teacher education programs should focus their attention on the latter, not the former. The question is not whether . . . teachers have the "right" personal beliefs but whether, if the dispositions required by the profession are at odds with their personal beliefs, the former will override the latter.
>
> (p. 41)

For this reason, we will explore teacher dispositions that have, through research, been accepted as those that most effectively help teachers put their knowledge and skills into practice. As you read, we encourage you to begin examining your personal beliefs in relation to these dispositions.

As dispositions can be contextual, for instance, a specific disposition may apply more readily to one situation over another, it may be helpful to consider dispositions in larger, more inclusive categories. One particularly effective way this has been done is to consider dispositions as they relate to the domains of (a) intellectual dispositions, (b) cultural dispositions, and (c) moral dispositions (Schussler et al., 2010; Stooksbury, Schussler, & Bercaw, 2009).

Intellectual dispositions are defined as "teachers' inclination to process knowledge of content and pedagogy, their awareness of what the educational context requires for desired learning outcomes to be reached, and their inclination to put their knowledge and awareness to use accordingly in the classroom" (Schussler et al., 2010, p. 352). These include dispositions toward instruction, curriculum, learning expectations, beliefs about learning, and the teacher's role as a professional. An instructional disposition might include ideas about the use of content and delivery to maintain student attention. One such disposition would suggest that if you teach to the individual differences of students and find ways to keep them engaged in meaningful and relevant content, classroom management issues will be minimized. Armed with this disposition, a music teacher would use her knowledge to find class materials that are both content-rich and meaningful to the students in her classroom. Additionally, she would use her skills to design and deliver instruction in ways that connect students to the material.

Cultural dispositions are defined as "teachers' inclination and desire to meet the needs of all learners in the classroom" (Schussler et al., 2010, p. 352). There are three elements to consider in this domain. Rooted in research on culturally relevant pedagogy (Gay, 2000), these include: (a) the teacher's understanding of his or her culture and its effects on student learning, (b) an understanding of the students' cultures and their effects on learning, and (c) the intersection between these many cultures and how the relationships generated at this point effect student learning. These dispositions might include ideas related to teacher identity, student identity, and the ability to alter or modify instruction. A teacher holding the disposition that Western art music does not celebrate the identity of students from disadvantaged backgrounds may not engage in the traditional practices found in most middle-school instrumental music programs. Further, his identity as a versatile musician who is capable of understanding and performing a wide variety of music might help him examine the intersection between his musical understandings and the musical identities of his students. Through this investigation, the teacher could decide to change the content and practice of the standard instrumental music classroom to focus on hip-hop. The teacher would make use of his knowledge of musical structures and instrumental performance to develop means to study the content in educationally sound ways that would respect the students' identities. His skills would allow him to teach students how to produce music of this type in their classroom.

Moral dispositions entail "teachers putting aside their own needs to help another reach her or his potential" (Schussler et al., 2010, p. 353). Teachers cannot escape their own moral value systems as they make teaching decisions and we are not suggesting that they should. However, "Because teachers make hundreds of decisions daily that are packed with assumptions about the purposes of education and how students should be educated, their dispositions act as a value-laden guide that frames their thinking and actions" (p. 353). The key for effective teachers is for them to recognize their value systems and understand how these systems affect instruction and learning. These dispositions might include care and concern for all pupils, the desire that educational outcomes are advantageous to the students' wellbeing beyond the immediate classroom, and that all students have access to quality education. If a high-school orchestra director holds these dispositions, she might work with community members to develop an orchestra league that would raise money to support the purchase of high quality step-up instruments for students whose families may not be financially capable of doing so. Her desire to make sure that what students learn in her classroom is applicable to their lives outside the classroom and perhaps beyond high school might drive her to collaboratively design a service learning project with her orchestra members that allows these students to take peer-coached chamber groups to perform at homeless shelters around the community on a recurring basis. Much of her knowledge and skill would be put to use in accomplishing these goals.

BLOG ON . . .
Dispositions

What dispositions did your *most influential teacher* model for you? Were these evident to you at the time you were in his or her classroom or studio? What dispositions do you believe will be most difficult for you to develop? Why?

PUTTING IT ALL TOGETHER: KNOWLEDGE, SKILLS, AND DISPOSITIONS

We have explored knowledge, skills, and dispositions separately throughout this chapter. This approach was necessary so that we could discuss each without confusing it with another. However, in the actual practice of music teaching, each of these areas is enacted interdependently with the other two. Changes in a disposition might require the teacher to acquire new knowledge or develop new skills. Consider the example of the middle-school instrumental teacher's desire to develop a music curriculum focused on hip-hop. The decision to make this change likely required the teacher to study the background and history of hip-hop from its genesis in Brooklyn, New York, to its current practices as a mainstream musical art form. He may have needed to acquire some technology skills in music production to adequately instruct students in their class projects composing and performing their own songs. With new knowledge and new skills, new dispositions may emerge as well. Figure 3.2 is adapted from a model used to study values, skills, and knowledge (VSK) within education in Singapore (Chong & Cheah, 2009). We have changed their category of 'values' to 'dispositions' and have listed knowledge and skills that are applicable to music teaching. With those changes, this model can help you visualize how the dimensions of teacher knowledge, skills, and dispositions work together to inform your music teaching.

Throughout this text you will be challenged to continually examine the knowledge, skills, and dispositions you will need to be an effective professional music educator. This is a personal journey and will likely change many times in your schooling and career. The time to start is now and enjoy the excursion!

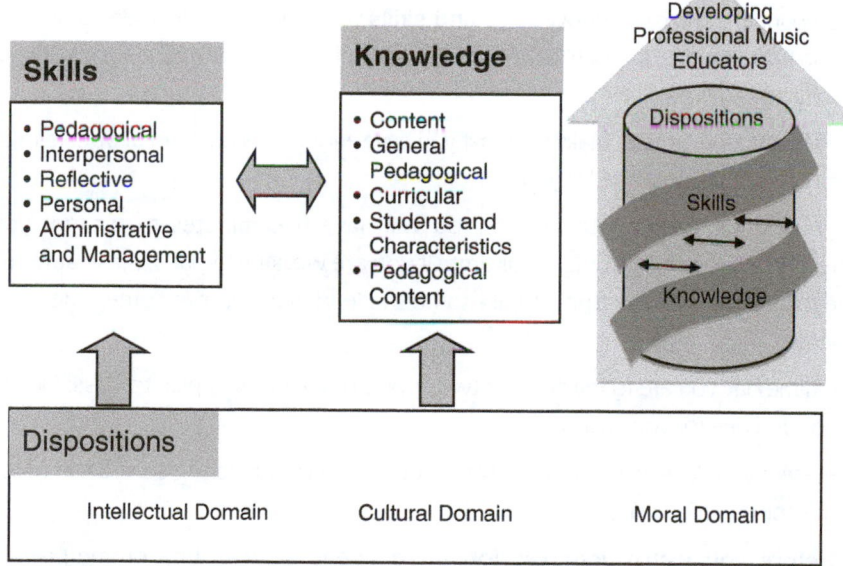

FIGURE 3.2 Knowledge, skills, and dispositions framework. Adapted from the National Institute of Education, Singapore—2005 Values Skills Knowledge Framework. The original model can be found in Chong and Cheah (2009). Adapted with permission.

CLASS ACTIVITIES

Class Activity 3.1: What If You Were to Teach a Skill?

The following are instructions for completing a short (i.e. 5–7 minute) teaching episode that we call a 'Micro-Teaching Episode' (MTE). An MTE can be accomplished by an individual or in pairs. For this activity, you should complete the following steps:

- Decide on your 'subject matter'—**what you will teach**—make it a simple skill that you can teach in five minutes. People have taught how to tie shoes, make a PB&J sandwich, etc. BE CREATIVE!

- Write an initial step-by-step plan for **how you will teach** this skill.

- Decide if this plan is appropriate for your learners (classmates) and **how they might learn best**.

- Assess, as best you can, if your learners will have the necessary **prerequisite knowledge and skills** to reach the objective of your plan.

- Based on **what** you are teaching, how you believe your **learners learn best,** the amount of preexisting **knowledge and skills** you believe your learners to possess, and **how** you plan to teach this skill, assess your plan, and make any adjustments you think to be necessary.

- Gather your materials. Make sure that you have enough materials for all your learners to be ACTIVELY engaged in your lesson.

- Practice delivering your lesson. You will have five minutes to present your lesson. This should be plenty of time. If you are working in pairs, make sure that each partner has the opportunity to be the lead instructor at some time in the lesson.

- On the day you are to teach, bring two copies of your lesson plan to class: One for you and one for your instructor.

- Present your lesson. If at all possible, video record your teaching so you can review the episode after class.

- **Before you watch your session**, make an entry in your blog on the planning procedure, what your thoughts were before you taught, and how it felt to teach.

- Watch the video of your session.

- **After you watch your session,** make another blog entry and address what you saw and heard in your video. Make special note of the things you did that were effective. You should also note areas you believe could be more effective. Finally, describe any surprises (i.e. anything you noticed on the video that you did not notice during or after your teaching).

Class Activity 3.2: What Do You Need to Know and Do?

In small groups (3–4 people), take a poster-sized sheet of paper and a marker and make a list of the things ALL music teachers need to **know** to be effective professional music educators. After you have made this list, turn the paper over and make a list of the things that ALL music teachers need to **be able to do** to be effective professional music educators. After this list is complete, go back to your first list and discuss ways that you could categorize music teacher knowledge. With your second list, discuss how you might categorize music teacher skills. Be prepared to share your thoughts with the class.

 # Part I: Self Concerns

At the end of each of the three parts (i.e. Part I—Self Concerns, Part II—Teaching Concerns, and Part III—Student-Learning Concerns) of this text you will find a chapter titled *Connecting to the Profession.* These contain collections of resources to enhance your understanding of the concepts presented within that entire part of the text. Each begins with a list of *terms and concepts* listed by chapter. These are what we consider to be the primary points from each chapter. There will also be a section titled *connect to research.* These are recent research articles on the primary topics from each of the chapters in each respective part. If there are concepts that are of particular interest to you, these articles will help you understand those ideas in greater depth than presented in the chapter. The section titled *connect to professional journals* also provides you with more information on these topics, but are not research studies. These are articles informed by research, but are not reporting the results of a particular research study. In the *connect to the web* section, you will find on-line resources. There are on-line articles and a number of video resources to help you further explore the concepts presented in the part. Finally, the *connect to the classroom* section lists a number of questions you could use as you view the classroom teaching videos on the textbook website.

TERMS AND CONCEPTS

Chapter 1

Teach

Learn

Professional

Technician

Talent

Active Learning

Passive Learning

Reflection

Chapter 2

Teacher Belief

Metaphor

Target

Source

Ground

Cognitive Dissonance

Perennialism

Essentialism

Positivism

Progressivism

Humanism

Constructivism

Chapter 3

Knowledge

Skill

Disposition

Content Knowledge

General Pedagogical Knowledge

Curriculum Knowledge

Knowledge of Learners and Their Characteristics

Pedagogical Content Knowledge

Knowledge of Educational Contexts

Administrative Knowledge

Common Content Knowledge

Specialized Content Knowledge

Personal Skills

Pedagogical Skills

Administrative Skills

Musical Skills

Intellectual Disposition

Cultural Disposition

Moral Disposition

CONNECT TO RESEARCH

Chapter 1

Teacher Identity/Role

Haston, W., & Russell, J. (2012). Influences of authentic context learning experiences on occupational identity development of preservice music teachers. *Journal of Research in Music Education, 59*(4), 369–392. doi: 10.1177/0022429411414716

The purpose of this study was to examine the occupational identity development of undergraduate music education majors as they participated in a year-long authentic context learning (ACL) experience situated within a professional development school (PDS). Five undergraduate music education majors enrolled in either a string pedagogy class or an instrumental methods class were required to teach in the band or string projects at the PDS. The authors utilized a multiple case study method and collected data from interviews, observations, and participant written reflections. The transformation of data included transcribing interviews and indexing student reflections. The authors identified four emergent themes: the development of general pedagogical knowledge, knowledge of self, performer/teacher symbiotic outcomes, and professional perspectives. The impact of the perceived positive or negative ACL experiences as well as interactions with peers was mediated by either adaptive or maladaptive participant responses to ACL experiences. Participants' descriptions fit the framework of an extended apprenticeship of what the authors labeled a critical apprenticeship of observation. Based on these findings, the authors developed a conceptual diagram in order to describe the impact of the ACL experiences on teacher occupational identity development.

Miksza, P., & Berg, M. (2013). A longitudinal study of preservice music teacher development: Application and advancement of the Fuller and Bown Teacher-concerns model. *Journal of Research in Music Education, 61*(1), 44–62. doi:10.1177/0022429412473606

The purpose of this study was to investigate the development of preservice music teachers' concerns using Fuller and Bown's model. Participants were eight instrumental teachers who participated in the previous Berg and Miksza (2010) study. Data sources included goals essays, journals, a midterm growth plan, and teaching observation reports with accompanying lesson plans that were collected over a 1.5-year period. The participants expressed less concern for self-survival and more concern for making an impact on students as time progressed from their junior-level practicum experience to the end of student teaching. Concerns regarding basic competencies and professionalism ultimately gave way to specific contextual aspects of the participants' teaching placements and more nuanced instructional issues. Results indicated that the focus of the participants' concerns also was affected greatly by their teaching context. Implications for music teacher preparation as well as extensions of Fuller and Bown's model are discussed.

Active Learning

Schmidt, M. (2010). Learning from teaching experience: Dewey's theory and preservice teachers' learning. *Journal of Research in Music Education, 58*(2), 131–146. doi:10.1177/0022429410368723

Teachers often claim that they learn more from teaching experience than from coursework. In this qualitative study, the author explored the value that six preservice teachers attributed to peer teaching, early field experiences, student teaching, and self-arranged teaching experiences engaged in during their university education. Consistent with Dewey's theory of experience, as the participants interacted with their teaching experiences, they each created continuity among and derived their own meanings from them. This individualized aspect of learning was enriched as they also experienced the value of learning within a community of educators. Meaningful learning from all types of teaching experience appeared to be fostered by a balance between doing (action) and undergoing (reflection), both individually and in community. Dewey's theory of experience proved useful in illuminating possible reasons for similarities and differences in the teaching experiences that each participant valued.

Reflection

Delaney, D.W. (2011). Elementary general music teachers' reflections on instruction. *Update: Applications of Research In Music Education, 29*(2), 41–49. doi:10.1177/8755123310396193

A qualitative study was completed to identify and study the content of selected elementary general music teachers' evaluations of their own instruction and the instruction of another elementary general music teacher. Participants represented a variety of educational backgrounds and teaching experience: Teacher A (9 years teaching Grades 4–6 at current school), Teacher B (2 years teaching K-5 general music at current school), Teacher C (completing third year teaching Grades 4–6 general music), and Teacher D (completing first year teaching K-4 general music and strings). Through viewing four videotape recordings of lessons and use of an open-ended interview process, participants were able to explain teaching strategies used and reflect on their teaching and the teaching of another elementary general music teacher. The participants recommended that videotape recordings of instruction accompanied by the interview process be used for professional development and to discuss teaching strategies with other teachers.

Chapter 2

The Use of Metaphor in Teacher Education

Lin, W., Shein, P., & Yang, S. (2012). Exploring personal EFL teaching metaphors in pre-service teacher education. *English Teaching: Practice and Critique, 11*(1), 183–199.

Metaphors are significant in teacher education, because they can provide insights into complex concepts of teaching and learning and thus provide a window into the comprehension of teachers' personal experiences. This study employed metaphorical analysis to investigate how preservice teachers view English as a Foreign Language (EFL) courses at the beginning of their teacher education programs. Forty student teachers in a teacher certificate program in secondary education were asked to provide metaphors of how they conceptualize themselves as EFL teachers. Findings revealed that the teachers' metaphorical conceptualizations appeared to be more student-centered, reflecting beliefs about teaching practice and generally stemming from personal and school experiences. Overall, the written metaphors provided access to preservice teachers' preconceived notions of teaching prior to entering the classroom. Metaphors thus provide a framework with which to assess teaching and a means for teachers to enhance self-awareness and professional development. This study leads to several conclusions that highlight some implications for teacher education and to ideas for further investigations.

Pinnegar, S., Mangelson, J., Reed, M., & Groves, S. (2011). Exploring preservice teachers' metaphor plotlines. *Teaching and Teacher Education: An International Journal of Research and Studies, 27*(3), 639–647. doi:10.1016/j.tate.2010.11.002

This study explores how entering female preservice teachers position themselves— the plotlines, obligations, responsibilities, and duties they are prepared to enact, the expectations they hold for students, and the implications these have for teacher education. Using positioning theory, the authors analyze application letters of 20 elementary preservice teachers to uncover metaphor plotlines for teaching. Preservice teachers' application letters contained 12 metaphor plotlines presented here in terms of the definition, the role of teacher, and the role of student. The paper explores implications for the content of teacher education, development as a teacher, and the ability to engage students.

Stylianou, M., Kulinna, P., Cothran, D., & Ja Youn, K. (2013). Physical education teachers' metaphors of teaching and learning. *Journal of Teaching in Physical Education, 32*(1), 22.

This study was informed by the literature on teaching metaphors and the theory of occupational socialization. Its purpose was to examine in-service Physical Education teachers' initial (before entering the profession), current, and ideal metaphors of teaching, related factors, and potential differences in participants' metaphors based on their teaching experience. A mixed-methods approach was employed for this study, including a modified version of an existing survey ($N = 66$) and interviews ($N = 13$). Descriptive statistics indicated that while participants predominantly embraced teacher-centered metaphors initially, about half of them reported their current and ideal metaphors as student-centered. Constant comparison and analytic induction techniques revealed three themes and several subthemes: (a) fluidity (own definitions, combination of metaphors), (b) formation of initial views of teaching (acculturation, professional socialization), and (c) evolutionary forces and constraints (experience, pressure of test scores, time allocation, resources). These results have implications both for preservice and in-service teacher education programs.

Teacher-Centered and Student-Centered Instruction

Andrews, K. (2013). Standing 'on our own two feet': A comparison of teacher-directed and group learning in an extra-curricular instrumental group. *British Journal of Music Education, 30*(1), 125–148. doi:10.1017/S0265051712000460

This practitioner-based research, undertaken by the author in her own teaching context with herself as participant, explores how autonomous learning skills and motivation can be fostered in primary-aged instrumentalists. A primary school extra-curricular recorder group was observed participating in two stages of lessons: the first, teacher-directed, and the second, focused around group learning. Lessons were videoed and transcribed for analysis and pupils' views on the two styles of lessons gained through interviews. The teacher-directed lessons were considered in the light of the apprenticeship conception of the teacher's role, with its potential to balance direction and facilitation, and scaffolding was observed to be used in various ways, both promoting and restricting pupil autonomy. The group learning lessons used aspects of the Musical Futures informal learning approach, particularly self-directed learning in friendship groups, using aural models on CD, with the teacher's role facilitative rather than directive. These lessons were considered in the light of theories of group learning, with pupils observed providing mutual support, scaffolding in different ways to a teacher, and engaging in transactive communication. Pupils, though positive about both stages, valued the opportunity to learn independently in the group learning lessons, gaining a sense of flow through the challenge involved. Findings suggest that whilst both teacher-directed and group learning can be effective, music teachers could develop their pupils' capacity for autonomous learning by taking opportunities to adopt a more facilitative role, providing the learning context and assistance when required, but allowing the pupils to direct their own learning.

Killian, J., Dye, K., & Wayman, J. (2013). Music student teachers: Pre-student teaching concerns and post-student teaching perceptions over a 5-year period. *Journal of Research in Music Education, 61*(1), 63–79. doi:10.1177/0022429412474314

In this descriptive study, self-reported concerns of 159 music student teachers pre- and post-student teaching were examined, over a period of five years. Resulting comments ($N = 867$) were analyzed on the basis of (a) stages of teacher concern (focus on self, subject matter [music and teaching], and students) modeled after Fuller and Bown and (b) emerging categories of concern compared with those identified by Madsen and Kaiser (1999). Stages of concern were reliably identifiable across all comments. Teachers, as predicted, began student teaching with more self (56 percent) and fewer student (4 percent) comments. Post-student teaching comments resulted in fewer self (33 percent) and more student (20 percent) mentions. Categorization of concerns indicated that pre- and post-student teachers shared some concerns (applying knowledge, discipline, confidence) but showed marked differences in other areas (cut out for teaching, information about students, administrative duties). Pre-student teaching categories were similar to those reported by Madsen and Kaiser a decade earlier; post-student teaching comments differed.

Chapter 3

Music Teacher Knowledge

Bauer, W.I. (2013). The acquisition of musical technological pedagogical and content knowledge. *Journal of Music Teacher Education, 22*(2), 51-64. doi:10.1177/1057083712457881

Technological pedagogical and content knowledge (TPACK) is a conceptual framework for the teacher knowledge necessary to effectively integrate technology into teaching and learning. The purposes of this study were to (a) develop and administer an instrument to measure music educators' TPACK, (b) examine how music teachers acquire their TPACK, and (c) determine if a relationship existed between those teachers' TPACK and their reported integration of technology. Participants ($N = 284$) were music teachers who completed two questionnaires, one designed to measure their TPACK (Musical TPACK Questionnaire [MTPACK-Q]) and another to describe the level of technology integration in their classroom (Concerns-Based Adoption Model–Levels of Use [CBAM-LoU] instrument). Scores on the technology-related domains of the TPACK model were lower than content, pedagogical, or pedagogical content domains. A moderate, significant, positive correlation ($r = .51, p \le .01$) was found between the participants' MTPACK-Q score and the level of technology integration in their classroom as reported by the CBAM-LoU.

Haston, W., & Leon-Guerrero, A. (2008). Sources of pedagogical content knowledge: Reports by preservice instrumental music teachers. *Journal of Music Teacher Education, 17*(2), 48-59. doi:10.1177/1057083708317644

The purpose of the study was to better understand what influences preservice instrumental music teachers' acquisition of pedagogical content knowledge (PCK). Research questions were as follows: (a) Are there identifiable applications of PCK in the preservice teachers' interactions with students? (b) To what source—apprenticeship of observation, methods classes, cooperating teachers, or intuition—do preservice teachers attribute these applications of PCK? Video recordings of preservice teachers conducting a rehearsal were collected and analyzed for events that demonstrated PCK. Exemplary excerpts were selected and reviewed with each participant. Interviews revealed a substantial amount of identifiable PCK. Apprenticeship of observation, methods courses, and cooperating teacher were each cited by two participants as their primary source of PCK. One participant cited intuition and methods courses equally. Determining where preservice teachers go to access PCK is the first step in redesigning college methods courses to better account for previously learned PCK.

Music Teacher Skills

Kelly, S. N. (2010). Public school supervising teachers' perceptions of skills and behaviors necessary in the development of effective music student teachers. *Bulletin of the Council for Research in Music Education, 185,* 21.

The purpose of this study was to investigate: (a) What specific skills and behaviors are considered most important by public school supervising teachers in the development of effective music student teachers; and (b) Are there differences between instrumental (band/strings) and choral/elementary music supervising teachers on those skills and behaviors? A survey was constructed, consisting of 35 items and representing a variety of teacher skills and behaviors. The respondents, public school music teachers who were experienced in supervising student teachers ($N = 112$), rated each survey item from 1 (not very important) to 5 (very important) regarding the degree each skill and behavior was considered important in the development of music student teachers. The findings showed the highest rated traits may be considered more social in nature and are frequently associated with an individual's personality or personal belief (e.g. honest and ethical). Traits receiving the lowest ratings did not require direct use of musical skills or knowledge (e.g. playing the piano; provide accompaniment), or instructional techniques (e.g. dealing effectively with student discipline). The findings suggest that music student teachers should be aware of high expectations placed on personal characteristics by supervising teachers during the student teaching experience.

CONNECT TO PROFESSIONAL JOURNALS

Chapter 1

Teacher Identity/Role

Hesterman, P. K. (2012). Growing as a professional music educator. *General Music Today, 25*(3), 36–41. doi:10.1177/1048371311435274

Education is a lifelong adventure that is ever-changing and active. Educators continually adapt their practices to meet the needs of an ever-changing population of children flowing through the schools. It is advantageous for teachers to be committed to lifelong learning for their own professional and personal development. As a novice teacher becomes more adept in the profession, new reflections and new perspectives can bring into focus additional ways to improve one's teaching, classroom demeanor, and the like. Professional interactions with other teachers are important for the music teacher to facilitate a dialogue for growth for the music teacher. Teachers who are learners throughout their careers realize that they are not the source of all knowledge pertaining to music. Good teaching practices are defined according to current educational thought, especially when the educator incorporates learner analysis and reflection into teaching and not only the acquisition of knowledge and imitation.

Joseph, D., & Heading, M. (2010). Putting theory into practice: Moving from student identity to teacher identity. *Australian Journal of Teacher Education, 35*(3), 75–87.

As teaching is a highly skilled and complex profession, preservice teachers need to develop a series of attributes for their practice in relation to pedagogy, content, student learning, classroom management, and their ability to engage in reflection. Through reflective narrative, this article seeks to share how a tertiary music educator prepares her generalist primary preservice teachers to engage, explore, and experience music education within the Bachelor of Education (Primary) course at [Unnamed] University. It also presents one preservice teacher's experience of teaching music during her school placements in 2009 in what she calls "putting theory into practice," moving from student identity to teacher identity. Although the "hands-on" approach to teaching and learning on-campus and when on school placement provide preservice teachers with knowledge, skills, and understanding, the continued support of professional learning is well recognized and will be an ongoing process as preservice teachers create their own professional identity.

Active Learning

Davis, V. (2011). What middle school students need from their general music class (and how we can help). *General Music Today, 24*(3), 17–22. doi:10.1177/1048371310373457

The middle-school general music class is a course that holds many possibilities and challenges. In this research-based article, teachers are encouraged to "teach for transfer," to create worthwhile learning activities that prepare students for music making in the adult community. Three needs of the middle-school music student are discussed: active, hands-on learning challenges, which involve the student in music making; in-depth exploration of focused listening, which acquaints students with the availability of listening opportunities and teaches them what to listen for; and opportunities for social connection, drawing together students and teachers in a community of music makers.

Mudd, T. (2012). Developing transferable skills through engagement with higher education laptop ensembles. *Journal of Music, Technology and Education, 5*(1), 29–41. doi:10.1386/jmte.5.1.29_1

This article argues that ensemble playing forms the backbone of transferable skills development in higher education music courses, and demonstrates how laptop ensembles, as well as being musically engaging projects in their own right, can be a useful way of integrating such skill development into more technologically oriented music degrees. The fact that such ensembles have few established modes of practice allows them to be particularly open to student engagement in a variety of roles and can help to promote an active learning environment. Approaches to structuring the organization of such an ensemble to promote these pedagogical aspects are discussed and related to the four stages laid out by David Kolb's experiential learning model.

Scott, S. (2010). A minds-on approach to active learning in general music. *General Music Today, 24*(1), 19–26. doi:10.1177/1048371309354432

Minds-on engagement in active learning is explored through the experiences of Margaret Sanders, a general music teacher. Minds-on learners think about their experiences. They are actively involved as questioners and problem solvers while they complete musical tasks and reflect on their work after it is completed. Minds-off learners focus on their actions but not on the thinking required to complete a given task. This idea is explored in relation to the use of classroom routines to direct instruction. Routines serve a valuable function in moving students through their school day, assisting their progress from class to class to their dismissal at the end of the day. However, teachers may assume that students are involved in minds-on learning when, due to instructional routines, students' responses represent a minds-off engagement in their learning. Teachers of general music must constantly challenge students in unexpected ways to maintain their minds-on engagement in music.

Reflection

Snyder, D. W. (2011). Preparing for teaching through reflection. *Music Educators Journal, 97*(3), 56–60. doi:10.1177/0027432111399348

University programs often require preservice music educators to complete some small- or large-group instruction before beginning student teaching. One of the tools used to deepen these preservice teaching experiences and consequently the pedagogical knowledge for these teachers is to have them reflect on their teaching episodes. Video reflection allows preservice teachers to examine their own teaching. This article presents excerpts of video reflections taken from preservice music teachers. Some of the areas where video reflection proved effective in improving instruction were (1) reducing the amount of teacher talking and increasing the amount of student playing, (2) structuring of the lesson, and (3) attention to student playing errors. Applications taken from this research are also presented.

Chapter 2

Teacher-Centered and Student-Centered Instruction

Blair, D. V. (2009). Stepping aside: Teaching in a student-centered music classroom. *Music Educators Journal, 95*(3), 42–45. doi:10.1177/0027432108330760

While the teacher is still the coordinator and designer of classroom musical experiences, the teacher does not need to direct every activity every moment. The teacher's role is important, but it changes to shift the focus of classroom instruction from what the teacher will do to what the students will figure out. This includes carefully crafting lessons that "allow for" and—in order to be successful—"necessitate" that students be creatively engaged with the music. Such lesson design requires finding ways that allow students to "be" composers, listeners, or performers—to express new musical ideas through composing, to find broad and specific musical ideas when listening, to interpret music when performing. This "allowing for" is quite intentional, and requires that the teacher step back and no longer be the center of the musical experience, responsible for all the thinking and doing and musical decision-making. It requires the teacher to trust and enable the students' budding musicianship, rather than requiring students to mimic their teacher's musicianship.

Block, D. (2011). Student-centered instruction is a means of creating independent musicians. *Teaching Music, 19*(1), 66.

The article discusses student-centered instruction in secondary music education. The author comments on music teachers' roles in facilitating independence in young musicians. Other topics explored include improving students' musical vocabulary, development of musical knowledge and theory, and the challenges of a performance-based class structure.

Philosophy

Branscome, E. E. (2012). The impact of education reform on music education: Paradigm shifts in music education curriculum, advocacy, and philosophy from 'Sputnik' to Race to the Top. *Arts Education Policy Review, 113*(3), 112–118. doi:10.1080/10632913.2012.687341

President Obama recently described America's current economic, societal, educational, and technological circumstances as "our generation's 'Sputnik' moment." If history repeats itself in the twenty-first century, music educators may face a situation similar to that which developed in the 1960s concerning the impact of education reform on music education. The purpose of this article is to identify possible trends in music curriculum, advocacy, and philosophy that may have developed in response to U.S. education reform, and to identify ways in which these trends may help music educators prepare for future innovations.

Chapter 3

Music Teacher Dispositions

Campbell, M., Thompson, L., & Barrett, J. (2012). Supporting and sustaining a personal orientation to music teaching: Implications for music teacher education. *Journal of Music Teacher Education, 22*(1), 75–90. doi:10.1177/1057083711427587

This article provides a conceptual argument for considering a personal orientation as a guiding framework for music teacher education. The potential strength and impact of this philosophical stance is underscored in the research on preservice and in-service teacher beliefs. Tools and dispositions that facilitate integrating a personal orientation into current programs are presented, discussed, and illustrated. Among these tools are methodologies for exploring self, methodologies for exploring school contexts, and methodologies for exploring teaching and learning. Principles for creating program coherence are also offered.

CONNECT TO THE WEB

Chapter 1

Is Teaching a Profession?

http://www.guardian.co.uk/teacher-network/2012/jul/31/is-teaching-a-profession
A short but thought-provoking article exploring the question "Is teaching a profession?" The piece was published in the *Guardian*, a British national daily newspaper; therefore some of the terminology is specific to that country.

Newteacherstalk's Channel

http://www.youtube.com/user/newteacherstalk/videos

A series of videos on YouTube from the United Kingdom discussing the questions surrounding teaching as a profession and then listing several aspects of teaching that Alan Newland terms "the teaching code."

Promoting Active Learning

https://utah.instructure.com/courses/148446/wiki/active-learning

A list of activities that can be used in any classroom to promote active learning.

What is Active Learning?

http://www.youtube.com/watch?v=UsDl6hDx5ul

Mark Trego from Northwest Iowa Community College discusses what active learning is and provides examples of how active learning can be used in both face-to-face and online classes.

Chapter 2

Changing Education Paradigms (Factory Model)

http://www.youtube.com/watch?v=zDZFcDGpL4U

Sir Ken Robinson speaks about the current paradigm of education and how it is affecting student learning. He addresses the "factory model" and the assumptions upon which it is based.

Learner-Centered Education in Maine

http://www.youtube.com/watch?v=7z9-f5qDoqY&list=PL49DDA11960CC8 70F

A series of six videos on concepts of developing student/learner-centered instruction.

Jack C. Richards on Learner-Centered Teaching

http://www.youtube.com/watch?v=dP2lXaQwfXQ

A concise discussion about the foundations of student/learner-centered instruction.

Chapter 3

Teacher Skills in a Digital Age

http://www.youtube.com/watch?v=R_BJcRVYQsE
Don Knezek describes shifting attitudes about what makes an effective teacher in today's technological world. Don Knezek, PhD, CAE, is Chief Executive Officer of the International Society for Technology in Education.

Effective Teacher: Professional Skills and Abilities (Putting it All Together)

http://www.youtube.com/watch?v=jC3D7O-ByLE
Are you a teacher or an educator? This is an interesting exploration of these two ideas.

 ## CONNECT TO THE CLASSROOM

Prior to watching one of the teaching videos available on the website, familiarize yourself with the questions below. As you view the video, take notes on what you see and hear. We suggest that you either download the video observation form from the text website or simply use a sheet of paper that has been divided into two columns. On the left side, list the events you see and hear taking place in the classroom. On the right side, make short notes about why you believe the teacher chose to use these events during the lesson. You may find it easiest to list all the events and then go back and make your notes on why the teacher chose those events as part of his or her instruction. After you watch the video, address the questions below.

1. What things did this teacher do that demonstrated his/her abilities as a professional music educator? (See Table 1.1, p.12, in your text.)
2. What teacher qualities did this instructor exhibit?
3. How did this teacher make use of active learning in his/her classroom?
4. What metaphor would best describe this classroom and why?
5. What was your general impression of this class? Why?
6. What teacher knowledge (i.e. subject matter, pedagogical, curricular, student learning) did you see this teacher demonstrate? What was the most effective example you observed?
7. What skills did the teacher demonstrate as he/she taught the class? (See Chapter 3, Figure 3.2, p. 55.)

PART II

DISCOVERY OF TEACHING

What is Your Classroom?

4

There are many different music classroom and rehearsal settings existing in schools today. When listing your more recent experiences as a music student, you would likely include large ensemble classes such as band, choir, or orchestra, and possibly experiences with some specialty ensembles such as jazz band, madrigal singers, or any number of the many different types of chamber groups possible. You may have considered music theory or music appreciation courses, and if you thought about your earlier experiences, you might have listed beginning band/strings or even elementary general music class.

Each setting is unique because of the skills being developed and knowledge being learned. For example, experiences in a high-school string orchestra rehearsal are markedly different than those in an advanced placement music theory class. Many of the same students might attend both types of classes and both classes might be taught by the same teacher, yet, the students' experiences are distinctly unique to each setting.

In this chapter, we will present Schwab's '**four common places**' model (Schwab, 1983) as a tool for examining the music classroom. Then, we will explore the strengths and the challenges facing American music education today, followed by a step back in time to consider how today's traditions of teaching music in schools came into being. Looking ahead, we will consider our profession's strengths and challenges in light of evolving contemporary influences. Finally, we will ask you to consider aspects of current music teaching settings that are working well and those aspects you believe need to be changed, allowing you the opportunity to begin crafting your vision of how music education could look in *your* future classrooms.

4.1 NAME THOSE MUSIC CLASSES

How many different settings can you think of and list in which music is taught in schools today (e.g. high-school wind ensemble, advanced placement [AP] theory, elementary general music)? (see Class Activity 4.1, p. 95)

CURRENT SETTINGS FOR TEACHING MUSIC IN THE SCHOOLS

School teaching settings are comprised of distinct physical and social characteristics conducive to delivering the particular subject matter being learned. Joseph J. Schwab, a

Note: Parts of this chapter are based on an article by Teachout (2007) titled "Understanding the ties that bind and the possibilities for change," appearing in *Arts Education Policy Review*. Used with permission from Taylor & Francis Ltd, http://www.tandf.co.uk/journals

pioneer of curricular reform during the second half of the twentieth century, established the 'four common places' of education, which include "teacher, student, what is taught [subject matter], and milieu of teaching–learning" (Schwab, 1983, p. 241). Schwab envisioned the common places model as a simple, yet elegant paradigm representing four critical perspectives required for planning any educational endeavor (see Figure 4.1). Furthermore, he saw the four common places as interdependent components such that characteristics of one component influence how each of the other components are perceived and how they contribute to the particular educational goals at hand.

To understand Schwab's model better, we will explore essential characteristics of each common place individually and then examine the rich interactive nature of the model as a whole.

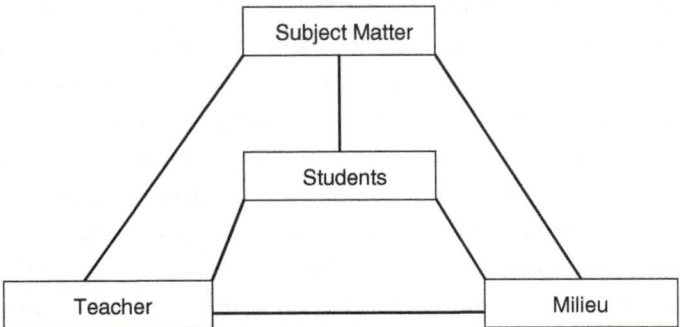

FIGURE 4.1 The four common places.
Source: Schwab, 1983.

The students. According to Schwab (1959/1978), teachers should possess a general knowledge of the student age group as well as specific knowledge of the particular group of students being taught. General knowledge includes knowing students' developmental levels, particularly regarding levels of physical, cognitive, emotional, and social development (Bjorklund & Blasi, 2009). Based on their age, which is typically correlated with general developmental progress, what are students able to do? What do they already know? What are they ready to learn? What is the degree to which they care about what they know and can do? Finally, how do they express these abilities in relation to others? Answers to these questions can help greatly with understanding differences among students across a broad range of ages.

Specific knowledge is information a teacher possesses about the students in the particular setting under consideration and how those students might be *different* from similar children of the same age (Schwab, 1959/1978). For example, knowing the home environment of your students can help you understand whether or not they might receive support for learning outside the classroom. How many and which students might have a learning disability? Are there students in your class who are gifted in a particular area? What motivates each of your students? What are their learning styles? Answers to these and a multitude of other questions aimed at learning the unique characteristics of the particular students you teach will help you to know them well. Furthermore, attending to the combination of general and individual characteristics will help you create effective learning experiences for all your students. We will explore student characteristics more thoroughly in Chapter 8.

The teacher. In Chapter 3, we examined the types of knowledge, skills, and dispositions needed to be an effective teacher (see Figure 4.2). The primary question pertaining to the 'teacher' common place is: To what degree are these three areas developed in the teacher?

Knowledge

Of Subject Matter

Of Learners

Of General Pedagogy

Of Curriculum

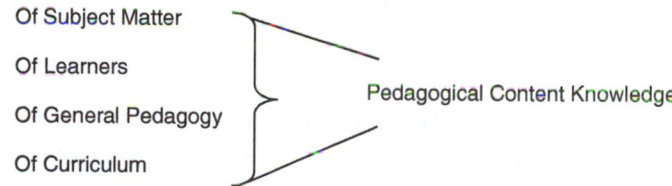

Pedagogical Content Knowledge

Skills

Personal Skills
Teaching Skills
Musical Skills

Dispositions

"There is always something new I can learn that will make me a better teacher."

*Additional dispositions may include:
    Ethical
    Responsible
    Maintain high standards of personal and professional conduct
    Inclusive and affirming of diversity
    Collaborative
    Reflective
    Receptive to feedback
    Self-efficacious
    Engaged and committed to teaching as a profession

FIGURE 4.2 Knowledge, skills, and dispositions needed to be an effective teacher. Note: *Additional dispositions are drawn from the "Candidate Dispositions Assessment Process" rubric, which can be found at: http://www.uncg.edu/art/pdf/art%20ed%20 student%20resources/Candidate_Dispositions_Assessment_Process.0916.11.pdf

From Chapter 3, we learned there are four types of teacher knowledge: knowledge of subject matter, of learners, of general pedagogy, and of the curriculum. Pedagogical content knowledge, a fifth type of teacher knowledge, exists at the intersection of where the other four meet and provides a more complete perspective than does any one of the other types of teacher knowledge alone (see Figure 3.1).

Skills that music teachers need to develop, as mentioned in Chapter 3, fall under the categories of personal skills, teaching skills, and music skills. As with types of knowledge, teacher skills require deliberate practice to develop, and such skills will improve over time with an intentionality of purpose.

Unlike knowledge and skills, which typically take a concerted effort over time to develop, one can adopt a mature set of dispositions from the start of his or her career. Assuming the attitude 'there is always something new I can learn that will make me a better teacher' will help you to improve as a teacher. Similarly, how you interact with your students can have a profound effect on the classroom atmosphere. As a young teacher, Haim Ginott (1972) wrote the following:

> I have come to a frightening conclusion. I am the decisive element in the classroom. It is my personal approach that creates the climate. It is my daily mood that makes the weather. As a teacher I possess tremendous power to make a child's life miserable or joyous. I can be a tool of torture or an instrument of inspiration. I can humiliate or humor, hurt or heal. In all situations it is my response that decides whether a crisis will be escalated or de-escalated, and a child humanized or de-humanized.
>
> (pp. 15–16)

The knowledge, skills, and dispositions you, as the teacher, bring to a teaching environment play a critical role in contributing to effective learning experiences for your students.

The subject matter. Music is an art form associated with human civilization since prehistoric times and woven inextricably within the fabric of all cultures (Merriam, 1964; Wallin, Merker, & Brown, 2000). Music *education* is concerned with the teaching and learning of music and is a discipline encompassing both breadth and depth. A wide range of knowledge, skills, and associated dispositions is taught across all music classes. Furthermore, many of those classes explore particular aspects of that range with great depth, developing highly complex understandings and skills sets in students. In 1994, the National Standards for Arts Education were recognized as part of the Goals 2000: Educate America Act, providing a set of content standards specifying what students should know and be able to do in each of the arts disciplines. Although the standards provide a comprehensive 'road map' for what should be taught about music, inclusion of these standards in the music classroom is entirely voluntary. Consequently, few individual music-teaching settings address all nine music content standards, and no particular implementation protocol exists ensuring all students will experience the kinds of music learning implied by the 'spirit' of the national standards (Conway, 2008; Williams, 2007). We will explore this particular concern later in the present chapter and examine subject matter in a more detailed manner in Chapter 9.

The milieu. The milieu (or environment) of music teaching and learning constitutes the general atmosphere in the classroom and is affected by many interactive variables that include experiences in the classroom as well as influences from within the school and from the community. Additionally, expectations for music teaching and learning (e.g. the type and frequency of music performances, whether or not participation in music contests is typical, etc.) exist at each of these three levels (see Figure 4.3), all of which work together to impose their influence on the ways content will be taught and learned.

Within the classroom, has the teacher established an environment where trusting and respectful relationships can be established? What kinds of peer relationships exist? Do the students know each other from prior experiences or do they begin as strangers?

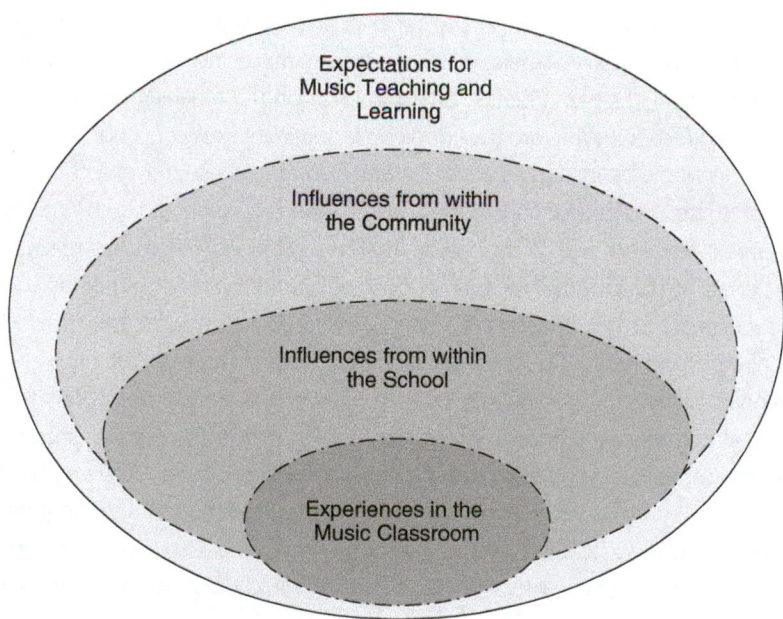

FIGURE 4.3 Influences on the milieu of music teaching.

Physical teaching spaces and the resources in those spaces also affect the classroom environment; however, the teacher can and should work to overcome any obstacles to learning. For example, we are reminded of a music teacher in an inner-city high school who wanted to start a piano class, but did not have the needed instruments. He shared the idea with his concert audiences and with many of the local music instrument dealers. Before long, he began receiving donations of used pianos, which he placed in the music rehearsal spaces, practice rooms, and even in some of the hallways nearby the music area. He now runs a piano course every semester. Class periods typically begin with all the students gathered around his piano as he gives instructions. Then, students go off in teams to work on their assignments, and return at the end of class to play for one another.

At the school level, the milieu is affected by the degree of cohesiveness and interaction among the teachers, and by the type of leadership exhibited from the school administration. How well do the teachers work with one another and with the school administration? Are there opportunities for students to encounter music as an interdisciplinary experience? Is music perceived as a valuable component of the school's curriculum?

The influence the community imposes on a music-learning setting is not dictated simply by socio-economic status, although the resources made available by the community can impact learning substantially. Rather, a community's influence is affected by the nature of various overlapping groupings, including socio-economic status, religion, cultural origin, education level, and political perspective, just to name a few. Schwab (1959/1978) succinctly encapsulates the influence of community on the teaching environment with the following question, "What are the conditions, dominant preoccupations, and cultural climate of the whole polity and its social classes insofar as these may affect the careers, the probable fate, and ego identity of the children whom we want to teach?" (p. 367).

As *music* teachers, we must realize that expectations for music teaching and learning occur at the community and school levels, and those expectations ultimately affect experiences in the classroom. Here, we would like to broaden the idea of community beyond 'where people live' to include the community of music-teaching professionals within that geographic location. In some places, expectations from the professional community reflect a strong sense of tradition for regular presentations of public performances. In other places, the professional community may emphasize the development in students of creative expression, artistic perception and judgment, and understanding relationships between music and other areas. Experiences in the music classrooms for students in each of these scenarios would likely be vastly different from each other.

The four common places as an interactive dynamic. An understanding of each component in Schwab's model provides an incremental strategy for observing and noticing various teaching/learning interactions in the music classroom. During your initial observations, you might consider each component individually. In most classroom settings, there is usually enough depth in any one of these areas to make for a rich exploration. Eventually, you should examine two areas simultaneously, noticing how changes in one area might affect the other area. For example, when observing a teacher work with several classes of students, one might notice ways the teacher changes her approach with each class based on the make-up of the students in each of those classes. Conversely, if you have the opportunity to follow a student in several different classes, you might notice how that student behaves differently relative to each different teacher. As you begin to consider the addition of subject matter and environment simultaneously in your observations, you can see easily that the dynamic relationships among all four areas are complex and multifaceted.

BLOG ON . . .

Common Places in School Music Offerings

Go back to your list of music teaching 'settings' generated at the beginning of the chapter, choose two distinctly different settings, and describe each in terms of the four common places. For each setting describe (a) general characteristics of the students, (b) the knowledge, skills, and dispositions required of the teacher, (c) what is being learned, and (d) characteristics of the environment. How do the common places differ between the two settings? Next, choose one setting and speculate how changes in one common place might affect the other three.

TYPICAL SCHOOL MUSIC OFFERINGS: A CHRONOLOGY

At the elementary level, the most common type of school music offering is the general music class. Although such weekly classes do not meet as frequently as 'tested' subjects such as math and reading, school music is typically a required subject at the elementary level. Consequently, participation is nearly universal (Richmond, 1997). At the 6–8 Grade levels, schools may continue to offer general music. However, this is also when many beginning band and string programs are introduced and choral ensembles such as treble choir and mixed chorus are started. Once students reach high school, the most common music-learning settings occur as large ensembles such as bands, choirs, and orchestras. Although related smaller ensembles are offered beginning at the secondary level, as are academic music classes such as music theory or music appreciation, neither small ensembles nor academic music classes typically serve the number of students in one setting as is found in large ensembles.

PERFORMANCE EMPHASIS AND INFORMANCE EMPHASIS ENVIRONMENTS

Another way to look at typical school music offerings is to consider the primary outcomes of each course. Most recently, you likely participated in a large ensemble of some type. In that setting, your music education largely consisted of preparing pieces for public performances of one type or another. In addition to the large ensemble, you may have been involved in chamber music groups consisting of smaller, non-conducted ensembles like string quartets, brass quintets, and chamber choirs, or mid-sized conducted ensembles such as percussion ensembles, steel drum bands, mariachi bands, or jazz choir. Because the primary outcome of ensemble and chamber experiences is a performance, we label such offerings as 'performance-emphasis' classes. Non-performance components may occur in performance-emphasis classes; however, they are usually included only to the degree they contribute to the quality of the performance. For example, a middle-school concert band, preparing the piece *Fanfare, Ode and Festival* by Bob Margolis, has an opportunity to explore hallmarks of the Renaissance period. Students could be exposed to listening examples of other Renaissance pieces, particularly those by the sixteenth-century composer Claude Gervaise upon whose work *Fanfare, Ode and Festival* is based. Such listening experiences help students to adopt authentic performance practices. Similarly, students could learn about modal music, presenting tonal alternatives to the ubiquitous major and minor tonalities that they hear most often. Such learning can aid the effort toward playing 'in tune' as an ensemble. In performance-emphasis courses, learning that is ancillary to the performance is included as it aids the particular pieces being rehearsed; however, such learning is not typically intended to ensure a comprehensive curricular approach for learning music.

As an alternative to performance-emphasis classes, you may have taken a music class that did not revolve around producing a performance result. These might include courses in music theory, music composition, or music history. For these classes, the emphasis was on becoming increasingly *informed* as a musician. We label these offerings as 'informance-emphasis' classes. Here, we acknowledge that the term 'informance' has been used in other contexts, primarily as a designation for performances that are also intended to 'inform' the audience. Examples of such events may include beginning instrumental concerts that are also used to inform parents about expected home practice activities or elementary music programs that inform the audience about music concepts being learned. Nonetheless, our use of the term 'informance' depicts coursework that is primarily intended to 'inform.'

Performance may be one of several outcomes in informance-emphasis classes; however, it is more often a means to accomplishing the primary goal of increased musical understanding. For example, a high-school music composition course might include a project early on in the class requiring students to compose a melody and apply basic harmonic treatments (i.e. I, IV, V) to that melody. An expansion of that project might ask students to propose additional harmonic alternatives. In uncovering new harmonic treatments, the students are exposed to new sounds, raising new questions about those sounds. It is in the asking and answering of those questions that learning takes place. An associated activity might be for the class to sing through each melody several times, while the teacher performs each of the harmonic accompaniments. In this scenario, performance is not essential to learning; however, it provides a tangible product through which the students can experience what they have learned. Such an activity might evolve into a public performance of composed pieces at the end of the term. Once again, the goal of the course is to learn the craft of composing music. In such a course, public performance becomes an activity that enhances the experience, but does not usurp the primary goal of learning about the craft of composition.

DISCUSSION BOARD
Performance Emphasis and Informance Emphasis

Using the list of settings that you generated at the beginning of this chapter, post the settings on the discussion board and label them as either performance-emphasis or informance-emphasis classes. Remember, there can be aspects of both in a particular setting, but ultimately the outcome of that setting is either one or the other. Read at least two other lists of your colleagues and comment about settings that are congruent with yours and ones that differ from what you designated.

STRENGTHS OF AMERICAN MUSIC EDUCATION

The music teaching profession has a strong presence in today's education system. Music is offered in nearly all the of nation's schools and instruction is taught by a music specialist 93 percent of the time at the elementary level and 97 percent of the time at the secondary level. At both levels, music instruction is offered in more schools than are any of the other arts (Parsad & Spiegelman, 2011).

Although there is no national music curriculum in the United States, music education at the elementary level typically utilizes a sequential conceptual approach in which musical elements are explored as "the substance for contemplation, consideration, and analysis" (Landis & Carder, 1972, p.112). Furthermore, most elementary music curricula reflect the voluntary National Standards for Arts Education, which call for instruction in the broad areas of creating, performing, responding to music, and understanding relationships to music (Consortium of National Arts Education Associations, 1994). Additionally, a wealth of music teaching materials for the elementary level has been published that supports both a sequential conceptual approach and implementation of the National Standards (see Silver Burdett Making Music, 2008, and Spotlight on Music, 2011, for specific exemplars). With a relatively balanced and sequential approach and readily accessible materials to support that approach, general music at the elementary level exists as a cohesive content area, "based on music outcomes, goals, and standards" (Erwin, Edwards, Kirchner, & Knight, 2003, pp. 40–41). Consequently, general music can be characterized as "the comprehensive study of music for all students" (from Boswell, as cited in Erwin et al., 2003, p. 40).

At the secondary level, music has a long history and strong tradition of performance excellence in all three major ensemble areas. Although greater numbers of students enroll in band and choir than in orchestra, all three enjoy a well-deserved reputation for producing performing ensembles of high quality. Contributors to this phenomenon include the music merchant industry, formalized professional organizations, and an implicit, but strong sense of tradition. Throughout the last half of the twentieth century and the beginning of the twenty-first century, the music merchant industry has responded to the growth of school performance groups with a number of accommodations, including manufacturing beginner and intermediate models of instruments, offering beginning model instruments through rental-purchase agreements, and publishing graded music across a wide variety of difficulty levels. Such accommodations have provided accessibility of instruments and literature appropriate for the various levels of school-aged children. Professional organizations specific to each performance area (e.g. American Choral Directors Association, American School Band Directors Association, American String

Teachers Association, etc.) generate opportunities for music teachers to share ideas about teaching and literature through their websites, professional publications, and conferences. Often, these groups and their many state-level chapters have collaborated with the music merchant industry to produce state-sanctioned music lists that guide teachers in choosing appropriate large and small ensemble literature for their students.

The strong tradition of performance is due in no small part to the activities and ideas shared at professional organization conferences. Often at these gatherings, professionals meet to hear presentations from experts on a wide variety of ensemble teaching topics and to hear performances of some of the newest literature available. The Midwest Clinic, for example, is a week-long gathering of approximately 15,000 band and orchestra teachers from across United States and over 30 other countries occurring every December in Chicago. Over 80 clinics are presented, providing new ideas on all areas of instrumental music teaching. In addition, approximately 40 concerts are performed by groups from all levels of experience, ranging from grade school through the professional level (About The Midwest Clinic, n.d.). Attendance at events like the Midwest Clinic and the hundreds of similar smaller professional gatherings has become an unspoken expectation among most music educators. As a result, the indoctrination of new and seasoned professionals alike regarding the importance of producing performing groups of high quality has been substantial.

Overall, music education has prospered in the United States, primarily because of its early inclusion in the schools. With the addition of formal music teacher education programs providing a steady supply of educated professionals, the unwavering advocacy efforts of the National Association for Music Education (NAfME, formerly MENC) highlighting the continual need for program support and resources, and the establishment of standards for what every child should know and be able to do, music education has become a stable component of the American education system.

CHALLENGES FACING AMERICAN MUSIC EDUCATION

With its established position notwithstanding, a close look at American music education and specifically at typical music courses and the students they serve reveals two troubling trends. First, the percentage of the student population involved in school music drops dramatically between the elementary and secondary levels. At the elementary level, music is offered in 94 percent of the nation's elementary schools as a required subject. By the time students reach high school, nearly all music offerings are elective. Consequently, of the 91 percent of our nation's schools that offer secondary level music instruction, only

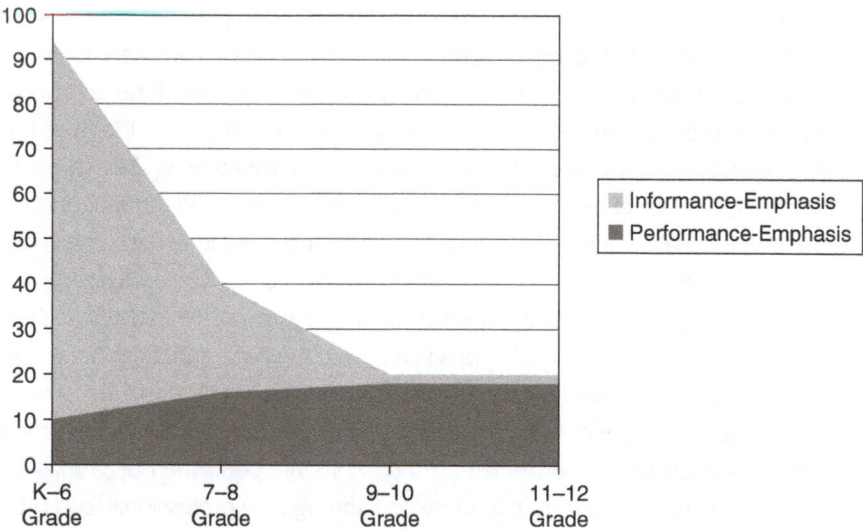

FIGURE 4.4 Percentage of informance- and performance-emphasis music course offerings across grade levels.

Note: Performance-emphasis courses at the K-6 levels represent the propensity of some programs to begin instrumental or choral ensemble instruction in the latter grades (i.e. fifth and sixth grades). Informance-emphasis courses at the 7-8 grade levels reflect state laws in 18 states that mandate music. Data are extrapolated from Richmond, 1997.

15–20 percent of the students in those schools participate in any type of music offering (Parsad & Speigelman, 2011; Richmond, 1997). Second, the type of outcome shifts from primarily informance-emphasis experiences at the elementary level to primarily performance-emphasis experiences at the secondary level (see Figure 4.4).

Each of these trends gives reason to question how well we, as a profession, are achieving a fundamental goal of the National Association for Music Education, which is "to ensure that every student has access to a well-balanced, comprehensive, and high-quality program of music instruction . . ." (National Association for Music Education, 2011). If music teachers are in contact with only 15 percent to 20 percent of the student population after eighth grade, our current model is not reaching "every student." Likewise, if the vast preponderance of secondary level music learning experiences occurs in performance-emphasis courses, one must wonder about the degree to which all secondary level music experiences are "well balanced" and "comprehensive."

Performance-emphasis experiences are important. After all, music is a performance art. We dare say that few of us would have pursued music as a career if it were not for the profoundly stirring moments we have all experienced many times as performing musicians. However, few performance-emphasis courses consistently provide students with a sense of relevance connecting what was learned in music class to the many cultural opportunities that surround their lives. Although the performance quality of school music ensembles from other countries rarely exceeds the performance quality found in school music ensembles from United States, few students leave our programs with a thorough understanding of the music they have played and with an individualized ability to make creative music performance decisions from an informed theoretical, historical, and cultural perspective. Students are not leaving our programs with the same confidence in their personal musicianship as they have in their ability to incorporate understandings of math, reading, and science to function productively in society (Teachout, 2005, 2007; Williams, 2007). One needs simply to notice the few numbers of students who make the transition from school performance ensembles to any type of adult music-making activity to question the impact school music programs are having on students (Cavitt, 1995). How did we, as a profession, get to this point?

To best understand current practices, they must be examined in light of the circumstances that preceded them. The current model of school music education is the product of several pivotal influences, including historical precursors and the traditions that have arisen from those precursors. The following section presents a brief historical overview of music education in the United States. For a more complete historical perspective, readers are encouraged to explore the original resources cited throughout the section.

HISTORICAL PRECURSORS REINFORCING TRADITIONAL ENVIRONMENTS

Education in music began in the United States as a pragmatic reaction to poor singing occurring in church congregations during the early 1700s. Subsequently, when the secular singing school movement developed during the eighteenth and early nineteenth centuries, so did the bonds tying musical development to our nation's social activities. The opportunity to come together and enjoy each other's company through making music provided a welcome reprieve from the harsh realities of frontier life. Thus music education started in the United States with a natural emphasis on improving the quality of ensemble performance and providing an important opportunity for social contact. Since those beginnings, music education has deviated little from those purposes.

Pestalozzian principles and the beginning of school supported music. Around the beginning of the nineteenth century, the theories of Johann Heinrich Pestalozzi permeated educational thought in the United States. A forerunner of John Dewey,

1700s	1800	1838	1850	1900 - - - - - 1940	1957
Music study begins as a reaction to poor singing in church congregations. The singing school movement begins.	Pestalozzian principles begin to permeate educational thought.	Lowell Mason establishes public funding for music education in the schools.	Music education continues to be a small-scale private endeavor.	Child Study Movement begins. Instrumental music education takes hold and is modeled after professional ensembles. Population explosion.	Launch of Sputnik raises concerns about education in the U.S. Little has changed in U.S. music education since 1957.

FIGURE 4.5 Timeline of pivotal points in U.S. music education.

Pestalozzi believed that the only true foundation of human instruction was that acquired through direct participation (see Pestalozzian principles listed at the end of Chapter 7). Such ideas were easily interpreted to support a performance-based approach to teaching music. In 1810 Hans Georg Nägeli incorporated Pestalozzi's objectives in *The Theory of Instruction in Singing*, an influential text that opened a new era in music instruction to children and was used as the foundation for vocal music teaching offered by Lowell Mason at the Boston Academy. Thus, the die was struck to define music education in the United States as something involving active participation, the proof of which to be a *performance* result.

In 1838, **Lowell Mason** became a pivotal figure in music education history when he convinced the Boston School Committee that music should be included in the school curriculum. As it happened, Mason's landmark achievement was characterized by its emphasis on performance. A successful public concert, presented by Mason and the children of the Hawes School in South Boston on August 14, 1838, convinced many people that music should be included in the school curriculum. Fourteen days later, the Boston School Committee approved a motion to appoint a teacher of vocal music in the public school of Boston, marking the first time that the teaching of music was supported with public funds (Mark & Gary, 1992).

For many years following the official induction of music in the schools, music programs consisted of instruction only in the primary school grades. Music reading skill development remained the chief goal as it had been in the singing schools prior. The post Civil War era was marked by a surge of graded music texts published to provide a systematic and sequential method for developing music reading skill (Labuta &

Smith, 1997). The emphasis was squarely on developing the tools for participation and performance with little thought of how that participation and performance might be employed as the means to the greater end of enhanced musical understanding.

Throughout the second half of the nineteenth century, secondary education was largely a small-scale private endeavor. Vocal music was part of the curriculum in most places, the content usually consisting of singing the great choruses of the European masters. Instrumental music education developed in the early twentieth century from a strong ensemble performance tradition heavily influenced by the professional orchestras and the military bands of the nineteenth century. In fact, all major modes of instrumental music education found in today's schools, with the exception of jazz ensembles, gained an important foothold in the curriculum between 1893 and 1915 (Humphreys, 1992).

Progressive education and music education. The existing educational approaches at the start of the twentieth century were rooted in social efficiency, emphasizing classroom control, management, obedience to authority, and a structured curriculum that focused on memorization and rote skills. A new approach to education, however, was beginning to take hold. The **Progressive Education** Movement, most closely associated with **John Dewey**, was an outgrowth of the Granville Stanley Hall's Child Study Movement. Hall related child educational readiness to psychological and physiological stages of development and suggested that the curriculum should come from the child and be based on his or her interests and needs. Dewey, a student of Hall, promoted the idea that students should be encouraged to be critical thinkers, creative beings, and expressive about their feelings. What was learned needed to be experienced directly and subjected to scientific inquiry by the student in order to be understood fully.

The idea of direct experience fit well with the active nature of how music was being taught at the time. "Music, more readily than the academic disciplines (of the time), complied with the principle of experience made useful in actual performance . . . In musical performance . . . there is constant application and instant evaluation of many facts and beliefs" (Leonhard & House, 1972, p. 62). However, there were limits to just how far music educators at the time would apply Dewey's ideas.

[Music educators] were comfortable with [students] learning to read music and singing patriotic songs, but they were suspicious of sensitizing children to beautiful sound and color. Also suspect were teaching methods that spent time motivating children, or worse allowing them to decide what they would do on a given day. Dewey's pragmatism fit in with the "can do" attitude developed on the frontier, but many of the subtleties of the new relationship between teacher and learner did not. Often the teachers themselves, despite the benefits of workshops, graduate study, and lectures and demonstrations at MSNC [now NAfME] and other professional meetings, did not change the atmosphere of their classrooms.

(Mark & Gary, 1992, p. 198)

It appears that the music teaching profession was afforded an opportunity to transcend its functional beginnings, yet seemed to masterfully take what supported the status quo and sidestep what might have profoundly changed the course of music education.

Informance-emphasis courses of the early twentieth century. Other modes of music teaching existed during the early 1900s that sought to provide students with an education in music beyond what was being delivered in school ensemble rehearsals. The term 'music appreciation' was used to describe these courses, with some apology and often for want of a better term (Keene, 1987). We humbly offer the term 'informance-emphasis' courses in the effort to capture the comprehensive nature of what was being taught and learned in those courses. Describing what was perhaps the first informance-emphasis course in the U.S. public schools, Mary Regal stated in a 1910 National Education Association publication that the purpose of her course was "to cultivate such a love and knowledge of music as would enrich the mental and emotional nature just as the love and knowledge of literature or painting or any other of the fine arts does" (Keene, 1987, p. 231). Frances Elliott Clark, Will Earhardt, Peter Dykema, and others who promoted informance-emphasis courses sought to facilitate lifelong musical involvement among their students. Further, the music memory contests, musical discrimination contests, the young people's concerts, as well as the use of the phonograph and the radio for teaching music might all be cited as roots of what would later be known as comprehensive musicianship. These programs were unique and innovative; however, their impact was limited by the nature of high school at the time. Unlike today, high school was largely considered to be a preparatory step toward college and was not compulsory. As such, a much smaller percentage of students attended than does today (Abeles, Hoffer, & Klotman, 1996).

Population expansion and the entrenchment of the large ensemble. Between 1910 and 1940 a dramatic expansion and subsequent geographic population shift worked to solidify large ensemble performance as a primary teaching mode of secondary music education. In that time, the percentage of high-school-aged children who attended school increased from 10 percent to 75 percent, creating a need to calibrate curricula to accommodate this expansion in the secondary school population. For music offerings, large ensembles served such a purpose well. Further, population shifts from rural to urban areas resulted in a deficit of trained school music teachers. To remedy the situation, professional performers were often hired to teach in the schools. "These musicians held 'rehearsals' much as one would in a professional group, and their whole orientation was directed toward performance" (Abeles et al., 1996, p. 18). By the middle part of the twentieth century, the model of public school music was characterized by music instruction at the elementary level providing basic conceptual development, and then primarily ensemble participation at the secondary level.

The large ensemble performance-based mode of music education was further entrenched by the advent of music contests, a characteristic of public school music that exists today. From the onset, competitions provided a tangible method of generating excitement among the public for music education. In promoting the first national band contest in 1926, its organizers exclaimed, "a good school band can add more than perhaps anything else to the prestige of its school and town" (Mark & Gary, 1992, p. 273).

With such high expectations, contest results soon became, and still are, an expedient way for administrators and the public to evaluate the effectiveness of a secondary school music program and, in an unspoken but very real way, the effectiveness of the teacher. Given that assessment dictates instruction, the practice of music education at the secondary level had become increasingly about achieving higher and higher levels of the large ensemble performance quality. Not surprisingly, justifications for the inclusion of music at the secondary level often included elements that promoted a successful large ensemble performance result rather than elements that facilitated students to mature along their individual roads toward musical independence. To this day, the typical academic year for a high-school music ensemble consists mostly of preparing for concerts and for district- and state-level contests, with more thoughtful consideration afforded the question 'What technical challenges do I need to prepare my students to accomplish so that we can perform the literature?' rather than the question 'How can I best utilize encounters with the literature to facilitate musical independence in each student?' (Kelly, 2009).

SOME AVENUES TOWARD A MORE COMPLETE MUSIC EDUCATION

Being aware of how and why the profession adopted particular music teaching traditions and practices allows you an important opportunity to consider carefully how you might move beyond the status quo in your future music classroom. To assist you with this task, we would like you to consider a possible evolution of American music education through three particular lenses. Each lens offers a 'big picture' idea to consider when planning and implementing music learning experiences.

Group versus individual. We propose that an educationally sound music-learning setting involves a balance between individual and group opportunities for students to engage in music making and learning. Throughout American history, however, music education has been primarily a group endeavor, particularly at the secondary level (Kelly, 2009). This phenomenon has only been solidified by a reward system of contests and festivals acknowledging group outcomes enthusiastically celebrated and echoed by parents, administrators, and the general public. Missing is an equally weighted opportunity for individuals to discover their unique relationship to music and for that to be celebrated to the same degree. Particularly missing are opportunities for students to be empowered as independent music decision-makers. Reimer (2009) depicts the need for students to be given such an opportunity when he discusses the relationship between performance teachers and performers (students):

> Performance teachers must be able to help their students internalize musical models—inner representations of appropriate musical expression—which form the basis for independent artistic decisions carried out in acts of performance . . . When [performers'] actions are based only on their teachers' internalized models rather than their own, the performers remain dependent on others for artistic decision making. When they are helped to gain and appropriate within themselves the musical models they need to call upon they are enabled to become independent musicians/artists.
>
> (p. 209)

 School music versus 'student' music. In an editorial, Raiber (2011) posed the question, "Why is it that students walk from class to class literally plugged into music all day, but are not interested in the music offerings at their school" (p. 16)? Perhaps the music material studied and the standardized instrumentation necessary for participation in traditional band, choir, and orchestra classes is so narrowly specialized that the experience is perceived as being irrelevant or inaccessible to most students. One might argue that school music should explore primarily the canon of art music and masterworks in the effort to bring students to new understandings and perceptions about music. Although this perspective appears laudable, it misses the logistical reality that most students are not initially drawn to such an experience. Furthermore, today's students have access to an inexhaustible amount of music spanning an unlimited number of styles from all over the world, a substantial portion of it being of very high quality, all within a few keystrokes of one's digital device of choice. Additionally, all students have greater access than ever before to non-school-related music-making experiences through digital technologies. Conceivably, it is possible for today's students to tap and develop an amazingly rich musical identity and never set foot in a school music classroom, an outcome we would be sad to see happen. We are not suggesting the elimination of traditional large ensembles or rejecting the music that is studied in those groups. On the contrary, we affirm the solid foundation that has been established in school music by those groups. Rather, what is missing is the recognition and acceptance of a growing body of 'student' music and opportunities to incorporate that music as an entry point to the school music experience. Perhaps a balance is needed between the musical experiences taught traditionally and what students might bring from outside the classroom.

Conformity versus creativity. A common experience for students participating in a large ensemble involves primarily following the conductor's directions. In fact, much of music teaching involves the teacher telling the students information (Kelly, 2009).

> In the rehearsal setting, the teacher performs nearly all decision-making actions. "Trumpets, that's a B-flat not a B-natural." "Sopranos, sing that top pitch softer." "No, violins—you are rushing the tempo; let's try it again, and hold back this time." Meanwhile students obediently follow the teacher's instructions, hoping to eventually receive some indication they have achieved the goal.
>
> (Teachout, 2007, p. 20)

Often, music education is focused primarily on performing, listening to, and analyzing music, with little attention to creativity (Stavrou, 2012). What seems to be missing, particularly at the secondary level, are frequent opportunities for students to develop their creative abilities. It is ironic that an arts-related classroom traditionally avoids the facilitation of creative musical decision-making by students. Though describing a pedagogy for facilitating creativity in students is beyond the scope of this text, Woodward (2005) has suggested that a teacher's responsibility in such an endeavor would include ensuring a safe environment to make mistakes and encouraging risk-taking and divergent thinking on musical problems. Few of these approaches are particularly common to most music classrooms at the secondary level, but such practices might need to be reconsidered.

A reasonable alternative regarding all three issues mentioned above might be the inclusion of a wide diversity of course offerings that attract large numbers of students. Building on the traditional foundation of large ensembles, small ensembles, and theory class, a contingent of new offerings could help to allow for individualized musical development, a wider exploration of music and instrumentation, and the cultivation of student creativity. Kelly (2009) described such possibilities:

> A more diversified contemporary music curriculum may include non-traditional opportunities such as music composition, electronic music including MIDI, popular music performance ensembles (yes, even rock and roll ensembles or country and

western bands), music appreciation classes, and world music ensembles. Students could receive individual instruction in guitar, piano, or any traditional wind, percussion, or string instrument.

(pp. 65–66)

HOW MIGHT *YOUR* FUTURE CLASSROOM LOOK?

Over the course of this chapter, you learned about aspects of current school music settings that are working well and other aspects that need to be remedied. Changing the educational status quo is often met with resistance, particularly regarding funding, facilities, and scheduling. For the time being, let us suspend those concerns and imagine what your future classroom might be. Kelly (2009) offers some solutions to the three possible barriers mentioned above. However, he proceeds to describe what he considers the greatest challenge to changing music education practice—"the music teachers themselves" (p. 67). Kelly states:

> Like other school personnel and community members, teachers have been enculturated to what traditionally constitutes music education . . . Consequently, teachers must consider music education in ways that are very unfamiliar with the result that there will be numerous challenges to overcome. While maintaining a focus on traditional forms of music making, teachers will need to overcome enculturated attitudes about what is 'good' music.

(p. 67)

He goes on to say:

> So often, teachers who are open to new experiences create opportunities that result in an expanded music curriculum while maintaining a traditional focus and increased student participation.

(p. 67)

When you are open to new possibilities, you are limited only by that which you can imagine. When you have done all you can imagine, it is time to imagine more.

4.2 YOUR FUTURE CLASSROOM

Think of an area (band, choir, or strings) and a grade level, and then consider the following questions:

(a) Which aspects of traditional music education for your scenario would you keep? Why?

(b) What aspects of traditional music education for your scenario would you change? Why?

(c) How would you change them? (see Class Activity 4.23, p. 95)

CLASS ACTIVITIES

Class Activity 4.1: Name Those Music Classes

Individually, think of and list as many different settings as possible in which music is taught in schools today (e.g. high-school wind ensemble, advanced placement [AP] theory, elementary general music, etc.). Afterward, pair with a partner and share lists, adding to your list as necessary. Finally, share these ideas with the class.

Class Activity 4.2: Your Future Classroom

Assemble in groups of 3–4 students. Each group should choose an area (band, choir, or strings) and a grade level. Discuss the following questions within the group: (a) Which aspects of traditional music education for your scenario would you keep? Why? (b) What aspects of traditional music education for your scenario would you change? Why? (c) How would you change them?

5 How *Will* You Present Instruction?

Good teaching is one-fourth preparation and three-fourths pure theater.

(Gail Godwin)

When you think about it, proficient teachers often employ skill sets usually associated with good actors. Effective professionals of both types deliver material so the audience, or class, will take notice and be affected intellectually and emotionally. For the actor, the material is the collection of lines the playwright has written. For the teacher, the material is the subject matter of the lesson. To communicate content successfully, actors and teachers must know their material and present it in such a way that they 'reach' their audiences. So, just what is it that makes an actor effective? What acting skills can teachers use to improve their effectiveness?

DIFFERENCES BETWEEN ACTING AND TEACHING

We believe effective actors use several specific delivery skills that could benefit teachers. Before we explore acting skills that teachers might use, however, it is important to acknowledge two substantive *differences* between acting and teaching. First, actors have a different relationship with their audience than teachers have with their students. Actors usually perform for a new audience each evening, while teachers engage the same groups of students on a regular basis and across a variety of situations. The job of an actor is to use his acting skills to convince an audience of the character he is portraying. Successful actors present convincing performances of each new character they portray. A good actor develops a memorable, sometimes intense, but always a short-lived relationship with his audience. The successful teacher, on the other hand, forms a deep bond of trust with his students. Such a bond is established when students know that the teacher cares about them and about their journey as learners. The bond is further strengthened when students encounter the degree of consistency and authenticity that comes only

5.1 LEVELS OF EXPRESSIVE-NESS

If you were to share one of your favorite quotes with someone in as dramatic a fashion as possible, how would you use your voice, body, face, eyes, and hands to facilitate this expression? What would change if you wanted to present this same quote in as 'low key' fashion as possible? (see Class Activity 5.1, p.113) from the teacher presenting his genuine self. Teachers develop rapport with students not by playing a role, but by presenting their authentic selves. For the actor, delivery skills are the primary 'tools of the trade' one uses and develops to achieve increasingly greater levels of acting achievement. For the teacher, delivery skills are used to enhance the genuine connection that is being established with students. Rather than as tools engaged in the process of reinventing one's self, we believe acting skills for teachers can be utilized best in the service of *highlighting and projecting aspects of one's genuine nature*.

Second, actors have a different relationship with their 'content' than teachers have with the content they teach. Good actors may invest months learning background information on a character and weeks learning a specific script, only to start over on a new role once the current production has reached completion. Effective teachers, on the other hand, 'live' their content most of their lives. This is particularly true of effective music teachers. More than likely, you have performed music most of your life and now you are enrolled in a degree program in which you will study music in many different ways. Remarkably, this study is in addition to the coursework and co-curricular experiences aimed at helping you learn to *teach* music to others, and all this work occurs prior to entering the profession. Once in the classroom, effective teachers strive continually to learn increasingly more about their content. Rather than delivering a specific script, teachers must be ready to move in any number of different directions with their content depending upon the needs of the students. Such an improvisatory environment requires that teachers know a large degree of both the breadth *and* depth of their subject matter, the study of which usually continues over the entirety of one's career.

THE ROLE OF ENTHUSIASM

There exists a type of energy or enthusiasm, if you will, in the classrooms of excellent teachers, creating a positive atmosphere that is conducive to student learning. Not only do students self-report they learn more from teachers exhibiting enthusiastic behaviors (Christophel, 1990; Richmond, Gorham, & McCroskey, 1987), but researchers have found objective evidence for enthusiastic teacher behaviors positively affecting student learning (Kelley & Gorham, 1988), students' on-task behaviors (Bettencourt, Gillett, & Hull, 1983), and students' intrinsic motivation (Patrick, Hisley, & Kempler, 2000). This last point is especially important because it affirms that a teacher's enthusiastic delivery has profound implications for the students developing the habit of lifelong learning.

We believe the enthusiasm effective teachers bring to the classroom is sourced in two places: enthusiasm for the content and enthusiasm for teaching that content (and for students learning that content). In a very basic sense, it should be fun to share your ideas about music with others. Highet (1989) best describes this enthusiasm. "If you enjoy the subject, it will be easy to teach when you are tired, and delightful when you are feeling fresh" (p. 20). Hopefully, you can recall many former teachers who were particularly excited about their subject areas. Pick one and try to visualize how he or she talked and moved during the act of teaching. Did it seem like he or she had endless energy? More than likely, that person was *enthusiastic* about the subject being presented.

While one may possess a high degree of enthusiasm for subject matter, enthusiasm for *teaching* that content to others must also be present in teachers. Many professional musicians are excited and enthusiastic about the music they play and about performing in general. However, their enthusiasm for music does not guarantee they are or would be successful *teachers* of music. As we stated earlier, effective teachers care about students and their learning. This caring, however, goes well beyond simply establishing a bond or being excited about leading students. Effective teachers are devoted to their students and are motivated more so by what they give to students than what they received from the interaction. A kindergarten music teacher becomes just as excited when her students are initially able to clap a steady beat as the middle-school orchestra director becomes when a student first understands how to transpose a melody to a new key center or a high-school band director becomes with his ensemble as they begin to achieve consistency at applying principles of just intonation across multiple pieces of music. In each of these three scenarios, the teacher's intrinsic reward comes from having successfully facilitated students with gaining a skill or an understanding that supports those students' growing musicianship.

BLOG ON . . .

How Did Your Teachers Show Enthusiasm?

When thinking about memorable and effective teachers in your past, what did they do that let you know they were enthusiastic about the content they were teaching? What were some ways they demonstrated their enthusiasm for teaching in general?

DELIVERY SKILLS

The development of delivery skills for teachers can be compared to the development of technique and executive skills for performers. When musicians perform, their primary goal is to communicate expressive musical ideas to their audience. Much thought goes into decisions such as when to push through a phrase, when to hold back, how loud should a particular crescendo reach, etc. The maturity of one's musical ideas and expressiveness constitutes his or her level of musicianship. Proper technique becomes the conduit through which one is able to present those musical ideas effectively. Consequently, without proper technique, a musician rarely is able to convey the musical content in the exact manner he or she wishes. Ultimately, however, technique is pursued in the service of mature musicianship. If one has developed outstanding technical facility, but has nothing to say, few will listen for very long. Likewise, one with a seasoned and well-developed sense of musicianship can greatly improve his or her ability to express those ideas by working regularly on skill development.

Just as proper technique enables musical performers to express a sophisticated level of musicianship, delivery skills serve teachers with helping them effectively present the genuine enthusiasm they have for their content and for teaching. Many music education researchers have found that students' perceptions are affected by the way music teachers deliver their lessons (Cassidy, 1990; Hamann, Baker, McAllister, & Bauer, 2000; Juchniewicz, 2010; MacLeod & Napoles, 2012; Madsen, 2003; Madsen & Geringer, 1989; Rohwer & Henry, 2004; Yarbrough, 1975). When discussing the importance of delivery skills with others, however, we have heard arguments that 'students can easily detect when someone is "acting the part"' or that 'teachers are paid to educate, not entertain.' We agree with each of these arguments. Although we present delivery skills as the primary focus of this chapter, effective delivery skills alone cannot make one a good teacher. For example, when teachers engage students, but treat those students simply as viewers of the action, the students are being entertained, but they are not necessarily learning content. Only when one is genuinely enthusiastic about the ideas being shared, and equally enthusiastic about how students will receive and learn those ideas, will enhanced delivery skills positively affect one's teaching.

By now, we have presented two important points. First, the enthusiasm you bring to the classroom can have a profoundly positive effect on your students and on their learning. Second, effective delivery skills can enhance your projection of the genuine enthusiasm you have for music and for teaching. Sometimes teachers may possess a great deal of enthusiasm for what they know and do, but need to work on delivery skills to maximize their communication with students; this is especially true of those new to the profession. The good news is you can learn particular vocal gestures, physical gestures, and room staging ideas that will help you. In the following sections we will isolate and describe some of those skills and ideas. As you read the material, keep in mind that, similar to the way music performers develop their technique, you should probably work on each of these techniques individually before thinking of ways to combine them. At first, isolating them might feel awkward and/or unconnected to the 'real' practices of teaching. Remember that many successful music performers spend hours in the practice room working on isolated technique-building exercises that eventually come together, forming an amalgamation of skills that make the stage presentation of musically sophisticated musical ideas possible.

As you work through the following pages, you may find there are aspects that come more naturally than other aspects. To gain the maximum benefit, pay attention to those aspects that come easily to you and take note of others that may require concerted effort to master. As a performer, you know how tempting and rewarding it is to play or sing repeatedly through the passages of a piece that you already know and can perform well. Yet, in all honesty, you probably also know that long-term progress and growth comes only from attending regularly to those parts that really need your attention the most. We invite you to assess your delivery skills and devise an individualized plan for facilitating and maximizing your growth in this area. As you work your plan, you will most likely find your development accelerating. In Chapter 1 we discussed the idea that good teaching is a skill that can be developed rather than a talent that is fixed and unchangeable. Similarly, we would advise you to approach your delivery skill development with the idea you can improve no matter where you are on your personal continuum of development at the moment.

ANYONE . . . ANYONE? THE IMPACT OF VOCAL EXPRESSION

The title of this section refers to an infamous scene from the movie *Ferris Bueller's Day Off* (Jacobson & Hughes, 1986) in which Ben Stein's character, the economics teacher, presents a lecture to high-school students demonstrating what could easily be considered the very poorest use of vocal delivery skills. Stein utilizes minimal levels of pitch inflection and volume variation while maintaining a monotonous word delivery pace. On one level, the scene is a marvelously effective comic portrayal of the typical 'boring lecturer' because of Stein's exaggerated lack of vocal variety. On another level, sadly, the scene works so well precisely because the iconic image of the boring lecturer is common to most people's schooling experience. We hope that with attention to your vocal delivery skills, you might never be perceived as the typical 'boring lecturer.'

By now, you are probably becoming aware that *how* you use your **voice** can have a great impact on your teaching. In the following section, we will offer some specific categories in the area of vocal expression. We will also provide some tips and basic activities that we hope will help to raise your awareness of the particular issues you might need to address. Tauber and Mester (2007) offered four logical categories of vocal expression: pitch, volume, quality, and rate. As you discuss the voice components on your list, you may have noticed that many of your observations fit into these four categories.

Vocal pitch. In the English language, as in many languages, variations in vocal pitch have particular meanings. For example, when you raise the pitch of your voice at the end of a sentence, it sounds like a question. When you lower the pitch at the end of the sentence, it sounds like a statement or an answer. Quite often, young teachers unknowingly undermine their own authority by ending statements with a rising tone, as if asking permission from the students. Using a lowered vocal pitch at the end of a directive adds a sense of authority. Pitch variations are also used in the middle of sentences:

> "Everybody SING this time." (instead of just speaking the lyrics)
> "EVERYBODY sing this time." (instead of just the sopranos)
> "Everybody sing THIS TIME." (perhaps frustrated that some did not sing last time)

Vocal habits are developed over a lifetime, and there are as many different 'normal' voices as there are people. Each person, within a particular range of pitch variation, must find out what feels and sounds natural for him or her and what others perceive as effective communication. It is a good idea to consciously change your pitch variation patterns to develop flexibility and effectiveness. Seize opportunities to record yourself as you teach in different settings, and listen—and have other teachers listen—to your vocal pitch to keep it exciting and effective.

Vocal volume. Volume is one of the most effective tools you can use to portray authority. A strong resonant voice conveys a sense of confidence, which typically evokes a positive response in students. A good rule of thumb is to maintain a volume that can be heard and understood from anywhere in the room.

A good projected voice is the product of good vocal technique. Professional voice training is beyond the scope of this book, but you can easily learn specific techniques for achieving maximum resonance with minimum effort. Hopefully professional vocal training is part of your curriculum as a music education major. Remember that your vocal health

5.2 VOCAL PITCH VARIATION

How does the way in which you end your sentences affect the impact of what is being said? Does a lowered tone at the end make a difference? What does a raised tone at the end indicate? Are there other elements besides pitch that affect the meaning of what you say? (see Classroom Activity 5.2, p. 114) is paramount. If you strain your voice by overdriving it in an attempt to be heard in the classroom for six or seven hours each day, you risk suffering permanent damage.

Once you establish an effective basic volume level, however, you can use variations in volume to maximize your teaching effectiveness. Most often, it is the *change* in volume that catches the listener's attention. By moving around the room and speaking softly at times, you can often draw in the students' attention as they concentrate harder to hear you. A deliberately soft voice can also be effective at times in getting control of an excited class. Calm, deliberate, soft (but loud enough to be heard) directives from you can help young students make the transition back to their 'inside' voices.

Vocal quality. As mentioned above, good projection must be the product of good vocal technique, which also produces a nice vocal quality. Vocal quality can be compared to the timbre that musical instruments produce. Each of us possesses our own unique vocal quality (nasal, raspy, resonant). It is important, however, to determine if you have any distracting or unhealthy vocal quality habits. If you have any annoying tendencies, your students will notice. In extreme cases, a distracting vocal quality can detract from learning. If you have any unhealthy habits such as stridency, breathiness, etc., over time, you will probably feel the painful effects on your throat.

Good vocal health is important for teachers. When you are teaching every day, for several hours a day, you will be using your voice almost constantly. Adopting a few good habits can go a long way toward protecting your voice.

1. Speak at your own pitch. To find your most natural voice, say "umm-hmmm" as if you are genuinely agreeing with someone. Use a rising inflection with the lips closed. If you are doing this correctly, you will feel a tingling or vibration around the nose and lips. This means that you are achieving a healthy oral-nasal resonance. If your pitch is too low, you will feel the vibration in the lower throat (Cooper, 1996).
2. Inhale at the belly. When you inhale, your air should go to the bottom of your lungs. Then, it is ready to be supported properly by the diaphragm muscle.
3. Support your voice for both singing and speaking. When you speak, your voice needs the same amount of support as it does when you are singing.
4. Consider using a personal amplification system, particularly when teaching large classes. Students will hear you teaching with a calm demeanor and you will be saving your voice.
5. Get plenty of rest.
6. Drink plenty of water throughout the day.
7. Avoid trying to be heard at noisy places like large crowds, sport arenas, etc.
8. Try to minimize vocal disturbances such as coughing or clearing your throat.
9. Treat your voice like the valuable instrument that it is!

Given that you have achieved a healthy, and generally pleasant, vocal quality, you can use variations to occasionally provide emphasis to the material being taught. For example, when discussing the difference between a rich full instrument timbre and a thin raspy timbre, you could change your voice to reflect the type of timbre being discussed. This brief exaggerated variation can be an effective way to emphasize the point.

Vocal rate/timing. There are clear differences regionally in the United States regarding rate of speech. These regional dialects have a number of characteristics, such as specific vowel pronunciations and emphases; extreme dialects can be very difficult to understand by people from a different region of the country. During the rise of radio and television in the United States, however, a standard American pronunciation developed. National network commentators, news people, and weather reporters are perhaps the best practitioners of this dialect. Because their job is to ensure listeners understand the content being conveyed upon the initial delivery, their speech is marked by clarity of consonants, neutral vowels, and a medium to slow rate of speaking.

Beyond clarity, it is the *change* in the rate of speech that produces the strongest emotional effects. After a while, speaking slowly at a constant rate can produce the same mind-numbing effects as speaking too quickly at a constant rate. Therefore, it is important to alter your rate of speech occasionally. Furthermore, the timing of words can greatly facilitate clarity and expressiveness. A strategically placed pause can be an important and valuable communicative tool, creating the suspense that draws the listener in to a particular point. To achieve the maximum effect, place a pause just before the word or thought being emphasized. For example, if you want to emphasize the particular day

INDIVIDUAL ACTIVITY
Deliberate Speaking

An example of slow, deliberate, concise, clear speech can be heard when listening to the hourly new reports on National Public Radio (NPR) or most nightly news shows. The reporter's job is to successfully communicate many complex ideas in a succinct fashion. The rate of speech that is used by reporters on NPR or other news shows is usually slower and more deliberate than the rate that would be found in typical conversational speech. Listen to a report, turning the volume down occasionally to repeat what the reporter just said. Be sure to maintain the same rate of speech as the reporter. Notice how it feels to speak at a slightly slower rate than conversational speech.

when an exam is being given, you might say, "You will be given a theory exam on (pause) Wednesday." Pauses are also used to emphasize items in a series. "The test will cover (pause) key signatures, (pause) time signatures, (pause) and (pause) expressive markings." Still, another way of changing the rate of speech is to elongate the duration of a single word or, perhaps, even a single syllable. "Don't forget. TOMORROW we will take a field trip to hear the orchestra." In general, rate and timing of speech is the most easily manipulated vocal characteristic and, as a result, has the greatest potential for vocal expression.

Although we have looked at these basic characteristics of vocal inflection in isolation, they are rarely used apart from the others in real life. When trying some of the ideas presented for each specific voice component, it is still likely that you varied more than one component at a time. This is natural. When used deliberately in particular combinations for specific purposes, they can produce dramatic results. Take some time to try intentional variations with each of the components and then practice them in different combinations. As with all aspects of teaching, the key is to practice, evaluate, and practice some more.

EVERY MOVE YOU MAKE—THE IMPACT OF PHYSICAL EXPRESSION

By this time, you should be well sensitized to many different ways that vocal expression can affect your teaching. As you become more vocally expressive, physical gestures, body language, and facial expressions will also begin to change. This is a part of natural human communication; and although we will study the physical techniques separately, ultimately our aim is for you to pull vocal and physical characteristics together in a naturally expressive presentational style.

As you pay closer attention to the physical expression of your communication, you may begin to notice particular ways in which you use your body to communicate. More than likely, you will see variations in your stance or posture. Perhaps, you gesture with your arms or hands. Notice how you vary the expression on your face. You may even use eye contact to a greater degree as you become more expressive. As with variations in vocal expression, each of these physical adjustments can help you to become an increasingly effective communicator. In the following pages, we will break down physical expression into four categories: (a) eye contact, (b) facial expression, (c) gestures, and (d) posture.

Eye contact. Effective eye contact occurs when meaningful engagement and communication is experienced by looking into the eyes of another person. Eye contact is a powerful tool in the classroom. We can, in an instant, communicate that we are being attentive to the students and, consequently, can command their attention. Because eye contact can be used to establish such a powerful bond, we need to be aware of some common mistakes. Often, young teachers will visually direct their attention only to the center of the class, as if suffering from tunnel vision. To counter this, it would be beneficial to purposely and systematically train yourself to look into the eyes of each student regularly. You can retrain your habits by periodically conducting a simple exercise. First, ask all the students in your class to raise their hands and keep them up. Then, instruct them to lower their hands only after they felt you established meaningful eye contact with them as individuals. Begin and proceed to establish eye contact with each individual in any order, moving back and forth, row by row, until all hands are down. You might even want to time yourself to see how quickly you can reach all the students. Once you start teaching regularly from a score and video record your teaching, you will become particularly sensitive to the need for knowing the score well enough to maintain eye contact. If you engage the students consistently with genuine visual communication, they will be more likely to understand the information you are sharing through your words and with your conducting gestures.

Facial expression. Facial expression is another tool used to convey emotions. The four parts of the face that help to communicate emotions are the forehead, eyes, mouth, and head angle. In our culture there are common interpretations for particular combinations of forehead, eye, mouth formations, and head angle. Notice how powerfully a slight change in one of the four parts can affect the emotion being conveyed.

Sometimes, you may not always be aware of the emotional messages you are sending. Therefore, it may be beneficial to become sensitive to how you are using your face. One way to do this is to video record your teaching. Leave the camera on long enough for you to forget that it is there. When viewing the recording, look for instances in which you are especially effective or ineffective in portraying an emotion. In either case, try to remember what you were thinking and feeling at that point in the class. How did your thoughts and emotions contribute to your particular facial expression? If you can make the connection between what you are feeling on the inside and how you are expressing those feelings on the outside, you can begin to make adjustments. Another helpful exercise would be to look into a mirror and experiment with intentionally changing your facial expression to convey a variety of emotions including anger, sadness, contentment, surprise, fear, etc. Notice how much, or little, movement is needed to achieve a particular emotion. This type of work can help you maximize your facial expressiveness.

Gestures. Hand, arm, and body movements are effective tools for emphasizing material being presented. The most effective types of gestures are ones that are natural, flowing, and appropriate to the situation. Your enthusiasm for the music will commonly show itself in gestures that highlight and clarify particular points you want to communicate

> **5.3 FACE READING**
>
> What parts of your face can you use to communicate without saying a word? Can you imagine what a person might be thinking or saying based on his facial expression? (see Class Activity 5.3, p. 114)

in a given lesson. However, there are times when you may need to emphasize a point by using a quick, compact, hand movement or maybe a sweeping arm motion. These exaggerated motions can be effective if they appear to be genuine. Rather than offering a specific repertoire of exaggerated gestures to practice, we suggest that you begin to observe excellent teachers, public speakers, actors, etc. Notice how they use exaggerated gestures to emphasize a point. Try out some of these gestures in your own teaching.

Posture. There is a 1960 Peanuts cartoon where Charlie Brown is standing with bowed head, hunched shoulders, and a glum expression. He says to one of his friends, "This is my depressed stance. When you're depressed, it makes a lot of difference how you stand." Then, after straightening up, Charlie Brown declares, "The worst thing you can do is straighten up and hold your head high because then you'll start to feel better." He slumps again and says, "If you're going to get any joy out of being depressed you've got to stand like this."

INDIVIDUAL ACTIVITY
Practicing Posture

Stand up. Slouch your shoulders forward. Tilt your head downward or to one side and look downward. How do you feel? Energized or weakened? Now straighten up. Stand tall. Lift your shoulders up and back. Look upward. How do you feel now? For the two positions described above, take time to incorporate each into your posture at various times throughout the day for a substantial period of time. Notice how you feel when you slouch as you sit, stand, and walk. Also notice how you feel using a tall, supported posture as you sit, stand, and walk.

BLOG ON . . .
How Does Your Posture Make You Feel?

Is it possible to move yourself into a new way of feeling? Take a moment and discuss how your energy changes as you adopt each of the two stances over various activities. Also, notice when you see others and how their postures portray their emotions.

Interestingly, your posture can have a profound effect on the energy level you feel inside and, consequently, on the message you project outward. It is amazing to notice just how much our internal feelings and outward physiology are linked. You probably know when someone is emotionally 'down' by their slumped shoulders, hanging head, and downwardly focused eyes. You can also detect an energized person by their lifted, upwardly projected posture. It is commonly accepted that outward appearances are a reflection of inward feelings. Could the opposite be true? Is it possible to enhance your level of energy and confidence by changing your posture? We believe that the answer is a resounding 'yes.' According to Madsen and Madsen (1974), "You can act your way into a new way of thinking faster than you can think your way into a new way of acting" (p. 213).

One of the most effective ways to achieve an energized state of feeling is to act 'as if' you are energized. How is this done? First, adopt the uplifted upper-body posture that we described above. Second, get yourself into the habit of using 'open' rather than 'closed' arm positions. When you fold your arms in front of your body you are communicating non-verbally that you are protecting yourself or hiding something. This kind of communication makes it difficult for others, your students included, to trust you. On the other hand, an open arm position projects a sense of vulnerability. This vulnerability communicates to your students that you are confident with what you have to offer and that you trust them. In turn, they will tend to trust you more easily.

A third way of 'acting your self into a new way of feeling' is to maintain your upward lift while moving. A fast-paced walk with a raised upper body and a raised head projects a sense of purpose. The next time you are walking among other people, try walking 'with a sense of purpose' and observe just how quickly others notice you and move out of your way. Similarly, if you move throughout your classroom with a sense of purpose, your students will notice.

AM I BELIEVABLE?—CONGRUENCE OF PHYSICAL AND VOCAL EXPRESSION

As we have said before, in real life the basic characteristics of vocal and physical expression are never used in isolation. Try to look for some effective combinations that happen naturally and that you can use in your own repertoire of delivery skills. For example, practice giving a directive such as "Trumpets, use a stronger accent at letter B." Combine a loud volume and a slow rate of speaking with raised eyebrows and a strong physical gesture like extending your hand. When you combine all aspects of a strong clear vocal delivery with the physical aspects of good posture, strong gestures, confident facial expression, and engaging eye contact, you will experience something we call a congruent delivery. Why is a congruent delivery so powerful? Researchers have found that when spoken words were *incongruent* with vocal tonality and body language, words convey only 7 percent of the communication, while tonality of the voice conveys 38 percent, and body language conveys 55 percent. Said a different way, when communicating feelings and attitudes, your students will trust the predominant forms of communication such as vocal tonality and body language, more so than the literal meaning of the words, especially when your words are not congruent with your vocal tonality or body language (Mehrabian, 1981). A congruent delivery helps your words 'connect' with students.

STAGING THE TEACHING SPACE

Music teachers teach in a variety of venues, including large ensemble rehearsal rooms, well-equipped music rooms, cafeterias, gymnasiums, auditorium stages, football fields, and, occasionally, broom closets. Although it is important to work continually toward acquiring the most ideal space for the type and level of music learning being facilitated, teachers may not have control over the choice of space where they teach. However, they do have control over *how they use* the space they are assigned. Similar to delivery skills used effectively to enhance one's genuine enthusiasm, the imaginative use of classroom space can also facilitate communication of that enthusiasm resulting in positive learning outcomes for students.

The way one uses and stages the teaching space can help to achieve several important outcomes. Proper staging can help the teacher capture students' attention and, consequently, facilitate the desired relationship between the teacher and his or her students. Proper staging also can help one to emphasize the most important ideas of the lesson, thus positively affecting student learning (Tauber & Mester, 2007). To maximize these outcomes, however, one must ensure the basic environment is set logistically.

Staging to support logistics. Two fundamental logistical concerns for staging a classroom are acoustical and visual accessibility. Students must be able to see and hear the teacher clearly, especially when the teacher is delivering instruction. However, music-teaching spaces vary widely. Some spaces are designed for particular types of music learning, while others are not. Most large ensemble rehearsal rooms and music-specific specialty rooms have been designed or retrofitted to ensure optimum acoustical flexibility. That is, the sound level produced by musical instruments or voices is mitigated to reduce the possibility of individuals acquiring hearing damage, while still allowing students to hear the teacher's directives when music is not being produced. Other venues, like gymnasiums and cafeterias, are not intended primarily for music teaching and learning. Typically they allow too much reverberation, requiring the teacher to devise a plan to minimize unwanted echoes.

Optimizing visual clarity for students is relatively easier than ensuring acoustical quality, because you are able to see what the students see. One basic rule holds true here: If you cannot see a student, he or she will not be able to see you. After attending to the more obvious issues such as ensuring proper lighting or that there are no obstructions in the room, a teacher should identify places in the room where he or she is able to be seen by the greatest number of students and those places that inhibit students in particular areas from seeing the teacher. Being sensitive to such places will allow the teacher to balance opportunities for varying her proximity throughout the room with ensuring that she does not remain outside the sightline of a particular student or group of students for very long. Another issue of visual accessibility involves content projected onto a screen or posted on the walls that is intended for students to see from their seats. Letters, numbers, and icons large enough to be seen easily will facilitate students with learning and understanding the information being presented.

Staging to facilitate student engagement and learning. One of the most effective tools available for engaging students, and often one of the most underused, is the act of varying one's proximity to the students. Because most teachers remain in the front of the room for the duration of the class period, those teachers who choose to move throughout the room will automatically raise students' attention by piquing their curiosity. When movement becomes deliberate, purposeful, and strategic, student engagement improves significantly (Hastie, 1998). For example, approaching an off-task student and simply delivering your content while standing beside the student's chair will most likely result in the student changing behaviors. Further, this subtle type of communication gives the student the opportunity to self-regulate his behavior without being called out by the teacher, and it allows the teacher to continue teaching without interrupting the flow of the lesson.

How does such a subtle gesture work? The answer is found in the study of **proxemics**, the science of how humans use space within the context of culture (Hall, 1966). Hall asserted that people use space to communicate non-verbally and that the type of relationship we share with others and particular cultural norms dictate how that communication is perceived. According to Hall, social distance among people is highly correlated with physical distance and people interact consistently within one of four parameters, depending upon the type of relationship: (a) 'intimate distance' for the closest of relationships (i.e. 6–18 inches), (b) 'personal distance' among good friends (i.e. 1.5–4 feet), (c) 'social distance' among acquaintances (i.e. 4–12 feet), and

(d) 'public distance' among strangers. Further, people of different cultures maintain different standards of personal space.

In the classroom, you can use the principles of proxemics to establish trust and/or reinforce power in your relationship with students. To establish trust, for example, one might approach a student by respecting his or her personal space and only moving into it when such movement is an understood and expected aspect of the teaching-learning situation, such as moving close to review some written work or to help adjust a student's hand position on an instrument. Congruently combining a number of non-verbal gestures can accelerate the trust-building process—for example, approaching the student with a warm smile to indicate acceptance, arms at your side to suggest openness, stooping down to eye level to imply equality, and working beside the student rather than in front of him to signify collaboration. At the other end of the spectrum, let us recall the off-task student mentioned above. Moving close to the off-task student lets him know you are aware of his behavior and that you are willing to invade his personal space. This powerful non-verbal message communicates to him that you are in charge and is particularly reinforced if the student is sitting and you are standing.

Music class settings, especially those involving large ensembles, pose a challenge to teachers wanting to employ proxemics as an engagement strategy. Strong traditions associated with ensemble settings place the teacher in the front of the room on a podium, physically removed from the students who are arranged typically in successively larger concentric arcs of seats. In the instrumental classroom, this arrangement requires multiple numbers of students to share music stands. The close-knit arrangement of students' seats and music stands enforces an impenetrable barrier, keeping the teacher from venturing beyond the first row of students. Although such an arrangement may be appropriate for performance, it is clearly not conducive to effective teaching and learning, especially if it is used exclusively.

One alternative might be to insert an aisle through the center of the traditional arrangement running from the front to the back of the room. The teacher would be able to move easily to just about any place in the room within a matter of two or three seconds. Such increased accessibility accomplishes several goals. Most obviously, it allows the teacher to individualize instruction more easily than would be possible in a traditional set-up. Equally important, however, students tend to respond differentially to seating arrangements that allow the teacher to vary his or her proximity to individual members of the group (Gump, 1987; Marx, Fuhrer, & Hartig, 1999). Researchers have confirmed that, compared to those seated in the back or at the sides, students seated in front or central positions communicate more (Levine, O'Neal, Garwood, & McDonald, 1980; Montello, 1988), and show different non-verbal behaviors (Breed & Colaiuta, 1974), and more interest, enjoyment, and motivation (Millard & Stimpson, 1980). When teachers insert aisles in a traditional seating arrangement, essentially increasing the teacher's accessibility to all students, learning is affected in powerful and positive ways. Simple temporary adjustments to the rehearsal seating arrangement can help students hear and notice multiple dimensions of the music being rehearsed. The possibilities may include:

- For a portion of the rehearsal, maintain the traditional arc but ask students to sit anywhere they choose. Subsequently, students may return to the original set-up.

- For a portion of the rehearsal, place those with similar musical material in close proximity (e.g. those with similar melodic lines, countermelodies, etc.). Then ask students to return to the original set-up.

- In a choral setting, place students in small mixed ensembles (e.g. an octet comprised of two sopranos, two altos, two tenors, and two basses).

- Set up concentric *circles* as an alternative to concentric arcs.

144 SOCIAL PLACE

Staging the Classroom

Quickly list as many different ways you can think of to stage the classroom you are in currently. Note how learning might be affected by these changes. What are the limitations of staging options in this room?

CONTINUING TO DEVELOP YOUR SKILLS

Think for a moment of the most effective teachers that you have had. More than likely, their words were often reinforced by the energy in their voices and the deliberate actions of their physical expression. They probably were fortunate to have many great models of effective teaching to emulate as they developed. Although some teachers bring a tremendous amount of natural teaching ability, the most effective ones continue to hone their skills throughout their careers. If you are interested in speeding up your own process, our best advice is to find great teachers who you respect, and then learn to do what they do. Each one of us is a unique mixture of the people who have most strongly influenced our lives. We all tend to pick up habits along the way. Many times this influence happens passively and unconsciously. However, if you choose models you want to emulate and apply a concentrated effort towards identifying and re-creating their effective habits, you will not only speed up your own development, but you will empower yourself by taking responsibility for your own future.

Look for opportunities in your coursework to practice honing delivery skills. Conducting class presents a particularly effective opportunity for you to work on facial expression and to coordinate that dimension with physical gestures of the arms and upper body, all inspired by the artistic elements of the music being conducted. Some degree programs require courses that are labeled 'speaking intensive' (i.e. speech class, Oratory, etc.). Similarly, you could enroll in a theater class. Such courses present fabulous opportunities to improve characteristics of vocal delivery and to practice combining various vocal and physical components to produce particularly powerful moments in the classroom. As you begin to accumulate a repertoire of what works for you, you will also begin to notice that new effective ways of presenting yourself to others will feel increasingly natural.

As you proceed through your degree program, you will undoubtedly engage in many hours of early field experience. Take the opportunity to video record yourself presenting instruction and review it for voice characteristics of pitch, volume, quality, and timing. Also notice physical characteristics such as posture, gestures, facial expression, and eye contact. Many professional speakers practice their craft by video recording their presentations and carefully reviewing those recordings to notice when their delivery skills are working together and when they are not. They take the time to practice various vocal inflections or rates of speech, perhaps slowing down to make a particular point. They practice coordinating these vocal characteristics with hand and arm gestures and with particular facial expressions. You need to practice your craft with the same degree of intensity. Just like the process of improving your technique as a musician, you need to practice the delivery skill techniques that will make you a better teacher.

CLASS ACTIVITIES

Class Activity 5.1: Levels of Expressiveness

Choose a sentence of about 10 words from any printed material that you have with you . . . it might be a textbook, course syllabus, or magazine. Take turns, in class, reading your sentence three ways: (a) be as boring as humanly possible, (b) talk in a normal conversational tone, and (c) 'ham it up' as much as you can, perhaps like a radio DJ or automobile dealer on TV. As each person demonstrates three levels of expressiveness, take notes and try to determine just what changes occur in the voice, body, face, eyes, hands, etc., for each level of expressiveness. Be specific when describing physical characteristics and changes. These lists should be saved for class discussions as you go through delivery skill categories throughout this chapter.

Class Activity 5.2: Vocal Pitch Variation

Write a list of three requests that you might use as a teacher. For example, an orchestra director may say, "Open your folders and take out the overture." A general music teacher may say, "Pat the beat on your knees with me." A choral teacher might say "Sopranos, please hold the pitch out until my release." A band director may say, "Trombones, you've got to take your mutes out before the repeat." Form groups of four to five people, and practice saying the items on your list, ending each with a lowered vocal pitch. Also try them with a questioning, or rising, ending. Talk about the emotional effects of each version. What other elements, besides pitch, contribute to effectiveness of requests?

Class Activity 5.3: Face Reading

In small groups of four to five people, discuss the emotion being portrayed by each face below and try to reach group consensus for each one. In your discussion, determine how various facial components (e.g., eyes, forehead, mouth, angle of head, etc.) contribute to the particular emotions being conveyed (see Figure 5.1 on p. 114).

FIGURE 5.1 Face-reading photo.

How Will You Design Instruction?

6

While exploring the elements of effective music teaching, we have examined the varied worlds in which music is and can be taught (Chapter 4) and uncovered some common actions that help music teachers convey ideas effectively (Chapter 5). Now, as we continue our exploration, we will investigate common structures that support effective learning in the music classroom. Music teachers need to be adept at creating such structures both inside and outside their classrooms.

The assumptions teachers hold regarding students, music, learning, and teaching drive their decision-making as they consider the structures they will put to use in their classrooms. These assumptions can be outwardly expressed ideals or philosophies such as "All children should have the right to enjoy and study music." Some of these assumptions may not be expressed outwardly but may be better described as taken-for-granted beliefs (see Chapter 2) such as "All students learn best when instruction is presented in a logical sequence by the teacher." While some students may learn well within such a structure, others may not. It may be that none of them learn 'best' in this structure. To teach without examining your ideals, philosophies, or assumptions is to consider them to be 'truth' or 'just the way things are.' Many assumptions purported to be 'truth' support the 'factory' model of schooling that was discussed in Chapter 2. As we learned from that discussion, these 'truths' should not be taken for granted, but examined closely so that informed decisions can be made.

BLOG ON ...

My Advice to Me

Refer back to the metaphor that you wrote in Chapter 2. **Read this as though another teacher had written it.** In your blog, give some advice to this teacher concerning his or her assumptions. What assumptions are implied but not outwardly expressed in the metaphor? Do you believe the assumptions (both expressed and implied) will serve that person well in the classroom? If so, why? If not, what would you suggest as a change or addition to the metaphor that might help this teacher become more effective?

CURRICULUM—ASSUMPTIONS AT THE FOUNDATIONAL LEVEL

When constructing learning experiences, most teachers start with the idea of a *curriculum*. The word 'curriculum' is used often in educational settings, which would seem to imply that its definition is simple and clear. Unfortunately, this is not the case. From its Latin roots, 'curriculum' literally means 'to run a course.' This definition helps us begin to understand the meaning; but it is still rather vague. More specifically applied to music, Hanley and Montgomery (2005) define curriculum as the process of "establishing educational outcomes and selecting appropriate learning experiences to help students achieve these outcomes" (p. 17). The authors continue by asserting that others define curriculum as, "teaching methods, materials and tools" (p. 17). Still others define it in three ways, "as skills—what students must be able to do; as knowledge—what students must know as a result of schooling; and instructional methods—Orff, Kodaly, Gordon and so on" (p. 17). While these ideas are more specific than our first definition, they do not bring us any closer to a clear understanding of 'curriculum.' Instead of attempting to define curriculum, it may help to consider questions about its construction. Benedict (2010) listed the following for consideration:

> Is curriculum a course to be run or set of experiences that shape us? Are there fundamentals, basics or essentials that each of us should 'know?' Is curriculum a way in which to address social justice? Is there a difference between the stated and operationalized curriculum? What does teaching have to do with curriculum? And finally, yet hardly finally, who is curriculum for and who has been left out?
>
> (p. 144)

Many of these questions address important issues that we will explore more completely later in this text. However, you may ascertain from this short discussion that curriculum is complex and not easily defined. So, rather than defining curriculum, we believe it is most important to be mindful of how *your* expressed and implied assumptions about curriculum can influence the construction of learning in your classroom.

When uncovering these assumptions, knowing something about curriculum theory is helpful. While an exhaustive examination of curriculum theory is well beyond the scope of this text (and perhaps beyond your desire to know right now), there are some basic concepts common to most types of curriculum construction that can help us understand its structure. There are four basic ways to think of curriculum. These are:

- curriculum as a body of **knowledge to be transmitted**

- curriculum as a **product**

- curriculum as **process**

- curriculum as **praxis** (Smith, 1996, 2000).

If we think of curriculum as a *body of knowledge to be transmitted* to students, we are likely to make our curricular decisions focused exclusively on content. We would examine the content of what is to be learned and, once the details are ascertained, we would make decisions about the process for transmitting or delivering these details to students by the most effective methods possible (Blenkin, Edwards, & Kelly, 1992). Approaching curriculum in this manner assumes that the students have no prior knowledge of or experience with the content. They are 'empty vessels' waiting to be filled by the teacher. This approach also assumes that all students can and should learn the content in the same way at the same time. Because the curriculum is only concerned with transmitting content, there is no concern for how students construct learning experiences. In this sense, education is something that is 'done to' students.

A *product-based curriculum* is concerned about students, but views them as a product or outcome. This approach views education as a technical exercise where objectives are set, a plan devised, then applied, and the outcomes (products) measured. Product management theory strongly influences this approach with concepts like (a) a greater division of labor with jobs being simplified, (b) managerial control over all elements of the workplace, and (c) assessment based on systematic study of time and efficiency. The attractiveness of this approach in education is that curriculum can be the product of systematic study that can be applied uniformly to large groups of students (Smith, 1996, 2000).

There are several issues to be considered with the product-based approach. One is the limited voice of the learner in the process. Learners are told what they must learn and how they will learn it. The success or failure of both the program and the individual learner is often judged on the basis of whether pre-specified changes occur in each learner according to standardized measurements. Another issue is the 'de-skilling' of teachers. As a result of simplifying job requirements and exercising more managerial (i.e. administrative) control, teachers are limited to making fewer and fewer professional decisions in the process of designing and delivering instruction. One example of this de-skilling process might include prewritten curriculum programs in general music that have attempted to make students' experiences with these materials 'teacher proof.' Very detailed plans are included with all necessary materials and even scripts for teachers to use for the delivery of instruction. Some schools mandate the use of such curricula. The logic of this approach is for each student to receive the same instruction regardless of his or her situation. To ensure such uniformity, the curriculum is designed in great detail so that it can be delivered to groups of students who are assumed to engage equally with the material. Teachers must deliver the prescribed materials in the same ways to all students. Individualized instruction is not possible. Product-based curricular approaches can force professional educators into roles as teaching technicians who are not expected to make educational decisions. It can also dehumanize students' roles in the classroom, as they are viewed as objects to be acted upon.

In both the transmission and product models, the curriculum is often thought of as a set of documents used for teaching. Another way to think about curriculum is to consider it as a *process*. In this sense, curriculum is not a physical thing, but rather the interactions among teachers, students, and what is to be learned. Hence, curriculum is what actually happens in the classroom and what people do to prepare and to evaluate instruction. There are a number of contrasts in this curricular model when compared with the transmission and product models. First, where the other models approach teaching as a craft and teachers as expert technicians who apply that craft, the process model places teachers in roles as informed professionals who use their professional knowledge, skills, and dispositions to enable optimal learning experiences in their classrooms through active experimentation. Thus, a curriculum is not a package of materials to be *covered*, but rather a process in which professional educators take informed ideas about content and practice and share them with learners in ways that will help those learners *uncover* meaning through interactions with the content, the teacher, and their environments (including other students). Therefore, the curriculum is unique to each classroom setting and is not a program that can be delivered uniformly. Learners are active partners in the curriculum and are not objects to be acted upon by others or by the content.

Two issues are most often raised when process-based curriculum is called into question. First, there is the possibility of a severe lack of uniformity among students regarding what is learned. The potential exists for different content to be studied in each learning environment. It is also likely that many different approaches to understanding the same content will be employed. These irregularities confound the normal process of examinations. Efficiently measuring the learning of such varied content in so many different forms with conventional assessment practices is simply not possible. This issue can be disconcerting because many students and their families need some valid and reliable measure of student learning for participation in future endeavors like college entrance. The second concern is that curriculum as process relies heavily on the quality of the one who facilitates learning. The approach is entirely dependent upon the cultivation of meaning making in the classroom. If the teacher is unable to facilitate the process, there will be limitations to what can occur educationally. In essence there will be little or no curriculum.

A fourth way to think about curriculum is as *praxis*. Praxis is action that is informed by, and committed to, certain ideals. A praxial approach to curriculum suggests that it is not simply a set of plans to be implemented, but rather is constituted through an active process in which planning, delivery, and evaluation are all reciprocally related and integrated into the process. Each part of the process occurs simultaneously and informs the other two. Hence, evaluation is not simply a test at the end of instruction, but an integral part of the curriculum that occurs along with planning and delivery. The curricular goal is to teach students to deal efficiently with the contemporary world. Curriculum as praxis should include the students' preconceptions and should incorporate how the student views his or her own world. This type of curriculum should allow the student to build an orderly sense of the world in which he or she lives.

Concerns with the praxis model are similar to those within the process model and revolve mostly around accountability. If the curriculum is to be responsive to the individual needs of each child, how is one to measure student achievement with standard examinations? Most who address this question suggest that alternative assessment strategies can be used to assess meaningful outcomes when curriculum is constructed in this manner (Barrett, 2005; Cohen, 2012; Mills, 2009; Robinson, 1995). (Note: We will discuss much more about assessment in Chapter 11.)

Exploring this brief overview of four ways to think of curriculum may raise a question about which is best. The answer to this question is as complex and multifaceted as curriculum itself. While you may feel there are advantages to certain curricular approaches and some 'fit' better than others, you may not have a choice regarding which approach is being used in your teaching environment. Most likely, no single approach is used. Rather,

DISCUSSION BOARD
Curricular Thoughts

Describe the curricular approaches you believe were used in your school music experiences and why you think they were used. It may be that a combination of approaches was employed, so feel free to indicate that in your posting. Read your colleagues' posts and comment on how your experiences were either similar or dissimilar to theirs.

some combination of each is being employed. So, beyond trying to decide which is 'best,' it may be more valuable to understand the strengths and shortcomings of each approach so you can construct learning experiences in the most effective manner possible.

MUSIC CURRICULUM

Curriculum construction in music has a long historical foundation. While we will not detail much of this history, we will examine the assumptions brought to curriculum construction from this background.

Traditional curriculum. The first approach is based upon assumptions of **technical rationality** or what some call a **positivist** approach (Barrett, 2005; Benedict, 2010). This approach is "one in which faith in science and reasoning and that which can be observed and measured is favored over all other models of engagement" (Benedict, 2010, p.146). This approach with its historical foundations is often referred to as "traditional curriculum" (Barrett, 2005, p. 22). Most traditional curriculum design has been based historically on four questions (Jorgensen, 1988). These are:

- What educational purposes should the school (teacher) seek to attain?

- How can learning experiences be selected which are likely to be useful in obtaining these objectives?

- How can learning experiences be organized for effective instruction?

- How can effectiveness of learning experiences be evaluated? (Tyler, 1949, p. 1)

Many professional music educators have used these questions, or others very similar to them, to construct curriculum for the music classroom (Conway, 2002; Russell, 2006; Standerfer & Hunter, 2010; Woods, 1982). Conway (2002) suggests there are a number of different models for constructing a traditional curriculum in music. She cites an **objectives-based** model as the approach most commonly used. "This is a four-phase process that involves (a) developing objectives, (b) sequencing those objectives (often referred to as 'scope and sequence'), (c) designing activities to meet the objectives (lesson plans), and (d) designing evaluation tools to assure that learning takes place (tests)" (p. 56). She notes that effective teachers often mix activities in the sequence rather than implementing this approach in a strict linear process. A **literature-based** approach is founded on the repertoire chosen for study. Obviously, this approach can be used for performance-based classes, but it is recommended that other curricular approaches be used as well (Conway, 2002). A **skills-based** approach focuses on what students should be able to do and would include skills like "singing, moving or playing on instruments . . .

and musical concepts such as tonality and meter" (p. 56). This approach is based exclusively on students' abilities and does not include elements like musical understanding or students' attitudes and preferences about the music they are using to develop their skills. A **knowledge-based** approach would focus on theoretical and/or historical understanding of musical elements and events. Conway notes that, "Although this is an important part of music class, the [teacher] should be careful to balance knowledge with skills" (p. 56).

With the advent of the *Common Core State Standards* (CCSS) in 2010, much curriculum work in the United States has been refocused on a **standards-based** approach. As of the publication of this text, 45 states have adopted the CCSS. "These standards define the knowledge and skills students should have within their K-12 education careers so that they will graduate high school able to succeed in entry-level, credit-bearing academic college courses and in workforce training programs" (Common Core State Standards Initiative, 2012). Currently, standards addressing English language arts and mathematics are the only sets of standards that have been completed and adopted by these states. Others are in development. Addressing the question of why educational standards are needed, CCSS states that:

> Standards are a first step—a key building block—in providing our young people with a high-quality education that will prepare them for success in college and work. Of course, standards are not the only thing that is needed for our children's success, but they provide an accessible roadmap for our teachers, parents, and students.
>
> (p. 1)

Music education has a long history with standards-based curricular approaches. As we noted in Chapter 4, the National Standards for Music Education are a set of nine voluntary standards that were published in 1994 as part of the National Standards for Arts Education, addressing "what students should know and be able to do in the Arts" (National Association for Music Education, 2012). Currently the National Coalition for Core Arts Standards is examining and reconsidering all these standards and music standards are part of this consideration. New standards are expected to be published in the next few years. Many states have also developed subject area standards and some states (e.g. Michigan, New York) have district-level music curricula that were intended to align with both state and national standards. Conway (2002) cautions, however, to remember that standards are not the curriculum, but a list of knowledge and skills on which to base curricular decisions. She goes on to suggest that "When aligning a curriculum with state and national standards, the [teacher] should write the local curriculum first" (p. 57).

After the curriculum is drafted, it can then be compared with the standards. If there are gaps between the standards and the curriculum, these gaps should be addressed in professional development for teachers so they have the knowledge and skill necessary to implement the curriculum.

The entire scope of standards-based curricula is currently changing so quickly that it would be impossible to address its entire nature with any clarity in this text. You are encouraged to work with your professors and others in the educational community to gather information about the impact of standards on the construction of effective music learning experiences.

While traditional approaches to curriculum have impacted and will likely continue to impact construction of musical learning experiences, some assumptions on which these approaches are founded have, however, been called into question (Barrett, 2005; Benedict, 2010: Hanley & Montgomery, 2005; Reimer, 2012). The primary arguments are similar to assumptions associated with curriculum as transmission of a body of knowledge and curriculum as product. Barrett (2005) depicted the curriculum construction process from this perspective (see Figure 6.1).

> Like a series of actions in a chain reaction, the diagram . . . conveys that curriculum planning is a rational, orderly, and sequential process that culminates in student learning. Students participate in the curriculum that teachers deliver and demonstrate that they have 'got it.' The assumption is that if we get the front end of the chain right, the rest will follow.
>
> (Barrett, 2005, p. 22)

This top-down approach to instruction carries with it a number of other assumptions as well.

There are times in this approach when students are considered to be 'empty vessels' or 'blank slates' that bring little or no experience with music into the classroom. This is not an expressed assumption. Teachers do not often tell others that they hold this belief, but

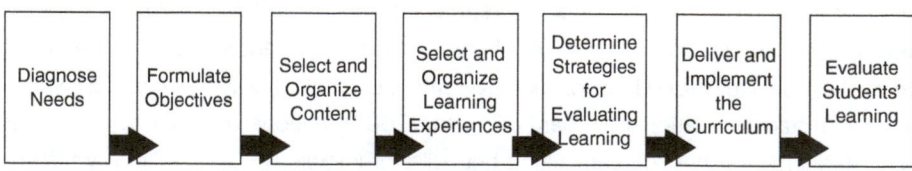

FIGURE 6.1 A positivist approach to curriculum planning.
Note: This figure is from Barrett, 2005, p. 22, and is reprinted here with permission.

when one examines the ways in which music is sometimes formally taught, it seems clear that the assumption can drive curricular decision-making. For example, let's consider the presentation of *Mary Had a Little Lamb* in many beginning band method books. The notation found in most beginning method books looks like Figure 6.2.

As long as your students have grown up within typical American society and attended schools within this culture, they likely learned to sing this tune as a young child as it is notated in Figure 6.3.

When a student plays *Mary Had a Little Lamb* as he remembers singing it—as his experience with this music informs his performance—he is likely told that it is 'wrong.' The notation in the method book (Figure 6.2) does not represent what the student is likely to play (Figure 6.3). Rather than consider the performer to be wrong, however, the teacher could consider the notation to be 'wrong' because it does not consider the students' past experiences with this tune. This is an interesting change in perspective from transmission of knowledge and product to a more process- and praxial-based approach.

Parker Palmer (2007) calls this linear model of knowing represented in Figure 6.1 **objectivist**, meaning that knowing moves from the object (knowledge) through the expert (teacher) to the amateur (student). Experts are allowed to have access to the object due to their abilities to know and to teach. Amateurs do not have direct access to the object. Their role is to receive information about the object provided by the expert. The object is believed to be well beyond the reach of the amateur who must rely on the expert

FIGURE 6.2 *Mary Had a Little Lamb*—standard notation in beginning band methods.

FIGURE 6.3 *Mary Had a Little Lamb*—students' prior knowledge of the tune.

at the center of the model to provide what is needed. Therefore, "in this myth, truth is a set of propositions about objects; education is a system for delivering those propositions to students; and an educated person is one who can remember and repeat the experts' propositions" (Palmer, 2007, p. 101).

As we noted earlier, teachers do not often express such thoughts when stating their teaching beliefs, ideals, or philosophies. These beliefs are more likely expressed in the assumptions that influence instructional decision-making. As an example, think of a typical large ensemble rehearsal in a middle-school, junior-high-school, or high-school setting. The object (music most often selected by the teacher with no student input) is studied by the expert (score study by the teacher aimed at 'knowing' the piece) and the information extracted from this examination by the expert is imparted to the amateurs (ensemble members) during rehearsal. The ensemble members' responsibilities are to take the information given them and remember it (do it) during a performance of the piece. This model is constructed so that information will flow from the object through the expert to the amateur as efficiently as possible. This efficiency requires that information flow in only one direction—from the object to the amateur—as flow in the other direction could cause delay or confusion.

As noted earlier, "These ways of teaching and their resultant curriculum are influenced by modes of rationality that have potent, formidable historical roots" (Benedict, 2010, p. 144). Secondary music education in the United States has long been grounded in the standard large ensemble performance model and instructional design has been founded on models of efficient practice. Bennett Reimer (2012), noted music education philosopher, states, "At the secondary level we have put practically all our eggs in the basket of performing music in large ensembles and have had admirable success with it" (p. 25). We, the authors of the text, continue to support the idea that there is a place for large ensemble performance within the curriculum. However, as we will discuss next in this chapter, there may be other ways to construct the learning process within these and other settings.

Curriculum reconstructed. In recent years, questions concerning the assumptions of a traditional curricular approach have been raised. These include:

Should music education be teacher centered, subject centered or learner centered? Should we focus on skill development or the development of musical understanding? Should we emphasize musical learning or cross-curricular connections? Should we be trying to improve our students' musical tastes or welcoming the diverse kinds of music relevant in their lives? Whose interests should guide decision making?

(Hanley & Montgomery, 2005, p. 18)

Answers to these questions and others suggest a need to reconsider or reconstruct the assumptions upon which curricular decisions within music education have been made. These questions have raised such concern that a special focus issue of *Music Educators Journal* (March 2005) was published with articles addressing these concerns. Some suggestions by the authors of these articles included moving away from positivist assumptions of learning to more **constructivist** assumptions (Hanley & Montgomery, 2005), basing curricular decisions on the actual lived experiences of students rather than on predictive outcomes (Barrett, 2005). Authors' suggestions also include bringing both the content and pedagogy of music that students choose to engage with outside the classroom into school music endeavors (Green, 2005). While these suggestions are not exhaustive in the ways to reconsider construction of music curricula, they each offer some interesting ideas.

In the previous section, we noted that traditional curriculum construction is founded on positivist assumptions. These include beliefs that the best model for knowledge is found in the closed system of the scientific process where variables are controlled and procedures are logical and orderly. Applied to curriculum, this model assumes that learning is best facilitated through similar controls and order. Another positivist assumption is that to have meaning, concepts or ideas must be experienced through the senses and, once internalized, these concepts or ideas must result in some measurable behavior. Therefore, all learning should be outwardly experienced and measurable (Henderson, 2011; Watson, 2009). Finally, knowledge is considered to be an object that must be transmitted from an expert to an amateur, hence teachers are active transmitters and students are passive receivers in the learning process (Palmer, 2007).

Constructivist assumptions about knowledge and learning are quite different from those of positivism. First, learners are assumed to construct knowledge actively as they call upon their past experiences to help construct meaning for what is occurring presently. With this assumption, knowledge is not an object to be transmitted, but is constructed within each learner *by* each learner. That this process of construction often takes place during activities with others is another assumption of constructivist learning, thus students need to work in collaborative groups and learn from peers as well as from the teacher. Finally, learners play an essential role in assessing their own learning, and the outcomes of learning are often varied and unpredictable (Hanley & Montgomery, 2005). Applying this assumption to curricular construction, alternative means of assessment are needed—ones that place the student at the center of the process.

Barrett (2005) suggests that music curricula should be reconstructed by placing the 'lived experiences' of students at the center of consideration. "The ways that students make sense of the school experience and relate it to their lives outside of school become the focal point for creating the curriculum" (p. 23). She provides a model (see Figure 6.4) that demonstrates this approach. Barrett acknowledges the dual musical lives of students and that lifelong engagement in music will not take place in school. Students in school music programs, as well as those not in school music programs, will continue to engage with music for a lifetime. Our goal as music educators should be that the experiences of those who have enjoyed a comprehensive music education are enriched through the knowledge, skills, and dispositions they acquired as a result. To this end, Barrett suggests that the construction of music-learning opportunities should place students' actual experiences with music at the center of the process and teachers should acknowledge all influences, both in school and outside of school, on the students' musical engagement and understanding. This approach does not allow for preconceived outcomes, nor can curriculum be constructed without the student. Barrett states:

> A curriculum centered on meaning provides time for students and teachers to reflect on music and its value, uses an array of instructional strategies to promote inquiry,

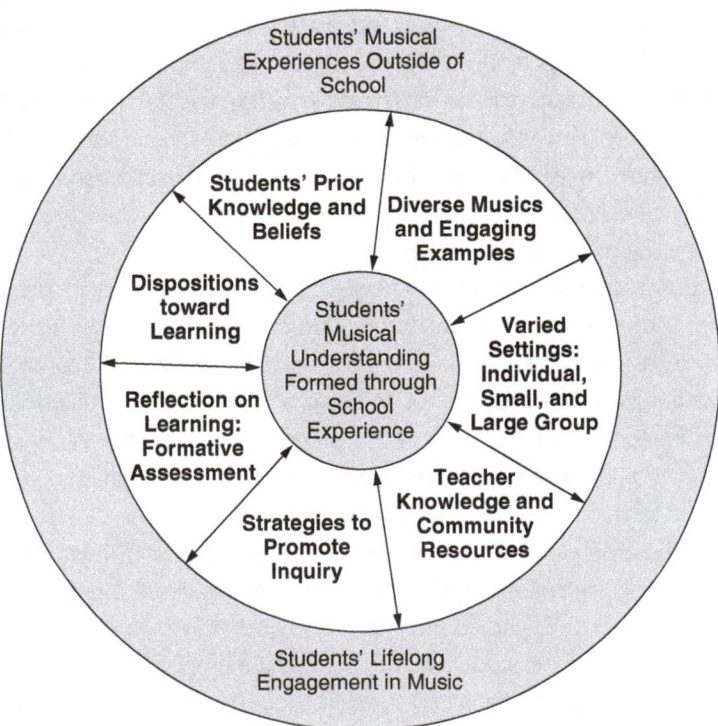

FIGURE 6.4 A reconceptualized view of curriculum.

Note: This figure is from Barrett, 2005, p. 23, and is reprinted here with permission.

features varied settings to promote independence, and offers plentiful avenues for exploring diverse musics in school and community settings. Essential questions for teachers to consider include the following: How can classroom experiences directly engage students' musical thinking? How can the curriculum foster students' abilities and desires to relate to music as a lasting presence in their lives? What is the essence of a musical experience with this sort of power?

(p. 23)

Green (2005) also considers the dual musical lives that many students are living in her construction of musical learning opportunities. She states that "Music educators in many countries have attempted to close the gap between two musical worlds: that of pupils' musical culture outside school and that of the classroom" (p. 27). The difference in her considerations is that she not only advocates for the inclusion of music that students choose to listen to outside of school as part of the school music curriculum, but that this change in content also be accompanied with a change in pedagogy. Undoubtedly, many of you have had the experience of performing an arrangement of a 'popular' or 'vernacular' piece in a school ensemble. Green's contention is that this change in musical content alone does not connect students to 'their' music. Teaching popular or vernacular music in the same manner as one would teach traditional ensemble repertoire, with the same performance protocols and expectations, not only misses the mark of allowing students to have experiences with their music in school, but it is often insulting to the students' actual musical experiences with this content. Green suggests that popular/vernacular musicians learn music differently and this pedagogy can be applied effectively to the music classroom. In articulating these differences between what she calls *formal* and **informal music pedagogy**, she states:

Learning practices of these [popular/vernacular] musicians differ from the teaching and learning strategies associated with formal music education, insofar as they involve the following:

- Learning based on personal choice, enjoyment, identification and familiarity with the music, as distinct from being introduced to new and often unfamiliar music
- Recorded music as the principal, aural means of musical transmission and skill acquisition, as distinct from notated or other written or verbal instructions and exercises
- Self-teaching and peer-directed learning, as distinct from learning with adult supervision and guidance, curricula, syllabi or external assessment

- Assimilating skills and knowledge in haphazard ways according to musical preferences, rather than following a progression from simple to complex
- Integration of listening, performing, improvising and composing throughout the learning process, as distinct from their increasing differentiation.

(Green, 2005, p. 28)

Green's process begins by asking students to bring recordings of music they choose to listen to with them to class. She then enacts a four-rule process. The first rule is that students must form groups of three to six members and they may choose with whomever they wish to work. Secondly, all members of the group must be involved musically in the process. Third, they are to choose a recording that all group members enjoy. Finally, they need to 'cover' the tune they have chosen by aural means using only the recording as a reference. They may not seek out notation of any kind. With groups formed and rules in place, she sets the students free to work on their own to prepare a performance of their cover for the class.

Through extensive research with a number of students, Green (2005) has found that similar aspects occur consistently as students engage in this process. The process usually starts with chaos, which is not dissimilar to the actual ways that popular/vernacular musicians work. There is a great deal of individual experimentation and improvisation. Eventually, group members begin sharing ideas. They listen to each other and offer critiques of ideas, referring back to their reference recording as they work out the musical ideas they are hearing and attempting to re-create. This endeavor is not usually orderly, but musical ideas are exchanged, analyzed, and evaluated throughout the process. The process often leads to a group composition activity where ideas are shared, modified, and discarded as the cover takes shape. Green is clear to state that this is not a linear process. Groups move in and out of each of these stages at all times. The groups then perform for each other and offer ideas and feedback to the other groups.

Green notes that teachers' greatest concern with this process in the classroom is the lack of teacher control and a fear that students will not be engaged, exhibiting off-task behaviors. Through her research, she has found that teachers who learn to interact with students in the process at appropriate moments and in appropriate ways are successful. These teachers often take a position outside the group and listen to exchanges between group members. These teachers do not usually offer solutions to the group's problems, but guide groups in discovering their own solutions when needed. Such teacher/student interactions continue to acknowledge the student's ownership of the music they are producing. On-task student behavior is also noted in most groups. At times, there are groups that do not function as a complete unit initially, but as time passes this problem tends to dissipate. She does note that teacher guidance is sometimes needed to solve some of these engagement issues.

The scenario described above is the beginning step in a much more complex process. Even with the short description, you can see the impact this approach could have on the reconstruction of music learning opportunities. There are resources in the *Connecting to the Profession* chapter at the end of this section addressing Green's entire process. We would encourage you to look at these resources to get a more comprehensive picture of this approach to reconstructing the music curriculum.

These are just a few examples of how some professionals are reconstructing music-learning opportunities. As you consider them, note that they all suggest a movement away from thinking of curriculum as transmission of a body of knowledge or as product. Rather, they address curriculum as process and praxis. We encourage you to carry these thoughts with you to the last section of this chapter.

144 SOCIAL PLACE
Reconstruction Thoughts

Using 144 characters or fewer, share one way you might be able to reconstruct learning experiences for your students that would be different from the experiences you had in school.

CONSTRUCTING MUSIC-LEARNING OPPORTUNITIES

The discussions of four ways to think about curriculum and traditional vs. reconstructed curriculum will not do much to help you construct meaningful learning experiences for your students if you do not have a means to take these theories and apply them to your actual practice of teaching music. There are many different ways to construct curricula in music. It may be that you are provided a curriculum guide as you enter your position. While this is not as common as it is in other subject areas, formal music curricula are likely to become more common as reform initiatives such as No Child Left Behind, Race to the Top, and Common Core State Standards impact music education (Reimer, 2012). The following is the outline of an approach to constructing curriculum from the inception of broad learning concepts to the actual delivery of instruction in the classroom. As a framework, we believe this can be helpful in either constructing a curriculum for a class or in applying ideas within a curriculum guide to your classroom.

Jorgensen (1988) (see Table 6.1).

> an approach to curriculum design in music which, while taking account of important external factors, establishes the teacher's experience as a central element in the process and implies that the teacher's task is a professional as opposed to merely technical one and an artistic rather than simply a craftmaking enterprise.
>
> (p. 94)

The first stage requires the music educator to establish **general objectives** for her music-learning environment. This requires the teacher to call upon her own internal knowing including her attitudes, beliefs, values, subject matter knowledge, cultural background,

TABLE 6.1 Stages of curricular development.

Stage of development	Considerations
General objectives	• Professional training • Cultural background (both teacher and students) • Attitudes, beliefs, and values (both teacher and students) • Subject matter knowledge • External influences (e.g. national standards, state standards)
General program outline	• Sketch of major elements • Framework on which to hang ideas • Several major units of study • Consider student desire and needs • Consider community desire and needs • Begin to balance preference with practical
Specific objectives	• Begin to decide what elements to include and in what balance • Consider student experience • Both rational and intuitive objectives
Specific curricular plan	• List of activities/projects or repertoire to be studied • A plan, not an imperative • Dynamic and not static • Tension between the desirable and the possible continues
Specific lesson strategies	• Break down content into 'learnable' units • Make decisions on method • Consider developmental appropriateness
Translation to instruction	• Consider changes necessary as teaching and learning interact

Source: Jorgensen, 1988.

and professional education. It also requires her to consider external factors such as national and state standards. At this stage, the teacher begins to reconcile her internal preferences with the external standards that may be imposed upon the curriculum.

The product of this examination leads to the development of a **general program outline**. Jorgensen describes this step as a sketch of the major elements or a framework upon which to hang more specific ideas. As the music educator works her way through this outline, several major units of study emerge. For example, an elementary general music educator may consider units focused on pitch (high versus low) and beat (internalizing steady beat) for her first-grade learners. As the music educator is working through this process, a tension rises between what the music educator would like her students to learn and what can practically be done given factors such as instructional time, student backgrounds, and community desires. Again, the music educator must make professional decisions about what to include and how to balance what 'should' be done with what 'can' be done.

These decisions lead the music educator to construct **specific objectives** that take all these forces into consideration. The music educator makes rational decisions about the scope and sequence of the materials that will be presented in the classroom. Jorgensen also suggests that the music educator makes intuitive decisions that are informed by her experiences with the subject matter, the students, the school, and even time of year. Returning to the example of an elementary music educator involved in this process, she may decide that in the first quarter of the semester, first-grade students will be able to (a) distinguish between high pitch and low pitch, and (b) be able to move to a steady beat. She considered that she sees these students for 60 minutes of instruction each week and that they will also be expected to sing with the other grades in the all-school assembly in late September.

Given these objectives, the teacher develops a **specific curricular plan** that lists activities, projects, and/or repertoire that can be used for instruction. Jorgensen suggests this plan is not set in concrete, but is a guide to be used by the teacher. Again, the teacher calls upon her knowledge, experience, and education to construct these elements, but also realizes that elements may change due to changes in both internal and external forces. The tension between what is desirable and what is possible continues to exist and the music educator must work continually to achieve a balance she believes will help students learn best.

At this point in the process, the music educator breaks down the content within each unit into learnable chunks and constructs **specific lesson strategies**. Decisions about how to construct these strategies are based often upon the instructional method the teacher chooses to use. (Note: there is much more discussion about specific methods later in this text.) Teachers also consider the developmental level of the students as they design this instruction. For example, to introduce the concept of high and low pitch, our elementary music teacher chooses to use a floor graph with a blue line on top and a brown line on the bottom. Blue is high 'like the sky' and brown is low 'like the ground.' Knowing her students learn well though movement, she plays *Hot Cross Buns* on the piano, changing octaves between each measure. Students are asked to move to the blue line when they hear high sounds and brown line when they hear low sounds.

These specific strategies are then **translated to instruction**. This is the moment when the theory of constructing lesson plans meets the actual practice of delivering instruction. The music educator continues to make professional decisions in the process of delivering instruction that informs her of any necessary changes for the instruction to be as effective as possible. For example, as our elementary teacher enacts her plan with the floor graph, she notes that students are moving back and forth between the blue and brown lines as the pitches descend in each measure of *Hot Cross Buns.* As a result she changes her instruction and uses four repeated pitches in one octave and then four in another. Later, she will help students listen for groups of notes in pitch classes of high and low.

Jorgensen (1988) affirms the necessity of this entire process in the professionalization of music educators:

> This paradigm of curriculum design also dignifies the teacher's task. The curriculum becomes a way by which music teachers express their professional judgments as to why, what, how, when and where aspects of music should be taught. Rather than being treated as technicians who use prepared methods without examining which fit best with their objectives in a given set of circumstances, teachers can select the approaches that are, in their professional judgment, appropriate for their personalities, professional training, and experience, the particular and changing circumstances in which they find themselves, and the perceived needs of their students.
>
> (p. 105)

What may be most important for you to gather from the information presented in this chapter is that opportunities for meaningful learning experiences do not often occur without thoughtful work. The professional music educator in the classroom must construct these opportunities, as he or she is the only one who has all the information necessary to construct an appropriate curriculum that will enrich each student's musical life for years to come.

6.1 WHAT IF . . .?

How might you be able to reconstruct some of the ways music is commonly taught? Is it possible to construct these music-learning experiences so traditional requirements of the 'program' are met while enabling students' personal connections with music to grow? (see Class Activity 6.1, p. 133)

CLASS ACTIVITIES

Class Activity 6.1: What If . . . ?

Special Note on Setup

This activity uses a 'card-storming' process. To set up for the activity, take a plastic tablecloth and attach it to a flat surface or a wall. Placing it over a chalk or white board works well. Spray the cloth with a light coat of standard spray adhesive. This will form the card-storming screen. Standard index cards can be stuck to the screen and then un-stuck, moved, and re-stuck to the screen. Hand out a number of index cards and markers to each group.

Process

Divide into groups in which you would likely have common music-learning experiences. Items you might consider for this grouping would be (a) primary ensemble experiences (i.e. choir, band, orchestra), (b) size of school and community, (c) setting (i.e. rural, urban, suburban), and (d) other items that may be unique. Once you have formed groups, if they are larger than six, divide them into smaller groups of three to five members.

In these groups, discuss the music-learning experiences you believe impacted your musical learning most. Decide on one experience that the group would like to share. On the index cards provided, describe the curricular approaches you believe were used to construct this learning experience. What assumptions guided the instruction? Once you have your ideas on the cards, bring them to the front and stick them on the screen.

After you have stuck your first set of cards on the screen, discuss other learning experiences in your music education you believe either did not impact your musical learning or impacted your musical learning in a negative manner. Pick one experience from the group and write a set of cards that addresses how these experiences were constructed. What assumptions drove this instruction? Once you have your ideas on the cards, bring them to the front and stick them onto the screen.

Gather at the screen and read over the comments from all groups. If it is possible, collect the cards in common approaches, assumptions, or ideas about music learning. Which of these had a positive, meaningful impact on music learning? Which did not? Are there some that were simply necessary because of requirements placed upon the teacher by external forces?

Finally, clear the screen of all cards and consider a way that the instruction in either of these examples could have been reconstructed to help it impact your musical learning in the most meaningful manner possible. Is it possible to construct these music-learning experiences so that traditional requirements of the 'program' are met while enabling students' personal connections with music to grow? Write your answer on your cards and stick them to the screen. Gather and discuss these ideas as a class.

How Will You Teach for Musical Competence?

7

Music teachers are constantly making decisions about how they will teach, and many factors influence this process. In this chapter, we will discuss what information is available to help music teachers decide how to approach their teaching. Often, past experiences are cited as a primary influence on novice teacher decision-making. These experiences could include interactions with high-school teachers, applied teachers, college ensemble conductors, college music education professors, the student teaching cooperating teacher, the university student teaching supervisor, and the content and activities of college courses (Bauer & Berg, 2001; Wiggins, 2001). While such interactions can provide new insights, many teachers admit to simply teaching the way they were taught. We must be clear that making decisions based solely on past experience may or may not lead to effective decision-making. Effective teachers may teach as they were taught, but typically do so only after having considered the approach carefully. This careful contemplation should include consideration of all four 'common places' (teacher, student, subject matter, and milieu) (Schwab, 1983). Teachers who make decisions based solely on how he or she learned the subject matter omit consideration for the students and the learning environment. Without considering all four common places, the potential for teacher decisions to affect student learning positively is diminished.

If effective music teachers are to consider elements beyond their own experiences to inform their decision-making, what other information is available? Before answering this question, we would urge caution as you consider additional sources. There is no shortage of publications and media that erroneously suggest teachers only need to follow the supplied scripted directions for student learning to occur. In the recent past this was called '**teacher-proof curriculum**' (Taylor, 2010). This flawed view of curriculum assumes there is one right way to organize and teach the subject matter, and if the teacher has a curriculum that embodies this right way, students will learn well. Music teaching is not immune to this approach. Some examinations of texts and materials for music teaching from elementary general settings to secondary instrumental settings reveal similar assumptions (Regelski, 2002). These approaches effectively de-professionalize music teachers by limiting their impact in the decision-making process. When each

---

7.1 TEACHER DECISIONS

When teaching, what information does one use to decide how he is going to present the subject matter?

As you make decisions about how to teach a skill, what might you consider about each of the following: (a) the teacher, (b) the subject matter, (c) the student, and/or (d) the environment?

What other information might be available to you as you make decisions about how to approach your teaching? (see Class Activity 7.1, p. 151)

teaching and learning decision is made for the teacher, he or she is relegated to the role of technician rather than professional (see Chapter 1). The difference between the roles is that technicians deliver curriculum while professional music educators use all their teacher knowledge (see Chapter 3) to make informed decisions that facilitate each student's musical learning through the curriculum. We urge you to consider approaches that enhance your professional role in the classroom.

There are resources that can help music teachers organize their teaching while acknowledging music teachers' professional roles in making decisions that affect their students' learning. These are most often referred to as **methods** of music teaching. Most professional music educators note the need for a methodical approach in the teaching of music, but that every music teacher need not use the same method. Professional music educators must use the information available to them to make decisions about what method or combination of methods is best for them, for their students, for the subject matter, and for the given environment. At this point, it may be best to define what we mean by 'method.' The definition we support suggests that a method should have four recognizable characteristics:

(1) an identifiable underlying philosophy (in others words, a specific set of *principles*);
(2) a unified body of pedagogy unique to it (a body of well-defined *practice*);
(3) goals and objectives worthy of pursuit; and (4) integrity (its raison d'être must not be commercial).

(Choksy, Abramson, Gillespie, Woods, & York, 2001, p. 2)

There are a number of methods of music teaching that fit this definition. Most of these methods are primarily concerned with music teaching and learning for young children and are often addressed in elementary music education courses. This fact often causes some preservice music teachers not planning to teach at the elementary level to disregard them. We would urge you to reconsider this position. Those music educators who choose to teach at the secondary level, be it in general music or in ensemble settings, will benefit from the approaches to instruction espoused in these methods. We also believe all professional music educators can benefit from an examination of the foundations that support these methods regardless of the level or type of music teaching undertaken. We have found that the goals and objectives for all levels and types of music teaching are similar and that savvy professional music educators can make use of the foundations from these methods to inform their particular teaching situation at any level.

We should also note that some music educators who practice these methods prefer to call them **approaches** rather than methods. They note that the term 'method' suggests a practice that is rigid or prescribed and that these approaches do not condone a mindless application of method (Choksy et al., 2001). We agree with this assessment, but will use the terms 'method' and 'approach' interchangeably based upon terms used most often in the literature from each area.

METHODS AND APPROACHES FOR MUSIC TEACHING

In this section, we will examine four particular methodological approaches to music teaching. These include methods and approaches attributed to (a) Zoltan Kodály, (b) Carl Orff, (c) Emile Jaques-Dalcroze, and (d) Edwin Gordon. None of these examinations are exhaustive, but are intended to provide you with information concerning how designers of these methods answered the basic question of how one might choose to teach students to understand and make music. After each is introduced, we will consider any similarities in foundations between the four. These foundations may help inform your decisions about how you may choose to teach music.

Kodály

Zoltan Kodály's concept for music teaching and learning emanated from his desire to provide skills in music reading and writing to all members of a society (Landis & Carder, 1990a). Kodály wished for a unified system of music education in Hungary capable of helping everyone, from the youngest child to the oldest adult, develop a love and knowledge of music. The approach that evolved from this desire is based on singing, on the study of artistic music, and on a system of relative solmization (movable-Do Solfège) (Choksy, 1999).

The philosophical foundation of the Kodály method is comprised of three elements: (a) child development, (b) experiential learning, and (c) sequential instruction (Choksy, 1999). Instruction founded on **child development** considers normal children's abilities and experiences at various stages of growth when making decisions. Conversely, a subject-logic approach organizes instruction according to what seems reasonable for the content. In music, a subject-logic approach to teaching rhythm often uses notation beginning with a common time whole note that is divided into half notes and then to quarter notes and so on. A child developmental approach considers that people relate rhythm to movement and internal feeling rather than notational logic. Thus, rhythms related to single pulse patterns are more easily understood than those that are sustained over multiple pulses. Hence, instruction in common time would start with quarter eighth patterns first before expanding to other patterns that include longer durations.

Experiential learning refers to a belief that children learn best through direct experience rather than through abstract representations like books. Children need to touch, feel, and manipulate materials to learn about the world around them. In terms of music education, this means that children need to learn *through* music making rather than *about* music making. They need to manipulate musical materials while making meaningful music decisions that are appropriately leveled for their musical experiences. Many of the materials used in the Kodály method have been developed so that students can construct their understandings of music by arranging these materials to represent the abstract musical concepts being presented. An example of this approach would be to allow students to construct their understanding of rhythmic content of a song through using craft sticks. Single sticks would represent a common time quarter note and two sticks barred across the top by a third stick would represent two eighth notes. Using this 'notation,' students could construct what they believe to be the rhythm of the tune. They could then read this notation and put it in their bodies using body percussion or clapping.

Sequential instruction refers to a pedagogical approach such as a belief that learning is best facilitated through a step-by-step approach to instruction. In the Kodály method, music learning is accomplished through a five-step sequence that begins with the '*prepare*' phase. In this phase, students experience a new concept primarily through listening or moving. The experience is repeated in a number of ways so students become familiar with attributes of the new content. Next, in the '*make conscious*' phase, students name now-familiar musical content and often associate visual symbols as well. From there, instruction moves to the '*reinforcement*' phase where students put this new material to work within their music-making activities that includes other familiar content. In the '*practice*' phase students explore new content in unfamiliar materials like new songs. They also apply this content with familiar materials on other instruments such as recorder or barred percussion. In the final phase, students use the new content to '*create*' new materials through improvisation or composition.

In this sequence certain philosophical beliefs about teaching and learning are expressed. The instruction moves from **sound to sight**. Musical ideas are first presented aurally and children are encouraged to learn them though their aural explorations. The instruction moves from **simple to complex**. Ideas are presented in their most simple form and then combined with other ideas and skills so that a complex understanding of the content is achieved. Instruction moves from the **known to the unknown**. Ideas are presented in relation to what the students already experience in their own lives and then are moved to unknown contexts. Finally, instruction moves from the **concrete to the**

abstract. Students begin learning content through activities that allow them to touch and see materials and then move to more abstract understandings like improvisation.

Orff-Schulwerk

Carl Orff (1895-1982) was a German-born composer whose original vision was the perfect combination of music and dance for the theater. Basing his work on folk traditions, he combined the orchestra and dancers on stage for productions. Dorothee Günther, a friend of Orff, began using his materials and ideas in the training of dancers and gymnasts at her school. It was from this beginning that the approach was adapted for children's music learning. The approach makes use of speech, singing, and movement along with simple instruments to help learners engage in music-making activities that are most appropriate for them.

A basic foundation of the approach is that experience should precede conceptualization. In terms of music learning this means that novice learners should not be required to deduce musical meaning through notation before experiencing music making. Rather, musical learning should be part of an inductive process where learners engage in multiple experiences through speech, rhythm, singing, and playing so that the learner is a musical participant first. Notation is then used as a means of remembering what has been done in the experience (Choksy et al., 2001).

Materials used for instruction include poems, rhymes, games, songs, and dances. These can be traditional works or those written, designed, or choreographed by students or teachers. Orff educators also make use of a number of instruments in the classroom. These include recorders and a collection of keyboard instruments such as xylophones (soprano, alto, and bass), metallophones (soprano, alto, and bass), and glockenspiels (soprano and alto). In addition, many traditional percussion instruments such as castanets, tambourines, triangles, cymbals, and timpani are put to use when composing and/or improvising accompaniments.

Learning in the Orff-Schulwerk approach is process oriented, meaning it is the outcome of a learner's exploration and experimentation of space, sound, and form through musical play. Learners explore space through creative movement that allows them to engage with the qualities of movement such as light and heavy, down and up, or smooth and jagged. Exploration of sound begins with elemental sounds such as a door slamming, a cell phone ringing, or a car driving by. This exploration moves from these unorganized sounds to more organized sounds like patterns of drumbeats. Qualities of sound such as hard sounds, soft sounds, solid sounds, and rattle sounds are also explored through creative play often using simple instruments and the voice. Form is explored by arranging movement and sounds into patterns. These patterns are then organized into larger units. Movement patterns are organized into dances and sound patterns are organized into compositions.

The primary pedagogical approach of Orff-Schulwerk enables learners to move from imitation to creation. Learners begin by *observing* a model, often presented by the teacher, and then *imitating* the model as closely as possible. As the process continues, the teacher begins to lessen his or her central role by providing frameworks for learners to *experiment* with content they had imitated previously. In this experimentation phase, learners begin to gain ownership of the content by manipulating qualities of movement and sound while forming content into new patterns or form. This final step enables learners to *create* musical ideas that are new to them and, ideally, free of teacher input (Shamrock, n.d.).

Other important foundations of Orff-Schulwerk include: (a) moving from the **simple to the complex**, (b) moving from **part to whole**, and (c) moving from **individual to ensemble**. Similar to Kodály's ideas, child development is considered before subject logic when making instructional decisions. This approach results in instruction that transitions from simple content and skills to complex combinations of the same. To accomplish this transition, teachers start by introducing single parts that involve all the learners in unison. As more parts are added learners gain independence through performing multiple parts at the same time until the whole composition or dance is complete. A final important component of this approach is that learners have opportunities to move from being individual music makers to becoming members of an ensemble. This process allows music learners to understand both their individual contribution to the whole and the contribution of the whole to their individual music making.

Dalcroze

Emile Jaques-Dalcroze believed that rhythm was the primary element in music and that the natural rhythms of the human body were the source of all musical rhythm (Landis & Carder, 1990b). With this idea, he devised a method that included **Eurhythmics**—a process that includes movement and music attempting to combine what the ear hears to what the body feels and senses along with what the brain evaluates, imagines, and corrects. The other two elements in this method are Solfège and improvisation. The method was originally designed to meet the needs of conservatory musicians who needed a more complete connection to their musical experiences than their traditional instruction was providing.

In addition to meeting the needs of conservatory musicians, Dalcroze also questioned the manner in which music was currently being taught. He noted the musical, physical, and emotional needs of his students and the 'dullness' of the teaching materials being used and began to ask questions about the philosophies and teaching methods of the time. Some of the questions he pondered were:

- Is there any way to arouse and develop musical awareness, understanding, and response simultaneously with training the musical ear?
- Can mere finger technique . . . be considered a complete musical education?
- Why is it that the qualities that characterize real musicians are seldom felt in music class?
- What can be done about music lessons in which students are permitted to perform without understanding; students are permitted to read without comprehension; students are permitted to write that which they cannot hear or feel?

(Choksy et al., 2001, p. 42)

To address these questions, Dalcroze adapted his conservatory approach to a music-teaching and learning method for children. In doing so, he maintained that humans learn best when learning takes place through multiple sources and he concluded that music should be taught through touch, movement, sound, and sight (Frego, n.d.). Additionally, he believed that music education should center on active involvement and begin with experience or **practice-before-theory**. This idea was contrary to the ways in which music was being taught at this time. Formal music instruction often started with music theory and notation prior to inviting students to be actual music makers. This theory-before-practice approach ignored the fact that many of the learners in the music classroom made music outside the classroom. The authentic, informal musical experiences of learners were not included as part of the music learning process.

Dalcroze also supported a **sound before sight or symbol approach**. He contended that instrumental study should be preceded by other music study and that, "It is veritable nonsense to have the child begin the study of instrumental music before he has manifested, ether naturally or by training, some knowledge of rhythm and tone" (Jaques-Dalcroze, 1921, as cited in Landis & Carder, 1990b, p. 9).

To address each student's knowledge of rhythm and tone, the Dalcroze approach makes use of three elements. Through the use of **Solfège** (fixed "do"), listening skills are developed so that notation can be realized in the musician's imagination before it is expressed aurally or on an instrument. Through the use of **improvisation**, students engage in spontaneous performance activities designed to improve their musical response time so that they can communicate effectively as musicians. Finally, through the use of **Eurhythmics**, symmetry, balance, and rhythmic accuracy in musical performance are obtained by addressing these same elements in movement to music (Mead, 1994). Using all three elements, teachers employing this approach seek to develop a complete musical understanding that is expressed through each musician's responsiveness to musical stimuli.

144 SOCIAL PLACE

Contemporary Questions?

Consider the questions Dalcroze proposed and address whether you think these questions are applicable to music education in today's schools. If you believe they do apply, what leads you to this conclusion? If you believe these do not apply, how have they been addressed?

Music Learning Theory

Edwin E. Gordon has conducted extensive research in music aptitude and music achievement. Through this work, he has made many contributions in the study of music learning and development. From 1979 to 1997 Gordon was the Carl E. Seashore Professor of Research in Music Education at Temple University in Philadelphia, where he developed his ideas for Music Learning Theory (Valerio, n.d.). Gordon's approach is based upon how humans learn music through a process he terms **audiation** (Gordon, 2007). Audiation is defined as ". . . musical thinking. When [learners] audiate, they do more than remember pitches, intervals, durations, or rhythms. They think in tonal patterns and rhythmic patterns in terms of tonality and meter" (Valerio, n.d.). Through his research, Gordon contends that audiation is the foundation for music aptitude and achievement. He defines **music aptitude** as a measure of a student's potential to learn music, while **music achievement** is a measure of what a student has learned in music (Gordon, 2007). Gordon's research suggests that aptitude is developmental and that certain types of music instruction can affect a change in a child's aptitude up to roughly age 9. He also notes that achievement can be affected at any age though a combination of instruction and student engagement. Because audiation is the foundation of both aptitude and achievement, teachers should develop learners' abilities to audiate music. Gordon suggests that this can be accomplished through specific sequential instruction.

Gordon (2007) proposes that learning music is similar to learning language. When a child begins to engage with the world, he or she starts by listening and attending to the sounds within the environment. With repeated exposure, the child organizes these sounds so that they have meaning for him or her. As the child desires to communicate with those within the environment, he or she begins to experiment with these sounds to express a need. A grunt or squeal comes to have meaning with those in the child's environment. As the child grows, specific sounds begin to have specific meanings and they are organized into meaningful patterns, phrases, and sentences that communicate with growing complexity. In short, the child develops an aural and spoken vocabulary. At this stage of development, the child is working with two vocabularies: the vocabulary used to communicate and express ideas, and a thinking vocabulary. The thinking vocabulary is more complex than the expressive vocabulary partly due to the motor skills necessary to express sounds accurately as words. Using both vocabularies, the child begins to associate certain sounds and ideas with certain symbols or words, resulting in the development of a reading vocabulary. In addition, the child develops a written vocabulary to express complex ideas in words. Ultimately, the child learns to use his or her vocabulary to communicate spontaneous ideas through the spoken and written language.

To parallel music learning with language acquisition one must recognize that learners live in worlds of music and they attend to musical sounds at very young ages. Learners, in ways that are meaningful to them, organize the musical sounds into listening vocabularies of familiar tunes and songs. As they grow, learners use these listening vocabularies to develop performing vocabularies allowing them to outwardly express musical thoughts. As with language acquisition, two vocabularies are at work: a performing vocabulary and an audiated vocabulary. The audiated vocabulary is the more complex of the two, due in part to the executive skills necessary to create musical sounds. At this stage in their development, learners are capable of associating the familiar sounds in their vocabularies with symbols that represent what they hear. They can learn to read notation for music they know, thus developing a music reading vocabulary. They can also develop a written musical vocabulary. Using their aural, visual, and written musical vocabularies, students can perform, improvise, and compose music.

From this understanding, Gordon developed a sequence of instruction that makes use of a learner's natural vocabulary development. The sequence is presented in two parts, **discrimination learning** and **inference learning**. For the purposes of our limited discussion we are only going to present the discrimination sequence. Table 7.1 shows the entire discrimination sequence in terms of the vocabulary it is intended to address. Within this sequence, learners expand their musical vocabularies through the use of tonal and rhythmic patterns. Just as language is not simply an alphabet, music is not isolated notes and rhythms. Tonal and rhythm patterns become the musical 'words' and 'phrases' on which a musical language is built. As with language learning, musical sounds are not removed from the context that makes them meaningful. To maintain musical context, tonal patterns are always related to an aural tonal center and rhythmic patterns are always presented in relation to meter. Additionally, instruction starts with presenting the *whole* and then moves to understanding the *parts* before taking this increased understanding back to the *whole*.

TABLE 7.1 Discrimination learning sequence with vocabulary addressed.

Language vocabulary	Music vocabulary	Sequence of instruction	Examples
Listening	Listening	Aural/Oral	Patterns and tunes are taught on nonsense syllables like 'bum.' Learners listen and imitate.
Speaking	Performance	Verbal association	Patterns and tunes are labeled with tonal and rhythmic Solfège. Learners listen and imitate using Solfège.
Thinking	Audiated	Partial synthesis	The first two stages are combined. A pattern or tune is given aurally to learner on nonsense syllables and he or she repeats it back on Solfège.
Reading and written	Reading and written	Symbolic association reading and writing	Tonal and rhythm patterns are now associated with tonal and rhythmic notation. Students read and write patterns and tunes using notation.
Reading and written	Reading and written	Composite synthesis reading and writing	Tonal and rhythm patterns are now put together into meaningful series and relationships are made apparent (e.g. tonic and dominant, duple and triple).

DISCUSSION BOARD

Foundations of Your Past

As you consider the music learning endeavors in which you have been involved, do you think your teachers, particularly at the elementary level, used any of the methods or approaches exclusively? If so, which and why do you think so? (Provide examples if possible.) If your teachers were not influenced such that they founded their instructional decision-making entirely in any single method, do you see any philosophies, pedagogies and/or instructional designs within any of these methods or approaches that may have influenced the musical instruction you received? Are there any philosophies, pedagogies, or instructional designs that you believe would help you make and understand music more completely than you do? What are they and why do you think so? Do you believe a music teacher should have a method or approach? Why or why not?

COMMON FOUNDATIONS FOR TEACHING MUSIC

We started this chapter with the question about how you might choose to teach music in your classroom and, as one means to address the question, we have investigated some common methods/approaches used to teach music. As you were reading about each method, it is likely you began to notice some similarities among them. Perhaps, an investigation of these similarities would help as you begin to consider how you might teach music in *your* classroom.

Sound before symbol (or sight). This approach was shared by all the methods we discussed. In practice, this idea requires music learners to develop an aural understanding of the music before notation is introduced. Thus, learners would not be expected to read notation before they are capable of bringing an aural understanding to the notation they see on the page. If this foundation were applied to instruction within a beginning band classroom, students would not simply open their method books to page 1 and begin reading notation as they learn to play their instruments. Students might begin by singing tunes they already 'know' (those they bring to class from their previous experiences with music) and learn to play them on their instruments without notation. To expand their aural vocabulary, students could aurally learn increasingly complex tonal and rhythm patterns. After performing these tunes and patterns on their instruments, students would then learn to read the same from notation. This practice allows the students to read with understanding because they are bringing their aural understanding to the notation. Similar to reading words or phrases in language, these beginning band students are more likely to read musical patterns than students who are taught to read notation without aural understanding. Learners who are equipped to bring their aural understanding to notation are less likely to be phonemic music readers, 'sounding out' what they see note by note as they perform. Music learners who are taught via a sound-before-sight approach are equipped to read and perform music with understanding.

Experience (or practice) before theory. This approach was also shared by all the methods in our discussion. When put into practice, learners are engaged in music-making activities first and then theoretical understanding is brought to the activity after the learner begins to own the experience. If this approach were to be applied to teaching improvisation, a teacher might show the musicians in his high-school performing ensemble five pitches they can choose from as they begin to form melodies over a given accompaniment. The students would be allowed to experiment, with teacher guidance, with these pitches in various combinations until they have demonstrated the ability to perform an improvised melody that 'fits' the accompaniment. After this experience, the teacher would 'uncover' the knowledge and skills demonstrated by the students and discuss how they used the pitch content of an F pentatonic scale to improvise over an F blues accompaniment. Because students have experienced the act of improvising prior to the discussion and explanation of the theory, they have context for the theoretical information being presented. They can learn from their personal experience with improvisation. Such practice often increases motivation for learning, as students develop a 'need to know' from combination of practice and theory. As students develop greater theoretical understanding, they desire to apply it to the actual musical practice. More practice leads to a need for greater theoretical understanding. Thus, the practice before theory learning cycle leads to effective and long-term music learning.

Teach from the known to the unknown. Again, all the methods we investigated include this approach that begins the learning process by uncovering what the learner already knows or can do and then relates that to new knowledge and skills. If applied in a middle-school choral classroom a teacher could ask students to sing the beginning of "Here comes the bride." After several successful attempts of the students singing the familiar opening to this tune, the teacher could then label the opening interval as a perfect fourth and note that this is the same interval used to open the piece they are beginning rehearsal with that day. The teacher would then ask the students to look at the music and sing the perfect fourth they now have in their tonal memory, transferring the familiar sound to unfamiliar notation.

Sequential instruction. Most the methods we discussed include some form of sequential instruction. Whether it is the Kodály sequence:

prepare → make conscious → reinforcement → practice → create

or the Orff sequence:

observe → imitate → experiment → create

or the Gordon sequence:

aural/oral → verbal association → partial synthesis →
symbolic association → composite synthesis,

music learning can benefit from a systematic approach. Each of these sequences applies the concept of teaching from the **simple to the complex**. The sequence begins with activities that allow learners almost immediate engagement with simple music-making tasks and then adds one new element at a time until learners are taking charge of their own experience. In each sequence, learners are ultimately charged with using their newly acquired musical knowledge and skills to create something original. No matter the level of the learner or the type of music being taught, sequential instruction can lead to very powerful musical outcomes.

As an example, a high-school band director may choose the Kodály sequence to teach the *Hoy, Nazan Eem* portion of Alfred Reed's *Armenian Dances Part 1.* This portion of the work (mm 69–185) is notated in 5/8 and often alternates between 2+3 and 3+2 subdivisions. To *prepare* for this repertoire, the teacher introduces aural rhythmic patterns that alternate subdivisions in the same fashion as the Armenian folk tune. The teacher models the patterns using neutral syllables (no rhythmic Solfège) and the students sing and then play them in various combinations on their instruments. Once students are comfortably playing these patterns on their instruments, the teacher labels or *makes conscious* what they are doing with rhythmic Solfège. To *reinforce* this learning the teacher visits with the school tennis coach and borrows enough tennis balls for the members of his ensemble to use as they count the pattern with Solfège while bouncing the tennis balls to the macro (2+3, 3+2) pattern. As ensemble members develop the skills to count and bounce the balls in time, the teacher asks them to do the same as he plays a recording of the work. Immediately, students are asked to read the notation on their parts as they move their heels to the macro-pulse and tap the micro-pulse on their collarbone. As they continue to *practice*, students are asked to perform the notation as it is written. Realizing that students will not 'own' their learning until they can use their understanding and skill to *create*, the teacher allows a portion of time in rehearsal for the next week for students to form quartets and compose 16-bar tunes using the same rhythmic pattern as is in the folk tune. Each quartet will perform their compositions for the class in the next week.

Child development vs. subject logic. Many of the methods discussed in this chapter suggest that instructional decisions are most effective when they are based on what the students are ready to learn and not necessarily on how the subject matter is internally organized. Teachers who work from a child development perspective may begin their teaching with material that, according to the organization of the subject matter, does not start at the beginning. As an example,[1] internal logic for rhythmic concepts suggests that the teacher start with the longest duration first. After all, one does not know the duration of a half note until she understands the duration of a whole note. Using this logic, a middle-school choir director might begin teaching rhythmic reading by having students complete a 'rhythm tree' (see Figure 7.1). Students would learn the durations of all the notes in the tree to understand their mathematical relationships to one another. The teacher would help students transfer this understanding to reading rhythmic notation in repertoire the ensemble is sight reading. A teacher using this approach is likely to find

---

[1] This example assumes that these students have not had previous instruction in rhythmic reading. Ideally the foundations of rhythmic reading would have been taught in a comprehensive elementary music classroom and students would bring this understanding with them to the middle-school choral classroom.

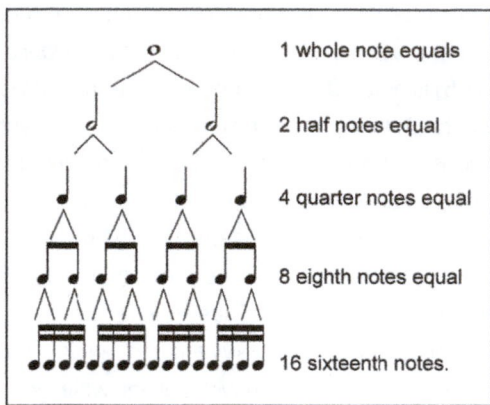

FIGURE 7.1 The rhythm tree.

that it is difficult for students this age to transfer these mathematical concepts to reading notation.

Another middle-school choir director might begin his rhythmic instruction by having students sway to a given pulse and then echo chanted rhythmic patterns given to them by the teacher. The patterns chosen by this teacher contain durations of no more than one macro-beat (e.g. a quarter note in common time) or two micro-beats (e.g. two eighth notes in common time). This teacher is working from an understanding that these learners need to 'feel' rhythm before they read rhythm. Learners need to bring this feeling to rhythmic patterns that begin with durations that outline macro- and micro- patterns, as these patterns are easier for them to feel. Once these patterns are embodied, the learners can successfully experience longer durations. These patterns are then transferred into the repertoire the class is sight reading. Finally, students learn the mathematical relationships of the various durations beginning with the notation representing the macro-beat. They learn to add macro-beats for longer durations, while dividing macro-beats for shorter durations. These students will also be more likely to understand rhythmic reading when notation changes (e.g. cut time) because they have learned the relationships of macro- and micro-beats rather than "a whole note gets four beats."

THE OLD IS NEW AGAIN

In Chapter 4 we discussed some of the historical influences that have affected our current practices in music education. Once again, some historical insight might help our perspective. William Channing Woodbridge was one of the country's earliest and greatest advocates for the inclusion of music education into the American education system. He studied instructional methods in Europe and was particularly inspired by the method employed by George Nägeli. Nägeli's instruction design was based upon general educational principles put forward by Johann Heinrich Pestalozzi in the late eighteenth and early nineteenth century. Modified for music, the principles were:

1. To teach **sounds before signs**—to make the child sing before he learns written notes or their names.
2. To lead the child to observe, by hearing and imitating sounds, their resemblances and differences, their agreeable and disagreeable effects, rather than explaining these things to him. By this principle, the child was to be an **active, rather than passive, learner**.
3. **To teach but one thing at a time**—rhythm, melody, expression are taught and practiced separately before the child is called to the difficult task of attending to all at once.
4. To make children **practice each step** of each of these divisions, until they master it, before passing on to the next.
5. To give the **principles and theory after practice**, and as in induction from it.
6. To analyze and practice the elements of articulate sound in order to apply them to music.
7. To have the names of the notes correspond to those used in instrumental music.

(Mason, 1843, pp. 25–29, as cited in Mark, 2008, p. 33)

As you consider each of these seven principles, note how many are similar to the common principles we extracted from our brief investigation of the four methods/approaches presented earlier in this chapter. Even though these principles were first presented in the mid nineteenth century (Mark, 2008) it would seem that they have contemporary applications as you consider how you might teach music in your classroom of the future. While you may choose to use interactive white boards, smart phones, electronic tablets, and/or laptop computers in your classroom, it will still be your responsibility to construct activities that help students make and understand music. Based on what we know about various methods and approaches to teaching music, it would seem that these principles may help you as decisions are being made.

BLOG ON . . .

How Will You Teach?

Consider the seven principles presented above and those we extracted from the methods we investigated. Combine those considerations with your personal convictions and understandings about teaching music and answer the question this chapter focuses upon. How will you teach students to understand and make music in your classroom?

ONE FINAL THOUGHT

There has been a subtle and deliberate shift in the focus of this chapter and we would like to assist you in noting this change. While the title of chapter asks how you are going to teach, you might notice, in the end, the answer relies on student learning. This shift from a focus on teaching to a focus on learning is very important. Robert Duke (2005) makes this point clear when he states:

> Focusing primarily on the activities in which teachers and students engage without carefully considering the learning that teaching is intended to bring about is decidedly disadvantageous, because teaching and learning are not inextricably linked. Teaching is neither necessary nor sufficient for learning. People can learn without being deliberately taught and a teacher can inform, instruct, explain, and demonstrate in the presence of students without the students' learning what the teacher intends to teach.
>
> (p. 12)

In the first part of this text the questions we presented focused on you: who you are and who you might become as a professional music educator. From there, we moved the focus to teaching, the environments in which music teaching takes place, the ways teachers construct curricula and lesson plans, and the design of the instruction as teachers present each lesson. In the final section we move our focus to the students, who they are, what they learn, how they learn, and how we know that they learn. It is important that you not journey into the next section without the understandings and insights you may have gained from the first two sections. Instead, take your understandings of who you are becoming as a professional music educator and what knowledge, skills, and dispositions you have or will need to develop as a music teacher with you as you discover who you might be in your classroom. Balancing all three of these perspectives will help you construct the music educator you wish to be.

CLASS ACTIVITIES

Class Activity 7.1: Teacher Decisions

Pair up with another student in the classroom. You will need one shoe with laces. Take turns and teach each other how to tie the shoelaces. The partner who is tying the shoelaces should not do anything without instruction, only completing the actions of what he or she is being told to do. After each partner has had a turn, address the following questions:

1. When you were teaching, what information did you use to decide how you were going to teach your partner how to tie the shoelaces?
2. Which of the following did you consider as you were making decisions about how to teach this skill: (a) the teacher, (b) the subject matter, (c) the student, and (d) the environment?
3. What other information might be available to you and inform your decisions about how to tie shoelaces?

CONNECTING TO THE PROFESSION

 ## Part II: Teaching Concerns

This is a collection of resources to help you build deeper understandings of the material presented in the chapters in this part of text. A detailed explanation of the structure of the *Connecting to the Profession* sections can be found at the beginning of *Connecting to the Profession—Part I*.

TERMS AND CONCEPTS

Chapter 4

Four Common Places of Education
  Subject Matter
  Teacher
  Student
  Milieu
Performance Emphasis
Informance Emphasis
Singing Schools Movement
Pestalozzian Principles
Lowell Mason
Progressive Education
John Dewey
Group vs. Individual
School Music vs. Student Music
Conformity vs. Creativity

Chapter 5

Delivery Skills
  Voice
    Pitch
    Volume
    Quality
    Rate
Physical Expression
    Eye Contact
    Facial Expression
    Gestures
    Posture
Congruence
  Staging Space
    Logistics
    Engagement

Proxemics

Chapter 6

Curriculum

    Transmission

    Product

    Process

    Praxis

Technical Rationality

Positivist

Objectives-Based

Literature-Based

Skills-Based

Knowledge-Based

Standards-Based

Objectivist

Constructivist

Informal Music Pedagogy

Curriculum Planning

General Objectives

    General Program Outline

    Specific Objectives

    Specific Curricular Plan

    Specific Lesson Strategies

    Translated to Instruction

Chapter 7

Teacher-Proof Curriculum

Method

Approach

Zoltan Kodály

Child Development

Experiential Learning

Sequential Instruction

Sound to Sight

Simple to Complex

Known to Unknown

Concrete to Abstract

Orff-Schulwerk

Part to Whole

Individual to Ensemble

Emile Jaques-Dalcroze

Eurhythmics

Practice-Before-theory

Music-Learning Theory

Audiation

Music Aptitude

Music Achievement

Discrimination Learning

Inference Learning

CONNECT TO RESEARCH

Chapter 4

Large Ensembles in Music Education

Elpus, K., & Abril, C. R. (2011). High school music ensemble students in the United States: A demographic profile. *Journal of Research in Music Education, 59*(2), 128–145. doi:10.1177/0022429411405207

The purpose of this study is to construct a national demographic profile of high-school band, choir, and orchestra students in the United States using evidence from the 2004 follow-up wave of the Education Longitudinal Study of 2002. Results indicate that 21 percent of seniors in the United States' class of 2004 participated in school music ensembles. Significant associations were found between music ensemble participation and variables including gender, race/ethnicity, socio-economic status (SES), native language, parents' education, standardized test scores, and GPA (Grade Point Average). Certain groups of students, including those who are male, English language learners, Hispanic, children of parents holding a high-school diploma or less, and in the lowest SES quartile, were significantly underrepresented in music programs across the United States. In contrast, white students were significantly overrepresented among music students, as were students from higher SES backgrounds, native English speakers, students in the highest standardized test score quartiles, children of parents holding advanced postsecondary degrees, and students with GPAs ranging from 3.01 to 4.0. Findings indicate that music students are not a representative subset of the population of U.S. high-school students.

Heuser, F. (2011). Ensemble-based instrumental music instruction: Dead-end tradition or opportunity for socially enlightened teaching. *Music Education Research, 13*(3), 293–305. doi:10.1080/14613808.2011.603043

Public school music education in the USA remains wedded to large ensemble performance. Instruction tends to be teacher-directed, relies on styles from the Western canon and exhibits little concern for musical interests of students. The idea that a fundamental purpose of education is the creation of a just society is difficult for many music teachers who dream of conducting student musicians in polished performances. This paper describes a middle-school band program in which students teach instrument lessons to similarly aged children in a homeless shelter. This qualitative study is grounded in the writings of Maxine Greene and shows how teachers might 'break through' the frames of custom and touch the consciousness of those we teach.

Parker, E. (2010). Exploring student experiences of belonging within an urban high school choral ensemble: An action research study. *Music Education Research, 12*(4), 339–352. doi:10.1080/14613808.2010.519379

The purpose of this action research study was to describe adolescent singers' experiences of belonging within one urban high-school choral ensemble. Understanding student perspectives on belonging within music ensembles can assist choral educators, parents, and administrators in order to more fully support adolescent emotional and social development in school. Tenth- through twelfth-grade students were selected from one northeastern high-school choral program in a large city within the U.S. Twenty-six participants, in small groups of three to four students each, were asked to describe their experiences of belonging within the ensemble. Interview data were open, descriptively and analytically coded. Codes were gathered into categories. Five themes were developed, including choral experience as uncompetitive, sectional bonding as social bonding, singing as shared experience, chorus as safe space, and trips as pivotal bonding experiences. Suggestions for future research include examining student belonging as part of choral teacher practices, studying school choral participation as stress reduction, and investigating social belonging as embedded within group singing environments.

School Music vs. Student Music

De Vries, P. (2010). What we want: The music preferences of upper primary school students
      and the ways they engage with music. *Australian Journal of Music Education, 1*, 3–16.
This article examines the current music preferences of Grade 6 children (12- and 13-year-olds) in an Australian primary school and the way these children engage with music. Data were collected in three phases, comprising a written questionnaire administered to all 86 students, focus group interviews with 12 of these children, and observation of students' engagement at school, both in class and out of class, over a five-week period. This article focuses on the latter two phases. Results revealed: students prefer contemporary popular music to other styles of music; new media technology such as digital music players play a significant role in their engagement with music; music plays multiple roles in the students' lives; they are aware of the diverse ways music is present in the world, both in and out of school; the students valued choice, particularly in terms of repertoire, in music activities at school; school can stifle potential engagement with music; and students involved in extra-curricular music groups at school valued the experience.

Chapter 5

Delivery Skills

Hamann, D.L., Baker, D.S., McAllister, P.A., & Bauer, W.I. (2000). Factors affecting
      university music students' perceptions of lesson quality and teaching effectiveness.
      Journal of Research in Music Education, 48(2), 102–113. doi: 10.2307/3345569
The purpose of this study was to determine what effect, if any, music teacher classroom delivery skills or lesson content had on university music students' perceptions of lesson or teacher appeal by student academic standing. Participants, 511 university students

studying music at three moderate-size universities, viewed one of two videotapes that contained four randomly placed teaching episodes of approximately four minutes in duration. Each of the two tapes contained four lessons, as follows: one lesson with good classroom delivery skills and good lesson content, one with good skills and poor content, another with poor skills and good content, and one with poor skills and poor content. Subjects were directed to evaluate each teaching episode immediately after it was viewed using a researcher-developed questionnaire. The researchers found that students liked and found teaching episodes with good teacher delivery skills to be more interesting than those lessons with poor teacher delivery, regardless of lesson content quality. Whether enhanced student liking and increased interest in classroom lessons improve student learning and retention remains to be determined.

Madsen, K. (2003). The effect of accuracy of instruction, teacher delivery, and student attentiveness on musicians' evaluation of teacher effectiveness. *Journal of Research in Music Education, 51*(1), 38–50. doi:10.2307/3345647
This study is an examination of whether accuracy and delivery of teacher instruction and student attentiveness would affect evaluative perceptions of teacher effectiveness. Participants were 168 musicians and were grouped according to experience level: (a) Grades 6–8, (b) Grades 9–12, (c) undergraduate, and (d) experienced teachers. Participants viewed and evaluated a videotape of eight teaching segments for teaching effectiveness. A two-way ANOVA with repeated measures indicated significant differences due to experience level and teaching segments. Results indicated that the secondary students rated a teacher giving inaccurate instruction relatively high when the teacher demonstrated high delivery and the class was attentive. Analysis of the descriptive data suggested that the four groups attended to the delivery of the teacher more than any other variable.

Napoles, J., & MacLeod, R.B. (2013). The influences of teacher delivery and student progress on preservice teachers' perceptions of teaching effectiveness. *Journal of Research in Music Education, 61*(3), 249–261. doi:10.1177/0022429413497234
The purpose of this study was to examine how teacher delivery and student progress influenced preservice teachers' perceptions of overall teaching effectiveness. Experienced teachers (N = 6) were videotaped teaching mini applied lessons under four conditions: (a) high teacher delivery and more student progress, (b) high teacher delivery and less student progress, (c) low teacher delivery and more student progress, and (d) low teacher delivery and less student progress. Preservice teachers (*N* = 75) viewed these teaching excerpts and rated each for teacher delivery, student progress, student musicianship, teacher knowledge of subject matter, and overall teaching effectiveness. Participants

rated teachers with high delivery as more effective than teachers with low delivery, irrespective of student progress. There was a moderate positive correlation ($r = .53$) between perceptions of teacher delivery and student progress. Multiple regression analysis revealed that teacher delivery was the best predictor of perceptions of overall teaching effectiveness, followed closely by student progress.

Chapter 6

Informal Music Learning

Green, L. (2008). *Music, informal learning and the school: A new classroom pedagogy.* Burlington, VT: Ashgate.

This is the author's third book in a longitudinal study of popular music pedagogy and its possible applications to the music classroom.

Jaffurs, S. E. (2004). The impact of informal music learning practices in the classroom, or how I learned how to teach from a garage band. *International Journal of Music Education, 22*(3), 189–200. doi:10.1177/0255761404047401

This ethnographic study is an investigation of the environment that students create when making music that is meaningful to them. The initial purpose of the study was to describe a developing 'rock group,' and the factors that contributed to its creation. The significance of the study may be in the discovery of ways to subvert dominant traditions in many formal environments. The author reflects on the lessons of informal music learning practices and the implications for her own classroom environment. A broader perspective on the informal/formal dichotomy may help teachers establish more diverse learning practices.

Woody, R., & Lehmann, A. (2010). Student musicians' ear-playing ability as a function of vernacular music experiences. *Journal of Research in Music Education, 58*(2), 101–115. doi:10.1177/0022429410370785

This study explored the differences in ear-playing ability between formal 'classical' musicians and those with vernacular music experience ($N = 24$). Participants heard melodies and performed them back, either by singing or playing on their instruments. The authors tracked the number of times through the listen-then-perform cycle that each participant needed for accurate performance. Participants retrospectively reported their thoughts and provided biographical information related to vernacular music experience. Analyses indicated that singing required fewer trials than playing on instruments and that vernacular musicians required fewer trials than formal musicians. The verbally reported thoughts indicated that participants used different strategies for encoding the melodies. Vernacular musicians applied a more sophisticated knowledge base to generate accurate expectations; formal musicians used less efficient strategies. Formal musicians devoted more conscious attention to physically producing the melodies on their instruments (e.g. fingerings), a process that was executed more automatically by vernacular musicians.

CONNECT TO PROFESSIONAL JOURNALS

Chapter 4

Group vs. Individual—Large Ensembles

Neidlinger, E. (2011). Idea bank: Chamber music within the large ensemble. *Music Educators Journal, 97*(3), 22–23. doi:10.1177/0027432111400002
Many music educators incorporate chamber music in their ensemble programs—an excellent way to promote musical independence. However, we rarely think of the large ensemble as myriad chamber interactions. Rehearsals become more productive when greater responsibility for music making is placed on the individual student. Here are some ways you can engage a large ensemble in chamber-like interactions.

Informances

Kerchner, J.L. (2010). Mapping performance as general music informance. *General Music Today, 23*(3), 15–19. doi:10.1177/1048371309359647
Music ensemble teachers use informances as means of illuminating less visible student rehearsal experiences that serve as cornerstones for the ever-visible musical performances. How might teachers apply this tool of advocacy and education to the general music classroom? In this article, the author provides a description of action research that she conducted in middle-school general music classes in rural Ohio. Specifically, the author suggests that informances need not be limited to music ensemble concert settings but can be applicable to general music classes in elucidating music listening skill development experiences vis-à-vis music listening map creation and performance.

Large Ensembles

Mantie, R. (2012). Striking up the band: Music education through a Foucaultian lens. *Action, Criticism, and Theory for Music Education, 11*(1), 99–123.

Large ensembles (e.g. choirs, orchestras, bands) have become prominent fixtures in most secondary schools and university schools/faculties of music in Canada and the United States. At the secondary school level, large ensembles have become, in effect, practically synonymous with the words 'music education.' This article derives from the author's own experience with and interest in wind bands as a means of enacting music education. Specifically, the author interrogates, through a Foucaultian discourse lens, the kind of relationship with music fostered in and through what he terms the "pedagogical band world" (p. 99)—the world comprising school and college/university wind bands that has developed from around the middle of the twentieth century. Based on an intensive examination of pedagogical band world discourse and a consideration of the historical appearance and evolution of bands, the author argues that as bands became entrenched as the primary medium for music instruction in secondary schools (and concurrently became a major component of university schools/faculties of music), and as education increasingly became the target of state concerns over 'progress,' the discourse of band performance changed from one of supplying music in order to create a sense of community and personal enjoyment to one of edification through exposure to Art (i.e. great repertoire).

Williams, D.A. (2007). What are music educators doing and how well are we doing it? Traditional large-group performance may not be the best goal of music education when the way society experiences music is changing. *Music Educators Journal, 94*(1), 18–23. doi:10.1177/002743210709400105

Paul Lehrman mentioned in Mix Magazine that school music programs, which traditionally have given students the precious opportunity to hear what real instruments sound like from both the player's and listener's perspective, are "in the toilet" (p. 18). Some within the profession have voiced similar concerns. K-12 music teachers historically have had very little motivation to modify programs, especially classroom activities such as large-group ensembles. Many music teachers seem to focus solely on large-group performances, adding pressure on teachers to sustain the size and quality of performance groups. In this article, the author observes how large-group performance has limited music teachers' access to their students. The author suggests that teachers should be brave enough to offer opportunities for students to find music interesting and relevant.

Creativity vs. Conformity

Brinkman, D.J. (2010). Teaching creatively and teaching for creativity. *Arts Education Policy Review, 111*(2), 48–50. doi:10.1080/10632910903455785

This article provides a brief review of generally accepted ideas about creativity, followed by examples of music teachers teaching creatively and teaching their students to be more creative. Implications for teacher education and policy recommendations for music education are discussed.

Norris, C.E. (2010). Introducing creativity in the ensemble setting: National standards meet comprehensive musicianship. *Music Educators Journal, 97*(2), 57–62. doi:10.1177/0027432110387934

This article explores realistic ways with which ensemble conductors can facilitate the conceptual acquisition of their students via creative activities. Creativity, as included in the National Standards, is presented through the 'eyes' of comprehensive musicianship.

Chapter 5

Effective Delivery Skills

Hoffman, A.R. (2011). Do you hear what I'm sayin'?: Overcoming miscommunications between music teachers and students. *Music Educators Journal, 97*(4), 33–36. doi:10.1177/0027432111405341

There is a substantial body of literature on music education in urban settings; however, few resources are available to music educators working in other increasingly diverse school districts across the United States. This article offers a discussion of language barriers and miscommunications between music teachers and students whose cultural backgrounds differ. Through an understanding of the ways cultural differences might lead to miscommunications and frustrations, music educators can begin to better serve the students who are often made invisible in our suburban as well as urban school districts. Included are samples of words and phrases commonly used by students and misunderstood by teachers. The article also suggests ways in which teachers can help students better navigate school music programs.

Chapter 7

Sound Before Sight

Woody, R.H. (2012). Playing by ear: Foundation or frill? *Music Educators Journal, 99*(2), 82–88. doi:10.1177/0027432112459199

Many people divide musicians into two types: those who can read music and those who play by ear. Formal music education tends to place great emphasis on producing musically literate performers, but devotes much less attention to teaching students to make music without notation. Some would suggest that playing by ear is a specialized skill that is useful only to jazz and popular musicians. There are, however, many reasons to reconsider this position. Around the world, aural transmission of music and ear-based performance are the norm. Music pedagogues have described ear playing as a necessary developmental precursor to becoming a truly fluent music reader. Research supports the idea that playing by ear is a foundational skill that contributes to other aspects of musicianship, including improvising, sightreading, and performing from memory. Ear playing has even been shown to be a contributor to skilled performance of rehearsed music, the traditional mainstay of school music. Ear-driven activities can involve student musicians in composing and arranging, musical collaboration with peers, and lifelong individual artistic expression.

CONNECT TO THE WEB

Chapter 4

Do Schools Kill Creativity?

http://www.youtube.com/watch?v=iG9CE55wbtY
Sir Ken Robinson makes an entertaining and profoundly moving case for creating an education system that nurtures (rather than undermines) creativity.

Musical Creativity

http://www.davidelliottmusic.com/praxial-music-education/musical-creativity/
A book review by David J. Elliot with some interesting ideas about what it means to teach creativity via music education.

Fostering Individual Creativity Within the Large Ensemble

http://leadingnotes.org/2012/02/06/guarr/
On-line article concerning ways to move away from teaching conformity and enhancing creativity in the large ensemble.

Learning Platforms in Action—Promoting Creativity in Children

http://www.youtube.com/watch?v=jSLCXRCsfjs
Video from actual use of an on-line learning platform being used to promote creative music making among children.

Chapter 5

'Anyone, Anyone' Teacher from *Ferris Bueller's Day Off*

http://www.youtube.com/watch?v=uhiCFdWeQfA
The scene from the classic movie.

Proxemics

http://www.cs.unm.edu/~sheppard/proxemics.htm
A quick guide to the understanding and the use of proxemics.

Seinfeld and Proxemics

http://www.youtube.com/watch?v=tgO8V6TdAKM
A comical look at the idea of personal space.

How a Teacher's Voice Affects Pupil's Behavior

http://www.teachingexpertise.com/articles/your-voice-your-job-669
The connection between the use of voice and classroom management.

How is Your Teacher Voice?

http://www.write-out-loud.com/teachers-voice.html
More good advice on how to use your voice effectively in your teaching.

Top Tips for Trainee Teachers: Use Your Body Language to Control the Classroom

http://careers.guardian.co.uk/top-tips-for-trainee-teachers-use-your-body-language-to-control-the-classroom
Quick advice on using your body language to help classroom management.

Body Language: Creating Bonds

https://www.teachingchannel.org/videos/creating-relationships-with-students
Great video series on the effective use of physical expression in teaching.

Chapter 6

Common Core State Standards

http://www.corestandards.org
The home page for the CCSS initiative.

National Standards for Music Education

http://musiced.nafme.org/resources/national-standards-for-music-education/
Part of the NAfME site that addressed the current (1994) national standards.

National Coalition for Core Arts Standards

http://nccas.wikispaces.com
Site for information on the development of the updated national standards.

Use a Learning Theory: Constructivism

http://www.youtube.com/watch?v=Xa59prZC5gA
Short video on the foundations of constructivism.

Formal and Informal Music-Learning Contexts in Schools and Communities Internationally

https://www.youtube.com/watch?v=924TqUSfuVs
A 90-minute presentation on the topic from four internationally known presenters proctored by Gary McPherson.

Musical Futures—Informal Music Learning in the Formal Curriculum

https://www.musicalfutures.org
Musical Futures fundamentally consists of two pedagogical approaches: non-formal teaching and informal learning. Through Musical Futures these approaches have been

tried and tested in many classrooms, by classroom teachers often operating in isolation. Any teacher or practitioner is free to adopt and adapt these approaches to suit their teaching environment. Here are provided some suggestions on getting started with doing this.

Musical Futures—Canada

http://musicalfuturescanada.org

Musical Futures is a new way of thinking about music making in schools that brings non-formal teaching and informal learning approaches into the more formal context of schools.

"When I'm Gone"—Class Project

**http://www.youtube.com/watch?v=8G9Ult6SHI0&context=C4dd30b3ADvj
    VQa1PpcFOuXK_MIm_LNKusLrvWD0pSotLTmUEgVR8 =**

This is an actual product from a two-week unit on informal music learning at the University of Oklahoma. Here is what the students said: "4 of us friends are instrumental education majors and we're studying a unit on informal teaching. Students can be the driving force of their own education. We are examples of that with this project. We chose a song, learned the parts on instruments other than our primaries (flute, violin and clarinet) and performed it for the University of Oklahoma School of Music. We're definitely not professionals on these instruments, but we had a good time playing. Hope you enjoy!"

Informal Music Learning in Polk County, Florida

**http://www.clipsyndicate.com/video/play/2915366/musical_futures_debuts
    _in_polk_county**

A news clip from a band program in Polk County, Florida, that is incorporating informal music learning.

Chapter 7

Choral Sight Reading in Concert—Solfège and Kodály Handsigns

http://www.youtube.com/watch?NR=1&feature=endscreen&v=3rAyv5zR46w

A sight-reading Solfège demonstration with a high-school choral program on a concert . . . an informance.

Teaching a New Melody According to the Kodály Concept

http://www.youtube.com/watch?v=LSJVoZ7wojw
Singing a new melody according to Z. Kodály's Concept. This video was prepared for the Kodály Institute, Kecskemét, Hungary.

Orff-Schulwerk

http://www.youtube.com/channel/HCFw-bRoY2qWU
The Orff-Schulwerk channel on YouTube—many different and varied videos.

Dalcroze Eurhythmics Channel

http://www.youtube.com/watch?v=C9fimEkKGtU&list=PLspxoHiyxG4lVmdq Mjr75iODGzb3fiaoV
Several exercises demonstrated with college-age students.

Edwin E. Gordon Music-Learning Theory Overview Part 1

http://www.youtube.com/watch?v=XRUCZp9uYOM
Dr. Edwin E. Gordon presents an overview of Music Learning Theory to students, faculty, and guests at Rhode Island College.

Music-Learning Theory Practical Applications Part 1

http://www.youtube.com/watch?v=QUaqEkmJ1Ys
Applications of MLT to various settings of music.

Center for Music Learning

http://cml.music.utexas.edu/research-programs-in-the-center/music-teaching -and-learning/
This is the research page for the center housed at the University of Texas, Austin.

CONNECT TO THE CLASSROOM

Prior to watching one of the teaching videos available on the website, familiarize yourself with the questions below. As you view the video, take notes on what you see and hear. We suggest that you either download the video observation form from the text website or simply use a sheet of paper that has been divided into two columns. On the left side, list the events you see and hear taking place in the classroom. On the right side, make short notes about why you believe the teacher chose to use these events during the lesson. You may find it easiest to list all the events and then go back and make your notes on why the teacher chose those events as part of his or her instruction. After you watch the video, address the questions below.

1. Describe each of the 'four common places' as you observed them at work in this classroom. Which of the common places were strongly connected? Which of the common places were not as strongly connected? Why do you think this occurred?
2. Would you classify this setting as more performance-based or more informance-based? What led you to this conclusion?
3. What delivery skills (i.e. voice, body, face, gesture) did this teacher demonstrate in class? What was the most effective moment you observed related to effective use of delivery skills?
4. What curricular approach(es) (transmission, product, process, praxis) do you believe are in place in this classroom? Why do you think so?
5. What evidence of teacher planning do you see?
6. Was there any evidence of particular methodological approaches (e.g. Kodály, Orff, Dalcroze, Music Learning Theory) in the video? Describe the scene and the evidence you found. If none were found, describe how you believe the session might benefit from a particular method or approach.
7. What evidence did you observe that this teacher was making use of the common foundations for teaching music? (See Chapter 7.)

PART III

DISCOVERY OF STUDENT LEARNING

The Students: Who Are They?

8

We begin this exploration of P–12 students by first asking you to take a close look at someone you should know pretty well . . . *you*! The better you know yourself, the better you can get to know your students. So, what is *your* background? Do you identify with a particular ethnic heritage, set of cultural traditions, and/or religious practices? What about your parents or grandparents? Did they emigrate from another country to the United States? You do not have to go back far to learn about the first generation of your family to set foot in this country. What traditions and practices were, or are, important to them? Maybe your family did not move here from another country, but rather are Native Americans. Do you know your family's origins? If not, perhaps it might be good for you to explore your ancestry. Everybody comes from somewhere (how profound) and most places of origin have some pretty interesting ways of living life, usually involving food, dance, music, art, clothing, rituals, and beliefs. You may have a particularly rich lineage and not even know it.

In addition to your ethnic, cultural, and religious background, you have been shaped to some degree by your accomplishments and the challenges you have encountered. Perhaps you overcame a substantial emotional obstacle and have evolved to become a stronger, more capable individual. Maybe you live with a disability or a particular medical condition that others may or may not notice readily. Perhaps you have cultivated a unique skill or talent and take pride in being a painter, sculptor, chef, gardener, comic, actor, orator, writer, gymnast, golfer, or bowler. You may be heterosexual, lesbian, gay, bisexual, transgendered or questioning, and, because of your sexual identity, have experienced unfortunate incidences of prejudice that occur all too often, even in today's society. Each facet of your background has contributed in some way or another to the unique individual you are today.

There are myriad aspects of your life and your history, each one of which has touched you in a profound way. Together, they have culminated to shape you into the person you are at this moment. A thorough and introspective self-reflection will bring to the surface many interesting and treasured characteristics that you may not have acknowledged previously. These should be recognized and celebrated. Likewise, such an exploration is bound to reveal unconscious biases and prejudices that may require you to consider how they are

> **8.1 KNOWING YOUR STUDENTS**
>
> What does it mean to know about your students (facts) versus *knowing* your students such that they feel you 'know' them? Why might each way of knowing be important? How do teachers get to *know* their students? (see Class Activity 8.1, p. 196)

affecting you and ways they might affect your interactions with future students. As you progress through your undergraduate degree program, you will accumulate knowledge and acquire skills associated with teaching music. Additionally, you should be developing a set of dispositions about teaching and learning that will help to ensure your success. One such disposition involves cultivating an attitude of **inclusiveness** that affirms the diversity of the students whom you teach. To enact this disposition fully, teachers are impelled to, as Jensen (2000) states, "live acceptance" (p. 133). Only after you have taken the opportunity to acknowledge who you are, and what shaped your path, are you best ready to learn about your students with the empathetic perspective needed to facilitate their learning wisely.

Each young person who enters your classroom brings a unique 'story.' An important component of your job is to learn all your students' stories. When you have taken the time to get to know about your students, and they believe you know them and what is important to them, they will tend to feel affirmed by you and trust in what you have to offer. Covey (2004) presented an idea he called the 'emotional bank account,' which he depicts as "a metaphor that describes the amount of trust that's been built up in a relationship" (p. 188). When you invest in learning about your students, you are, in effect, making deposits into the emotional bank account that exists as an aspect of the relationship shared between you and your students.

What you learn about your students will help you to act and respond in ways that ensure each student has the same opportunity to learn as the rest of the class. For example, giving a student more time than average for processing directions because of a learning disability is as important as providing an extra challenge to a 'quick learner' to keep her fully engaged. Likewise, what you know about your community might present opportunities to enlighten your students about some aspect of their background. For example, if you teach in a community that includes a particular immigrant population or heritage, you might want to plan a learning experience or activity that honors some of the traditions of that group. We are reminded of a band director who taught in a suburb of Minneapolis, which included many families from Nordic descent. One September afternoon, while attending a local folk festival, Jim (a pseudonym) was enjoying the performance of a mother/daughter singing duo. As they sang sets of traditional Norwegian folk songs, he began to hear melodies he recognized from Clare Grundman's band composition, *Norwegian Folk Rhapsody*. Immediately, he conceptualized a plan to program the Grundman piece and invite the duo to make a presentation to the band students. On the day of the visit, the duo arrived dressed in bunads (traditional Norwegian costumes from the mid 1800s). They talked about Norway and about Norwegian folk songs. They described traditional Norwegian foods, discussed some unusual customs, and talked about the seasons and weather patterns and how they affected life's activities. Finally, they performed and taught the band students several Norwegian folk songs and some traditional dances. The band director even found a bakery that delivered Norwegian krumkake (a thin, crisp cone-shaped cookie, usually made during the Christmas holidays). On the evening of the concert, the mother/daughter duo was invited back to sing and dance for the audience and, in the true tradition of folk singing, taught and led the audience through a Nordic folk tune sing-along. In this process, the students learned something about their own heritage and the experience was shared with the community.

Music teachers are responsible for educating students so those students develop comprehensive competence with an array of musical knowledge and skills (Consortium of National Arts Education Associations, 1994). The choice of *how* one goes about fulfilling that responsibility can mean the difference between lessons that are forgotten by the time students are on their way to their next class or experiences that may touch them for the rest of their lives. When you consider who your students are, their backgrounds, their talents, what challenges them, and what is important to them, you are in a position to teach with compassion and to provide instruction that resonates fully. In Chapter 4, we referred to 'the students' as being one of Schwab's (1959/1978) four common places of education. Below we will take Schwab's lead and discuss general characteristics of students, and then explore strategies for getting to know the specific group of students you might be teaching at any point in time.

GENERAL CHARACTERISTICS: DEMOGRAPHICS

So, just who are the students attending P–12 schools today? Broad labels are typically used to classify groups of people and individuals in our society, including race, ethnicity, religion, sexual orientation, and poverty level, among others. These labels provide important reference points, but they also represent a limited understanding of the students. As Jensen (2000) stated:

> Knowing any or all of those labels might help you to know about the child, but not to know the child. To *know* the child you would have to get beyond the labels to the individual. However, not to know pertinent information about a child is to risk assuming that all backgrounds are the same.
>
> (p. 138)

Later on in this chapter we will explore getting to *know* your students. However, we will first explore some of the more general classifications.

DISCUSSION BOARD
What Do You Notice?

In preparation for this exploration, take a moment and describe as much as you can about the students you see in Figure 8.1. What overt elements of diversity do you see being represented? What unseen issues regarding diversity *could* be present among this group of students? Once you have posted your response, read at least two other responses and comment on what they noticed. Did they see elements you might have missed?

FIGURE 8.1 Mixed children's chorus.

Race. According to the National Center for Education Statistics, the U.S. population has become increasingly racially diverse over the past several decades, as the populations of Hispanics and Asians have increased more rapidly than those of all other races. In 1980, Caucasians represented about 80 percent of the total U.S. population. This share decreased to 69 percent in 2000 and to 66 percent in 2008. Conversely, the Hispanic population increased from 6.4 percent in 1980 to 12.6 percent in 2000 and to 15.4 percent in 2008 (Aud, Fox, & KewalRamani, 2010).

Between now and 2025, these patterns of population change are expected to continue. For example, the Hispanic population is expected to grow at a faster rate than most other races, with 21 percent of the population expected to be of Hispanic origin by 2025. In addition, the growth rate for Caucasians is expected to be slower than the rate for other races, decreasing their share of the total population to 58 percent by 2025 (Aud, Fox, & KewalRamani, 2010). Furthermore, a milestone was reached on July 1, 2011, as 50.4 percent of our nation's population younger than age 1 was from minority classifications. This event marked the first time a 'minority-majority' (population greater than 50 percent minority) had been reported as a nationwide characteristic for an age group (U.S. Census Bureau, 2012). These numbers represent national averages and do not account for differences in population distributions among geographic locations, for example, inner cities, suburbs, and rural areas. Nonetheless, all locales, and the schools situated in those locales, are bound to experience an increase in racial diversification over the next several decades.

Likewise, there exists a substantive difference between the racial make-up of teachers and students. Nationally, while minority students make up 40.7 percent of the public-school population (Keigher, 2009), minority teachers represent only about 16.5 percent of the teaching workforce (Coopersmith, 2009). In music, this chasm is even greater, with minority music teachers representing slightly less than 10 percent of our profession's flagship organization membership—the National Association for Music Education (see Eureka Facts, 2004, as cited by McKoy, 2009). As a teacher, you must be aware of the possible differences that exist between you and your students, and you must work to understand experiences common to students that may not be common to you.

Ethnicity. Ethnicity and race are two distinct categories. Race refers primarily to a person's appearance and is determined genetically (e.g. skin color, eye color, hair color, bone and jaw structure, etc.). Ethnicity, on the other hand, is a cultural phenomenon that is reflected in elements such as language, religion, regionality, ancestry, clothing, customs, and rituals (Nagel, 1997). Often, race and ethnicity are considered a single means of identification in people's thinking. This is primarily because both have strong ties to geography, particularly prior to the current era of globalization. People of a particular geographic location tend to share physical characteristics (think light-skinned blue-eyed Swedes or dark-skinned brown-eyed Hispanics). Because people of a particular geographic location live and interact with each other, they also tend to coalesce around social customs and norms they have developed. These elements of ethnicity typically hold strong emotional significance because people ascribe common values and meanings to them. Music is often a cultural element that serves to unite people and can reinforce ethnic identity. In 1964, Alan P. Merriam proffered 10 functions of music that exist across cultures, including:

1. Communication
2. Emotional expression
3. Symbolic representation
4. Aesthetic satisfaction
5. Entertainment
6. Physical response
7. Encouraging conformity to social norms
8. Validating social institutions and religious rituals
9. Contributing to the continuity and stability of culture; and
10. Contributing to the integration of society.

(Merriam, 1964)

Most of Merriam's functions affirm music as a reinforcing element of cultural identity. In music classrooms, lessons designed around Merriam's ideas can be used to affirm students' ethnic identity or to help them uncover aspects of their heritage they might not know.

BLOG ON ...

Racial and Ethnic Diversity

Figure 8.2 depicts a group of racially and ethnically diverse string musicians and their teacher. How might the music content they explore be used to enhance or unintentionally disregard their racial or ethnic identities?

FIGURE 8.2 Teacher talking to high-school orchestra students.

Religion. Religion is also intertwined with ethnicity. The beliefs and rituals of an ethnicity tend to include religion, often to a strong degree. Like connections between race and ethnicity, religion is also somewhat associated with geography in that many places exist where people of a particular religion are more prevalent than those of other religions (think Irish Catholics or Middle Eastern Muslims). Nonetheless, we discuss religion in its own category because belonging to a particular religious tradition is not dependent upon belonging to a particular ethnicity or race. Although there are many disparate religions in the world, the major tradition in the United States is primarily Christianity, with Protestants and Catholics comprising more than 75 percent of adults in the United States (Pew Forum on Religion and Public Life, 2008; see Table 8.1).

Contrary to the seemingly stable nature of these numbers, however, a closer look at the data reveals a diverse and extremely fluid nature to religious affiliation in the United States. According to the Pew Forum on Religion and Public Life (2008):

More than one-quarter of American adults (28%) have left the faith in which they were raised in favor of another religion—or no religion at all. If change in affiliation

TABLE 8.1 Percentage of major religious traditions in the United States.

Christianity -- 78.4%	
Protestant	51.3%
Catholic	23.9%
Mormon	1.7%
Jehovah's Witness	0.7%
Orthodox	0.6%
Other Christian	0.3%
Other Religions ----------------------------- 4.7%	
Judaism	1.7%
Buddhism	0.7%
Islam	0.6%
Hinduism	0.4%
Other world religions/ faiths	1.4%
Unaffiliated ----------------------------------- 16.1%	
Atheist	1.6%
Agnostic	2.4%
Nothing in particular	12.1%
Don't Know/Refused ----------------------- .8%	

Note. From "Summary of Key Findings" in *U.S. Religious Landscape Survey* (2008) published by the Pew Forum on Religion and Public Life. Reprinted with permission. Due to rounding, figures may not add to 100 and nested figures may not add to the subtotal indicated.

from one type of Protestantism to another is included, roughly 44% of adults have either switched religious affiliation, moved from being unaffiliated with any religion to being affiliated with a particular faith, or dropped any connection to a specific religious tradition altogether.

(p. 5)

As you plan your curriculum, lessons, and performance programs, you should consider the general landscape of religious affiliations in your region of the country as well as specific trends in your community. In some areas for example, Wednesday evening is as sacrosanct as Sunday morning regarding *not* scheduling rehearsals or performances. The religious climate in your community is an important characteristic to consider when planning the activities and content that comprise your music program.

144 SOCIAL PLACE
Religious Diversity

Figure 8.3 depicts a group of Muslim children. Although Christianity is the primary religious tradition in the U.S., likely there will be children of other faiths in your music classroom. Using 144 characters or fewer, list some issues you think should be considered when planning music-learning activities and content involving these children.

FIGURE 8.3 Muslim children chanting the Qur'an.

Sexual orientation and identity. Sexual orientation is the sexual attraction individuals have for the other sex, for their own sex, or for both (LeVay & Baldwin, 2012). Consequently, primary sexual orientation categories include heterosexual, homosexual (lesbian/gay), and bisexual, and they exist across a natural continuum (Vrangalova & Savin-Williams, 2012). Of the three, heterosexual is by far the most common orientation, a fact that has been used to perpetuate the insidious societal assumption that heterosexuality is 'normal,' while all others are 'abnormal (Hogan & Hudson, 1998).

Sexual identity refers to how one *thinks* of him- or herself in terms of his or her sexual orientation. The idea of sexual identity is important, particularly because one may be unaware of, or questioning, his or her sexual orientation. Thus you might encounter students whose sexual identity may not be fully formed or acknowledged. Cass (1979) posed a six-stage model of homosexual identity formation that ranges from a budding awareness to a fully integrated concept of one's self; the stages include (a) confusion, (b) comparison, (c) tolerance, (d) acceptance, (e) pride, and (f) synthesis. Because each individual is unique, Cass's model may not describe the specific journey of identity discovery for every person with a minority sexual orientation. However, the model does explain students' thoughts, feelings, and behaviors, and therefore might help you to know how to support students through a period of sexual identity development.

In addition to lesbian, gay, and bisexual, transgender is a fourth minority category, one in which individuals see themselves as a different gender (male or female) than what corresponds to their sex at birth (American Psychological Association, 2011). Transgender does not imply any particular sexual orientation because the term does not depict sexual attraction. Rather the term is related to sexual identity in that a person who is transgender experiences an internal sense of being male, female, or something else that does not correspond to his or her sex at birth.

In two efforts employing nationally representative samples, researchers attempted to determine the percentage of the U.S. population in minority sexual orientation categories. In the first study, Laumann, Gagnon, Michael, and Michaels (1994) found 2.8 percent of the men and 1.4 percent of the women identified themselves as homosexual. In the more recent work, researchers found 8 percent of men and 7 percent of women identify as gay, lesbian, or bisexual (Herbenick et al., 2010). Likely, an uptick in the more recent investigation is due in part to an increasingly greater acceptance of the lesbian, gay, bisexual, and transgender (LGBT) community—with a greater likelihood to self-identify—and because the sample included both homosexual and bisexual respondents. These numbers are important because, as a music teacher, you will likely be working with large numbers of students and a substantive portion will identify as being part of the LGBT community. Why is this important?

Let's look at another set of statistics. According to a 2007 report by the Gay, Lesbian, and Straight Education Network (GLSEN):

- nine of ten LGBT high school students were verbally harassed because of their sexual orientation;

- 60 percent of LGBT students feel unsafe because of personal characteristics, such as sexual orientation or race/ethnicity, compared to one out of five students in the general population;

- about a third of LGBT students are absent or miss class for safety reasons, compared with 5 to 6 percent of students in general;

- almost half (44.1 percent) of LGBT students experience harassment or assault; and

- nearly two-thirds of LGBT students heard homophobic remarks from school personnel (see Bergonzi, 2009, p. 22).

As Bergonzi (2009) points out, life is much different for the LGBT student as compared to his or her heterosexual counterpart. Whereas society has generally recognized a responsibility to facilitate students' developmental needs and schools have been designed to fulfill this responsibility, LGBT students are frequently left out. "Too often . . . high schools are developmental wastelands for youth in sexual orientation minorities" (p. 21). Bergonzi (2009) goes on to describe the ways that unconscious assumptions in schools and in music programs play out in behaviors that favor a heterosexual perspective, and marginalize others. LGBT students navigate through a system of education that can be both overtly and covertly hostile. Yet, for some, music class can offer a respite and possibly a way of thinking which might benefit all students. Nichols (2011) conducted a case study of a gay student named 'Ryan.' According to Nichols:

> Ryan described his school music classes as 'safe places' and valued the opportunities they provide for musical and emotional expression as well as social connection. For Ryan, the ensembles function as communities of practice where mutual participation in achieving mutual goals 'connected the participants to each other in ways that [were] diverse and complex.'
>
> (p. 43)

Along with students who self-identify as LGBT, you may encounter students who question their sexual identity. Given the implicit societal stigma and overt expressions of hostility toward those with a minority sexual orientation, individuals questioning their sexual orientation are in particular need of support from parents and others, including their teachers. According to the American Psychological Association (2008):

> Young people who identify as lesbian, gay, or bisexual may be more likely to face certain problems, including being bullied and having negative experiences in school . . . On the other hand, many lesbian, gay, and bisexual youths appear to experience no greater level of health or mental health risks. Where problems occur, they are closely associated with experiences of bias and discrimination in their environments. Support from important people in the teen's life can provide a very helpful counterpart to bias and discrimination. Support in the family, at school, and in the broader society

helps to reduce risk and encourage healthy development. Youth need caring and support, appropriately high expectations, and the encouragement to participate actively with peers.

(p. 4)

BLOG ON ...
Sexual Identity

What kind of climate do you envision for your students? How could your classroom be a place where LGBT (and questioning) students, like the ones show in Figure 8.4, might thrive?

FIGURE 8.4 Students from Northampton High School marching in the 30th annual LGBT March, Northampton, MA.

Poverty level. A persistent achievement gap continues between students living above and those below the poverty line (Hopson & Lee, 2011). A family of four (two adults, two children) that earned less than $23,550 in 2013 was living below the poverty line

(U.S. Department of Health and Human Services, n.d.). In 2011, 16.39 million or roughly 23 percent of the children in the United States were living in poverty (Kids Count Data Center, n.d.). Students living in poverty tend to drop out of school 10 times more often than those not living in poverty (Cataldi, Laird, & KewalRamani, 2009). Additionally, under-resourced learners score lower on standardized tests (Caldas & Bankston, 1997; Payne, 2008), experience higher rates of behavioral issues at school (Becker & Luthar, 2002), and achieve lower GPAs overall (Malecki & Demaray, 2006). Income or socio-economic status substantially affect a child's ability to be successful in school.

Poverty, however, is more complex than lack of income. Karelis (2007) states that poverty is "Having insufficient resources to meet what are typically seen as basic needs in that place and time, whether those needs stem from our animal nature or not" (p. 3). Resources may be physical (supplies, clothing, food, or shelter) or other aspects necessary for student success, including a sense of belonging, a stable social environment that provides a safe place to live and learn, and parental (or a caring surrogate's) guidance (Templeton, 2011). Why might these resources be lacking for children living in poverty? A few less than obvious contributors include:

- Constant mobility—Families in poverty move often. Many live in temporary housing (e.g. shelters or motels). These children often live in a constant state of fear not knowing what the next day will bring and where they will live.

- Overcrowded living conditions—It is common for some children to live in a two-bedroom home with more than eight people who may, or may not, be related to them. Children living in this situation may have learned they must be loud to be heard and must be overly assertive to get needed attention—traits not often valued in school.

- Parental interaction—When parents play with young children, lessons are often instinctively inserted in the play. For example, a father might say, "Please, show me the yellow toy." In this exchange, the child is learning concepts of "yellow" and "toy" as well as the polite and inviting nature of the request. Some parents living in poverty do not have the energy or background to engage in such exchanges regularly to help their children learn. As poverty is often generational, current parents may not have had any model of such an exchange. Templeton (2011) notes that parents' lack of connection with formal education in their own experiences also contributes to this issue. She states, "If parents had an unpleasant experience with school, their attitude may affect their children's outlook toward school. If parents repeatedly received the direct or indirect message that they were stupid, slow, or a failure, they may convey the same message to their children." (p. 71)

Access to arts education has been shown to impact at-risk students in a number of positive ways. According to a report by the National Endowment for the Arts on the impact of the arts on at-risk students, children with greater access to the arts tend to have better academic results, better workforce opportunities, and more civic engagement (Catterall, Dumais, & Hampden-Thompson, 2012). Additionally, these authors found that economically disadvantaged students with access to arts programs are almost twice as likely to have plans to attain a bachelor's degree than economically disadvantaged students who do not have access to the arts in school.

While we, as music teachers, can celebrate the findings of this longitudinal study, another study was released by the U.S. Department of Education, the first in the previous 10 years to examine who has access to arts in education (Parsad & Spegielman, 2012). These researchers found that access to arts education is not equitable. Statistics specifically related to music in elementary schools show improvement over the past 10 years in frequency of music offerings, availability of facilities, availability of music specialists, and specified curriculum in music among all public elementary schools. However, children in more affluent schools are more likely than children in high-poverty schools to enjoy all aspects of these improvements, particularly those in facilities that have availability of arts specialists.

If it is possible that music instruction can impact and perhaps counteract some of the devastating effects of poverty on students' learning, what is our responsibility as a profession to see that all children have access to quality music education? When at-risk students do have access to music education, how can we ensure instruction is of high quality and relates directly to their needs? These are questions you are likely to face in your own classroom, rehearsal hall, or studio.

DISCUSSION BOARD
Addressing Poverty

Consider the children pictured in Figure 8.5. Students will arrive in your music class from a number of home situations—some stable and others less so. What are ways you, as a music teacher, might help to ensure the activities in your class relate to their needs? Read at least two other posts from your colleagues and comment about ideas that may be similar to yours and ones that differ.

FIGURE 8.5 Children playing in a tenement house backyard.

GENERAL CHARACTERISTICS: DEVELOPMENTAL ISSUES AND EXCEPTIONALITIES

Human development manifests in a number of ways (i.e. cognitively, physically, emotionally, and socially). As a group, for example, kindergartners typically have a shorter cognitive attention span than, say, fourth-grade students. Therefore, one would need to plan many more activities, each of a shorter length, when teaching kindergartners, and fewer, but longer, more complex activities for groups of fourth-grade students (Boyer & Rozmajzl, 2012). Similarly, due to differences in developmental levels, beginning wind instrumentalists in fifth grade typically require a greater number of repetitions for establishing and coordinating the successful development of physical skills such as embouchure, hand position, and fingering, than do similar students in seventh grade. While both groups may be challenged at their optimum level of complexity, fifth graders will move through stages of cognitive and physical skill development more slowly than will seventh graders (Delzell & Doerksen, 1998). Human development is a complex issue involving the maturation of many different processes affecting the body and the brain. Woolfolk (2012) offers three general principles about development that most theorists would support: (a) people develop at different rates, yet (b) the order of the stages that learners experience is fairly consistent, furthermore (c) development takes place gradually.

Students who do not progress through developmental stages in a typical manner may have a 'developmental delay,' which is a type of disability or exceptionality. All children are 'exceptional' because each is a unique collection of talents, abilities, and limitations. However, students with learning disabilities or other challenges are called exceptional because they present particular issues that require special services to help them reach their potentials (Woolfolk, 2012). Approximately 13 percent of all children from ages 3 to 21 in the United States receive special education or related services (National Center for Educational Statistics, 2012). Students with specific learning disabilities comprise the most common group served, followed by those with speech or language impairments, and then those with other health impairments due to chronic or acute health problems (examples include a heart condition, sickle cell anemia, leukemia, and diabetes). Together these three groups account for approximately two thirds of all students receiving special education or related services (National Center for Educational Statistics, 2012). Autism— or autism spectrum disorder (ASD)—is one particular type of disability, currently on the rise in the United States. Individuals with ASD have difficulty with social interaction and communication, and often exhibit repetitive behaviors (Goldstein, Naglieri, Rzepa, & Williams, 2012). We mention ASD in particular because it is the fastest-growing developmental disability in the world, with diagnoses in the U.S. having risen from 1 in 2,500 in 1970 to 1 in 88 by 2008 (Randolph-Gips & Srinivasan, 2012). Chances are, you will have students diagnosed with ASD in your future music classes.

In 1975, the U.S. Congress enacted Public Law 94-142, which was subsequently recast and amended. It was reauthorized most recently in 2004 and is known currently as the **Individuals with Disabilities Education Act** (IDEA). According to IDEA, all public schools are required legally to develop and follow an individualized education plan (IEP) for every student who has a disability (see Table 8.2 for a list of IDEA disability categories). Further, all students with disabilities must be educated in the least restrictive environment possible. Such settings must be as similar as possible to ones in which children who do not have a disability are educated (Stantrock, 2008). Finally, a third major component of IDEA is the protection of students' and parents' rights. These rights include, among others, maintaining the confidentiality of students' records, making available to parents all records pertaining to the testing, placement, and teaching of their child, and providing parents written notification (in their native language) before any evaluation or change in placement is made.

TABLE 8.2 IDEA categories and students served in 2010-2011, ages 3–21.

Disability category	Number of students in 2010-2011	Percentage of these students who spent at least 40% of the day in regular school classes
Specific learning disabilities	2,356,621	91
Speech or language impairments	1,390,387	92
Other health impairments	713,669	85
Intellectual disability	447,113	45
Autism spectrum disorder	416,560	57
Emotional disturbance	388,626	60
Developmental delay	380,594	82
Multiple disabilities	129,808	29
Hearing impairments	77,912	73
Orthopedic impairments	62,728	70
Visual impairments	28,378	77
Traumatic brain injury	25,594	71
Deaf-blindness	1,467	35
Total	6,419,457	

Source: National Center for Education Statistics. *Digest of Education Statistics, 2012*. Chapter 2. Elementary and Secondary Education. Available online at http://nces.ed.gov/programs/digest/2012menu_tables.asp

In addition to IDEA, there are two other laws that address the education of people with disabilities. Section 504 of the Rehabilitation Act of 1973 (hereafter section 504) is a civil rights statute prohibiting discrimination on the basis of disability in programs, public and private, receiving federal financial assistance (U.S. Department of Health and Human Services, 2006). The Americans with Disabilities Act of 1990 (ADA), later revised in 2009, is a civil rights law that extended coverage of section 504 to include employment, public services (including transportation), public accommodations, and telecommunications, regardless of whether the entities receive federal funding.

Although most schools have special education teachers or other professionals who are responsible for compliance with these mandates, you should be familiar with each one and with your role as a teacher in helping to maintain compliance.

BLOG ON ...
Your Comfort with Exceptional Learners

Consider the children pictured in Figures 8.6a, 8.6b, and 8.6c. Most of the content present in the previous pages addresses children with disabilities. Yet, an important subset of the student population includes those who are exceptionally gifted, as depicted in Figure 8.6c. Write about your comfort level (or concern) with teaching children at each end of the exceptionality spectrum.

FIGURE 8.6a Music activities for children with learning disabilities.

Knowing the general characteristics of students in your community is an important backdrop to consider when planning and teaching music. The general make-up of the student body will differ greatly between, for example, an inner-city environment and a rural area, requiring differences in teaching approach and content. Beyond these generalities, however, it is critical that you get to know your students as individuals.

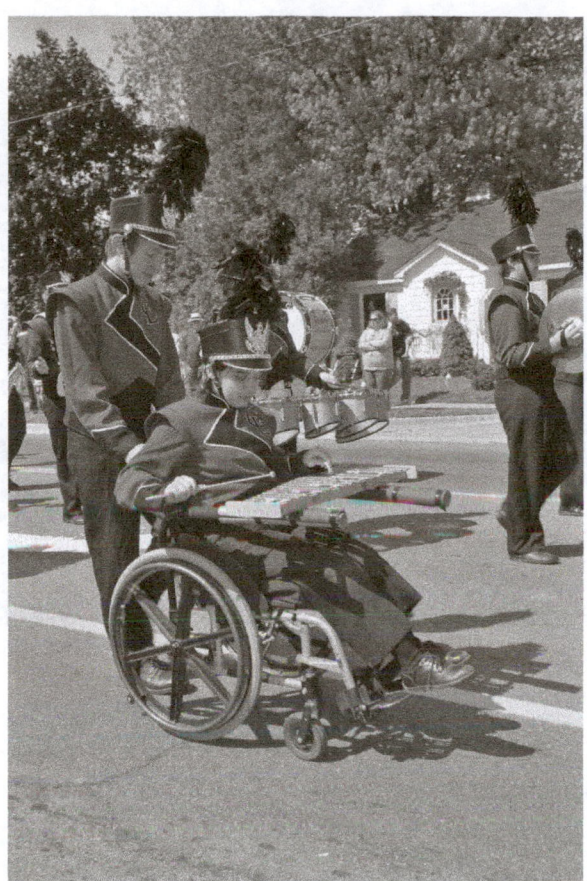

FIGURE 8.6b High-school band member pushing a fellow band member with a physical disability in a parade.

KNOWING YOUR STUDENTS—AS INDIVIDUALS

There exists an unlimited number of ways your students can be different from one another; however, each child's uniqueness is expressed primarily through his or her personality. Personality is comprised of the thoughts, feelings, and behaviors that guide how an individual adapts to the world (Stantrock, 2008). Psychologists have long sought to identify a core set of personality types that represent most of the possible variations. McCrae and Costa (1987) proffered the **Five Factor Model**, (FFM), based on characteristics thought to describe the main dimensions of personality. Each factor represents a particular continuum anchored at each end by two extremes. The five factors include:

FIGURE 8.6c Gifted student playing the violin.

- **Openness** (inventive/curious vs. consistent/cautious)

- **Conscientiousness** (efficient/organized vs. easy-going/careless)

- **Extraversion** (outgoing/energetic vs. solitary/reserved)

- **Agreeableness** (friendly/compassionate vs. cold/unkind)

- **Neuroticism** (sensitive/nervous vs. secure/confident).

Each of your students has personality characteristics that fall somewhere within each of the factors. The FFM can provide a framework for thinking about your students and about ways to make connections. Below, we offer strategies that can help you to get to *know* your students by discerning their personality differences.

Observe your students. Notice how students interact with one another. This can provide you with more accurate information about your students' individual characteristics than when they interact with you. Try to identify the 'leaders'—those students to whom the others tend to defer. Notice who takes charge in new situations and who holds back. Notice cliques and divides among your students. Be aware of students who do not get along with each other. Knowing your students as individuals will help you plan instruction that can meet each one's needs. When implementing team-based activities, try to include as much diversity within each group as possible regarding assets, liabilities, gender, ethnicity, leaders, followers, etc. Such diversity ensures each team possesses the range of experience needed to explore content from a variety of perspectives making the learning a rich endeavor (Fink, 2004). To that end, observing your students will help you to know their tendencies, giving you the information you need to facilitate their learning best.

Learn their names. The value of this suggestion is obvious; however, the task can be challenging with large ensemble classes or when you meet different classes of students each day of the week and see each class only once per week as is the case for many elementary general music teachers. Nonetheless, learning names and using them as early as possible will help you to affirm your individual relationship with each student. Below are a few techniques that may help you:

1. **Name tags:** A half-sheet of 8.5 × 11-inch piece of paper taped to the back side of a music stand with the student's first name can help instrumental ensemble teachers associate names with faces and with instruments. Adhesive name tags worn on clothing during the first week can help in choirs or in classes where students may move from one formation to another (think general music classes).

2. **Seating charts:** Prepare seating charts that include students' names, instruments or voices, and pictures. You can study these during your planning time and evening hours. When teaching elementary general music, have a 'home base' seating arrangement where students begin class and return in between movement activities.

3. **Picture flashcards:** Prepare sets of picture flashcards for each of your classes that include the students' pictures on one side and two or three categories of information that are relevant to your situation on the other side. For example, in an instrumental ensemble, include name, instrument, class (e.g. Freshman, Sophomore, etc.), and one interesting fact (e.g. is a member of the chess club). Keep the cards in class sets. Each evening during the first couple of weeks of the school year, shuffle a set and test yourself. If you are tech-savvy, you might try *Flashcard Deluxe*, a simple flashcard app you can use to test yourself with a computer.

4. **The Name Game:** With younger students, sit in a circle and tell everyone to pretend they are going on a trip. Then ask them to think of an object they would like to take along that begins with the first letter of their name. Start a chant by having a student say his or her name and the object—for example, "My name is Steve and I'm taking stamps." The next student responds with "His name is Steve, and he's taking stamps. My name is Ashley and I'm taking apples." Go around the circle making

yourself last. You will be amazed at how well you have names memorized by the time it is your turn.

5. **Use their names:** Force yourself to address students by name each time you see them both inside and outside your classroom. If you are wrong, they will tend to forgive you. Ask them to correct you immediately so you can learn quickly. Students recognize and appreciate that you are trying.

The most challenging aspect to learning students' names occurs when you see students out of context—in the lunchroom, on the playground, or at the grocery store. With a consistent effort, however, the task gets easier. Once you have been in a school for a year or two, you will know all the returning students. At that point, the main challenge comes with learning the names of the incoming new students.

Engage your students in conversation. Initiating conversation can be a one-on-one endeavor or it might involve interacting with small groups of students, all in casual conversation. The purpose is simply to open lines of communication. Initial conversations can begin with something as innocuous as "Tell me about the best part of your day." People generally like talking about themselves and open-ended questions get them to respond with more than a simple "yes" or "no". Once you are able to engage students and get them talking about something important to them, they will unconsciously communicate non-verbally as well as verbally. Look for the excitement in their voices and faces. As you see these signs, an occasional affirmation from you ("Wow, that is really exciting!" or "You must be really proud of your accomplishment!") will let them know you are invested in them as individuals. When they see you as someone who cares about them individually, they will begin to trust you to an increasingly greater degree—remember the 'emotional bank account.' Also look for closed gestures such as crossed arms or averted eyes. These are signals to slow down and bring the conversation back to a 'safe place.'

Conversations should go in both directions. If your students begin to share something about themselves, you should be willing to do the same. However, we advise that you keep the content of what you share about yourself to be 'relatable,' but not too personal. For example, it is OK to tell students you adopted a new puppy—they will relate easily to that—but not that you got into a fight with your boyfriend last evening—that is not appropriate, nor is it any of their business. The goal is to let them see your genuine personality and to learn about who you are as a person.

Ask students to write a biographical sketch. With older students, ask them to write on a 6 × 4-inch index card answering such questions as (a) Does anyone in their family play an instrument or sing in the choir? (b) What music do they like and listen to?

(c) Have they ever been to a live concert? or (d) How do they connect with music outside of school? For younger students, you might send home a form their parents can complete. The idea is to give students a chance to describe themselves to you.

Attend _their_ functions. Just as _you_ do, your students have lives outside of the music room. Some are involved in other arts activities such as drama, dance, painting, sculpture, or even other music activities. Others play sports. Still others might be involved in academic competitions such as the quiz bowl or spelling bee. Attending students' functions and cheering for them shows that you value them for more than simply what they can provide to you in the music-learning setting. Also, you get to see them in new contexts, which undoubtedly will change and broaden the way you interact with them.

Visit the school guidance counselor. The school guidance counselor is a trusted source of information about students. The role of the guidance counselor is to serve the overall wellbeing of students. Consequently, counselors rely on teachers because teachers are considered to be the "key adult figure[s] in the average pupil's school day" (Stelzer, 2003, p. 2). The interdependent relationship shared between the guidance counselor and teacher is one that is intended to benefit students ultimately. To that end, you need to learn as much as you can from your guidance counselor about the students you teach.

Knowing whether or not any of your students have learning or attention challenges, including delays in physical, cognitive, communicative, behavioral/emotional, or social/adaptive areas, can help you to understand and interact with them effectively. Similarly, knowing if you have students who are particularly gifted in one or more areas can help you to individualize instruction. To the degree your guidance counselor deems appropriate, find out if there are extenuating home life circumstances, for example, one or more parents losing a job or crowded living conditions. Some would argue that gathering information from the guidance counselor compromises the teacher's ability to treat all members of the class objectively and with a sense of fairness. On the contrary, we believe the more you know about your students, the better equipped you are to provide appropriate support that may be needed in any particular situation. That said, you should become familiar with the **Family Educational Rights and Privacy Act** of 1974 (FERPA), to ensure you remain in compliance as you gather information. Your guidance counselor should be able to help you.

Hold social events. Social events such as pizza parties or miniature golf outings are wonderful opportunities for your students to get to know you better and for you to get to know them. The following vignette conveys a particularly poignant event in the public-school teaching career of one of the authors.

SWITCHING ROLES

I am reminded of a particular Saturday afternoon in February at a local roller-skating rink that turned out to be a transformational experience for one of my low-level seventh-grade beginner clarinet students and for me. James (a pseudonym) had experienced difficulty with learning to play the clarinet since he started back in September. He was the last clarinet student of his peers to produce a sound on the instrument, the last to play down to low E, and one of the few who had still not managed to 'cross the break.' Relative to his peers, James was woefully behind. Each day he would arrive and try his best, but knew he was not making adequate progress. I secretly wondered whether he was going to stick with band.

Then came the February roller-skating party, an event I scheduled to bring the students together at a time in the school year that was well into the second semester, but nowhere close to the summer break. They needed a change of pace and so did I, and the skating event was the students' first choice. I was never a proficient skater and it was years since I had been to the rink. As I laced up my skates, I realized the only way I would make it around the oval was to cling to the side wall and inch my way. When I approached the gate to enter the oval, I looked up in time to see James skating like a pro. He was skating forward and backward. He could turn to the right and to the left. He performed jumps, holding his skates and landing back down without a hitch, and could stop on a dime. This kid was amazing. But what happened next was even more amazing. When he saw me starting to hobble my way around the wall, he skated right over to me, grabbed my hand and said, "Let me help you learn to skate! Let me be *your* teacher today." Without an ounce of self-consciousness, and thoroughly filled with pride, he spent the next 20 minutes helping me away from the wall and showing me that I could, indeed, skate my way around the oval, more than once! In those few minutes, the power differential between teacher and student had shifted completely. We both saw aspects of each other that were, up to that point in time, unavailable in the music class. He became the compassionate, patient teacher and I was the vulnerable, ever-trying but slow–achieving, student. After that day, James started to gain ground on his clarinet playing. I am not sure if his progress was due to a newly found confidence with the clarinet or if I was becoming a bit more patient—probably a bit of both. In any case, after that day at the skating rink we shared a new understanding—a unique bond of respect between teacher and student. James eventually remained in band throughout high school and became a much better clarinet player than I ever became a roller skater.

Up to this point, we have explored many ways you might get to know your students. Equally important, however, is that they get to know *you* . . . so they can learn to trust you. Once again we refer to Parker Palmer's (2007) wonderful book for teachers titled *The Courage to Teach: Exploring the Inner Landscape of a Teacher's Life*, in which he affirms, "good teaching comes from the identity and integrity of the teacher" (p. 10). He goes on to explain:

> In every class I teach, my ability to connect with my students, and to connect them to the subject, depends less on the methods I use than on the degree to which I know and trust my selfhood—and am willing to make that available and vulnerable in the service of learning.
>
> (pp. 10–11)

Your students will know you through the decisions you make and the actions you take on a daily basis. If those decisions and actions consistently communicate that you have their best interests and their learning as your highest priority, they will allow you to take them new places pedagogically. Your teaching can become particularly powerful when you align what you know about your students with the content you teach.

BLOG ON . . .
Establishing Rapport

Review the list of suggestions for getting to *know* your students as individuals. Can you think of examples in your own experience of one or more of these suggestions? Again, based on your past experience, is there a suggestion or two you can add?

CLASS ACTIVITIES

Class Activity 8.1: Knowing Your Students (What Do You Know About Your Colleagues?)

Since the beginning of this course, your instructor has learned information about you and your colleagues from your blogs. Your instructor has prepared and will distribute cards that include descriptions or characteristics of individuals in your class (e.g. left-handed, able to juggle, visited three foreign countries, practices Judaism, etc.). Once you receive a card, your task is to approach your colleagues individually and ask for the signatures of those whose characteristics are listed on the card. You will have a limited amount of time to complete this task. When finished, consider the following questions:

1. Did you learn new things about those with whom you have shared a course since the beginning of the semester?
2. What does it mean to know about your students (facts) versus *knowing* your students such that your students feel that you 'know' them?
3. Why might each way of knowing your students be important?
4. How do teachers get to know about and *know* their students?

The Students: What Do They Learn?

9

When you first consider what students learn from an education in music, you might think of answers that reflect some of the more ancillary benefits—self-discipline, staying with a task until it is accomplished, working with others effectively, etc. While these benefits may be gleaned from an education in music, they can also be learned through a number of other *non-music* experiences such as team sports, youth organizations (4-H, Scouts, etc.), or even involvement in other Arts such as dance or drama. A more accurate response to the question is found by considering only what can be learned *exclusively* in music. For that, we must look to the fundamental building blocks of music: the music elements.

MUSIC ELEMENTS

The elements of music are those components that can be perceived as having characteristics distinctive from one another (melody, harmony, rhythm, timbre, etc.). Further, they are usually classified as belonging to one of four broad categories: *tonal, temporal, expressive,* and *structural* elements. **Tonal** elements are associated with highness and lowness of musical sounds, including pitch, intervals, chords, melody, tonality, harmony, consonance, dissonance, timbre, etc. **Temporal** (or rhythm) elements are associated with perception of music across time, including steady beat, meter, subdivisions of beats, rhythmic patterns over the beat and subdivisions, syncopation, etc. **Expressive** elements are those aspects of music superimposed over tonal and temporal elements in the effort to communicate particular musical intentions. They include dynamics, phrasing, articulation, rubato, etc. **Structural** (form) elements provide the 'roadmap' or layout for a piece of music by positioning parts that either repeat or contrast each other. Parts can exist as simple phrase combinations like AB, ABA, and ABACABA or as complex sections like Exposition, Development, and Recapitulation, or something in between.

These particular lists of music elements are not definitive, nor are they inflexible. Given some time, you can probably construct a lengthy list of elements in each category and conceive of some elements as belonging to more than one category simultaneously. For example, some might consider timbre to be a tonal element because its various permutations are dictated by the presence (or not) of particular overtones. Others might think of timbre as an expressive element because of its deliberate uses for producing emotional affect—imagine the somber tone of a muted trumpet in a soft ballad being played by a small combo in an intimate jazz club setting. Similarly, phrase can be thought of as both an expressive element and a structural element. Each interpretation of timbre and phrase is accurate. Ultimately, how you determine the categories and ways of thinking about music elements should be a matter of what is most appropriate for the context in which you and your students are engaging with music.

None of these elements, however, exist in isolation. When engaging in activities that involve actual music (performing, creating, and listening), the elements are enacted together to generate particular musical ideas (e.g. it is difficult to think of a melody without simultaneously hearing the melodic rhythm). Therefore, the distinctive features of each element must be learned as well as the various ways elements work together to communicate musical ideas.

The primacy regarding the teaching of music elements is substantiated by the work of Howard Gardner (1993), who proffered the theory of multiple intelligences. Gardner's original seven intelligences included musical intelligence along with linguistic, logical-mathematical, visual-spatial, bodily-kinesthetic, interpersonal, and intrapersonal intelligences. The core operations associated with music intelligence are not those of instrumental or vocal performance ability. Rather, Gardner defines music intelligence as having sensitivity to the elements of music, particularly pitch and rhythm, and the ability to manipulate those elements to form artistic ideas and to communicate musically (Gardner, 1993). Therefore, an education in music should foremost include learning the basic elements of music and how they work together to produce musical and emotionally meaningful ideas.

> **9.1 THE MUSIC ELEMENTS**
>
> Considering the four 'broad categories' mentioned above, (tonal, temporal, expressive, and structural), what music elements belong to each? (see Class Activity 9.1, p. 218)

MUSICAL INDEPENDENCE

Student independence, a goal of every educational endeavor, has its roots going back to the Age of Enlightenment. Few would argue against the idea that a primary purpose of education is for learners to develop understanding of content, expertise to work with that content, and a sense of agency such that they are able to continue exploring content beyond initial schooling. In music, content is comprised of music elements and an understanding of how they operate together. Consequently, we suggest **musical**

independence is the capacity to enact artistically informed decisions when working with the elements of music.

Musical independence is demonstrated primarily through performing or creating music. However, musical independence also can be affirmed through other ways of interacting with music, such as analyzing and evaluating music or understanding relationships between music and other content areas. Think, for a moment, about the degree of musical independence one must possess to successfully negotiate the complex analysis of a Beethoven symphony or to explore ways that music has been affected by events of particular times and places and their associated cultural milieus. Indeed, musical independence applies not only to what one can do with music, but also how one thinks about and understands music relative to other aspects in life.

Facilitating musical independence in others is often an incremental pedagogical process that requires selflessness and patience on the part of the teacher. Selflessness is required because, for students to gain musical independence, the teacher must, little by little, relinquish control of music decision-making responsibilities. Patience is needed because the process of cultivating musical independence requires the teacher to offer frequent opportunities for students to exercise their budding sense of autonomy throughout their music education (see Figure 9.1).

In echoing John Dewey's thoughts on education, Woodford (2005), a Dewey scholar, advanced the idea that "Education should foster the *freedom of mind* such that students are empowered to exert some degree of intelligence or conscious control over experience" (p. 1). An education in music should include the cultivation of musical independence such

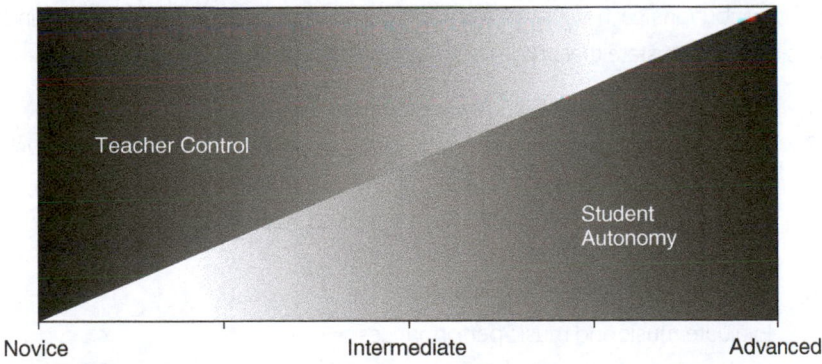

FIGURE 9.1 Model of student autonomy-teacher control change with growing expertise. Students' growing expertise requires increasing opportunities for autonomy and a lessening of teacher control.

that students have an understanding of music elements and how they work together and the capacity to use those elements as effective tools for artistic expression.

BLOG ON . . .
Musical Independence

Think back over your P-12 music education. In what way(s) was your sense of musical independence fostered? As a music major, you probably have a strong degree of independence regarding executive skills needed to perform with your instrument or voice, and with reading music notation. However, what other areas of musical independence may not have been facilitated in your P-12 experiences to the same degree? Now think about your classmates that did not go on to pursue a career in music. How would you characterize *their* musical independence?

THE NATIONAL STANDARDS FOR ARTS EDUCATION

The **National Standards** for Arts Education were developed as a declaration of what all students should learn and be able to do in the Arts (Consortium of National Arts Education Associations, 1994). Nine music content standards were developed to provide music teachers with a guide for what students should learn from an education in music. In the remainder of this chapter, we will explore the standards, with particular attention to the unique contributions each brings to a comprehensive education in music. The standards for music education state that students should be able to:

1. Sing, alone and with others, a varied repertoire of music.
2. Perform on instruments, alone and with others, a varied repertoire of music.
3. Improvise melodies, variations, and accompaniments.
4. Compose and arrange music within specified guidelines.
5. Read and notate music.
6. Listen to, analyze, and describe music.
7. Evaluate music and music performances.
8. Understand relationships between music, the other arts, and disciplines outside the arts.
9. Understand music in relation to history and culture.

(Consortium of National Arts Education Associations, 1994, pp. 26–29)

Although there is no hierarchical intent or dependent order to the standards, logical groupings seem to be apparent. Standards 1 and 2 emphasize **performance** as a tangible expression of musicianship. Standards 3 and 4 are avenues toward **creativity**. Standards 6 and 7 provide tools for developing music awareness and **response**. Standards 8 and 9 provide tools for **understanding relationships** between music and the other content areas, and to history and culture. Standard 5 does not fall squarely under any one of these categories exclusively, but rather can serve all four in some way or another.

We opened this chapter by asserting that students should learn the elements of music and gain the agency to make musical decisions independent of the teacher. For each area listed above, and for Standard 5, we will explore ways to help students uncover the music elements and gain musical independence.

PERFORMANCE AS AN EXPRESSION OF MUSICIANSHIP

> On the most fundamental level, it is clear that music making in the sense of singing and playing instruments lies at the heart of what MUSIC is and that music making is a matter of musical knowledge-in-action or musicianship.
>
> (Elliott, 1995, p. 72)

Of all the ways human beings express their musicianship, performance through singing or playing an instrument is the most immediate and visceral. Through performance, one figuratively and in some cases literally breathes life into a musical idea. For that to happen with any degree of consistency, however, attention must be given initially to the development of foundational executive skills. For this task, singing and playing instruments pose disparate challenges.

Almost everyone sings, whether alone (singing in the shower, singing along with songs on the radio while driving) or as a socially oriented activity—picture a group of middle-school girls gathered around an MP3 player singing popular songs or a church congregation singing hymns or a even a group of patrons gathered at a local Irish pub participating in a group singing along. In all of these instances, the voice is a 'taken for granted' tool for self-expression. The idea that the voice is a complex and fragile instrument needing regular attention is a thought that rarely crosses the minds of most people. Consequently, deliberate instruction is needed to sensitize students to the physical requirements for proper vocal development, including posture, breath support, phonation, resonant tone production, and diction (Phillips, 1996).

Unlike singing, children typically do not bring with them years of experience of playing wind, string, or percussion instruments upon entering school. Consequently, instrumental beginners require the teacher's guidance in helping them establish proper executive skills (posture and instrument carriage, fingering and hand position, breathing, embouchure formation, etc.) (Bachelder & Hunt, 2001; Combs, 2000; Hamann & Gillespie, 2004; Klotman, 1996; McClaren, 2006; Westphal, 1989). As you enroll in instrumental techniques courses, you might make opportunities to visit local beginning band and orchestra classrooms to take note of how and when executive skills are taught (see the website for protocols and ethics to consider when planning field visits to schools). From each visit, you will likely gain an increasingly clearer understanding of effective ways to establish these skills in beginning instrumentalists. Each visit should also produce additional questions, all in the constant effort to learn what works in each situation and why.

As students begin to develop a degree of sensitivity for proper vocal development or proficiency with instrumental executive skills, singing or playing an instrument can help them develop an ever-evolving sense of musicianship. Even the simplest of folk songs can be approached with a high degree of musicality. An important dilemma is posed when determining a balance between executive skill development and facilitating students' ability to express ideas musically. For example, it is unrealistic to expect a student to attempt phrasing or dynamics if he is not yet able to sustain a tone for any substantive length. Yet, dwelling on the development of executive skills exclusively for a prolonged time period may cause you to ignore ways that musicality might be used to break through temporary limits with one's technique.

McPherson (2005) found that young instrumentalists who used sophisticated strategies early on in their development—such as thinking how the melody would sound on their instrument, thinking how the pitches related to fingerings, and singing the melody while fingering on the instrument—were much more likely to subsequently achieve at the highest level than their non-strategic counterparts.

Perhaps engaging the students' sense of musicianship, for example having them sing a particular stylized musical phrase or articulate a rhythm using a specific combination of dynamics and rubato, might provide the alchemy needed to transform one's fledgling executive skills into a more sophisticated and capable vehicle for delivering the particular musical message at hand. A great resource that aligns with this idea is Duke and Byo's (2009) method book for beginning band, which is based on the idea that habits that produce characteristic tone, excellent musicianship, and beautiful playing, can be established from the first days of instruction. The book (with teacher's score and parts) is available for free through the Center of Music Learning at the University of Texas at Austin (http://cml.music.utexas.edu).

Music elements are not simply cognitive concepts such as high/low pitch or fast/slow tempo. Music elements also carry expressive attributes that correspond with physical feelings (e.g. the tension felt by a melodic line leading up to the 7th scale degree and finally resolving on a closing tonic or the weight associated with a beat pattern conducted at the tempo indicated by the term 'largo').

INDIVIDUAL ACTIVITY
'Feeling' Tempo

A slow tempo beat—e.g. 46 beats per minute (bpm)—has a corresponding feeling of great weight and much space. Try conducting a four beat pattern at a tempo of 46 bpm. You will likely find yourself using lots of space and conveying a feeling of great weight, similar to pushing and pulling your gestures through a pool of water, to correspond with the slow tempo. It is this particular relationship among time, space, and weight that produces the feeling of 'Largo' often associated with a tempo of 46 bpm. Now, change the tempo to 184 bpm and you will likely find yourself reducing your size of conducting pattern substantially smaller and expressing a much lighter feeling in your gestures to correspond with the much faster tempo, all resulting in a feeling of 'Presto.' If your students' concepts of steady beat include the attributes of time, space, and weight, they will eventually have the tools to perform a steady beat consistently without rushing or dragging the tempo.

Each of the music elements carries with it a sense of physicality. Some call this connection between music and the lived experience '**embodiment**.' In describing embodiment, Custodero (2010) writes, "Musical experiences are corporeal; they are located in the body. This means we experience the movement and associative aspects of music in correspondence with our physical being" (p. 62). The instrument or voice is the means through which students expresses their concepts of musical ideas. As they learn performance technique (breathing, articulation, fingerings, etc.), they should simultaneously develop and apply an understanding of and feeling for musical expressiveness (Duke & Byo, 2009).

Once students achieve a degree of musical stability and independence, they can make substantive contributions to, and learn from, the ensemble experience. In small independent groups, singers and instrumentalists can begin addressing the challenges of matching one another, specifically as they relate to balance (matching volume), blend (matching vowels and subsequently timbre), and intonation (matching pitch). Rhythmic precision, diction, articulation, and consonant placements all constitute temporal matching. As students become increasingly proficient they can apply all of these skills to their participation in ensembles of all sizes.

Once individual and ensemble responsibilities become increasingly refined and coordinated, students must be given opportunities to develop musical independence. Giving students increasingly greater autonomy allows them to grow their sense of musicianship. Small ensembles are wonderful opportunities for students to 'try on,' discuss, justify, and eventually reach consensus regarding a variety of musical options. In this environment students are simultaneously required to arrive prepared with their individual contribution to the ensemble *and* be willing to negotiate musical ideas from a thoughtful perspective. With each successive encounter, students hone their sense of and confidence in their own musicianship. A similar approach can be implemented in a large ensemble situation. The conductor can include members of the ensemble in musical decisions in the effort to facilitate their growing sense of musical independence.

144 SOCIAL PLACE

Fostering Musicianship with Performance

Using 144 characters or fewer, describe when you first felt you were capable of making artistic musical expressions on your instrument or with your voice? How did your teacher(s) facilitate this? Could it have happened earlier? Why or why not?

IMPROVISATION AND COMPOSITION AS AVENUES TOWARD CREATIVITY IN MUSIC

Creativity belongs at the heart of an education in music. The powerful feelings associated with developing an original musical idea and laying claim to it—"I did that!"—is the currency that gives profound meaning to music learning. Far from being superfluous to the more visible aspects of a music-learning experience, improvisation and composition complement students' performance experiences in ways that facilitate an awakened sense of musicianship. Pogonowski (2001) described the synergy that results when students are involved in both creative and performance endeavors:

When a student creates and performs, that student subsequently listens with a 'new' pair of ears, not only to his or her own music, but also to the music that others have produced. Critical thinking about music is an outcome of these equally weighted behaviors because of the personal investment that students make as they are engaged in them.

(p. 27)

Both improvisation and composition are highly creative ways to engage music learning; however, there is an important distinguishing characteristic that affects how each is pursued. True improvisation requires an extemporaneous 'in the moment' aspect to the process. There are no opportunities to go back and revise the work before its initial presentation. One might try an idea and then try it differently. However, to the degree that the process *is* the product, the second attempt would be a new product. Composition, on the other hand, implies the capacity to work with ideas over time—altering, adding to, taking away, reframing, etc.—prior to an initial presentation. So let's take a quick look at each individually.

Improvisation. A common misconception is that improvisation is something reserved only for 'jazz.' However, there are entire non-jazz-related musical traditions that incorporate the practice of improvisation. In fact, from the Medieval through the Romantic periods, improvisation was a highly valued skill among most composers and performers. The ability to improvise on a theme was a primary way one displayed knowledge and skill as a musician. In today's music classroom, improvisation can be a valuable tool to help students explore relationships among the different music elements.

Due to its extemporaneous nature, improvisation is as much a process as it is a product. The act of expressing one's self in the moment, without inhibition, can be a cathartic experience. However, moving from the primal stages to increasingly more exacting expressions of moods, emotions, physical sensations, and states of consciousness requires an evolving expertise with the 'language' of music (Dobbins, 1980). The challenge comes when attempting to facilitate students along this continuum. Few music teachers have developed high levels of improvisation skills, a situation that reduces the likelihood they will feel comfortable teaching those skills to their students. Fortunately, there are a number of approaches and associated materials that teachers can use to facilitate students along their exploration of improvisation (Azzara, 1999; Azzara & Grunow, 2006; Chappell, 2010; Green, 2001; Hintz, 1995; Marshall, 2004; Perlmutter, 2010; Scott, 2007; Volz, 2005). Kratus (1991, 1995) proffered a model of improvisation development that provides conceptual touchstones for planning instruction and monitoring student progress along seven levels: exploration, process-oriented improvisation, product-oriented improvisation, fluid improvisation, structural improvisation, stylistic improvisation, and personal improvisation. This broad-based perspective can offer those with little or no experience some guidelines for helping their students develop their improvisatory skill sets.

Composition. The primary goal for students engaging in composition and arranging activities is not for them to become full-fledged composers and arrangers, although some might go on to do just that. Rather, the aim is for students to "explore their innate emotional and intellectual capacities within and through an artistic frame" (Kaschub & Smith, 2009, p. 4). To this end, students should engage in composition and arranging as a form of personal expression through music. Along the way, they gain some rather important benefits. When composing and arranging, they work intimately with all the music elements, getting to know their expressive qualities through direct engagement and decision-making. Compositional decision-making promotes a form of musical independence. The following vignette describes a composition activity assigned during piano studio instruction. It offers a wonderful example of the ways that the decision-making aspect of composition can help students uncover and personalize qualities of the music elements.

ZACH'S COMPOSITION

Zach is a fifth-grade student who was composing a short piece about his vacation at the ocean the previous summer. When contemplating how he would depict the flurry of activity that seemed to surround him during his daily visits to the beach, he considered a number of rhythmic approaches, and eventually settled on a rather slow tempo (representing the constancy of the ocean and tides), with a melodic rhythm consisting mostly of sixteenth-notes and triplets (representing the frantic activity on and around the beach). Not only was Zach engaged with his feelings and thoughts about his experience, he had to decide on the most effective ways to use music elements and their combinations to express those feelings and thoughts.

Rather than detrimentally affecting the more traditional aspects of most music programs, compositional activities have been reported to *improve* students' contributions in all music-making efforts, particularly those in the large ensemble (Ginocchio, 2003; Hickey, 1997). In describing the benefits of incorporating composition in an instrumental music program, Ginocchio (2003) shared the following about the process in his school district that begins at sixth grade and continues through high school.

[Students] have band every day for forty-eight minutes. On average, they spend one day a week working on composition skills. While it takes time away from rehearsal for upcoming performances, the students' greater sensitivity to compositional methods and expression enhances their rehearsal skills. Furthermore, by notating music, they develop a greater understanding of rhythm and melody, thereby improving their music-reading ability.

(pp. 51–52)

There exists a variety of resources that will give you a fundamental grounding with teaching composition so you can get started when you are ready to have your own music classroom (Ginocchio, 2003; Hickey, 1997; Kaschub & Smith, 2009, 2013; Strand & Newberry, 2007; Wiggins, 1989, 2001). As a music teacher who is likely new to arranging and composing, you may feel a bit intimidated at the prospect of incorporating these components into your instructional curriculum. Therefore, when the time comes, we suggest you start with a small manageable project, one that would allow you to envision the project in its entirety *before* you begin. Upon completion, take time to notice what in the process needed improvement. Also, notice what worked, for you and for your students. Hopefully, the empowerment you see in your students from creating personally meaningful products, and from the enhanced musicianship that will undoubtedly spill over onto all other areas of their musical life, will motivate you to incorporate increasingly adventuresome compositional explorations into your music program.

New ears and new capabilities. The 'new ears' Pogonowski (1999) describes is a product of the direct interaction with and manipulation of music elements that occurs when one is improvising or composing music. Having wrestled with multiple ways to depict an idea, one becomes increasingly sensitive to the musical works of others, which enhances his or her ability to perform expressively. Similarly, 'critical thinking about music' is a form of musical independence that we, as music educators, strive to engender in our students. Despite these benefits, some would argue that genuinely creative experiences are rarely a deliberate and ongoing component of an education in music. We hope that the ideas and tools we described here will help you to envision how you might incorporate creative experiences in your future music program.

READING AND NOTATING MUSIC

The essence of *music* is what you hear and feel. *Music notation* is simply the set of associated written symbols used to communicate technical information (e.g. when, how high, how loud, etc.) to the performer, who then translates these symbols into sounds and feelings. Learning to read standard music notation is highly valued in the culture of Western music, which is pervasive throughout the United States. Therefore, reading and writing standard notation is an integral component of an education in music, as these skills can facilitate learning in each of the four broad areas under which the other standards are organized: performing music, creating music, responding to music, and understanding relationships between music and other areas.

Learning to read and notate music. If we, as music educators, took a cue from the ways children learn language, we would surround them with heard music at every opportunity, from the first days of pre-kindergarten. We would facilitate in them a growing expertise with the building blocks of tonality and rhythmic feeling (see Schleuter, 1997), as well as with expressive and structural elements. Our instruction would be aimed at helping them become confident in their ability to hear and understand foundational music elements and use those understandings to express themselves musically as singers and instrumentalists *prior to* notational reading.

Unfortunately, in the zeal to promote notational reading skills as early as possible, many music teachers do not establish a proper conceptual foundation before diving into notation (Grunow & Gamble, 1989; Jordan, 1989; Levinowitz, 1989). Rather, they unwittingly expect students to conceptualize music elements while simultaneously learning visual symbols, with the misguided idea that symbols will help conceptualization. This is similar to expecting toddlers to learn what a chair is by being introduced to the written word 'chair,' without having seen a chair, sat in a chair, or heard others refer to chairs and their uses.

Remember the years of corollary skill development in language learning *prior* to reading and writing? In a proper sequence, conceptual understanding is developed to the fullest *first* so that notation simply becomes a consistent set of visual labels representing the deep understanding that has already been established. In music, this involves students learning songs 'by ear' and singing and playing instruments by rote as strategies for facilitating conceptual understanding of the music elements and development of executive skills needed to express those understandings accurately. Some music educators avoid rote teaching, mistakenly thinking that the approach hinders music-reading skill development. Actually, just the opposite is true, but *only* if rote teaching is implemented carefully as one step in a deliberate strategy aimed at developing conceptual understanding and eventually associated notational understanding (Woody, 2012). One of the quickest ways for students to improve notational skills is for them to have a clear musical idea they want to remember. Then notation becomes a functional tool to facilitate the expression of musicianship.

TOOLS FOR DEVELOPING MUSIC AWARENESS AND RESPONSE

All education, and particularly music education, is concerned with student development across three primary domains: cognitive (what students know), psychomotor (what they can do), and affective (what they value) (Bloom, 1956; Hanna, 2007). Listening to, analyzing, describing, and evaluating music are tools to help students deepen their knowledge of music and improve their ability to discern quality and value, so they can apply that expertise to their performance and creative endeavors.

Listening to, analyzing, and describing music. Listening is an important music learning activity; however, its value is often underestimated. Perhaps because of music's ubiquitous presence, one might easily assume that people already make sense of what they hear. Similarly, listening seems to be such a natural (and passive) process that it appears not to require effort. As a result, music teachers often minimize music listening efforts so they can engage in more active-looking forms of music instruction such as performing or composing (Campbell, 2005). In reality, listening is a tool that can improve students' understanding of what they are performing or composing, thus facilitating development in all of these areas. Campbell (2005) proposed a three-phase "pedagogy of listening" that requires teachers and students to be involved actively in the listening process (p. 30). The model includes: (a) *attentive listening*, during which the teacher directs students' attention to various music events and structures, (b) *engaged listening*, which requires listeners to actively engage in music making (patting the beat, fingering through parts, singing along, etc.) while listening, and (c) *enactive listening*, during which the listener performs music, bringing a substantive knowledge base so she can attend to every musical nuance present in the music while performing it. This three-phase model depicts the kind of purposeful listening that can add a substantive dimension to what students know and can do in music.

Analyzing music helps students to notice rich musical ideas and the artistic connections that might not be readily apparent upon initial exposure to a piece of music. Analysis can occur as a listening activity, or with a notated score, or with both; however, it does require committed investigation into the inner facets of a composer's work so the underlying aspects might be discovered and elucidated. Analysis implies a deeper investigation into a piece of music beyond simple listening; Campbell's (2005) enactive listening, however, could be a type of analysis because it assumes the listener brings and applies a degree of knowledge to the activity. Score analysis provides an opportunity to see visually how various musical ideas are conceived to work together. It also allows the musician to engage a piece of music at a pace not dictated by listening to it in real time. Furthermore, score analysis provides a wonderful opportunity to apply audiation skill (the ability to hear music when the sound is not physically present) to parts of the work as it is being studied. Analysis involving listening *and* score study helps musicians connect what is seen to what is being heard.

The act of describing music also can be an effective learning tool. The vocabulary and verbal expressions one uses shapes his or her understanding of what is being studied (Winner, 1988). This is why describing music is such a powerful tool for helping students develop a consistent understanding of the musical ideas they encounter. When students are asked to describe a particular musical event or component in their own words, the teacher is provided an immediate window into the degree of understanding that may or may not exist. Furthermore, the act of considering all the possible ways to describe a particular musical idea and then settling on a specific word choice is a process that can sharpen one's thinking with each successive attempt (Bean, 2011). Verbal exchanges between the teacher and students can provide wonderful opportunities for the teacher to introduce and reinforce a technical vocabulary of music. As students begin to utilize such a vocabulary consistently, their descriptions will become more precise and their thoughts more accurate.

Evaluating music and music performances. Listening to, analyzing, and describing music are ways of taking in musical information and making sense of it. Evaluating music and music performances, on the other hand, involves using that information to form opinions, judgments, or otherwise assign value. By engaging in evaluative activities, students can develop an informed sense of quality regarding musical works and musical performances.

As with executive skills and the tools of creativity, facilitating development of an informed sense of quality is an incremental process. The first step involves having students form and express their opinions about what they hear musically. When students first offer their opinions, teachers can gain insight about the prior knowledge being brought to the classroom. For those students new to this process, they will learn that their opinion is something to be valued. Beyond forming opinions, however, students must engage in decisions about quality. For that, criteria are needed against which quality can be judged.

According to the national standards (Consortium of National Arts Education Associations, 1994), students should "develop criteria for evaluating the quality and effectiveness of music performances and composition and apply the criteria in their personal listening and performing" (p. 44). Involving students in the development of evaluation criteria will give them a 'voice' in process; however, the teacher's role also is essential. As students offer their ideas, the teacher must be there to interject an element of critical analysis, requesting clarification and justification (e.g. What do you mean? What would be an example of . . .? Why is this important? Why do you think so?). Criteria that students embrace are more easily applied to their personal listening and performance, although a degree of teacher reinforcement may be needed to establish the habit of consistent application.

Take, for example, the task of helping young singers produce characteristic tone quality. Although the job is mediated by students' physical development, establishing an aural conception of characteristic tone is imperative. You can help students with this task by demonstrating various qualities of sound (thin and airy, rich and full, etc.) and asking them to suggest descriptions in their own words (describing music) and then ask them to select which demonstrations sound better and why (evaluating music). Getting students to *apply* these newly discovered criteria consistently with their singing will involve helping them to solidify connections among their evolving executive skills, the sounds they are making, and the aural model they wish to achieve.

The example above is a simple application of developing criteria and applying those to one aspect of music performance (tone quality). A more complex version may involve developing and applying criteria to *multiple* aspects of a music performance. Here, criteria would involve quality of the presentation (e.g. Is it in tune? Is it rhythmically together? Are the parts balanced?) and appropriateness of the interpretation relative to the composer's intent within piece. Explorations into stylistic appropriateness open opportunities for many discussions addressing a variety of details. Co-creating criteria with your students will engender discussions that potentiate a wide vista of possibilities for student learning.

In addition to evaluating music performance, evaluating the quality of music compositions helps students understand the varying levels of quality in the literature they hear and may perform. For example, young students are often enthusiastic about preparing an arrangement of familiar music, but quickly grow weary of the piece *if* musical quality and substance are lacking. In fact, students seem to be somewhat intuitively perceptive about musical quality (Teachout, 1993). Therefore, deliberate explorations into the qualities of the pieces of music being studied will confirm for students their intuitions and provide a mechanism for generalizing what they learn from piece to piece.

Listening to and evaluating music are actions that can be embedded substantively into many music learning activities at all levels, kindergarten through high school. Used in tandem, they become important tools to help students form increasingly more accurate conceptions of music elements and facilitate the type of thinking and student inquiry that leads to musical independence.

DISCUSSION BOARD
Listening to and Evaluating Music

Think about a situation in which you would like to teach music. How might you make use of active music listening to help your students understand music? In what ways could you incorporate describing music into your instruction? Given that time is often limited, do you believe that these are of enough value that you would take time from performance instruction to include them? If so, why? If not, why not?

TOOLS FOR UNDERSTANDING MUSIC FROM MULTIPLE PERSPECTIVES

Understanding music in relationship to other content areas, history, and culture helps students experience and know music from multiple perspectives. At the core is the idea of '**interdisciplinarity**,' drawing upon two or more distinct disciplines in an effort to enhance understanding in all disciplines involved. According to Randle (1997), the brain is genetically designed to make sense from the cacophony of one's environment by seeking patterns. Conversely, it is slow to assimilate content that is fragmented, isolated, or lacks a personal connection. Based on Randle's description of how the brain works, "knowledge is learned more quickly and remembered longer when constructed in a meaningful context in which connections among ideas are made" (Ellis & Fouts, 2001, p. 24). When applied to music learning, the result is a rich multidimensional understanding that gives students a more comprehensive perspective of what is being learned than simply studying the musical properties alone (Burrack & McKenzie, 2005). For many students, interdisciplinarity provides the spark that makes music learning personal and lasting (Barrett, 2001; Barrett, McKoy, & Veblen, 1997).

Understanding relationships between music, the other Arts and the non-arts. Art is an expression of life. Consequently, each of the Arts draws upon a common source—the lived experience. This idea is similar to the concept of embodiment described earlier in this chapter. As a result of tapping into a common well of inspiration, there are similarities among the Arts regarding basic elements (color, line, form, pattern, etc.), artistic processes (inspiration, imagination, craftsmanship, etc.), and broader organizational principles (unity and variety, repetition and contrast, etc.) (Consortium of National Arts Education Associations, 1994). One way students engage with music is to identify, describe, and explain how these elements, processes, and principles "are used in similar and distinctive ways [among the Arts]" (p. 62). However, students need experiential activities to help them make the needed connections. Consequently, as a future music teacher, you would benefit by developing some degree of understanding about the other Arts, possibly through courses you could take while completing your present degree program. Having a command of some basic knowledge in each of the Arts can fuel a vision for the ways you can facilitate your students' growing understanding. If, however, you find yourself in your first job without a basic degree of comfort in the other areas, you might establish a collaborative relationship with a trusted colleague who possesses the needed expertise.

The nature of music's relationship to various non-Arts areas is unique to each area. Unlike the Arts, which share a common source of inspiration, music has an individualistic connection to such non-Arts areas as math, science (physical and biological), social studies, reading, history, and literature. In math, for example, the feeling of steady beat being grouped regularly by twos, threes, or fours, via musical applications of crusis, metacrusis, and anacrusis, can be related to mathematical concepts such as sets and subsets as well as addition and multiplication. In physical science, musical ideas of sound, dynamics, and pitch, can be related to the scientific concepts of vibration, amplitude, and frequency (UBEATS, 2011). In biological science, musical ideas such chord structure and harmonic progression can be related to protein patterns found in the human genome that operate similar to chords in a musical progression. In each of these three examples, music is being related to a non-Arts discipline in discrete ways, while the integrity of the conceptual content is preserved in each area and understanding in each area is enhanced through this relationship.

When integrating music with another area, care should be taken to ensure conceptual understanding is being developed in both areas and that music is not placed in a subordinate role, 'in service of' the other area (e.g. using music as a mnemonic device or simply as pleasant background sound). As Barrett (2001) affirms, "When connections between music and another discipline are valid, the bonds between the disciplines are organic; that is, they make sense without forcing a fit or stretching a point" (p. 28).

Understanding music in relation to history and culture. Biological evolution among humans reached its current state around 35,000 years ago as humans began to shape their environment rather than being shaped by it. For example, rather than evolving thick layers of blubber or heavy fur coats as did their aquatic and four-legged counterparts, humans living in arctic zones began to modify the environment by fashioning parkas from animal skins and building the first igloos for crude housing (Hodges & Seblad, 2011). Since that time, our evolution has been based primarily on cultural development rather than biological adaptation (Dubos, 1974). Consequently, what distinguishes humans from all other animals, and affirms our 'humanness,' is the existence of culture. Music has always been one of the invariant components of human culture. As Hodges and Sebald (2011) affirmed, "All people in all times and in all places have engaged in musical behaviors" (p. 5).

An exploration of culture and history must be foremost a study of culture. History provides a valuable chronological perspective for demarcating what happened when; however, the mere fact that a composer was born on a particular date and died on a subsequent date is trivial without additional context. Furthermore, history is always conceptualized in hindsight. For example, those composing in the Baroque era were not cognizant of a construct known as 'Baroque style.' It was only years afterward that those looking back on the music, and on the entire artistic milieu, labeled the period as being 'Baroque,' primarily based on a collective sense of cultural symbolism that existed during that time in history. Thus any reference to an historical period must be made relevant by exploring the cultural artifacts that affirmed people's 'humanness' at that time.

As a means of connecting music to history and culture, students should explore genres and styles of music from various historical periods and cultures. If you interpret this charge to mean a comprehensive perspective from *all* historical periods and cultures, you may be easily overwhelmed. If, however, you consider that the *spirit* of this charge asks you to help students understand music as an artifact of their 'humanness' experienced by people of particular time periods and affected by the events, politics, and technologies of those time periods, the task becomes a worthy and enlightening pursuit.

Barrett, McCoy, and Veblen (1997) created the 'Facets Model' for exploring works of music in a comprehensive and interdisciplinary manner (see Figure 9.2). Originally based on the metaphor that the Arts "are gems with many facets" (p. 77), this model can be used to explore the varied connections between a piece of music and the historical and cultural aspects that influenced it.

FACETS MODEL 1997

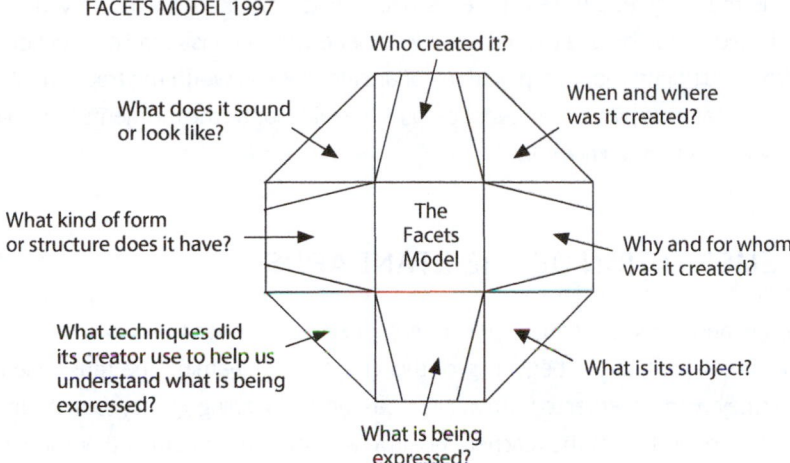

FIGURE 9.2 The facets model for studying artistic works.

Note: This model is from Barrett, McCoy, and Veblen (1997, p. 77) and is used here with permission.

The model places the piece of music at the center and surrounds it with questions that spark rich contextual explorations. An expanded version of the facets model adds questions that help to make meaningful connections to history and culture. These questions include:

> How and to whom is [the piece] transmitted?
> Who performs, dances, listens to, and values it?
> What is its function for individuals and groups?
> What does it mean to individuals and groups?
> What does it mean within historical/cultural contexts?
> How do differences in performance or interpretation change its meaning?
> How does it change through different interpretations or versions?
>
> (Barrett et al., 1997, p. 145)

With the original and expanded facets model questions, you can design individual activities, lessons, or entire units that help students make meaningful connections to the music they experience in powerful ways. These questions, however, require the use of music literature that matches, in quality, the type of deep learning that this approach potentiates. That literature could be from any tradition or style (classical, pop, bluegrass, etc.), but the primary consideration is that the music is of high quality. Likewise, a substantive exploration of culture and history will require an investment of teacher preparation and class time that may lead to fewer pieces being programmed through the year than is typical. However, we believe the memorable experiences and insightful connections that result from multidimensional explorations of artistic music is worth the tradeoff. After all, "Life is not measured by the number of breaths we take but by the moments that take our breath away" (author unknown).

IMPLEMENTATION OF THE STANDARDS

A thorough and complete education in music, one that achieves the two basic goals for students mentioned at the beginning of this chapter—(a) learning the music elements and how they work together to form music ideas, and (b) gaining agency to make musical decisions independent of the teacher—will involve a program of study that thoughtfully and interdependently engages all the standards. Imagine a situation in which students engage the music elements through creative explorations that involve listening and evaluating music, one in which their stylistic sensitivities and musical decision-making abilities are shaped by a growing understanding of music's connections to the Arts, to other content areas, and to history, and culture. Now, imagine all that influencing their development as singers and instrumentalists. How exciting would that be!

Yet, few programs currently incorporate every national standard in a meaningful way (Bell, 2003; Byo, 1999; Conway, 2008; Louk, 2002; Orman, 2002; Riley, 2009; Schmidt, 2000; Williams, 2007). The areas most consistently included are singing, playing instruments, reading/notating music, and listening to/analyzing/describing music (Orman, 2002; Schmidt, 2000), while the areas least consistently implemented are improvising, composing, evaluating, and understanding music in relation to other content areas, and to history and culture (Louk, 2002; Orman, 2002; Schmidt, 2000). The most common reasons for not implementing the latter group include time constraints (Bell, 2003; Byo, 1999; Riley, 2009) and a lack of training or a lack of expertise (Bell, 2003; Volz, 2005).

Time is a finite resource. Consequently, how music teachers choose to use it indicates their priorities. Many learning activities associated with the lesser-explored standards (improvisation, composition, etc.) require (a) giving students a degree of autonomy and (b) asking the teacher to prepare in ways he or she may not be accustomed—neither of which is within the comfort zone of most music teachers, and both likely require a teacher to invest time differently than is done with traditional approaches to music teaching.

Yet, when the *essence* of the standards is pursued, students become *better, more informed musicians* (Conway, 2008; Ginocchio, 2003; Hickey, 1997, 2003; Kaschub &

Smith, 2009; Pogonowski, 2001; Strand & Newberry, 2007; Wiggins, 2001). Whether your priority is primarily to produce performing groups of the highest quality (a performance-oriented goal) or to cultivate individuals to be well informed about music (an informance-oriented goal), perhaps a carefully implemented inclusion of all the standards would best ensure the development of student competence needed to reach either goal.

Maybe your background did not include experiences with improvisation, composition, or with most of the other lesser-explored standards. This is a challenge you should begin to address now. As a budding professional, you should be in the habit of taking stock of what you already know and what you need to learn to be an effective music educator. If, for example, improvisation is a challenge for you, begin to gather your resources and start practicing your craft. If you lack skill or understanding in the other Arts, take a dance class, theater class, or some sort of visual arts class.

When contemplating your role as a future music educator and thinking about your future students and what they will learn in music, we hope you consider that when the tools of all the standards are implemented interdependently, students gain a robust, dynamic, and multifaceted understanding of the music elements and . . . musical independence. Your success with addressing the national standards in your future classroom is dependent upon your understanding of and enthusiasm for the unique way each standard is intended to facilitate musical development in students.

9.2 COMBINING STANDARDS

Think of a particular grade level, teaching area (choral, instrumental, general, academic music class, etc.), and a particular piece of music. Can you envision an activity or project that would address performing and creating music as well as responding to and understanding the music's relationship to the world in which it resides? If so, what would it entail? If not, what are the issues preventing this vision? (see Class Activity 9.2, p. 218)

CLASS ACTIVITIES

Class Activity 9.1: The Music Elements

In small groups, decide on several broad categories under which to organize music elements. Then, independently, think of as many music elements as you can, relative to your group's categories. As you do this individual work, you might think of an element logically fitting two or more categories. Regroup and compare results. As you negotiate a final version that represents your group's consensus, realize your individual result may be different for your group's decision . . . and that is OK.

Class Activity 9.2: Combining Standards

Form small groups. Your instructor will prepare multiple slips of paper, each one listing three different music content standards. A representative from your group will choose one of the slips randomly (out of a hat). Your group's tasks are to decide on a grade level, teaching area (instrumental, choral, general music, academic music class, etc.) and a piece of music, and then design an activity, experience, project, etc. that would effectively address all three standards in combination to help students understand and/ or perform with understanding the music selection. Consider how students would learn about specific music elements in this process and ways you would facilitate musical independence.

INDIVIDUAL ACTIVITY
The KWL Chart

Before starting this chapter, make three columns on a piece of paper. At the top of the left-hand column, write "What I KNOW" and list everything you know about how people learn. At the top of the middle column, write "What I WANT to know" and list everything you would like to know about how people learn. Leave the third column blank. Then, make a copy for yourself and submit a copy (with your name at the top) to your instructor. We will revisit this chart at the end of the chapter.

MAKING LEARNING APPARENT

Susan, a young middle-school choral director, was well into the fall semester with a new crop of choristers. She had recently attended a staff development workshop and decided to try out something she heard in the session. Unlike in the past, when she typically would rehearse up to the very end of every class period, Susan began to take the last three or four minutes and ask the students, "What did you learn today?" On the first day of implementing this tactic the class responded initially with silence; they were not accustomed to thinking about what they were learning. Then, one brave student raised her hand and said in an unsure tone, "We learned a new way to breathe?" Susan immediately walked over and placed a gold star on the top of her choral folio. The student beamed with pride. The next day, she was the first to raise her hand and give an answer. By the fourth day of ending class this way (asking questions and rewarding correct answers with stars), Susan noticed that throughout the class period nearly all the students were taking notes about new ideas they were learning. By the second week, Susan would ask the question most days, but not every day, and continued with this inconsistent frequency for the next several weeks. Well into the second month, every student continued to shoot his or her hand in the air when asked, "What did you learn today?" Susan became completely convinced of the technique's effectiveness when, one day after class, one of the students came up to Susan and exclaimed, "I am amazed at how much I am learning in this class. I'm not learning nearly as much in math or English, but I am learning a *lot* in choir." Susan smiled and assured him, "Oh you are probably learning a lot in those classes, too. You just don't know it yet."

Learning implies change. As Woolfolk (2012) elaborated, "Learning occurs when experience (including practice) causes a relatively permanent change in an individual's knowledge or behavior" (p. 246). In the opening vignette, change occurred both in the students' behavior (taking notes about new ideas, identifying what they were learning) and in their thinking (becoming aware of *what* they were learning, concluding they were learning 'a lot'). Many theories have been developed to explain how people learn. Most of the ones that apply to classroom learning fall into one of two broad 'camps'—**behaviorism** and **cognitivism** (Hodges & Sebald, 2011). According to behaviorists, learning is explained by changes in a person's observable behavior that occur as a result of interaction with his or her environment. Cognitivists, on the other hand, view learning as changes in unobservable internal mental processes (thoughts, memory, feelings, motives, etc.) as a result of acquiring or constructing new knowledge. Table 10.1 is an 'advanced organizer' we will revisit periodically through the chapter to help you learn and remember the ideas being presented.

 With each type of learning, an important related issue is at play: the **motivation** to learn. Motivation involves processes that initiate a behavior, direct that behavior toward a particular goal, and sustain that behavior over time (Stantrock, 2008). All three aspects

TABLE 10.1 Behaviorism and cognitivism.

Behaviorism	Cognitivism
Primary people associated with each approach to learning	
Terms and ideas associated with each approach to learning	
Motivation types associated with behaviorism and cognitivism	

are needed for learning to occur. Take, for example, the prospect of starting a group of beginning instrumentalists. The students likely bring a great deal of genuine excitement to the classroom having received a new, shiny instrument and perhaps one they have always wanted to play. Directing that excitement toward learning specific instrumental skills might prove to be a bit more challenging than arousing their initial interest. Likewise, maintaining that interest over enough time so that proper habits will form and promote improved playing skills can also pose challenges.

You have learned to do a lot of different things over the years. When you do something because the activity brings you pleasure, you are experiencing **intrinsic motivation**. An intrinsically motivated task is enjoyable or worthwhile in and of itself. Conversely, when you perform a task to receive a reward that has little to do with the task itself, the reward serves as **extrinsic motivation**. The best classroom situation is one in which students learn because they are intrinsically motivated to do so. For most behaviors, however, the source of motivation falls somewhere along a continuum of being fully self-determined to being fully determined by others (Woolfolk, 2012). In the next section, we will explore each of the learning theories and discuss ways motivation affects student learning.

BEHAVIORISM

Around the beginning of the twentieth century, psychologists (behaviorists) began to embrace the study of overt behavior as the only evidence of learning; specifically, they began to investigate relationships between observable stimuli and the observable responses that resulted. They worked to establish universal principles that could be applied consistently across all human and animal species. The most entrenched behaviorists regarded the mind as a 'black box' of unknowable activity (Watson, 1925). Anything that could not be observed was dismissed. Two primary approaches to behaviorism are classical conditioning and operant conditioning. Both can play legitimate roles in the music classroom.

Classical conditioning. This type of learning occurs when two stimuli are presented at approximately the same time, become associated, and eventually elicit the same response. By nature, however, the 'learning' involved is involuntary. In the early 1900s, Ivan Pavlov conducted a now-famous experiment in which he successfully trained a dog to salivate at the sound of a bell by pairing an **unconditioned stimulus** (UCS) (meat powder) with a **neutral stimulus** (NS) (bell ringing) till the bell ringing alone eventually elicited the **conditioned response** (CR) (salivation).

Effective teachers employ classical conditioning often in the classroom, particularly as it can be used to establish unconscious habits that facilitate future learning (appropriate classroom procedures, correct physical habits, etc.). Take, for example, teaching beginning instrumental music students to adopt proper playing posture. Once students, learning to play woodwind or brass instruments, are taught two basic types of posture—'playing posture' (sitting at the front edge of the chair, with feet flat on the floor, a 90-degree angle at the knees, an open chest with shoulders down and relaxed, and head about 10 degrees above level) and 'relaxed posture' (same as playing posture, but seated at the back of the chair with the back being supported by the chair back), they are ready for some classical conditioning. Here is the simple key. When students experience playing posture *only* while producing a sound (blowing air through the embouchure), they will begin to unconsciously associate playing posture with producing a sound. In fact, after a few weeks, they will not feel comfortable in any other position except playing posture when producing a sound. The challenge is, during the conditioning period (about two to three weeks), the teacher must not allow any other associations to occur with playing posture except producing a sound (no teacher talk, no last-minute instructions, no reminders, nothing!). The teacher must reserve instruction for when the students are called to relaxed posture. With a few consistently applied pairings of an UCS (playing posture) with an NS (producing sound) the new CR of proper playing posture will be established *as a habit*.

Operant conditioning. Rather than associating stimuli to an unconscious response, a teacher implementing operant conditioning will utilize conscious associations of stimuli with target behaviors to induce or reduce those target behaviors. B. F. Skinner (1938) put forth the idea that behaviors that are reinforced tend to increase in frequency. Furthermore, he purposely used objective terms (e.g. 'reinforcement' instead of 'reward') to avoid inconsistent logic. 'Reward' implies something pleasant or desirable. However, something pleasant to one person may be unpleasant to another.

Skinner used four particular terms to outline most of his ideas: **positive**, **negative**, **reinforcement**, and **punishment**. Positive and negative refer to the act of either presenting/starting a stimulus (positive) or taking away/ending a stimulus (negative). Reinforcement and punishment refer to the effect on the target behavior. Anything that increases or strengthens the target behavior is called reinforcement, while that which reduces or stops the target behavior is labeled punishment. Together these terms can be used to describe four possible outcomes of operant conditioning: positive reinforcement, negative reinforcement, positive punishment, and negative punishment. The key to understanding operant conditioning is in identifying target behaviors and becoming familiar with the effects of various stimuli on those target behaviors. There are three parts to the model: target behavior, stimulus, and modified target behavior (see Figure 10.1).

	Target Behavior	Stimulus	Modified Target Behavior
	Occurs naturally or is the result of a directive or instruction	Something is presented or removed as a consequence of the presentation of the initial target behavior	Target behavior increases or decreases in response to the stimulus
Positive Reinforcement	Students verbalizing what they were learning	**Receives** a gold star	Verbalization of what they are learning **increases**
Negative Reinforcement	Productive classroom rehearsal	Requirement to enter the room in silence is **eliminated**	In-class rehearsal productivity **increases**
Positive Punishment	Stopping while sight reading	**Receives** a 'ribbing' from classmates	Stopping behavior **decreases**
Negative Punishment	Disruptive classroom behavior	Privilege to participate is **removed**	Disruptive classroom behavior **decreases**

FIGURE 10.1 Operant conditioning. This figure presents 'target behavior,' 'stimulus,' and 'modified behavior' as components of operant conditioning that occur across time, and it provides examples for each of the four possible outcomes of operant conditioning.

Positive reinforcement occurs when a stimulus, presented *after* a target behavior is exhibited, serves to increase that behavior (modified target behavior). Let's look to the opening vignette of the chapter for an example. One of the target behaviors described was 'identifying what they were learning.' When a student exhibited that target behavior, Susan presented her with a gold star. In this example, the gold star served as a positive stimulus, *not* because the student 'beamed with pride,' but because the star was being presented rather than being removed. The entire interaction exemplified positive reinforcement because the presentation of stars served to increase the target behavior. *Negative reinforcement* occurs when a stimulus, removed *after* a target behavior is exhibited, serves to increase that behavior. For example, the target behavior may be 'productive in-class rehearsals.' If the requirement to enter the rehearsal space in total silence is eliminated following the days the students do well in class (a negative stimulus because the requirement is being removed), the students will likely increase their productivity during class (reinforcement). *Positive punishment* occurs when a stimulus, presented *after* a target behavior is exhibited, serves to decrease that behavior. If, for example, the target behavior to be reduced is 'stopping while sight reading,' the student who receives a ribbing from his classmates for stopping while sight reading may likely work to reduce his 'stopping' behavior in the effort to avoid peer criticism. **Negative punishment** occurs when a stimulus, removed *after* a target behavior is exhibited, serves to decrease that behavior. After displaying disruptive behavior (the target behavior to be reduced), a student is removed from band class for the day. If removing that student from class successfully serves as negative punishment, that student will behave better in class upon his return.

In addition to the four possible permutations of positive/negative/reinforcement/ punishment, there are a number of principles associated with operant conditioning that are used often in the music classroom. Skinner (1957) found that **reinforcement schedules** play an important role in maintaining learned behaviors over a period of time. When introducing a new behavior, *continuous reinforcement* (reinforcing the new behavior with every occurrence) will result in a rapid change of behavior. However, persistence of that behavior is best accomplished by eventually moving to an intermittent reinforcement schedule that provides a stimulus at random and unpredictable time intervals. **Successive approximation** (or shaping) is another idea associated with behaviorism. When a target skill is too complex to learn in one step, the teacher needs to identify a series of smaller, more manageable approximations beginning with what students know or can do currently, and that incrementally approaches the target skill. This identification process is known as *task analysis*. Each step along the way should be mastered until all the students in the class can perform it before moving onto the next step. Duke (2005) described task analysis and successive approximation for teachers:

> As you are learning to teach, you should practice dividing instructional pathways . . . into the smallest increments imaginable, so that between the first, simplest approximation and the final task, there are many, many intermediate approximations. This is not to say that every one of these approximations will be included in the instructional sequence that is actually performed in the class every day. But it is important that you, the teacher, understand that the path between what students are able to do now and what you intend for them to do (the target goal) may involve any number of incremental approximations . . . How much more difficult or complicated or strenuous should the next performance task be? The answer: no more difficult than the least able students in the class can perform successfully within one to three attempts.
>
> (pp. 99–100)

Behavioral approaches to motivation. Because classical conditioning involves the formation of unconscious associations, it plays little if any role in our discussion of motivation (Ormrod, 2004). Operant conditioning, on the other hand, is the essence of behavioral motivation, particularly with its emphasis on external stimuli as components used to initiate, direct, and sustain desired behaviors. By definition, behavioral approaches to motivation are extrinsic in nature. Consequently, behavioral motivation should be thought of as a means to an end, but not as the end itself. Behavioral motivation can be used effectively to get students 'moving in the right direction.' However, it should not be the only way to explain why students do what they do.

Behaviorism in the music classroom. Students are continually affected by elements in their environment that generate automatic responses and increase or reduce particular behaviors. As a teacher, you must create and maintain conditions that consistently support the behaviors you want your students to acquire (Madsen, Greer, & Madsen, 1975; Madsen & Madsen, 1998; Madsen & Yarbrough, 1985). Behavioral learning principles are most often applied in the music classroom to support learning in two particular areas: the teaching of psychomotor skills associated with singing or playing instruments, and establishing and maintaining classroom-operating procedures. Psychomotor skills such as breathing, posture, hand position, embouchure, etc. represent physical proficiencies that you want your students to adopt *as unconscious habits*. Consequently, if you successfully apply classical conditioning principles so that your students can perform these skills accurately, they will be able to direct their attention to more complex aspects of music making. Similarly, classroom-operating procedures can be developed and maintained through a carefully applied series of operant conditioning techniques. If you are consistent with applying reinforcement schedules appropriate to the task and student experience level, you can establish a healthy supportive environment for student learning.

144 SOCIAL PLACE
Desirable Behaviors in the Music Classroom

Think of a particular music learning setting (grade level and area—instrumental, choral, general, etc.). Using 144 characters or fewer, list as many automatic physical responses as possible that you think would be helpful to establish in that particular music learning setting. Now, considering the same setting, start a second list. This one should be of the desirable behaviors you might get your students to adopt through systematic 'reinforcement.'

It is not a goal of this book for you to become immediately proficient at applying behavioral conditioning techniques in your teaching. However, you should be aware that these conscious and unconscious exchanges occur constantly during your interactions with students. As you take time to study the concepts mentioned here, in addition to more complex conditioning ideas you will undoubtedly encounter in future coursework, you should begin to look for ways that effective teachers use these ideas to affect student learning in their music classrooms. Table 10.2 is an expanded version of Table 10.1 we presented at the beginning of the chapter. It includes many of the ideas we discussed about behaviorism up to this point. See if you can use Table 10.2 to help you remember the main ideas about behaviorism.

Training automatic responses and shaping desirable behaviors can be effective ways to get students to adopt appropriate classroom routines and develop skill sets needed to engage in music activities successfully. However, there are limits to what behaviorism can explain about learning. A number of researchers have suggested behaviorism most

TABLE 10.2 Behaviorism: people, ideas, and motivation types.

Behaviorism		Cognitivism
Classical conditioning	Operant conditioning	
Uses unconscious responses to shape behavior effective for setting habits	Uses conscious associations of stimuli to increase or reduce target behaviors	
Primary people associated with each approach to learning		
Ivan Pavlov	B. F. Skinner	
Terms and ideas associated with each approach to learning		
Unconditioned stimulus (UCS)	Positive/negative	
Neutral stimulus (NS)	Reinforcement/ punishment	
Conditioned response (CR)	Schedules of reinforcement	
	Continuous/intermittent	
	Successive approximation	
Motivation types associated with behaviorism and cognitivism		
Extrinsic reward versus intrinsic reward		

appropriately explains the *performance* of learned behaviors rather than learning itself (Herrnstein, 1977; Ormrod, 2004; Schwartz & Reisberg, 1991). By the 1960s, behaviorism was being challenged as simply inadequate to explain the totality of learning (Tomic, 1993). Behaviorist principles could not explain instances of obvious complex learning. Language learning, for example, was recognized to occur at a rate in young children that could not be explained by behavioral principles alone. The time had come for psychologists to peer into the black box.

COGNITIVISM

From the cognitivists' perspective, learning is a change in *thinking* rather than in behavior. Learning is a result of internal brain functions such as perception, memory, information processing, and transfer. Effective teachers structure sequences of experiences and learning activities so they align with how the brain takes in and processes information. Information processing, an early cognitive theory, was developed to explain how the brain remembers content.

Information processing. Human beings take in information through the five senses and hold those perceptions in the **sensory register** (SR) for mere seconds before that information is either ignored or processed via working memory, otherwise known as **short-term memory** (STM). Information that is successfully processed by short-term memory is stored in **long-term memory** (LTM) (see Figure 10.2).

As teachers, we want the content we teach to be stored eventually in our students' long-term memory. Let's take a look at each of these three types of brain processes. We are constantly being bombarded by the sights, sounds, smells, tastes, and textures that surround us in our daily lives. Although there are not many implications for the classroom, the SR is the mechanism that allows the brain to experience these phenomena so that initial processing can occur (Bruning, Schraw, & Ronning, 1999). The amount of information

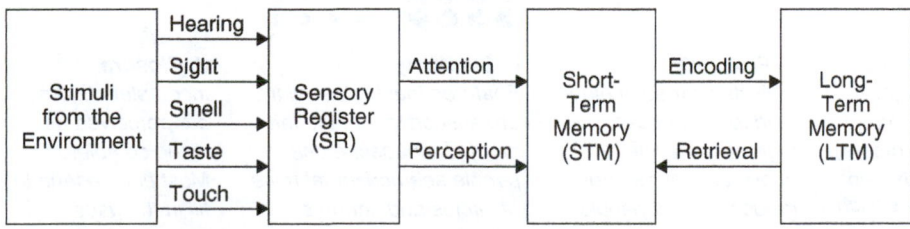

FIGURE 10.2 Information-processing model.
Source: Atkinson & Shiffrin, 1968.

entering the SR is vast, too vast to attend to everything. Therefore, we pay attention to particular stimuli and ignore most of the others. Attention is a 'weeding out' process that our brain conducts as part of the short-term memory process. Gestalt psychologists have developed labels to explain how the brain selects information based on patterns. Some of those labels include: figure-ground, proximity, similarity, and closure (see Figure 10.3).

Attention, however, has a limited capacity. Short-term memory typically has a capacity of seven units of information (+ or −2) and lasts between 3 and 18 seconds (Miller, 1956; Peterson & Peterson, 1959). Consequently, various encoding techniques can help move information from short-term to long-term memory, including *maintenance rehearsal* (repeating the information over and over—e.g., memorizing music phrases), *chunking* (grouping sets of information units together—e.g. linking several smaller musical phrases together to memorize long melodies), and *elaborative rehearsal* (associating new information with something already in long-term memory—e.g. associating the lyrics of a new song to words students commonly know already). Another example of STM's limited capacity is that you can attend to only one complex source of information at a time (Ormrod, 2004). Take the figure-ground diagram in Figure 10.3, for example. When attention is on the vase, it is difficult to simultaneously see the two faces, and vice versa. Teachers who are aware of these limitations will deliberately use their resources to draw students' attention to the ideas deemed most important. Colorful wall displays, purposeful seating arrangements, and even dressing up like as Mozart on a day you intend to explore his music are all ways to direct your students' attention and make a memorable first impression. Likely there were instances in your past that have had a lasting impact on you such that you remember details of those events to this day. These instances are excellent examples of long-term memory (LTM) and its seemingly unlimited capacity to store thoughts and memories.

   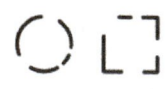

a. Figure-ground
Given a visual image, most people focus on a dominant shape (figure), Faces or vase—what do you see first? Now switch.

b. Proximity
Objects near each other tend to be grouped together. The lines above appear as three groups to most people.

c. Similarity
Features that look similar are associated. In the left group of shapes, most people see horizontal rows of circles and squares.

d. Closure
Incomplete figures are perceived as being complete. Most people tend to fill in the gaps.

FIGURE 10.3 Gestalt principles of perceptual organization: figure-ground, proximity, similarity, and closure. Gestalt principles explain how our minds are drawn to particular patterns of association.

An aspect of LTM, important to the classroom, is **semantic memory**, or memory for meaning, and it is often stored via **schemas**. Schemas are structures used to organize vast amount of closely connected ideas related to a specific object or event (Dansereau, 1995; Derry, 1996). For example, one's schema for 'Beethoven's 9th Symphony' might include ideas presented in Figure 10.4.

According to Ormrod (2004), "We learn information meaningfully by storing it in long-term memory in association with similar, related pieces of information. Meaningful learning seems to facilitate both storage and retrieval: The information is stored more quickly and remembered more easily" (p. 222).

Concept learning. According to Woolfolk (2012), "A concept is a category used to group similar events, ideas, objects, or people" (p. 299). When working with concepts, it is important to identify defining attributes, comparing what it *is* with what it *is not*. When we refer to a particular music concept such as *scale*, we mean the sequential pattern of ascending and descending pitches that typically utilizes half- and whole-steps and directs our ears to a home tone or 'resting tone.' We do not mean the instrument used to measure one's weight or one of the many small plate-like structures that cover fish. Patterns of ascending and descending pitches outline a tonality that may be based in major, minor, or in any of the other modes, but they all can be recognized as scales. If you explore further attributes of scales, you will likely recognize feelings of tension and release associated with particular scale degrees—consider, for example, the tension associated with the 7th degree of a major scale followed by the resolution felt when finally reaching the tonic.

Back in Chapter 9 we discussed music elements as being the fundamental building blocks of music. Each music element can be considered a concept. However, music concepts involve more than cognitive attributes; they also involve expressive attributes

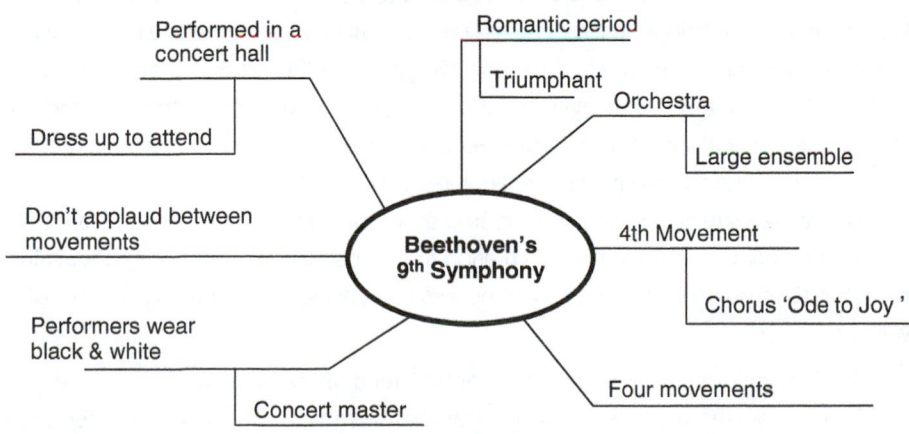

FIGURE 10.4 One possible schema for Beethoven's 9th Symphony.

that correspond to physical feelings. For example, cognitive attributes of 'steady beat' can be represented easily by the sound of a mechanical metronome, which involves an audible pulse presented at a regular interval. Yet, we all know that the metronome does not represent fully the feeling of steady beat, particularly at various tempos. A more complete version of the concept would involve expressive qualities of 'space' and 'weight' in addition to the fundamental aspect of 'time.' Remember the conducting activity we presented in Chapter 9? Music concepts include the combination of cognitive attributes and expressive attributes. To ensure your students gain a firm grasp of each music concept, you will need to ensure both types of attributes are experienced.

A schema, as we learned from information processing, is a way the brain stores information in long-term memory (LTM). Previously established schemas influence how we perceive and remember new situations and concepts. They also affect what we notice in those new situations and concepts. When teaching elementary music, for example, some students may have previously understood the concept of 'high' and 'low' to mean loud and soft (think of the expression 'Turn *down* the radio'). They will likely need extra attention to help them associate high and low with the direction of pitch rather than dynamics.

Concepts can be organized much like schemas through the use of concept maps, which are graphic tools for showing relationships among concepts (see the Introduction). As with schemas, you must ensure that previous misconceptions are corrected so that students gain an accurate and efficient understanding of what is being learned. Teachers operating from a concept learning perspective strive to organize their instruction so that concepts being learned are meaningful, as opposed to learning that primarily includes the rote memorization of facts. Structure and sequencing are key strategies used to ensure that the right connections are made most easily. Ausubel (1960), a champion of such structure, proposed the **advance organizer** (a general overview of the ideas to be learned and their relationships to previously learned material) as a strategy to help orient students' attention at the outset of a lesson. One version of an advanced organizer is the KWL chart you started at the beginning of this chapter and will complete at the end. By starting a lesson with an advanced organizer and revisiting it at the end, teachers provide support and context for the new information being presented.

Ultimately, learning should be structured and sequenced so that students are able to transfer what was learned in one situation to other situations. This is called **learning transfer**. Ormrod (2004) offered six principles influencing the probability that transfer will occur.

1. Meaningful learning promotes better transfer than rote learning.
2. The more thoroughly something is learned, the more likely it is to be transferred to a new situation.

3. The more similar two situations are, the more likely that what is learned in one situation will be applied to the other.
4. Principles are more easily transferred than discrete facts.
5. Numerous and varied examples and opportunities for practice increase the extent to which information and skills will be applied in new situations.
6. The probability of transfer decreases as the time interval between the original task and the transfer task increases.

(pp. 367–369)

10.1 TEACHING FOR TRANSFER

How might you use each of these six principles in a music-learning setting? (see Class Activity 10.1, p. 245)

Social cognitivism. While cognitivism involves taking in information and assigning meaning to that information via schemas and concepts, social cognitivism involves learning and forming concepts by *observing others*. Let's take a look back at the opening vignette. Operant conditioning occurred as Susan reinforced the target behavior of 'identifying what they were learning' by presenting the student with a gold star, which increased the target behavior in that student. It is likely that even by the fourth day, most members of the entire class were not rewarded individually, but by that time nearly everyone was taking notes throughout class period. They saw the reinforcement Susan gave to a few of the students and adopted the target behavior. The students who were not directly reinforced actually learned from watching the reinforcement their classmates experienced. This is a classic example of social cognitivism. Albert Bandura (1986), who is most closely associated with social cognitivism, also proposed that, although people may acquire a new skill through observation, they will not perform that skill until there is incentive to do so. Remember from the vignette that *nearly every* student took notes by the fourth day. We speculate that all students learned what to do, but a few did not have the motivation to act on that learning quite yet. Eventually Susan was able to get every student involved.

Cognitivism in the music classroom. Although behaviorism works well when the objectives are simple and straightforward, cognitivism can explain some of the more hidden processes of music learning, including memory, concept learning, and idea organization. In the music classroom, concept formation occurs primarily as your students experience and work with the music elements. For example, helping your students memorize fingerings is one way to get them to learn scales. However, if you help them to develop an aural concept of a major scale (the stepwise progression of pitches that includes half-steps between the third and fourth scale degrees and between the seventh and eighth scale degrees), you will be giving them a conceptual framework they can transfer to any starting pitch. When teaching psychomotor skills, like a proper bow hold, you can accelerate students' learning by providing accurate aural and/or visual models for what you want them to learn. Sometimes, all it takes for a young wind player to properly conceptualize the right combination of wind speed and embouchure firmness is to hear the teacher actually play a short passage using a good strong supported tone quality. When you can get a few students to perform accurate aural and visual models, all the better, because when students see peers succeeding at a skill that had been previously demonstrated only by the teacher, they tend to believe more strongly in their own capabilities to succeed at the skill (Schunk, 1987).

Cognitive approaches to motivation. Like cognitive learning theories, cognitive approaches to motivation explore changes in thinking rather than changes in behaviors. Furthermore, cognitivists believe behavioral changes are not due to external events, but rather to *interpretations* of those events. Cognitive theories emphasize intrinsic motivation as people become interested in solving problems that are personally relevant. One type of problem that nearly all people find personally relevant is determining explanations for their successes and failures. A theory that helps explain this issue is attribution theory.

Attribution theory. When faced with a situation that produces success or failure, a common response is to ask "Why?" This makes sense because you want to reproduce successful events and avoid future failures. Interestingly, how students answer the question (what they attribute their success or failure to) can affect how they behave in the future when facing similar circumstances. Weiner (1979, 1986) developed a model that characterizes attributed causes for successes or failures in terms of three dimensions: (a) **locus** (location of the cause being either internal or external), (b) **stability** (whether the cause stays the same or changes over time), and (c) **controllability** (whether the person can control the cause) (see Figure 10.5).

Stability	Locus			
	Internal		**External**	
	Controllable	**Uncontrollable**	**Controllable**	**Uncontrollable**
Stable	Long-term effort	Aptitude/ ability	*	Ease/difficulty of the task
Unstable	Skills/knowledge Temporary or situational effort for the task	Health on day of the task Mood	*	Chance

FIGURE 10.5 Achievement attributions by locus, stability, and controllability dimensions.

Source: Weiner, 1986.

Note: *External-controllable examples are omitted because, from the perspective of the individual, external causes are uncontrollable by definition (Bierhoff, 1989; Stipek, 1998).

Students who have the best chance for future success are those who attribute their current successes to internal-stable-controllable factors such as consistent effort, and attribute their failures to internal-unstable-controllable factors such as lack of effort leading up to the task (Pomerantz & Saxon, 2001; Weiner, 1984). Students who attribute their failures to internal-stable-uncontrollable causes (i.e. lack of ability) tend to give up easily. At worst, they can devolve into a state of *learned helplessness*. This happens when students, trying to overcome unproductive attributions, continue to fail no matter their efforts. They learn they cannot control the outcome, so why try?

Goal orientation and motivation. Another way to examine how motivation is affected by students' reactions to their successes and failures is to look at the way they approach goals. Goals increase motivation if they are specific, moderately challenging, and able to be reached within a reasonable amount of time (Pintrich & Schunk, 2002). However, students do not always approach goals similarly. Two primary orientations that dictate how goals are approached are *mastery orientation* and *performance orientation*. Students with a **mastery orientation** are concerned with mastering a task rather than how their performance measures up to that of others. They view making mistakes or 'failures' as acceptable aspects of the learning process. Because their goal is to learn, they tend to seek challenges and persist when they encounter difficulties. The often become completely absorbed by the task and lose track of time, similar to Csikszentmihalyi's (1990) flow experience. They are more likely to ask for help when needed, look for solution-oriented strategies, and remember what worked for them in the past (Butler & Neuman, 1995; Young, 1997). Those with a mastery goal orientation attribute their level of achievement to effort and tend to exhibit the attributional combination of internal-unstable-controllable.

On the other hand, students with a **performance orientation** are most concerned with how they perform and how that looks to others, rather than with the process of learning. They tend to be focused on winning and outperforming others. Consequently they adopt strategies that may unwittingly hinder learning (choosing to learn the easiest solos in order to ensure 'success') so they look good (Young, 1997). They are less willing to take risks and to try new tasks because they want to avoid the possibility of failure (Pintrich & Schunk, 2002). When faced with the impossibility of a successful outcome, they may choose defensive and failure-avoiding strategies such as pretending not to care or making a big deal out of 'not really trying' (Jagacinski & Nicholls, 1987; Pintrich & Schunk, 2002). Because performance-oriented students attribute their outcomes to ability rather than to effort, repeated failures result in a lowered sense of self-efficacy and can ultimately lead to a state of learned helplessness (Stipek, 2002).

Fortunately, new causal attributions and goal orientations can be taught or shaped through various instructional approaches (Raffini, 1988; Spaulding, 1992). For any

TABLE 10.3 Behaviorism and cognitivism: people, ideas, and motivation types (partial).

Behaviorism		Cognitivism	
Classical conditioning	**Operant conditioning**	**Information processing**	**Social cognitivism**
Uses unconscious responses to shape behavior effective for setting habits	Uses conscious associations of stimuli to increase or reduce target behaviors	Explains ways that information is processed through attention memory and thinking	Explains ways information is learned by observing others
Primary people associated with each approach to learning			
Ivan Pavlov	B. F. Skinner	Atkinson & Shiffrin	Albert Bandura
Terms and ideas associated with each approach to learning			
Unconditioned stimulus (UCS)	Positive/negative	Sensory register (SR)	Social = others serving as models/teachers
Neutral stimulus (NS)	Reinforcement/ punishment	Short-term memory (STM)	Cognitivism = thinking, expecting, anticipating, self-regulating, making comparisons and judgments.
Conditioned response (CR)	Schedules of reinforcement	Long-term memory (LTM)	
	Continuous/ intermittent	Chunking	
	Successive approximation	Maintenance rehearsal	
		Elaborative rehearsal	
		Schemas	
		Concept learning	
		Advanced organizer	
		Learning transfer	
Motivation types associated with behaviorism and cognitivism			
Extrinsic reward versus intrinsic reward		Attribution theory: locus, stability, controllability	
		Goal orientation: mastery orientation vs. performance orientation	

student with a non-productive attribution schema, the goal is to help him or her see failure as emanating from internal, unstable, and controllable causes. Approaches such as modeling, providing information about strategies and practice, and feedback can all be used to help a student to make the distinction between ability and effort (Stantrock, 2008). Rather than provide models of success with ease, Brophy (2004) recommends exposing students to models who depict struggle to overcome mistakes before finally succeeding.

It is time to revisit our advanced organizer. Table 10.3 includes all the information presented in Tables 10.1 and 10.2, and adds information we explored regarding information processing and social cognitivism. We also added information related to cognitive motivation. Before moving on, take a few moments to ensure you have a good grasp of the ideas and are familiar with the people listed in Table 10.3.

Up to this point, we have described cognitivist approaches to learning that are based on the **expository model**, an approach where the teacher is responsible for organizing the presentation and sequence of events so students receive the most useful content in the most expedient manner. A more current contrasting approach involves **discovery learning**, during which students explore their learning environments to discover general rules, concepts, and principles, rather than being passive recipients of the teacher's presentation (Schunk, 2008). In this approach, students construct meaning of new situations based on their previous experiences. This approach falls under a broader term—constructivism.

CONSTRUCTIVISM

Constructivism is a form of cognitivism because it defines learning as a change in *thinking*. However, unlike the other cognitive learning models, students learn by constructing their own perspective on the world based on prior knowledge and through new encounters with content, peers, and significant others. Constructivists would argue that learning does not actually take place until *the student* makes meaning of the content. Remember the Duke (2005) quote at the end of Chapter 7? Students will take greater ownership of learning through constructing their own meanings, leading to a stronger self-perception of competence and a deeper engagement with that learning, than they do with a direct instruction approach (Oldfather, 1999). Yet, a constructivist approach is not appropriate in all situations, particularly when students bring an insufficient background needed to contextualize new experiences. For example, when teaching a particular new psychomotor skill needed to play a musical instrument (embouchure, hand position, etc.), a constructivist approach would be terribly inefficient. For other goals, however, a constructivist approach is ideal. In the following pages we will provide some principles to help you consider student learning from a constructivist perspective.

Cognitive constructivism. Swiss psychologist Jean Piaget (1954) proposed that learners construct their understanding of the world through schemas and that these schemas are constantly changing. Two consistent functions that allow for such change are *assimilation* and *accommodation*. With **assimilation**, learners adjust their conception of the environment to fit their current schemas. Let's go back to our concept of a 'scale' for an example. When first learning scales, most likely students will encounter them in the major tonality. Therefore a child's schema for 'scale' likely includes: (a) ascending and descending patterns, (b) a feeling of a 'resting tone,' and (c) half steps that occur between the and scale degrees and again between the and scale degrees. When students learn a new major scale, their schema can remain intact while applying it to a new starting note and perhaps some new note names and fingerings. When learning new major scales, students change their environment (note names and fingerings) to match their current schema. Incidentally, this is a great way for children to experiment and learn new notes and fingerings, of course with the guidance of fingering charts. **Accommodation** occurs when children are faced with adjusting their schemas to make sense of their environment. When you introduce their first *minor* scale, students are faced with adjusting their schema of a 'scale' because the half steps are no longer in the same places as they were with major scales. Once they have adjusted their schema for 'scale' to include both major *and* minor scales, they have increased their understanding of scales. The act of going back and forth between assimilating content to match schemas and adjusting schemas to match new content is motivated by the need for *equilibrium*. The environment needs to make sense to the learner. When the environment does not make sense, learners adjust their thinking in order to resolve the internal conflict. They *construct* their understanding based on interactions between their schemas and the environment. The constant search for equilibrium while surrounded by a dynamic environment is what promotes change in thinking, thus learning.

Social constructivism. Cognitive constructivism explains learning from a perspective within the learner. Social constructivism, on the other hand, takes place in and among groups of people. Once again, changes in schemas are the mechanisms that promote meaning making. However, instead of the internal functions, social constructivists view *co-construction* of cultural knowledge with others as the primary way people learn. Leo (Lev) Vygotsky, the Russian-born psychologist most closely associated with social constructivism, believed that "human activities take place in cultural settings and that they cannot be understood apart from these settings . . . our specific mental structures and processes can be traced back to our interactions with others" (Woolfolk, 2012, p. 55). Specifically, learning is thought to take place as a two-step process. According to Vygotsky (1978), "every function in a child's cultural development appears twice: first, on the social level and later on the individual level; first between people (interpsychological) and then inside the child (intrapsychological)" (p. 57).

In the first of the two-step process, the learner gains skill or knowledge from interacting with others who are more proficient at the task or idea before being able to internalize the content and operate independently. This first step encompasses the range of tasks that cannot be performed independently, but can be performed with help. Vygotsky labeled this range the **zone of proximal development** (ZPD). Further, he believed children do not learn from performing tasks they can do already (below the ZPD). In fact, if students are not challenged beyond their comfort zone regularly, they can become disinterested and bored. Likewise, he believed children do not learn from being challenged consistently beyond their capability to perform successfully (beyond the ZPD). At this end, students can become confused and frustrated. Rather, Vygotsky believed learning is maximized when working within the ZPD and that the 'zone' creates the optimal learning environment (Murray & Arroyo, 2002). The level of engagement the learner experiences while in the ZPD can be compared to the concept of *flow* (Csikszentmihalyi, 1990), during which a person is completely occupied with the task at hand. Some characteristics of what it is like to be in the flow experience include: (a) being absorbed by the task, (b) having a distorted sense of, or losing track of, time, (c) losing one's sense of self-consciousness, and (d) relinquishing control of the situation (Chen, Wigand, & Nilan, 1999).

The type and level of support students require while working in the ZPD will vary, depending upon the learning that is occurring at any given point. **Scaffolding** is the process of providing and adjusting support as needed throughout the learning process. For example, students will likely benefit from direct instruction when first working on a new task. With increased experience, however, their skills and understandings improve and they require increasingly less help. Scaffolding requires teachers to be sensitive to students' evolving progress and to provide whatever support is needed to maintain optimal and appropriate challenges. When a teacher (or another more knowledgeable other) successfully serves to stretch and support a novice's understanding of a culture's skills, that relationship is known as a **cognitive apprenticeship** (Rogoff, 1990). Some literature refers to the two parties involved as 'teacher and student,' 'expert and novice,' or 'tutor and learner.' These labels are not tied to age, but rather to experience (Wiggins, 2001). Remember the vignette in Chapter 8 of the beginning clarinetist who was also an expert roller-skater and helped his music teacher learn to skate?

Scaffolding also can occur naturally as groups of people gather to engage in a common interest, forming **communities of practice** (Lave, 1991; Lave & Wenger, 1991). For example, when a group of amateur musicians meet for weekly 'jam sessions,' they likely are not all at the same skill level. Less skilled individuals will participate to the degree they are able, but often as 'periphery members,' while the more skilled members take on more substantive roles. As the once-novice participants gain experience, they will naturally take on increasingly more and varied musical roles and rely less on 'more knowledgeable others.' Often, the kind of learning that takes place in communities of practice is inherent to and socially embedded within the specific setting; this is known as **situated learning**. Take the jam session, for example. Participants are improving their musicianship skills regarding a particular practice that may not be easily transferrable to all music settings. If the group pursues Bluegrass, for example, they likely would not be improving their notational reading skills because that culture values 'playing by ear' more so than reading notation. Further, the instruments involved would probably include guitar, banjo, and mandolin, but not trumpet, saxophone, or bassoon.

Situated learning manifests in more ways than just learning content. Often, broad-based enculturation occurs when norms are adopted regarding behaviors, vocabulary, beliefs, attitudes, and values of a particular 'community.' As participants take on more substantial roles within the group their identity with that group strengthens. It is the need to preserve one's identity with a group that provides the motivation associated with learning content and learning group norms and values (Lave & Wenger, 1991). The community might be band, orchestra, or choir members; it could be street gang members or soccer players—any group that has specific ways of thinking and acting can become a community of learners in a situated learning context (Woolfolk, 2012).

Constructivism in the music classroom. Although students are constantly constructing meaning from their environment, music classrooms in which constructivist approaches are implemented will require the teacher to move away from the pervasive model of teacher-directed instruction and more toward that of facilitator and guide (Wiggins, 2001). In large-group settings, the teacher might adjust his or her role to allow for greater student decision-making than exists in most traditional settings. These enhanced student responsibilities could include selecting concert literature, providing feedback to the ensemble, and creating rehearsal objectives for subsequent rehearsals (Scruggs, 2009). Initiating such new roles will require attention to the degree of needed scaffolding. For example, the process for selecting concert literature might begin with the teacher providing a set of seven to ten appropriate pieces from which the students could select five. With subsequent experiences in choosing literature, justifying their choices, and consulting various resources for guidance (including the teacher), students would gain increasingly greater competence regarding characteristics that make particular pieces more and less 'appropriate.' This growing knowledge base would allow students to take on increasingly greater responsibility in choosing literature for the group.

Small-group work may involve providing a specific musical problem (e.g. compose a 16-measure piece for four voices) with defined parameters and the opportunity for groups of students to solve the problem. Each group would likely produce a unique product. The act of thinking through their resources, negotiating possible ways to utilize various music elements, and reaching consensus would likely bring the students to a greater understanding of and confidence with the composition process. Lucy Green's 'Musical Futures' project is a wonderful example of type of situated learning that occurs in a community of practice.

Common elements among constructivist perspectives. Woolfolk (2012) explored several constructivist approaches and found substantive differences among them. However, she also identified five key ideas that seem to be common among most constructivist approaches.

Complex learning environments and authentic tasks. Students should be given tasks that deal with 'messy,' ill-structured, real-world problems. The world beyond school rarely offers problems that can be solved with simple, easy, and straightforward answers. Rather, solutions are often complex, multidimensional, and often lead to more problems to be solved. If students never encounter such complexity in the controlled environment of school, they will likely be ill prepared to do so once they leave school. However, this idea needs to be balanced with appropriate scaffolding. The degree of 'messiness' needs to be appropriate to the students' level of experience. Music composition projects, for example, should begin with an appropriate number of parameters to ensure initial success. Subsequent projects can require increasing more decision-making on the part of students, posing issues of increasingly greater authenticity.

Social negotiation. Constructivists believe that increased mental processes develop through social negotiation; therefore students should have multiple opportunities to collaborate. Furthermore, working effectively and respectfully with others, making necessary compromises to accomplish a common goal, sharing responsibility for collaborative work, and valuing the individual contributions made by each team member are all elements of the 21st Century Skills framework (Partnership for 21st Century Skills, n.d.).

Multiple perspectives and representations of content. Students should experience multiple representations of the content using various strategies, examples, and analogies. When students experience content through many varied permutations, they acquire a whole, accurate, and complete conception of the material. This is similar to Bruner's (1966) idea of the **spiral curriculum** in which students are introduced to ideas first in their simplest forms, and then they revisit those ideas exploring content with increasingly more complexity at higher levels of difficulty and in greater depth. The National Standards for Arts Education are organized such that students experience simple versions of content standards in the lower grades, and then revisit those standards at each subsequent grade level with increasingly greater complexity and depth (Consortium of National Arts Education Associations, 1994). We also do this by utilizing various ways for students to interact with music (singing, playing instruments, creating, listening, dancing, etc.). In fact, this chapter may be your first exposure to many of the concepts and ideas being presented. In the spirit of the 'spiral curriculum,' we are presenting these concepts and ideas with the assumption you will encounter them repeatedly in more complex ways in future coursework and see them played out in your future field experiences.

Understanding the knowledge and construction process. Constructivists believe students should be aware of their own role in constructing knowledge (Cunningham, 1992). This is a form of **metacognition** (thinking about how one thinks). Because each student constructs his or her schemas and consequently reaches uniquely personal conclusions, each student should be aware of how those schemas are being influenced. Woolfolk (2012) stressed the importance of this process. "Students [should be] aware of the influences that shape their thinking; [so] they will be more able to choose, develop, and defend positions in a self-critical way while respecting the positions of others" (p. 365). In music, this can be accomplished with regular wrap-up discussions at the end of lessons about what was learned and how it was learned (see the vignette at the start of this chapter).

Student-centered instruction. Again, because students ultimately construct their own schemas, learning will be most meaningful when instruction is offered in ways that are sensitive to the students' interests, educational needs, and lives in general (McCombs & Whisler, 1997). According to Brown (2008):

> . . . student-centered instruction is when the planning, teaching, and assessment revolve around the needs and abilities of the students. The teacher *shares* control of the classroom . . . This does not mean that the students are in control of the classroom, but rather that they have some influence in the decisions that are being made about their learning.
>
> (pp. 30–31)

In music, teachers can acknowledge and facilitate students' schema formations in a number of ways. In the large ensemble settings, for example, teachers can pose questions that require students to analyze form, evaluate performance quality, or make decisions regarding expressiveness. It is important that "the teacher seldom gives out an explanation or the answer, at least not right away" (Brown, 1997, p. 33). Another form of student-centered instruction is peer-to-peer teaching. For example, pairing more competent musicians with less competent musicians to work on a specific musical passage will address both students' learning processes. The less competent learner will receive instruction from a peer who has likely experienced similar challenges in the recent past; thus the less competent learner will learn strategies that likely 'fit' his current schema. The more experienced learner will solidify his understanding because one learns content best when placed in a position of teaching it to others.

BEING 'SMART, SAVVY, AND SENSITIVE'

Although each theory has a place in the music-learning process, no one single theory can explain all of learning. When applying learning theories to various learning settings, Isbell (2012) advised music teachers to be "smart—understanding the nuances of various theories of learning, savvy—understanding their own learning style and how that may affect teaching effectiveness, and sensitive—understanding that teaching is situated in particular contexts" (p. 19). Being 'smart' not only means understanding the various theories, but also understanding that each theory (or combination of theories) is most appropriate to some situations, but not others. Various music-learning objectives (e.g. playing instruments, memorizing music, creating group compositions) involve unique types of learning. In addition to understanding her own learning style, the 'savvy' teacher will proactively develop and implement a plan to "expand out of [her] comfort zone to reach more students in different ways" (Isbell, 2012, p. 22). Likewise, the 'sensitive' teacher will be aware of how students are different from one another or how they may change with time and experience, and be quick to reframe her teaching approach to match the most current teaching/learning environment.

SELF-REGULATED LEARNING

In many ways, self-regulated learners represent the best of what we want our students to become, because they take charge of their learning, taking into account a sense of self-awareness such that they capitalize on their strengths and minimize their liabilities. They know what they want to accomplish when they read, study, or approach a task and typically tie these goals to longer-term aspirations. They plan their work, setting deadlines to ensure the work is accomplished with priority. Because they engage in work that is important to them, they are intrinsically motivated most of the time. However, they are able to recognize instances when they need to apply behavioral strategies to accomplish particular tasks ("I'll reward myself with some chocolate cake once I finish this paper draft"). That same self-discipline is applied when faced with distractions; they tend to establish work habits to avoid potential interruptions or other elements that can sabotage one's efforts (feeling anxious or becoming drowsy). They are selective about applying various learning strategies to particular situations, for example, knowing when either simple memorization or deep learning is most appropriate for a given situation. They monitor their progress to ensure they are making headway toward their goals or whether they are using the most effective strategy to achieve those goals, and they do not hesitate to switch strategies or adjust goals when considering a larger perspective.

As you may have guessed, self-regulated learning is rare in today's schools, perhaps in part because traditional instructional strategies do little to promote it deliberately. Although self-regulated learning likely develops from engaging in independent self-directed learning activities, it also can be facilitated in socially regulated environments like communities of practice. At first, more competent others (parents, teachers, peers with expertise) might help new learners by making apparent, through instruction or modeling, some of the hallmarks of self-regulation by setting goals, keeping attention focused on the task, suggesting a variety of learning strategies, monitoring progress, etc. Similar to moving from the periphery to the core of a learning community, students take increasingly greater responsibility for self-regulated learning processes. You likely know by now, our wish is for you to adopt the characteristics that describe the self-regulated learner so your students will do the same. Below we will revisit the KWL chart from the start of the chapter in the effort to support your developing habits of self-regulated learning.

INDIVIDUAL ACTIVITY
The KWL Chart REVISITED

Now, as you are finishing this chapter, bring out the chart you started at the beginning. At the top of the right-hand column, write, "What I have LEARNED" and list all you have learned from reading this chapter and engaging in the associated activities.

By completing the first column, you activated your prior knowledge about the topic 'how students learn.' The information in the second column allowed you to have some input

TABLE 10.4 Behaviorism and cognitivism: people, ideas, and motivation types (complete).

Behaviorism		Cognitivism			
Classical conditioning	Operant conditioning	Information processing	Social cognitivism	Cognitive constructivism	Social constructivism
Uses unconscious responses to shape behavior effective for setting habits	Uses conscious associations of stimuli to increase or reduce target behaviors	Explains ways that information is processed through attention memory and thinking	Explains ways information is learned by observing others	Explains how learners construct their understanding of the world through ever-changing schemas	Explains how learners co-construct meaning through collaborations
Primary people associated with each approach to learning					
Ivan Pavlov	B.F. Skinner	Atkinson & Shiffrin	Albert Bandura	Jean Piaget	Lev Vygotsky
Terms and ideas associated with each approach to learning					
Unconditioned stimulus (UCS)	Positive/ negative	Sensory register (SR)	Social = others serving as models/ teachers	Assimilation	Zone of proximal development
Neutral stimulus (NS)	Reinforcement/ punishment	Short-term memory (STM)	Cognitivism = thinking, expecting, anticipating, self-regulating, making comparisons and judgments	Accommodation	Flow
Conditioned response (CR)	Schedules of reinforcement	Long-term memory (LTM)		Equilibrium	Scaffolding
	Continuous/ intermittent	Chunking			Cognitive apprenticeship
	Successive approximation	Maintenance rehearsal			Communities of practice
		Elaborative rehearsal			
		Schemas			
		Concept learning			
		Advanced organizer			
		Learning transfer			
Motivation types associated with behaviorism and cognitivism					
Extrinsic reward versus intrinsic reward		Attribution theory: locus, stability, controllability			
		Goal orientation: mastery orientation vs. performance orientation			
		Self-regulated learning			

into what you might learn and allowed your instructor to tailor his or her instruction to your needs, expanding beyond the book if needed. The third column helped to solidify what you may have learned in this process. After you revisit the KWL chart and complete the 'Learned' column, take a look at Table 10.4 to see how many items you remembered.

We realize this chapter includes a lot of content, probably more than you can grasp completely in one sitting. Much of what you have read here, you will encounter again in future coursework and experience in your fieldwork. Our intent in this chapter is to give you an overview of the many ways children learn so you can begin to notice how these principles manifest in the music classroom. We also hope you are beginning to realize the complexity of teacher knowledge and skills required to be most effective in the classroom. Understanding the ways children learn and applying that knowledge is an important aspect of being a *professional music educator*.

Class Activity 10.1: Teaching for Transfer

In small groups (3 to 4 people) take a poster-sized sheet of paper and a marker and list each of Ormrod's six principles of learning transfer (see pp. 230–231). For the first principle, discuss what it means and some possibilities of how it could manifest in a music classroom, and then reach consensus on the best exemplar and write it on your sheet. Do the same for each of the principles. Once groups are finished, they should share their work with each other. Notice similarities and differences among the examples the groups develop for each principle.

11 The Students: How Do You Know They Learn?

Through this final section (Part III) of this text we have explored who the students in your classroom might be, what they might learn, and how they might go about learning. Our final question, regarding how you know if students are learning, is no less important just because it is the last one we ask. Evidence of student learning in your music classroom will be critically important to many different stakeholders for many different reasons (Orzolek, 2007). It will be important to your students, by providing necessary feedback to help clarify and solidify the knowledge and skills they are acquiring. It will be important to you (the teacher), by providing insight about the effectiveness of teaching strategies you employ. It will be important to parents who want to understand what their children are learning in your classroom. It will be important to your administrators who want to know if students are meeting curricular goals. It will be important to policy makers who need strong evidence of meaningful student achievement to substantiate investment of limited resources. In short, many important people will need to know about the quality of student learning taking place in your classroom. "Assessment has become inseparable from formal education—and it is here to stay" (Orzolek, 2007, p. 38)

There are, however, many misconceptions surrounding assessment, particularly in music education. Asmus states that, "For many teachers, assessment simply means grading" (1999, p. 19). As you addressed the questions about assessment in your blog, did you make this assumption? Were the positive or negative feelings you had about the process linked to a grade, rating, or placement? Did you assume that 'assessment' was equal to 'test' or 'audition' or 'contest?' Fautley (2010) suggests that this conception is due to what he calls 'a folk view of assessment.' He states that "The folk view of assessment is that it happens separately from a course of teaching or instruction, and represents a series of fixed points which demarcate the progression of a learner" (p. 3). In this view, assessment is something that is done to students who often have no active voice in the process nor receive meaningful feedback from it. Such assessment is often completed by an "unknown third party who has had little or no contact with the teacher or learner either beforehand or afterwards. This way of assessing learning in music detaches assessment from teaching, the learner from the learned, and the teacher from the taught" (Fautley, 2010, p. 3).

Before we move on with this discussion, it would likely help to differentiate between **grading** and **assessment**. Gusky and Jung (2013) state that grades are "the symbols, words, or numerals that teachers assign to evidence on student learning to signify different levels of achievement" (p. 64). Generally, the goal of *grading* is to communicate information about an individual student's learning and/or performance to various stakeholders (e.g. the student, parents, administration, the public at large). Although grades are sometimes treated as absolute representations of student learning, they are not always a reliable measure, as they may incorporate criteria—such as attendance, participation, and effort— that are not direct measures of learning. "In essence, grading is an exercise in professional judgment on the part of teachers. And because of the consequences grades can have, those judgments must always be thoughtful and informed" (Gusky & Jung, 2013, p. 65). This means that teachers should use multiple sources of evidence to support decisions made concerning students' grades. There are many factors that can affect student performance on any measure of student learning. Performance anxiety, a family tragedy, or an altercation with another student are a few examples of factors that can interfere with accurate evidence of student learning. To ensure these factors do not overly influence a student's grade, teachers should collect evidence of student learning in different ways and in different forms. There should be a clear purpose for each grade and this purpose should be shared with the students prior to the evidence-collecting process. Teachers should then weigh the evidence collected in terms of the purpose. This means that some evidence could be more representative of student learning than others. All information concerning how evidence will be collected and weighted should be communicated clearly via a grading plan to the stakeholders prior to the grading process taking place. It is beyond the scope of this text to discuss in detail the various approaches to grading and the development of grading plans. You can find more information on this in the *Connecting to the Profession* chapter at the end of this section. As you begin to consider all the elements and issues that impact grading, we believe one thought should guide your process. Professional music educators should

> always be able to defend the grades or marks they assign. In addition, they must have evidence on student learning to support their decisions. But their defense must be based on their defined purpose for the grade and their confidence in the validity of the evidence they use making their decision.
>
> (Gusky & Jung, 2013, p. 66)

Assessment is difficult to define, as there is no single agreed-upon definition. "Assessment can mean many things: performance evaluation (as in learning), value (as in property), or simply a judgment about something" (Orzolek, 2010, p. 38). These multiple definitions also affect the ways assessment is viewed in music education. Asmus (1999) states that assessment is "the collection, analysis, interpretation, and application of information about student performance or program effectiveness in order to make educational decisions" (p. 21). While Asmus considers assessment to be all aspects from data collection to the application of information, O'Toole (2003) considers assessment and evaluation to be separate yet interrelated activities. She states, "Assessment refers to the act of gathering data about learning (such as tests, journal entries, performance reviews) and evaluation is the process of analyzing or interpreting data in order to make judgments about what the data mean" (p. 70). Radocy and Boyle (1987) elect to not even use the word 'assessment,' but suggest that two other terms—'measurement' and 'evaluation'—more accurately describe the process. **Measurement** refers to the process of assigning "numerals to objects, individuals, or events according to specific systematic rules" (p. 6). After events are measured these measurements can be evaluated. **Evaluation** involves "making some judgment or decision regarding the worth, quality, or value of experiences, procedures, activities, or individual or group performances as they relate to some educational endeavor" (p. 7).

For the purpose of this text, we will consider assessment to include not just two actions but three: (a) the collection of data to **measure** student performance, (b) the **evaluation** of those data, and (c) **action**(s) taken resulting from information revealed by the evaluation (Shuler, 2011). By adding the third step beyond measurement and evaluation, we suggest effective assessment cannot be accomplished separate from the learning environment. In other words, assessment is not an interruption to the teaching/learning process. Rather, assessment is an essential part of meaningful teaching and learning. Effective music teachers are constantly assessing student learning and making adjustments to instruction based upon their evaluations. This process is most easily seen when teachers make use of **informal assessment**.

An informal assessment can be made by casually watching a student's behavior or listening to a response she makes. Informal assessments are different from **formal assessments**, such as standardized tests or graded formal exams, because the individual is less aware of the assessment in progress and because records of informal assessment are rarely kept. Examples of informal assessment would include a band director asking a student to play a passage so she could hear if the student is articulating clearly. An elementary teacher may have students echo sing their names on Sol-Mi syllables so he can quickly assess their use of singing voice and their pitch-matching abilities. A choral music educator may ask a student to sing the text of a work on a single pitch to assess his rhythmic reading ability. Music teachers make use of informal assessments regularly to adjust instruction and check for student understanding.

Use of informal assessment is most evident when teachers work in complete **teaching cycles** (Hammer, 1994). A teaching cycle consists of three major actions with the aid of informal assessment. Figure 11.1 is a graphic representation of a single teaching cycle. The cycle begins with a **set**. The set is an instruction given or request made of the learner by the teacher. A simple set to an ensemble could be "please, breathe together and start together." With the set given, the learners engage in the **follow-through** and attempt to demonstrate the skill or knowledge requested of them. As learners engage in this behavior, the teacher measures the students' abilities through observation—either visually, aurally, or both. Using this measurement, the teacher evaluates the outcome and provides a **response**. Based upon the evaluation, this response can be affirming, reinforcing the learners' correct behaviors, or it can be disaffirming, attempting to correct an invalid follow-through. Disaffirming responses can take one of three forms: (a) a reset, (b) a modified set, or (c) a release. If the teacher determines that learners are not achieving, but that this deficiency may be corrected simply through repetition, she may choose to give the set again with no further instruction. This reset is often used when teachers are working on skill-building such as finger patterns on violin or keyboard. If the teacher determines that some additional instruction is needed, she may choose to modify the set. These modifications may include additional pedagogical information such as "try that

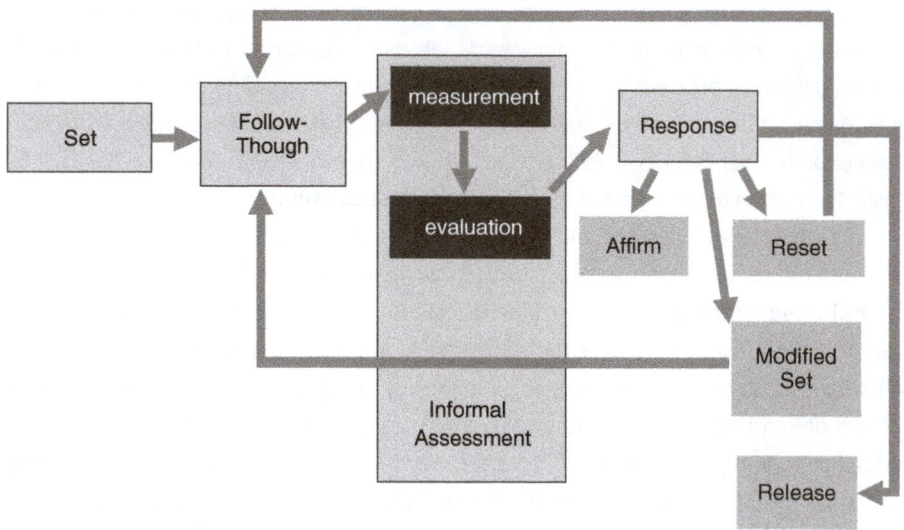

FIGURE 11.1 Teaching cycle model.

again and keep your chin pointed and flat" (instruction to a young clarinet student). The modification may be to simplify the original set like "sing that passage again, but only the rhythms on this single pitch." Should the teacher's evaluation note that the knowledge or skill requested of the learner in the original set is too far beyond his abilities regardless of instruction (beyond his zone of proximal development), the teacher may choose to release the learner from the original set with a statement like "OK, we are not quite ready for this yet. Let's try something new." These evaluations and instructional decisions often take place in less than a second. For these interactions to be effective, teachers must have a clear idea of the **standard** (or level of accomplishment) they are asking learners to achieve, often involving a visual behavior or an aural product. With the standard clearly in mind, the teacher measures the learner's response and compares it to the standard, evaluating ways the behavior or sound met the standard and ways it did not. He then uses this information to adjust his instruction so that the learner can achieve the desired outcome.

Viewed from this position, "assessment becomes an integral part of teaching and learning" (Fautley, 2010, p. 4). Shepard (2000) notes that this perception shift in the role assessment plays in the learning process allows all stakeholders to view assessment, "so that it is used to help students learn and to improve instruction rather than being used only to rank students or to certify the end products of learning" (p. 31).

144 SOCIAL PLACE

Assessment and Learning

In 144 characters or fewer, address some or all of following: What are your thoughts about using assessment to help students learn? Is it possible to use assessment to help students learn, given the amounts of testing that students experience? What might be some ways you could use assessment as an instructional tool in the music classroom?

THE PURPOSES OF ASSESSMENT

According to Shuler (2011), there are four primary purposes for assessment. While individual assessment activities are often contextualized according to the content, the learners, the teacher, and the milieu (i.e. the *four common places*) most all serve one or more of the purposes Shuler lists. The purposes are: (a) improving student learning, (b) improving teaching, (c) improving programs, and/or (d) informing stakeholders (students, parents, and policy makers).

"Improving student learning is the single most important reason for assessment" (Shuler, 2011, p. 11). Music teachers engage in assessment on a regular basis as they provide effective instruction in their classrooms. The use of informal assessment is essential to ensure effective instruction, but is not sufficient. Shuler states that "systematically measuring the extent to which students are achieving key learning outcomes requires advance planning: first to identify high-priority outcomes, then to design *formal assessments* for those outcomes" (p. 11). Music teachers must know what they want their students to learn, provide effective instruction toward these learning goals, and assess the outcomes of this instruction. Formal assessments provide the teacher with a record of student outcomes and achievements that can be analyzed for patterns to help improve instruction. For example, if, after a series of assessments, a middle-school choral director notes that many students do not achieve a given standard when singing minor tonal patterns, she can re-examine her instructional approach and/or materials to find ways to help students acquire the knowledge and skills necessary to meet the standard.

Records of formal assessments can also be used to assess the efficacy of a program. Asmus (1999) states that *program assessment* "examines a particular educational program, such as a choral program, a district-wide reading program, or the like, to

determine its effectiveness in meeting student, parent and community needs" (p. 20). Assessment of this kind is becoming increasingly important to support advocacy efforts and is likely to become a component of music teacher evaluation in the near future (see Teacher Evaluation resources in the *Connecting to the Profession* chapter at the end of this section). Informal assessments cannot fulfill the requirements of this reporting.

The need to report outcomes to various stakeholders also requires the use of formal assessments. As we noted earlier, many others outside your classroom need to be informed about the learning that is taking place within your classroom. Some argue that, due to the subjective nature of musical performance, no objective formal assessment can truly measure all the complexities of musical learning (Asmus, 1999). We tend to agree with this position, but realize that all teachers are increasingly being required to demonstrate growth in student achievement, and music teachers are no exception. The current movement in teacher evaluation is placing even greater emphasis on student achievement data (Darling-Hammond, 2012). In a number of states, 50 percent of a teacher's evaluation is based upon demonstrated growth in student achievement. Without records of formal assessments, music teachers cannot demonstrate such growth. Later in this chapter, we will discuss some ways you may be able to measure and evaluate student learning in your classroom in meaningful ways. The real challenge will be to find ways to incorporate formal assessments that do not interrupt the learning process in your classroom. This is yet another decision you will need to make as a professional music educator.

FORMS OF ASSESSMENT

Much of the discussion concerning assessment is confusing because different writers will label the same terminology in different ways. What one author may term a 'use' of assessment is called a 'purpose' of assessment by another author. So that we may share the same terminology in this chapter, Table 11.1 lists the terms we are using and how they are categorized.

Most of the literature recognizes three basic forms of assessment. They are: (a) **diagnostic**, (b) **formative**, and (c) **summative** (Asmus, 1999). While these are listed and will be discussed in this order, it is important to note that these are not hierarchical. Each form serves a different and important purpose. The choice of which form of assessment to use is determined by what information the assessor wishes to gather and how he or she wishes to use it. We will provide examples of each of these as we discuss their general characteristics.

TABLE 11.1 Assessment terminology.

Purposes of assessment	o To improve learning o To improve teaching o To evaluate programs o To share information with stakeholders	
Forms of assessment	o Diagnostic o Formative o Summative	These can be conducted formally or informally
Types of assessment	o Authentic o Alternative o Standards-based	
Uses of assessment	o Assessment of learning o Assessment for learning o Assessment as learning	

Diagnostic assessment takes place before instruction and provides information about what students already know and can do (Hale & Green, 2009). This essential information often serves two purposes: (a) to clarify the limits of a student's zone of proximal development (ZPD) (Vygotsky, 1978), and/or (b) to determine a student's musical aptitude (Gordon, 1998). As you may remember from Chapter 10, the ZPD is the space between what students can do without your help (what they already know and can do) and the *limit* to what they can do with your help (see Figure 11.2). Knowing a student's ZPD in a certain topic area allows the teacher to provide meaningful instruction. If instruction addresses what a student already understands or can do, he is likely to become disengaged due to boredom. If instruction addresses understandings or tasks that are beyond the learner's capabilities even with teacher help, he is also likely to become frustrated and disengaged. Knowing where these limits are, a music teacher can aim instruction within the ZPD so that students are engaged through appropriate challenges.

Music aptitude may play a role in diagnostic assessment. The concept of music aptitude and its effects on music learning have challenged music educators for many years (Reynolds & Hyun, 2004). Music aptitude is defined as "a measure of the student's potential to learn music" (Gordon, 1998, p. 5). Some believe this potential is only bestowed upon those with a special giftedness for music learning and music making. This is reflected in statements like "I can't sing" or "I can only play the radio," made by those who believe they are not 'musically talented.' Often, those expressing such ideas have limited exposure to music-learning opportunities. However, there is ample evidence that music aptitude is normally distributed across the entire population (Gordon, 1998). That is to say that, like most other endeavors, there is a portion of the population

Learner can accomplish tasks without teacher help	ZPD	Learner cannot accomplish tasks even with teacher help
Boring Zone	Learning Zone	Frustrating Zone

FIGURE 11.2 Zone of proximal development.

that have great potential, a portion of the population that have limited potential, and a the vast majority of the population that have varying degrees of potential within these two extremes. Most important for music educators is the realization that "everyone has at least some music aptitude" (Gordon, 1988, p. 11). With this information, a music teacher can make the case that everyone has the potential to learn music, not just those considered to be gifted or especially talented. However, knowing a specific student's aptitude for music learning has benefit for a music educator. Gordon (1998) contends that music aptitude is multidimensional and that people can demonstrate different aptitudes for rhythmic content and tonal content. Through research, tests have been developed to help measure the various dimensions within a person's musical aptitude (Gordon, 1998). A music educator who understands students' potential for learning in these various dimensions may be more equipped to meet students' individual needs than a teacher without this information. There is much more to understand concerning music aptitude as it applies to teaching music. We encourage you to visit the resources in the *Connecting to the Profession* chapter at the end of this section for more information.

Diagnostic assessment can be conducted either informally or formally. An elementary music teacher may take a role in one of the first class meetings by singing the students' names and asking them to sing it back if they are present. She can mark in her plan or grade book a '+' if the student matches pitch or a '–' if the student does not match. Because a record is being kept, this is an example of a brief formal diagnostic assessment of students' pitch-matching ability. A band director may ask each trumpet player to play a pattern on a single pitch at a quick tempo. His plan is to assess each player's ability to double tongue so that he can make decisions about the appropriateness of repertoire he is choosing to perform. Because no written record of this assessment is kept, this action would be considered an informal diagnostic assessment.

Formative assessment occurs either during or after instruction and is used to "elicit information which will be of use to the pupil and the teacher in deciding what ought to be done next in order to develop learning" (Fautley, 2010, p. 9). A primary feature of formative assessment is **feedback** (Havnes, Smith, Dysthe, & Ludgisven, 2012). Assessment without feedback does not fit the requirements for formative assessment. Fautley notes that the goal of providing this information back to the student is to facilitate future improvement. He states:

> The feedback given by the teacher influences the work which the pupils do in the next part of their work, which means that the feedback is focused on future improvement. It is for this reason that a number of commentators have renamed feedback to *feedforward*, as its intentionality is based upon forward development.
>
> (p. 11)

Teachers conducting large ensembles often make use of informal formative assessment. A choir director may ask the tenors to "sing that passage again and lead to the downbeat of bar four." After the tenors perform, he asks, "John and Max, would you sing that exactly as you did this last time? Everyone listen to the direction they create." After John and Max perform, the choir director states, "Excellent model! Let's all match that." Another example of informal formative assessment would be a music teacher moving from group to group, having a discussion with each about the composition task they are working on, and providing ideas or new questions to consider as they work. The key element to the teacher's assessment and feedback (or feedforward) is that she quickly assesses where each group is in terms of meeting the goal for the assignment and then she provides direction for future steps. This direction is not always a directive, with comments like "you might try a countermelody here." Often feedback can take the form of a question such as, "I wonder how you might be able to create more interest from bar 9 to bar 16?" Most often, formative assessment is conducted informally; however, as we will see shortly, formally conducted formative assessments are very useful.

Summative assessments occur after instruction has been completed and are used to determine what a learner may or may not know and/or can do independently at certain points in time. Because summative assessments do not include feedback, many associate them with standardized tests. Standardized tests are used at the national level, like the National Assessment of Educational Progress (NAEP), or at the state level, with End of Instruction (EOI) exams in certain subject areas. Standardized tests are conducted formally and can include either **criterion-referenced** or **norm-referenced** exams. If an exam is criterion-referenced the value of the learner's performance is determined by comparing it to a particular benchmark, established prior to the performance of the task (Asmus, 1999). It is possible for all who are assessed to receive 100 percent on a criterion-referenced test. On a norm-referenced test, the value of a learner's performance is determined by comparing it to a standard that is established from a large group of representative others that have taken the same test. The individual learner's outcome is compared to all the other outcomes. The individual's score represents how the learner performed in comparison to the others who were assessed with the same test. If a learner scored in the 90th percentile, it means her score was the same as or better than 90 percent of all who took or have taken the same exam.

Often standardized tests are called into question due to their **validity** and/ or **reliability**. Definitions of these measurement concepts can get very involved and complicated. For the purpose of our discussion, we will define validity as "the effectiveness of an assessment instrument in measuring what it is supposed to measure" (Asmus, 1999, p. 21). In addition to its ability to measure things accurately, validity also refers to the appropriate use of an assessment instrument. For example, if an orchestra teacher had taught his students to play a D major scale on their instruments, asking students to write a D major scale on manuscript would not be considered a valid test of their understanding. Performing and writing notation are constructed of two different (but related) sets of knowledge and skills. If the teacher taught D major scale performance, it would be most valid for him to assess this with a performance exam.

Reliability refers to "the consistency of an assessment instrument to obtain similar scores across time" (Asmus, 1999, p. 21). This is where performance exams are called into question most often. If criteria are not set clearly for the assessment of the learner's performance, scores of students who possess the same knowledge may vary widely for no apparent reason. Such scores are considered to be unreliable. Additionally, issues outside the control of the teacher, like the student being hungry or tired, may have an effect on a student's performance on an exam. Exam scores can also be affected by the time of the day they are given, the point within the school calendar they are given—for example, the day before a school vacation—even by the students' experience with the exam procedure. All of these issues can call in to question the reliability of the score to accurately reflect a student's understanding or skill.

Summative assessments are most appropriately used for **program assessment**. Asmus (1999) defines program assessment as "the determination of an educational program's strengths and weaknesses through a well-conceived and well-implemented plan of data collection and analysis" (p. 21). Such an assessment might allow a teacher to evaluate the effectiveness of a year-long curriculum in meeting the overall learning goals she established for her seventh-grade general music class. Program assessment may help a high-school band director evaluate a four-year curriculum in meeting the music learning needs of students who have been in the band program for their entire high-school tenure.

Some consider end of unit tests, mid-term playing tests, final composition projects, and even concerts or programs to be classroom-level summative assessments. If, as part of the process, no feedback is provided to the students concerning their performance and how they might improve future performance, this definition may be appropriate. We contend that this type of assessment at the classroom level serves little purpose. While accountability and systematic grading are necessary, formal formative assessments can be used for this purpose while providing information to the learner for improvement. For instance, it would be possible to move a concert from a summative event to a formative event by having ensemble members contribute to the construction of a rubric that will be used to evaluate a recording of the concert performance. Using student input, the teacher could construct the rubric and make it available to students prior to the concert so they are aware of the criteria being used to evaluate the performance. During the class period after the concert, students could use this rubric to evaluate their ensemble performance and to provide feedback to themselves and to their colleagues in the ensemble. A guided discussion concerning the feedback from this evaluation could lead to the corporate construction of new goals for the next performance by this group.

Garrison and Ehringhaus (n.d.) outline appropriate and inappropriate uses of summative assessment when they state:

> Although the information gleaned from [summative] assessment is important, it can only help in evaluating certain aspects of the learning process. Because they are spread out and occur after instruction every few weeks, months, or once a year, summative assessments are tools to help evaluate the effectiveness of programs, school improvement goals, alignment of curriculum, or student placement in specific programs. Summative assessments happen too far down the learning path to provide information at the classroom level and to make instructional adjustments and interventions during the learning process. It takes formative assessment to accomplish this.
>
> (p. 1)

Summative assessments can serve important purposes. As a professional music educator, you will need to determine what form of assessment is most appropriate for use in each situation.

ASSESSMENT TOOLS

We previously defined assessment as the process of gathering information or data concerning a learner's performance. Different types of data can be collected based

upon the type(s) of learning that are being facilitated during instruction. Learning types are often categorized in three different domains (Bloom, 1956). The **psychomotor domain** addresses learning associated with skills or the ability to do something. Learning required for a young percussionist to grip her sticks correctly would reside in the psychomotor domain. The **cognitive domain** addresses learning that is knowledge based. Understanding and being able to describe the common compositional techniques used in the Baroque era would be an example of learning in the cognitive domain. Learning that connects with feelings, emotions, motivations, and attitudes is addressed in the **affective domain**. An example might be, as part of the rehearsal and preparation of Ticheli's *Cajun Folk Songs*, that band students are asked to consider musical traditions and how they are preserved, changed, or lost. At some point the teacher may invite students to "share stories of music they might remember from their childhood that their own [future] children may never experience" (O'Toole, 2003, p. 276). It is appropriate and necessary for music teachers to address all three learning domains in their instruction. Data addressing all three domains should be collected as part of regular assessments.

During informal assessments these data are gathered through observation and listening. During formal assessments data are often gathered through the use of various tools. Each of these tools varies depending upon the amount and type of information they provide both to the teacher and the student. In Table 11.2 we list a few of the most common tools used in music teaching and the potential level of feedback each tool may provide. The table also includes the pros and cons of each tools use.

In the following section, we will briefly discuss the use of each assessment tool within the music classroom.

Pencil and paper tests. The use of written exams varies depending upon the classroom setting (Russell & Austin, 2010). Most ensemble classes do not engage in this type of assessment regularly. However, O'Toole (2003) notes that this is an efficient tool for assessing substantive knowledge (cognitive domain) about music. She also notes that there are two basic ways to collect data from written exams. One is through *selected response* (e.g. fill-in-the-blank, multiple choice, matching) and the other through *created response* (e.g. short answer, essay). In addition to collecting cognitive learning data, we believe it is also possible to collect affective data with created response questions that are well crafted. Written exams assessing common terminology, historical elements, and music theory concepts would be appropriate in any music classroom.

Checklists. When teachers collect psychomotor or performance data they often employ *observational* assessments. This means the assessor views or listens to the performance and records her observations. There are a number of tools that can be

TABLE 11.2 Assessment tools.

Tool	Data gathered	Possible feedback	Pros of use	Cons of use
Pencil and paper test	Depending on the type of answer required from the learner, all kinds of cognitive data can be gathered. Limited affective data may also be gathered	It is possible to provide detailed information back to the student	- Often easy to administrate - Detailed data can be gathered - Learners may be able to work at their own pace	- Is often an interruption to the normal daily activities in the classroom - Feedback is often removed from the task by an extended period of time
Checklist	It is possible to gather both cognitive and psychomotor data	Feedback exhibits only evidence of whether or not learning is demonstrated. There are no other levels of differentiation	- Administration is often easy and fast, serving large groups well - Can provide quick feedback to students	- Often not much information provided about how to improve - Does not work well when ranking is desired
Rating scale	It is possible to gather both cognitive and psychomotor data	Feedback is based on a scale, so that varying levels of achievement can be shared with the student	- Administration is easy and can work for large groups - Can provide quick feedback to students and help them understand the levels at which they are or are not achieving - Can work as ranking instrument	- Often does not provide much detailed information about how to improve

(Continued)

TABLE 11.2 (*Continued*)

Tool	Data gathered	Possible feedback	Pros of use	Cons of use
Rubric	It is possible to gather both cognitive and psychomotor data	Depending upon the specificity in the descriptors, it is possible to provide detailed feedback to the student	- It is possible to provide a large amount of information in a short time - Can be used in large groups - Can provide information about how to improve - Can work as a ranking instrument	- May be difficult to construct
Portfolio	Because these can exist in both hard-copy and electronic forms, all types (cognitive, psychomotor, and affective) of data can be collected. These data can also represent process and product over time	Portfolios are often used in conjunction with other tools (i.e. rubrics, rating scales). Along with narrative written feedback, much information can be provided	- Longitudinal data can be collected to assess growth - Can assess both product and process - Multiple forms of data can be collected	- Technology required for electronic formats may not be available - Evaluation takes time - Feedback may not be immediate - Can be cumbersome to store
Journaling	Because these can exist in both hard-copy and electronic forms, all types (cognitive, psychomotor, and affective) of data can be collected. These data can also represent process and product over time	Dependent upon the form of the journal and prompts used to elicit responses, a wide variety of information can be provided	- Longitudinal data can be collected to assess growth - Can assess both product and process - Multiple forms of data can be collected - Student's feelings and perceptions can be addressed	- Technology required for electronic formats may not be available - Evaluation takes time - Feedback may not be immediate - Can be cumbersome to store

used to record these observations. A checklist is one such tool. We especially note that many different assessors can use this tool in the classroom. The teacher can use it to assess student achievement, but a learner's peer(s) could also use it. Allowing students to peer-assess other students' learning provides added assessment possibilities in the classroom. These additions include (a) providing feedback to the learner from multiple perspectives and (b) providing an opportunity for the teacher to evaluate the quality of feedback given by the peer-assessors. In addition, this tool could also be used by the learner to self-assess, providing the teacher another opportunity to evaluate the quality of the learner's self-assessment. It would also be possible to use a combination of assessors. The teacher and student's peers could use this tool in a live evaluation of a student's performance. The teacher could then post a recording of the performance on a password-protected class website and the student could use the same tool at home to self-assess the recording of his performance. All the resulting evaluations could be combined to provide rich feedback to all those involved in the process. The possibilities of who uses this tool and how it is used are limited only by the teacher's imagination.

Regardless of who uses the tool, the key to effective assessment lies in the design of the tool being used during the observation. O'Toole (2003) reminds us that "The assessment design needs to be based on well-defined criteria to provide greater validity and reliability" (p. 77). A checklist notes specific elements or criteria that should be present when the learner performs successfully. The observer marks whether or not each element is present during the performance (see Figure 11.3).

The advantage of using a checklist is that criteria are clear and the tool is easy to use. Checklists work especially well when teachers are working with large groups of learners and need an efficient means to gather data. The greatest drawback in using checklists is that feedback is limited.

Rating scales. Similar to a checklist, a rating scale lists specific criteria for a successful performance. The difference is that the observer can provide more information to the learner by noting the level of performance for each criterion. Rating scales allow the learner to note not only the presence of the behavior, but the degree to which it is present, and thus providing more specific feedback to the learner.

There are many different types of rating scales that can be used to measure musical achievement (Gordon, 2002). These tools can be used by teachers, peers, and even by individuals, for self-assessment. The advantages are similar to those noted for checklists. The main disadvantage remains the limited feedback that is provided to the learner (see Figure 11.4).

Checklist—Flute assembly		
Student's name:		**Class period:**
The skill was observed		**Description of skill** **The student ...**
Yes	**No**	
		places the case on the floor right side up
		removes the body and the foot joint from the case
		holds the body in the left hand without touching rods
		holds the foot joint in the right hand without touching rods
		slides the foot joint onto the body with a slight twisting motion
		aligns the rod on the foot joint with the tone holes on the body
		holds the body in the left hand without touching rods and removes the head joint from the case with the right hand
		carefully slides the head joint onto the instrument with a slight twisting motion
		pulls the head joint out about a 1/4 inch from being "all the way in"
		aligns the embouchure plate with the tone holes on the body of the instrument

FIGURE 11.3 Checklist example.

Rubrics. Wesolowski (2012) describes a rubric as a "form of a criteria-specific performance scale. It is a set of scoring criteria used to determine the achievement level of a student's performance on assigned tasks" (p. 37). A rubric divides each task into constituent parts including details of various performance levels for each task, often organized from lower levels to higher levels. Each performance level is described in enough detail that the observer and the learner have clear ideas of what has or has not been accomplished in the performance. By reading the descriptors in levels above what was achieved during the assessment, learners can develop understandings of what needs to be done to improve their performance. Again, this tool can also be used for peer- and self-assessment (see Figure 11.5).

As with ratings scales, there are many different types of rubrics (Wesolowski, 2012). Teachers must be sure those criteria on the rubric accurately list each constituent area for the performance and that the descriptors for each achievement level in each area are accurate. Such accuracy is essential for assessment and evaluation to be valid. Wesolowski

Rating scale—Orff instrument performance—2nd Grade			
Student's name:	Class period:		
When you played, you…	Always	Rating Sometimes	Never
Kept a steady beat	😊 😊 😐 🙁 😣		
Played all the right rhythms	😊 😊 😐 🙁 😣		
Played all the right notes	😊 😊 😐 🙁 😣		
Kept your arms away from your body	😊 😊 😐 🙁 😣		
Played with alternating hands	😊 😊 😐 🙁 😣		
Played in the center of every bar	😊 😊 😐 🙁 😣		

FIGURE 11.4 Rating scale example.

(2012) lists several advantages to using rubrics for performance assessment stating that rubrics can provide the following:

1. Clear levels of accomplishment by defining tangible measures of individual achievement.
2. Clear indications of what students need to accomplish in the future to improve their individual performance.
3. A learner-centered approach to performing, learning, and assessing.
4. A bridge between student learning and teacher expectation.
5. Versatility in adapting to meet the needs of a specific curriculum, student age, ability level, style of music, and type of ensemble.
6. A valid and reliable form of individualized assessment and documentation of teacher accountability.
7. A quantitative means for evaluating and scoring qualitative, performance- based tasks.
8. A means for clearly implementing content standards and course objectives into the assessment process.
9. Valuable information for parents on their child's progress and needs for improvement.

(p. 38)

Score	4	3	2	1
	Above standard	**Meets standard**	**Approaching standard**	**Below standard**
Tone quality ____ Score	Tone is consistently focused, clear, and centered throughout the range of the voice	Tone is focused, clear and centered throughout the normal range. Extreme ranges sometimes cause tone to be less controlled. Tone quality typically does not detract from the performance	Tone is often focused, clear and centered, but sometimes the tone is uncontrolled. Occasionally the tone quality detracts from the overall performance	The tone is often not focused, clear or centered regardless of the range, significantly detracting from the overall performance
Pitch accuracy ____ Score	Pitches are consistently accurate as notated, enhancing the overall performance	Incorrect pitches occur rarely and without detracting from the overall performance	Incorrect pitches occur occasionally, detracting from the overall performance	Incorrect pitches occur frequently, detracting from the overall performance
Rhythmic accuracy ____ Score	Rhythms are consistently accurate as notated, enhancing the overall performance	Incorrect rhythms occur rarely and without detracting from the overall performance	Incorrect rhythms occur occasionally, detracting from the overall performance	Incorrect rhythms occur frequently, detracting from the overall performance
Diction ____ Score	The student articulates clearly and the text is understandable throughout all ranges	The student articulates clearly and the text is understandable, but there are some minor issues between ranges	The student articulates somewhat, but there are portions of the text that are not clearly understandable	The student rarely articulates the words and the text is not discernible
Technique ____ Score	Correct posture and breath mechanics are employed consistently, enhancing the overall performance	Correct posture and breath mechanics are usually employed. Lapses do not detract significantly from the overall performance	Correct posture and breath mechanics are employed often, but lapses do detract from the overall performance	Correct posture and breath mechanics are rarely employed, detracting from the overall performance
Total ____ score	20–18 = A 17–16 = B 15–14 = C 13–12 = D 11 and below = F			

FIGURE 11.5 Rubric for solo vocal performance.

Portfolios. Collections of evidence documenting each student's achievement in music can be organized into assessment portfolios (see Figure 11.6). With the help of technology, these portfolios can include written, video, and audio evidence of student learning. Mills (2009) notes:

> Because portfolio contents are usually selected by the students, portfolios require students to reflect on their work, assessing the work's quality and documenting their progress. In certain kinds of portfolios, students then formalize this knowledge through written reflections that become a guideline for reviewing the portfolio's contents. The process of creating a portfolio also provides opportunities for reflection as teachers and students engage in contextually rich dialogue.
>
> (p. 32)

Several types of portfolios exist, but they all generally fall into two categories as either *process folios* or *product folios* (O'Toole, 2003). Process folios document the learner's journey as he works to achieve particular skills and understandings. Artifacts in the portfolio demonstrate progress (or not) as these skills and understandings are being developed. A product folio is different in that learners are required to select representative artifacts that demonstrate their highest levels of achievement. The selection process is often coupled with student reflections concerning why they choose each artifact and how it demonstrates acquisition of certain skills or understandings. While portfolios can be used to collect rich data, other tools (i.e. checklists, rating scales, rubrics) are often used to evaluate portfolio contents. Using these tools, portfolios can be peer- and self-assessed as well.

Effective portfolio assessment takes good planning and management from the music educator. The details of this work are beyond the scope of this chapter, but Mills (2009) cites Linn and Miller's (2005) five 'key steps' for creating and using portfolios as a general guide. These five steps include: "(1) specify purpose, (2) provide guidelines for selecting portfolio entries, (3) define student role in selection and self-evaluation, (4) specify evaluation criteria, and (5) use portfolios in instruction and communication" (p. 33).

Journaling. Although they are not commonly used (Russell & Austin, 2010), journals can provide excellent insight into student learning. O'Toole (2003) states:

> journal assignments are a useful method for students to more freely express their musical knowledge and personal growth. Because [journal prompts] will more likely be open-ended, students will have more breadth to explore their thoughts and feelings than they would in a rubric or rating scale that focuses on specific skills or outcomes.
>
> (p. 84)

Anytown High School Orchestra
Portfolio Table of Contents
Marche Slave—**Study Unit**

The following should be included in your portfolio. Please label each folder with the same title (including number) as is listed in this table of contents. All materials must be posted to the portfolio website, by 7:00 p.m. on the due date. If you need to use the computer in the music library, schedule a time with Mrs. Jones.

01—Performance Assessment Recordings (PAR)—Include all three recordings from the assigned playoffs.

02—PAR reflections—Include all three of your self-assessment rubrics and reflections.

03—World History Collaboration —Include all artifacts from your collaboration with the students from Mr. Smith's world history class concerning the Serbian rebellion against the Ottoman Empire (minimum of two).

04—Protest Music Search—submit your annotated playlist of protest music from the 1960s.

05—Protest Song Composition Project—Submit the score, recording, teacher feedback, peer feedback, and your reflections for your quartet's 32-measure protest song composition.

06—Ensemble Performance Evaluation—Using the posted recording, complete the performance rubric/reflection and submit.

07—General Reflections—Submit your reflections concerning *Marche Slave* and this unit of study. Use the reflection framework posted on the website as a guide for this paper (500–750 words).

Note: It is recommended that you refer to the Portfolio Evaluation Rubric posted on the website as you make decisions about your portfolio contents.

FIGURE 11.6 Portfolio table of contents.

Depending upon the learner's developmental levels and the desired outcomes, journals can take on all forms, lengths, and types. Cohen (2012) uses journaling in her choral rehearsals and states that her goals for doing so are:

(1) to encourage participants to examine their experiences of singing through reflective writing in response to prompts that call for self-assessment and focused attention to elements of music, (2) to build camaraderie through written exchanges among participants, and (3) to provide opportunities for individualized instruction when members communicate directly with me about difficulties with musical learning and performing.

(pp. 43–44)

On a smaller scale, O'Toole (2003) suggests that teachers may want to "start with short, fun-to-answer questions" (p. 84). These could include questions like 'What point was the most clear part of today's class?' and/or 'What point was the muddiest part of today's class?' Some music teachers use journaling as means of documenting practice time outside of class. Beyond the practice card approach, which simply asks the student to list the times they have practiced, this assessment asks students to list their practice goals for the week, note what they did in their practice sessions to achieve these goals, and provide evidence regarding whether or not goals have been achieved. As with all formative assessments, it is imperative that students receive feedback on their journals in a timely fashion. Technology can help with this task, as some teachers are working with social media to help manage the process (Cohen, 2012). A particular advantage of journal assessment is that learners often have the opportunity to express their feelings, attitudes, and motivations in their writing. This affords the teacher opportunities to address learning in the affective domain. Other assessments do not allow for much work in this area. As always, creative teachers will find multiple ways to accomplish their goals. We encourage you to explore ways you can help bring this type of assessment into your classroom.

11.1 WHAT TOOL WOULD YOU USE?

If you were to teach your classmates to perform a simple task, what tool(s) would you choose to use to assess their understanding (cognitive domain)? What tool(s) would you use to assess their ability to perform the task (psychomotor domain)? What tool(s) could you use to assess their feelings about what they are learning (affective domain)? Is it possible to design one tool to assess all three learning domains? If so, what might that look like? If not, why not? (see Class Activity 11.1, p. 272)

TYPES OF ASSESSMENT

Assessment can occur in many different ways. If we return to Fautley's (2010) 'folk view of assessment,' we note that there are many who view assessment as separate from instruction. Often the content and forms of many assessments are so far removed from actual practice, learners have difficulty connecting assessment with the actual learning that is taking place in the classroom. Due to the amount of testing that takes places in today's American schools, students are often conditioned to think of testing as something that is done to them and that learning must stop so that assessment can take place. This 'testing culture' (Strauss, 2006) is difficult to counteract in the music classroom, but we believe it is possible and necessary to do so.

One means of addressing this issue is to make use of **alternative assessments** as much as possible. Asmus (1999) defines these as "any assessment technique other than traditional paper-and-pencil tests that uses strategies for collecting and analyzing information" (p. 21). Several of the ideas expressed in the previous section are forms of alternative assessment. We believe one of the most enjoyable parts of planning instruction is finding meaningful and engaging ways to assess student learning. Alternative assessments offer limitless opportunities to the creative music teacher.

Of particular interest and help to the music teacher is the idea of **authentic assessment**. These are "assessment techniques that gather information about students' ability to perform tasks that are found in real-world situations" (Asmus, 1999, p. 21). Authentic assessments are often active assessments where learners are engaged in thinking creatively and critically to solve real musical issues. They often take place collaboratively and require communication among students. When evaluating work in this manner, authentic assessments address what the Partnership for 21st Century Skills calls the 'four C's' (creativity, critical thinking, collaboration, and communication), as opposed to the traditional 'three R's' (that were never spelled correctly anyway!). The four C's propose to "help students master the multi-dimensional abilities required of them in the 21st century" (Partnership for 21st Century Skills, n.d.). Again, a number of the tools cited in the previous section can help you find ways to conduct authentic assessments in your classroom.

In Chapter 9, we addressed the question of what students should learn in your classroom. In doing so, we discussed the National Standards for Music Education. These are not the only music standards that exist. Many states also have published music standards. Similarly, there are some district-level curriculum guides that list music standards. Many teachers are required to demonstrate how their students are meeting the published standards for their subject area, but because music standards are often only recommended and not required, music teachers are not often held to the same requirements (Russell & Austin, 2010). In 2012-13 many states have been waived from the requirements of what has commonly come to be known as the No Child Left Behind act. With these waivers comes the requirement for increased teacher evaluation. As part of this evaluation, all teachers must demonstrate student growth within their subject matter. To accomplish this, **standards-based assessment** is being used in many subject areas.

Assessments designed to demonstrate student competencies in relation to published standards are being sought or developed by many educators in 'non-tested' subject areas (areas other than English language arts and math). While the scope of teacher assessment is well beyond this text, we encourage you to become informed about music assessment so that you can address this issue in ways that will provide for effective musical growth for your students, and not allow the 'testing culture' to be as pervasive in the music classroom as it has become in other subject areas.

USES OF ASSESSMENT AND EVALUATION

Considering all we have discussed thus far, effectively incorporating meaningful, valid, and reliable assessment in the music classroom is rather complicated. Our history as a profession does not suggest that music educators have been very successful in accomplishing this goal. Many issues are cited as causes, including large class sizes, performance demands, lack of training, and lack of administrative support (Russell & Austin, 2010). We understand these concerns are legitimate and solutions are not easy, but in the face of educational accountability, music educators must find ways to measure *each student's* growth in music learning.

To this end, we suggest that Scott's (2012) framework for the uses of assessment serves as a solid foundation from which to begin your work. Scott suggests that assessment serves multiple roles and lists these under three main categories: (1) assessment of learning, (2) assessment for learning, and (3) assessment as learning (See Table 11.3). **Assessment of learning** is "the traditional function assessment plays in providing a summative profile of what students have achieved as a result of instruction" (p. 32). This use of assessment places the students in a passive role, as they are forced to accept the evaluations of others. Often there is limited feedback from these assessments, resulting in the feeling of assessment being done *to* the students. Scott notes the advantage of this use of assessment is that it "provides a profile of students' achievement in terms of long-term out-comes" (p. 32). As we have discussed earlier in the chapter, this type of accountability is necessary for music educators in the twenty-first century. Among the disadvantages is the students' lack of internal motivation beyond the assessment. If the goal in class is to simply do well on the test, then the motivation to continue learning is gone once the test grade is received. As this is a common focus in many parts of the American educational community, music educators will need to be diligent in using assessment of learning sparingly and keep in mind the purpose this use of assessment serves.

TABLE 11.3 Uses of assessment.

Assessment of learning	Assessment for learning	Assessment as learning
"Done to" the student	"Done for" the student	"Done by" the student
Traditional	Constructivist	Self-reflective
Centered on the teacher	Centered on the student	Centered on self
Students as passive learners	Students as active learners	Students as active learners
Summative: occurs after instruction	Formative: intergrated with instruction	Formative: integrated with instruction
Administrative control	Helps students learn	Helps students learn
Competitive	Collaborative	Personal
Limited implementation of feedback to inform future learning	Implementation of constructive feedback from others to inform future learning	Implementation of feedback from self to inform future learning
Limited communication between teacher and students and among peers	Increased communication between teacher and students and among peers	Increased communication between teacher and students and among peers
Norm-referenced: criterion-referenced	Criterion-referenced	Criterion-referenced: self-referenced

Note: This table is from Scott (2012, p. 32) and is reprinted here with permission.

"**Assessment for learning** represents a constructivist perspective in which students, as active learners, use assessment feedback to extend their current levels of understanding" (Scott, 2012, p. 32, emphasis added). This use of assessment is always formative and is criterion-referenced. Student outcomes are not compared with others, but are shared between the student and teacher in relation to standards. In this manner, assessment is conducted *with* the students. By using assessment for learning, students can be involved in developmentally appropriate ways as assessment tools are being developed. Students can define criteria and levels of performance and, in so doing, increase their understandings of the subject matter and skill development. "Thus, the development of the assessment tools becomes an opportunity for learning" (Scott, 2012, p. 33). Notably in this process, the educator does not abdicate her responsibility to maintain high standards of assessment and evaluation by allowing students to make these decisions. Rather, through on-going informal assessment as students are collaborating on the design of assessment tools, the educator must facilitate student learning to meet the learning goals she has set.

The use of **assessment as learning** places the student in the central role as the assessor and evaluator of learning. It is a self-reflective process that is done by the learner. Scott (2012) notes that "Students monitor their own learning, reflect on what they have accomplished, and use this to inform future learning as they continually strive to perform at more sophisticated levels" (p. 33). As we discussed in the previous chapter, the ultimate goal of any educational endeavor is for the teacher to facilitate learning that becomes independent of the teacher, developing a self-regulated learner. Great educators work diligently so that it is possible for their students to surpass the knowledge and skills possessed by the teacher. Without this disposition, understandings and skill levels would never surpass the present. To achieve this goal, learners must be taught how to **self-assess** and **self-evaluate.** There are many obstacles to this endeavor. Today's students are often conditioned to value only external measures of achievement. To counteract this conditioning, you might try a process of **peer-assessment and evaluation.** Assessment tools and processes can be designed so that learners can assess their colleagues effectively. Again, these tools need to be implemented at developmentally appropriate levels for the learners, but they can serve as a bridge to help learners use assessment as learning. Once learners are accustomed to using assessment tools and making judgments about performance and achievement, you can help them learn to assess their understandings and skills such that they can steer their own learning in meaningful ways. With this approach, the potential for your students to be lifelong music learners is greatly increased. We hope that helping your students to be engaged with music for their entire lives is the ultimate goal of your teaching experience. Effective use of assessment is one very important step in achieving this goal.

CLASS ACTIVITIES

Class Activity 11.1: What Tool Would You Use?

In pairs, design a tool for assessing and evaluating instructional effectiveness. The instructional activity you are seeking to measure and evaluate is a five-minute lesson teaching this class a simple skill (e.g. tie a shoe, fold a paper airplane, sing a folk tune, etc.). This lesson will be team-taught and, as the assessor, you need to provide feedback in as many domains (i.e. cognitive, psychomotor, and affective) as possible directly to the instructors at the conclusion of the five-minute lesson. The essential question you are seeking to address in your assessment is, "What can these teachers do to provide the most effective instruction possible?" Once your assessment tools are designed, your professor may ask you to do some of the following:

- Exchange your assessment tool with another pair and each pair provide comments to the other on the design of this tool in relation to: (a) gathering valid and reliable evidence, (b) providing effective feedback, (c) addressing all three learning domains, and (d) the practicality of using this tool to assess a five-minute teaching episode.

- Submit your tools electronically to the professor, who will post them on a password-protected class website and: (a) invite comments about their use (see above) from the entire class, (b) invite class members to select which tool they would prefer was used if they were the one being assessed, and/or (c) invite class members to suggest modifications to a tool that they would prefer was used should they be the instructor who is assessed.

- Once a tool is selected, class members can develop simple five-minute skills-based lessons and present them to the class while the professor and/or other class members use the assessment tool developed in class as a means of formative assessment.

- The 'teachers' of the lessons could use this same tool for self-assessment and/or as a reflection framework.

 # Part III: Student-Learning Concerns

This is a collection of resources to help you build deeper understandings of the material presented in the chapters in this part of text. A detailed explanation of the structure of the *Connecting to the Profession* sections can be found at the beginning of *Connecting to the Profession—Part I.*

TERMS AND CONCEPTS

Chapter 8

Inclusiveness

Demographics

Race

Ethnicity

Religion

Sexual Orientation

Poverty Level

Developmental Issues

Exceptionalities

*Individuals with Disabilities
    Education Act*

Five Factor Model

*Family Educational Rights
    and Privacy Act*

Chapter 9

Music Elements

Tonal

Temporal

Expressive

Structural

Musical Independence

The National Standards

   Performance

   Creativity

   Response

   Relationships

Embodiment

Singing and Playing

Composing and Improvising

Music Notation

Music Awareness and Response

   Listening

   Evaluation

Measurement

Informal Assessment

Formal Assessment

Teaching Cycle

    Set

    Follow-Through

    Response

Standard

Purposes of Assessment

Forms of Assessment

    Diagnostic

    Formative

    Summative

Music Aptitude

Music Achievement

Feedback

Criterion-Referenced

Norm-Referenced

Validity

Reliability

Program Assessment

Assessment Tools

    Pencil and Paper

    Checklist

    Rating Scale

    Rubric

    Portfolio

    Journaling

Psychomotor Domain

Cognitive Domain

Affective Domain

Types of Assessment

    Alternative

    Authentic

    Standards-Based

Uses of Assessment

    Assessment of Learning

    Assessment for Learning

    Assessment as Learning

Self-Assessment

Peer-Assessment

Peer-Evaluation

CONNECT TO RESEARCH

Chapter 8

Diversity

Kindall-Smith, M. (2013). What a difference in 3 years! Risking social justice content in required undergraduate music education curricula. *Journal of Music Teacher Education, 22*(2), 34–50. doi:10.1177/1057083712450029

Preparing future music educators to teach diverse students in U.S. schools is essential; diversity is increasing, especially in urban schools. Music teacher education infused with social justice content promotes successful student learning and an understanding of diversity. This 3-year narrative includes social justice materials, successful pedagogical strategies, pitfalls, and students' comments. The 111 Caucasian students and 3 students of color were enrolled in three required music education undergraduate courses at an urban university. Students reflected about their cultural identities, created presentations with sensitive content, and revealed positive attitudinal changes about diversity. The risk for future music teachers was the requirement to learn a vast amount of traditional music education material plus social justice ideas. The risk for the professor involved breaking the canon of traditional music teacher preparation by teaching social justice content in required courses. What the author learned might persuade others to reevaluate their curricula and include social justice topics.

Race and Ethnicity

McKoy, C.L. (2013). Effects of selected demographic variables on music student teachers' self-reported cross-cultural competence. *Journal of Research in Music Education, 60*(4), 375–394. doi:10.1177/0022429412463398

The purpose of this study was to investigate the effects of race/ethnicity and school community setting for early field experience practica and student teaching on music student teachers' self-reported cross-cultural competence. Participants ($N = 337$) from 36 colleges and universities across the United States completed a survey designed to examine the extent of cross-cultural competence as specified by three constructs: (a) factors fostering readiness to teach in culturally diverse educational environments, (b) factors constraining readiness to teach in culturally diverse educational environments, and (c) educational experiences during teacher preparation relative to multicultural education and multicultural music education. The 'Foster,' 'Constrain,' and 'Teacher Preparation' dimension subscales served as the dependent variables. Results indicated no significant main effect of school community setting on participants' cross-cultural competence; however, a significant main effect of race/ethnicity ($p < .05$) was observed for the 'Constrain' subscale of the survey.

Special Learners

Salvador, K. (2010). Who isn't a special learner? A survey of how music teacher education programs prepare future educators to work with exceptional populations. *Journal of Music Teacher Education, 20*(1), 27. doi:10.1177/1057083710362462

As music educators are faced with an increasing number of students with various exceptionalities, their ability to differentiate instruction for those with special needs becomes paramount. The purpose of this survey was to investigate how music teacher preparation programs addressed the topic of differentiation for exceptional populations at the undergraduate level. Specifically, the survey asked if NASM accredited universities that granted doctoral or master's degrees in music education (a) required a course, (b) offered a course, or (c) in some other significant way systematically addressed the topic of teaching music to special populations. A link to a brief online survey was emailed to representatives of 212 institutions. Of 109 respondents, 29.6 percent required a course in teaching music to special populations, 38.9 percent indicated that this type of course was available, and 59.8 percent reported purposefully integrating the teaching of exceptional populations throughout their coursework. Respondent comments led to further literature review and discussion of the lack of consistent instruction with regard to this topic in undergraduate music education programs.

Physical Disabilities

Nabb, D., & Balcetis, E. (2010). Access to music education: Nebraska band directors' experiences and attitudes regarding students with physical disabilities. *Journal of Research in Music Education, 57*(4), 308–319. doi:10.1177/0022429409353142

Students with physical disabilities frequently are excluded from participation in instrumental music programs, yet the obstacles band directors face that preclude integration of these students have not been documented systematically. The primary purpose of this study was to measure Nebraska High School band directors' concerns regarding the integration of students with physical disabilities into their band programs. Results of a survey of 221 Nebraska high-school music programs suggested that awareness of options for ways to include students with physical disabilities, availability of adapted instruments, and the cost of acquiring such instruments are among band directors' primary concerns. Conclusions drawn from this survey serve as evidence that there is a need for adapted instruments and suggest that integration of students with disabilities and without disabilities in band would provide benefits for all.

Inclusiveness

Cassidy, J., & Colwell, C. (2012). University students' perceptions of an inclusive music production. *Journal of Music Teacher Education, 21*(2), 28–40. doi:10.1177/1057083711411714

A total of 130 undergraduate and graduate music education and music therapy students watched video of elementary children with cerebral palsy (CP) and typical peers preparing and performing in a musical production. The focus of the video was on preparation for inclusion, inclusive interactions, and the performance. Four questions addressing inclusion that required written responses from participants were posed. Responses were categorized for comparisons. Results indicated no significant difference due to training (music therapy majors, music education majors with and without class discussions on inclusion; $p > .05$). All groups focused on social more than academic benefits for all children. Participants noted the following: benefit of being in a musical play for the children with CP, that children without CP benefited from exposure to information about the disability, that children with CP gained from interacting with typical peers and from making a new friend and many of the techniques teachers used to prepare students for successful inclusion. More than a third were concerned that their future students would not accept children with disabilities in the classroom or that children with disabilities would be incapable. There is an apparent inability to make the transfer of using the identified teaching techniques to enable their own future efforts at inclusion to be successful.

Chapter 9

Composition and Improvisation

Beegle, A. (2010). A classroom-based study of small-group planned improvisation with fifth-grade children. *Journal of Research in Music Education, 58*(3), 219–239. doi:10.1177/0022429410379916

The purpose of this study was to examine and describe children's music improvisations and the interactions that transpired within their four-person groups during regular weekly music classes as they planned and performed music improvisations in response to three different prompts: a poem, a painting, and a musical composition. Participants were two classes of fifth-grade children at the elementary school where the researcher was the general music teacher. Sixteen children in four focus groups were chosen for closer observation and a series of interviews. Data were gathered over a 12-week period, utilizing audio- and video-recorded observations, daily field notes, and interviews following students' viewing of their own performances on video. The findings of this study demonstrate that: (a) all children utilized a similar planning process, and social roles and relationships were often correlated to musical roles and relationships; (b) children's music products differed based on the nature of the prompt, and children viewed prompts along a continuum of providing freedom of expression; and (c) children evidenced three specific strategies and expressed three valued considerations for planning and evaluating improvisation performances.

Bernhard II, H. C. (2013). Music education majors' confidence in teaching improvisation. *Journal of Music Teacher Education, 22*(2), 65–72. doi:10.1177/1057083712458593
The purpose of this study was to describe undergraduate music education majors' confidence in teaching improvisation, according to the National Association for Music Education K–12 Achievement Standards. Subjects were 196 undergraduate music education majors at a public university school of music. Combined subjects reported 'moderate confidence' for teaching Grade K–4 standards of improvisation, 'slight' to 'moderate confidence' for Grades 5 to 8 standards, and 'slight confidence' for teaching improvisation standards at the Grades 9 to 12 levels, and significant differences were found among the means for all three grade levels. Confidence increased by year in school (freshman, sophomore, junior, senior) and by primary instrument area (woodwind, brass, voice, piano, string, percussion). Subjects reported 'slight' to 'moderate confidence' in their own ability to improvise but 'moderate' to 'great interest' in learning more about how to teach improvisation. Implications for music teacher education are discussed.

Listening

Madsen, C., & Geringer, J. (2008). Reflections of Puccini's *La Bohème*: Investigating a model for listening. *Journal of Research in Music Education, 56*(1), 33–42. doi:10.1177/0022429408323072
A continuing line of research indicates that focus of attention is perhaps the most important attribute of actively participating in meaningful music listening and a model accounting for these findings has been developed. Music teachers are especially concerned with meaningful listening when having students discern important elements or attributes of music. Although newer listening devices offer sophisticated methods for continuous measurement, the educator usually does not have access to the advanced equipment used by researchers. This study is built on a previous investigation by examining the use of a paper-and-pencil drawing for recording aesthetic responses across time. The authors also asked the 50 university music major participants to reflect and write comments concerning their listening experiences. Findings indicate that a teacher using only a simple paper-and-pencil representation might be able to elicit and document an 'overall emotional effect' that provides almost as much information as using more sophisticated measuring devices.

Chapter 10

Information Processing

Bugos, J., & Mostafa, W. (2011). Musical training enhances information processing speed. *Bulletin of the Council for Research in Music Education, 187*, 7–18.

The purpose of this research was to examine the effects of music instruction on information-processing speed. The researchers examined music's role on information-processing speed in musicians ($N = 14$) and non-musicians ($N = 16$) using standardized neuropsychological measures, the Paced Auditory Serial Addition Task (PASAT) and the Trail Making Test (TMT). Results of a one-way ANOVA indicate significantly ($p < .05$) enhanced performance by musicians compared to non-musicians on the PASAT and TMT (Part A and B). These results suggest that musical training has the capacity to enhance processing speed of auditory and visual content. Implications for music educators stemming from these findings include the need for inclusion of rhythmic sight-reading exercises and improvisational activities to reinforce processing speed.

Self-Regulation

Hewitt, M. P. (2011). The impact of self-evaluation instruction on student self-evaluation, music performance, and self-evaluation accuracy. *Journal of Research in Music Education, 59*(1), 6–20. doi:10.1177/0022429410391541

The author sought to determine whether self-evaluation instruction had an impact on student self-evaluation, music performance, and self-evaluation accuracy of music performance among middle-school instrumentalists. Participants ($N = 211$) were students at a private middle school located in a metropolitan area of a mid-Atlantic state. Students in intact classes, Grades 5 through 8, were assigned to one of three treatment groups: self-evaluation instruction (SE-I), self-evaluation only (SE-O), or no self-evaluation (SE-No) for treatment lasting five weeks. All groups played through music used in the study at each lesson and heard a model recording of it. Participants in the SE-I group received instruction in self-evaluation, while students in the SE-O group self-evaluated their performances daily and the SE-No group received no additional instruction. Results suggest that instruction in self-evaluation had little impact on students; self-evaluation accuracy or music performance, although grade level did influence music performance. Additional time may be necessary for students to learn to evaluate their own performances effectively; however, it is interesting that students' music performance did not appear to suffer from time spent in self-evaluation instruction or practice. Music teachers may wish to consider implementing self-evaluation strategies to help students develop the skills necessary for successful self-regulation of music performance.

Miksza, P., Prichard, S., & Sorbo, D. (2012). An observational study of intermediate band students' self-regulated practice behaviors. *Journal of Research in Music Education, 60*(3), 254–266. doi:10.1177/0022429412455201

The purpose of this study was to investigate intermediate musicians' self-regulated practice behaviors. Thirty sixth- through eighth-grade students were observed practicing band repertoire individually for 20 minutes. Practice sessions were coded according to practice frame frequency and duration, length of musical passage selected, most prominent musical objective, and practice behaviors. The 600 minutes of video were parsed into 234 practice frames for analysis. Practice sessions also were rated for overall degree of self-regulation. Reliability of the observational procedures (three observers, 95 percent to 100 percent agreement) and self-regulation ratings (two raters, coefficients of 0.89 to 0.96) was excellent. Analyses revealed an average of 7.8 practice frames with a mean duration of 2 minutes and 45 seconds across sessions. Participants most frequently addressed the musical objective pitch accuracy and most commonly selected passages of nine measures in length or greater. The most common practice behaviors were varying tempo, repeating fewer than four measures, repeating more than four measures, and irrelevant playing. Significant relationships were found between self-regulation ratings and frequencies of the behaviors writing on music ($r = 0.55$), varying tempo ($r = 0.42$), repeating four or more measures ($r = 0.41$), and irrelevant playing ($r = 0.59$). Implications for future research and practical applications are discussed.

Chapter 11

Assessment

Darrow, A. A., Johnson, C.M., Miller, A.M., & Williamson, P. (2002). Can students accurately assess themselves? Predictive validity of student self-reports. *Update: Applications of Research in Music Education, 20*(2), 8–11. doi:10.1177/87551233020200203

The present study was designed to address the research question, 'Is there a relationship between the musical proficiencies students believe they possess and their performance on achievement tests designed to assess those skills?' Eight outcomes were selected from the content area 'melody' of a district-wide school music curriculum. Three test instruments were developed for the study: (a) a written student self-report questionnaire, (b) a music achievement test of musical knowledge that incorporated aural and visual recognition of melodic intervals and patterns, and (c) a music performance test devised to assess how well students could sing intervals and patterns as directed.

Ferguson, D. (2007). Program evaluations in music education: A review of the literature. *Update: Applications of Research in Music Education, 25*(2), 4–15. doi:10.1177/875 51233070250020102

Program evaluations can serve many goals. They can be undertaken in an attempt to determine a program's effect. They can be used as a tool for advocacy or as a justification for funding. Program evaluation can also be used as summative 'report card' or can be formative as an aid in decision-making. This study is a review of current literature concerning the various goals that program evaluations seek to meet.

Salvador, K. (2010). How can elementary teachers measure singing voice achievement? A critical review of assessments, 1994–2009. *Update: Applications of Research in Music Education, 29*(1), 40–47. doi:10.1177/8755123310378454

The first content standard of the National Standards for Music Education requires that students sing, alone and with others, a varied repertoire of music. Although state and district elementary music curricula vary widely, many are based on the National Standards for Music Education and therefore include singing as a primary content area and method of teaching and learning music. However, classroom assessments of singing voice achievement and development vary widely, and information about reliability and validity of these assessments is rarely reported. The purpose of this article was to identify and discuss measurements of singing voice achievement for elementary-aged students that have been used in research studies from dissertations and refereed music education journals since the publication of the National Standards for Music Education in 1994. The author describes each measurement tool, discusses its validity and reliability, and evaluates the practicality of each measure for classroom use by elementary general music teachers. Finally, recommendations for how one of these measures might be used to improve instruction in an elementary music classroom have been made.

Grading

McCoy, C. W. (1991). Grading students in performing groups: A comparison of principals' recommendations with directors' practices. *Journal of Research in Music Education, 39*(3), 181–190.

This article reports a study comparing Illinois high-school band and choral directors' grading systems with systems proposed by principals. Analysis suggested that principals placed more value on cognitive criteria and performance technique, but less on concert attendance and behavior than did directors. Findings suggest that music educators develop course and grading systems reflecting objectives deemed most important.

CONNECT TO PROFESSIONAL JOURNALS

Chapter 8

Inclusiveness

Fitzpatrick, K. R. (2012). Cultural diversity and the formation of identity: Our role as music teachers. *Music Educators Journal, 98*(4), 53–59. doi:10.1177/0027432112442903
This article encourages music teachers to consider the complexity of their students' cultural identities and the role these identities play in the formation of students' self-concept. The musical heritage students bring to the classroom may provide a rich foundation of experience for teaching and learning music. Readers are challenged to consider their own cultural backgrounds and experiences for possible preconceptions that may affect the classroom. Culturally relevant pedagogy is discussed as a way to improve the connection between school music curricula and student cultural identity, with specific suggestions and resources provided for the refinement of both curricular content and teaching.

Hoffman, A. R. (2012). Performing our world: Affirming cultural diversity through music education. *Music Educators Journal, 98*(4), 61–65. doi:10.1177/0027432112443262
This article describes a culturally responsive music curriculum through which students and teachers affirmed diverse stories of individuals present in our public-school community. An arts-integrated curriculum project helped make learning more meaningful while concurrently creating a safe learning space for students. This grant-funded project comprised three interwoven facets: a school-wide focus on world cultures and United States immigrant populations throughout the academic year; community celebrations of student learning through arts-based, experiential activities; and a core group of students who met weekly with teaching artists each week to disseminate knowledge via community informances. The themes connecting disciplines, content areas, and the school community served as lenses through which students gained artistic and academic skills as well as conceptual understandings about elements of language, culture, and community.

Religion

Hoffman, A. R. (2011). Rethinking religion in music. *Music Educators Journal, 97*(4), 55–59. doi:10.1177/0027432111404606

Much discussion concerning religious music in schools has been generated in our field. As we become increasingly sensitive to the diverse interests of the multiple stakeholders in public schools, issues of political correctness and pedagogical goals are raised. The author poses questions about religion and music education. To generate a different dialogue on this topic, four vignettes and alternate interpretations of the situations, as well as possible unintended consequences are examined. The author describes alternative approaches to music-learning contexts and offers questions to consider while keeping in mind the goal of music for all.

LGBTQ

Garrett, M.L. (2012). The LGBTQ component of 21st-century music teacher training: Strategies for inclusion from the research literature. *Update: Applications of Research in Music Education, 31*(1), 55–62. doi:10.1177/8755123312458294

Music is important to the development of multidimensional future adults. Students have self-reported the value of music in their lives. Music educators, therefore, have a unique opportunity to create inclusive learning environments. Music learning objectives are often rooted in development of rehearsal techniques and performance skills. However, teachers also impart personal values to students in the process. Diversity in contemporary school classrooms is represented by a variety of characteristics, including sexual orientation. Analysis of survey data indicates that a large percentage of lesbian, gay, bisexual, transgender, and questioning (LGBTQ) students are verbally and physically harassed at school. Teachers are often the first line of defense in situations involving harassment at school. This article is a synthesis of strategies for inclusion of LGBTQ issues in the music classroom, from research literature and oral histories.

Poverty

Bates, V.C. (2011). Sustainable school music for poor, white, rural students. *Action, Criticism, and Theory for Music Education, 10*(2), 100–127.

'Poor white trash' is likely the most enduring and degrading in a long line of 'stigmatypes'—'stigmatizing boundary terms that simultaneously denote and enact cultural and cognitive divides between in-groups and out-groups'—such as 'redneck,' 'cracker,' and 'hillbilly.' Some people apply these terms in reference to poor or working-class, usually rural (but not always), white Americans, conceived as strange, backwards, criminal, dangerous, lazy, inbred, diseased, dirty, malnourished, vulgar, promiscuous, ignorant, overly sentimental, and feeble-minded. There is also a tendency among upper- and middle-class whites to view poor, rural whites as a genetic and cultural threat. Many poor, white, rural students in the United States are subjected to the 'poor white trash' stigma. But the stigma also affects rural, working-class students, or rural whites whose household income is above the poverty line.

As opposed to conceiving 'poor-white-rural' people as a distinct group, it is more helpful, and accurate, to view 'poor-white-rural' as a complex intersection of dimensions between class, race, and/or geographical locations. In other words, the stigma that confounds white privilege with poverty and rurality extends well beyond a single demographic. In this article, the author explores, through the introspective lens of his own social-cultural-musical experiences in and out of rural schools, the potential oppression of poor, white, rural school music students in the United States. In the first section, he provides an overview of his family's home and school musical experiences, drawing attention to the clear distinction between the practices, aims, and musical outcomes of these two contexts. In the second section, he interrogates the 'common sense' belief that traditional school music practices in the United States are 'good for' children in the sense of fostering social mobility. His personal reflections and experiences as a teenager serve as an illustration in this regard. In the third and final section, he explores some ideas for how school music could be transformed in ways that might be more applicable, useful, and fair to poor, white, rural students.

Bates, V. C. (2012). Social class and school music. *Music Educators Journal, 98*(4), 33–37. doi:10.1177/0027432112442944

This article takes a practical look at social class in school music by exploring the manifestations and impact of three of its dimensions: financial resources, cultural practices, and social networks. Three suggestions are discussed: provide a free and equal music education for all students, understand and respect each student's cultural background, recognize the social forces that perpetuate poverty.

IDEA

Hammel, A., & Hourigan, R. (2011). The fundamentals of special education policy: Implications for music teachers and music teacher education. *Arts Education Policy Review, 112*(4), 174–179. doi:10.1080/10632913.2011.592463

The purpose of this article is to examine the fundamentals of the Individuals with Disabilities Education Act and its impact on music educators. Topics include: (a) zero reject, (b) non-discriminatory evaluations, (c) free appropriate public education, (d) least restrictive environment, (e) procedural due process, (f) parental involvement, and (g) response to intervention (RTI). Detailed explanations of policy are provided, along with strategies for implication in the music classroom.

Heikkila, E., & Knight, A. (2012). Inclusive music teaching strategies for elementary-age children with developmental dyslexia. *Music Educators Journal, 99*(1), 54–59. doi:10.1177/0027432112452597

Developmental dyslexia (DD) is more prevalent as an 'umbrella' disorder than many educators realize. The music educator can play a particularly useful role in helping children in the general or choral classroom cope with DD, given the temporal nature of cognitive issues inherent in the disorder. The purposes of this article are to provide a brief overview of DD and to offer teaching strategies for music educators to assist students with DD in the music classroom. Melodic and rhythmic activities are described and suggested as ways to engage children with DD as part of inclusive general music classrooms.

Special Learners

VanWeelden, K. (2011). Accommodating the special learner in secondary general music classes. *General Music Today, 24*(3), 39–41. doi:10.1177/1048371310396707
It can be challenging to know which accommodations for special learners can be used within the various secondary general music class settings. Fortunately, there have been several recent music education and therapy articles based on special education practices that have addressed techniques for working with students with special needs in music. These articles recommend using specific educational supports (e.g. written words, icons, color coding, other visual aids, assistive and supportive technology, echoing, and peer- mentoring) to help create successful learning experiences for all students. A synthesis of these educational supports and how they may transfer to secondary general music classes are defined and discussed.

Chapter 9

Composition

Guderian, L.V. (2012). Music improvisation and composition in the general music curriculum. *General Music Today, 25*(3), 6–14. doi:10.1177/1048371311415404
This article describes an approach to general music where assignments in music improvisation and composition are embedded into the curriculum. Creative assignments are given as an outgrowth of curriculum content and directly related to instruction and activities in conceptual learning and skill development in the classroom. Such an approach to general music education can make possible the teaching and learning of standards-based, sequentially designed curriculum and the nurturing of students' creative thinking in music, an almost simultaneous process. Included are practical suggestions for meeting National Standards Three (Improvisation) and Four (Composition) by embedding composition assignments into the general music curriculum per age categories of elementary-, middle-, and high-school learners supported by descriptions of examples from the field.

Improvisation

Beckstead, D. (2013). Improvisation: Thinking and playing music. *Music Educators Journal, 99*(3), 69. doi:10.1177/0027432112467822

This article explores and contextualizes improvisation in music from an educational perspective. First, recent brain research that sees improvisation as a distinct cognitive activity is examined and used to illustrate the importance and uniqueness of this often ignored area of music learning. Next, the implications for the music classroom are explored in light of the brain research findings as well as the common misconceptions associated with improvisation in music classrooms. Finally, some overarching principles to help guide the teaching of improvisation in any music classroom are offered.

Musical Independence

Neidlinger, E. (2011). Idea bank: Chamber music within the large ensemble. *Music Educators Journal, 97*(3), 22–23. doi:10.1177/0027432111400002

Many music educators incorporate chamber music in their ensemble programs—an excellent way to promote musical independence. However, we rarely think of the large ensemble as myriad chamber interactions. Rehearsals become more productive when greater responsibility for music making is placed on the individual student. This article lists some ways you can engage a large ensemble in chamber-like interactions.

Chapter 10

Learning Theory

Isbell, D. (2012). Learning theories: Insights for music educators. *General Music Today, 25*(2), 19–23. doi:10.1177/1048371311425684

Effective music educators often recognize that there is more than one way to teach a musical objective and understand that a specific approach may be more appropriate than another in a given setting. To meet contemporary demands, music educators need to be smart—understanding the nuances of various theories of learning; savvy—understanding their own learning style and how that may affect teaching effectiveness; and sensitive—understanding that teaching is situated in particular contexts. The music teacher's full potential may not be fully realized, however, unless that person is skilled enough to teach in a variety of ways. In this article, the author provides a basic overview and examples of diverse approaches to the classroom and offers practical suggestions for implementing these ideas in music classrooms.

Constructivism

Scott, S. J. (2011). Contemplating a constructivist stance for active learning within music education. *Arts Education Policy Review, 112*(4), 191–198. doi:10.1080/10632913.2011.592469

This article examines constructivist philosophies for learning with an emphasis on student-centered environments in education and the active involvement of students in learning as they relate new understanding to what they already know and refine previous skills in terms of newly acquired proficiencies. Active learning is explored from a constructivist perspective in which students adopt an analytic approach to questioning and problem solving. Through these processes, students extend their current understanding and emerge as independent musicians, actively engaged in their work as singers, players, composers, improvisers, and listeners. This approach is contrasted with student involvement in hands-on activities in which the focus is on the actions needed to fulfill a given task and limited awareness is devoted to the thinking required to complete the work. The author examines the implications of this approach for educational practice and call on policy makers to re-envision music education with attention to engaged learning as perceived within constructivist ways of knowing.

Scott, S.J. (2012). Constructivist perspectives for developing and implementing lesson plans in general music. *General Music Today, 25*(2), 24–30. doi:10.1177/104837131398285

Stacy McKenzie is challenged to find new ways to involve students in their learning. She begins this journey by developing a lesson-planning framework based on constructivist principles for learning. The perspectives Stacy applies in her program are shared in this article: first, by examining how she crafts a lesson framework that provides opportunities for students to build new understandings from what they already know through active involvement with music; and, second, by exploring how she uses questions to guide and support students' learning and how her students use questions as a means to assume an active role in their learning. This lesson is part of a larger unit of study using the piece 'Simple Gifts.'

Motivation

West, C. (2013). Motivating music students: A review of the literature. *Update: Applications of Research in Music Education.* doi:10.1177/8755123312473611

John Dewey knew that when students were actively involved in their learning they were more motivated and achieved higher. Unfortunately, our practices often negatively affect motivation, such as when teachers emphasize competition, social comparison, normative grading criteria, public forms of evaluation, and ability self-assessment. Most recently, researchers have begun exploring motivation through the lenses of: (a) how we attribute successes and failures (attribution theory), (b) reasons for achieving (achievement goal theory), and (c) ways in which we seek to satisfy our internal needs (intrinsic motivation theory). This article examines the music education literature within these three seminal social cognitive theories and discusses the implications to music education with respect to: (a) locus of control, (b) self-concept and achievement, and (c) motivational ways of engaging students. The article concludes with specific recommendations for increasing student motivation in the music classroom.

Chapter 11

Grading

Russell, J. A. (2011). Assessment and case law: Implications for the grading practices of music educators. *Music Educators Journal, 97*(3), 35–39. doi:10.1177/0027432110392051
Assessment continues to be a topic of discussion and concern for many music educators and music teacher educators. The discussion of assessment in music education can spark lively and passionate debate among music educators, music teacher educators, students, policy makers, and parents alike. This article offers a discussion of some of the litigation that has taken place in American courts that may significantly affect how many music educators assess their students now and in the future. Several steps are presented to help music educators create grading policies that meet legal guidelines as outlined by court rulings.

Assessment

Fisher, R. (2008). Debating assessment in music education. *Research and Issues in Music Education, 6*(1), 23–33.
Music education organizations achieved great success in Texas several years ago when legislation declared music as a part of the core curriculum. Similarly, more recent national education legislation like No Child Left Behind has recognized music as a core curricular subject. Since that time, little has been done to assess music students to ensure a set of basic skills and knowledge is being achieved. While national and state music standards exist, these standards, in many cases, are not mandatory and merely serve as a guide or recommendations for music educators to follow. Other core subjects endure severe oversight and rigorous testing at the state and local levels to measure whether or not students are attaining minimum standards. Some music educators are pushing for national

testing of music students to demonstrate that music has an academically measurable component. Yet other music educators are fearful that assessment of music education will have the same negative effects that other core subject high-stakes testing has had on schools. This article serves to discuss the current debate on national music assessment and to argue that music education's place in the core curriculum demands an increase in oversight through standardized music assessment of students in music education classes.

Silveira, J.M. (2013). Idea bank: Portfolios and assessment in music classes. *Music Educators Journal, 99*(3), 15–24. doi:10.1177/0027432112470071

The article offers information on portfolio and assessment in music education. It mentions that music portfolio provides a systematic approach to demonstrate and document the musical experiences of students, and can be a significant tool for music educators. It states there are several elements necessary in the creation of effective portfolios such as student self-reflection, selection of material, and criteria for judging student work. Moreover, one of the major strengths of portfolio assessment is the reflective process of continuous student self-evaluation that helps enhance evaluative technique.

Teacher Evaluation

Shuler, S. (2012). Music education for life: Music assessment, part 2—Instructional improvement and teacher evaluation. *Music Educators Journal, 98*(3), 7–10. doi:10.1177/0027432112439000

Educators are professionals. Teaching is not just a job; it is at least a career and arguably a mission. One important attribute of professionals is the constant quest for personal growth. Great music educators are lifelong learners who draw on a variety of sources to improve their expertise and effectiveness.

CONNECT TO THE WEB

Chapter 8

Eric Jensen on Teaching Kids in Poverty—Brain-Based Learning

http://www.youtube.com/watch?v=fSshAsUpeTI
Brain-Based Learning to overcome the challenges of teaching kids in poverty.

http://www.teachingwithpovertyinmind.com
The number one challenge for teachers and school administrators is teaching students affected by poverty. There is an element that the education community is powerless to

control—poverty. In the past two years, the rate of poverty has grown at an alarming rate and now even traditional middle-class schools are feeling the pressure that comes with the stress of poverty.

Dignity for All

http://www.youtube.com/watch?v=hWI3CYD16ho
Peter DeWitt Ed.D., Teach.com contributor, and author of *Dignity For All: Safeguarding LGBT Students*, talks about how schools can implement policies that protect LGBT students from bullying. Visit www.teach.com for more information.

Including Samuel

http://www.youtube.com/watch?v=Xfg1pswiOgM
Photojournalist Dan Habib rarely thought about inclusion before he had his son Samuel seven years ago. Now he thinks about inclusion every day. Habib's documentary film *Including Samuel* examines the educational and social inclusion of youth with disabilities as a civil rights issue.

Music for Special Needs

http://www.youtube.com/watch?v=PnPb_csb0ik
To improve the communication skills of students with profound special needs, including those with autism, Down syndrome, and cerebral palsy, Dr. David Lazerson and his co-applicant, Cindy Frost, implemented a music program in special education classes. The team used software to assist students in understanding the nuances of simple instruments, and, eventually, learning and playing songs. Students interacted with members of their community through song and dance performances at senior centers, other schools, and a local children's hospital.

Chapter 9

Embodiment: Resources and Definitions

http://www.embodiment.org.uk/definition.htm
Many different resources to understand the concept of embodiment in music.

Music Outside the Lines: Ideas for Composing in K-12 Music Classrooms

http://musicoutsidethelines.com

This website/blog will serve as an extension to Molly Weaver's recently published book that offers both practical and research-based ideas for teachers (anyone) to engage students in composition and improvisation. Dr. Weaver has been enjoying composition and improvisation work with children and adults of all ages and places for a very long time. Her conviction has only grown stronger over timel; that these creative music activities are among the most powerful that we can offer our students in music teaching spaces.

Murphy Hip-Hop

http://www.youtube.com/watch?v=4ccP7be0BF0&list=UUcVLML4Ehz1g PKllaArsvMQ

Video of original compositions from students at Ira A. Murphy school in Phoenix, AR. Robert Vagi, the band director, has instituted a hip-hop class where students create and record original compositions.

Expressing Visual Art Through Music

https://www.teachingchannel.org/videos/music-and-visual-art
Lesson connecting music and visual art.

Chapter 10

Use a Learning Theory: Behaviorism

http://www.youtube.com/watch?v=KYDYzR-ZWRQ
This short, light-hearted video explores the learning theory of behaviorism.

Classical Conditioning: The Office

http://www.youtube.com/watch?v=nE8pFWP5QDM
A comical look at Pavlov's theory.

Operant Conditioning with Sheldon Cooper

http://www.youtube.com/watch?v=dtWz8Ex8JKQ
A comical look at theories of Thorndike and Skinner.

Use a Learning Theory: Cognitivism

http://www.youtube.com/watch?v=hKIE6raT9M4b
This short, light-hearted video explains the learning theory of cognitivism.

Information Processing Theory

http://www.youtube.com/watch?v=zCLotWLfjd0
A fun look at information processing theory.

Schema Theory Example

http://www.youtube.com/watch?v=o4HHCgFmkcI
A great example of how schema theory works.

Bandura's Social Cognitive Theory

http://www.youtube.com/watch?v=OMBlwjEoyj4
Treading new ground in the field of social psychology, Albert Bandura's work has become basic to an understanding of how social forces influence individuals, small groups and large groups. From his early Bobo doll experiments, through his work with phobias, to his recent work on self-efficacy, Bandura has given us a sense of how people actively shape their own lives and those of others.

Use a Learning Theory: Constructivism

http://www.youtube.com/watch?v=Xa59prZC5gA
This short, light-hearted video explains the learning theory of constructivism.

Illustration of Schemas, Assimilation, and Accommodation

http://www.youtube.com/watch?v=3-A9SgbAK5I
Slide show about these three concepts from Piaget's theories.

Situated Learning and Communities of Practice

http://www.youtube.com/watch?v=roKJbwCLNBs
Short film on the theories of Lave and Wenger.

Musical Futures

https://www.musicalfutures.org
Musical Futures is a movement to reshape music education, driven by informal music learning research and theory. This is the home page for their website of considerable resources.

Musical Futures: Introduction to Informal Music Learning

**https://www.musicalfutures.org/resource/27235/title/informallearningfirst
    editionteacherpack**

This is a series of videos from the 'teacher pack' produced by Musical Futures. It should be noted that this is situated in the United Kingdom and curricular approaches to teaching music are different there than in the United States, but the content of informal music learning is made clear.

Brief Introduction to Metacognition

http://www.youtube.com/watch?v=mVE21QhY-lI
A short Prezi® on this topic.

Drive: The Surprising Truth About What Motivates Us

http://www.youtube.com/watch?v=u6XAPnuFjJc
This lively RSA Animate, adapted from Dan Pink's talk at the RSA, illustrates the hidden truths behind what really motivates us at home and in the workplace.

Chapter 11

Developing a Grading System

http://ctlt.illinoisstate.edu/resources/DYC/module9.php
This is a useful outline in developing a meaningful grading system aimed at university level teaching, but can easily be applied to the K-12 setting.

Individualizing a Grading System for a Student with LD and an IEP

**http://www.greatschools.org/special-education/legal-rights/1019-grading-
    system-for-a-student-with-ld-and-an-iep.gs**
Get expert advice on working with your students' IEP teams to develop a fair and equitable approach to grading.

Standards-Based Grading in the Music Classroom

http://musicstandards.blogspot.com
This blog shares ideas on standards-based processes from teachers all around the country.

Music Education Standards and Assessment

http://musicstandards.org

Access to all state and national standards for music education.

2012 Music Assessment Symposium—Assessment and Teacher Evaluation

http://www.youtube.com/watch?v=X3a9tk9dp-8

Opening remarks from NAfME past president, Scott Shuler, at the National Symposium on Music Assessment and Teacher Evaluation held in Baltimore, Maryland, on June 24 and 25, 2012.

http://www.youtube.com/watch?v=ivH4ghsKn7w

A presentation by Dr. Kelly A. Parkes, Associate Professor in Music Education, Virginia Tech, and chair of NAfME SRME Assessment Special Research Interest Group at the National Symposium on Music Assessment and Teacher Evaluation held in Baltimore, Maryland, on June 24 and 25, 2012.

http://www.youtube.com/watch?v=b5rkvOeXaSo

A presentation by Dr. Doug Orzolek, Associate Professor of Education, University of St. Thomas, chair of NAfME SRME Teacher Evaluation Special Research Interest Group, at the National Symposium on Music Assessment and Teacher Evaluation held in Baltimore, Maryland, on June 24 and 25, 2012.

http://www.youtube.com/watch?v=PgWHzM2yKrU

A presentation by Beth Cummings, Senior Coordinator for Music, Polk County Schools, and Dr. John Seybert, Associate Professor of Education, Southeastern University, at the National Symposium on Music Assessment and Teacher Evaluation held in Baltimore, Maryland, on June 24 and 25, 2012.

http://www.youtube.com/watch?v=KE8n3xLXas0

A presentation by Karol Gates, Content Specialist for the Arts, Colorado Department of Education, and John Epps, District Performing Arts Coordinator, Denver Public Schools, at the National Symposium on Music Assessment and Teacher Evaluation held in Baltimore, Maryland, on June 24 and 25, 2012.

http://www.youtube.com/watch?v=I7x2tdFOmlI

A presentation by Richard Wells, Performing Arts Supervisor for Simsbury Schools (retired), at the National Symposium on Music Assessment and Teacher Evaluation held in Baltimore, Maryland, on June 24 and 25, 2012.

http://www.youtube.com/watch?v=xXP1YdEP5co

A presentation by David Weatherred, Arts Coordinator, Spokane Public Schools, at the National Symposium on Music Assessment and Teacher Evaluation held in Baltimore, Maryland, on June 24 and 25, 2012.

http://www.youtube.com/watch?v=lHNUfWFDs7g

A presentation by Tom Dean, NAfME Eastern Division President, at the National Symposium on Music Assessment and Teacher Evaluation held in Baltimore, Maryland, on June 24 and 25, 2012.

http://www.youtube.com/watch?v=sPRJwJjezrM

A presentation by Frank Coachman, Deputy Director of the Texas Music Educators Association, at the National Symposium on Music Assessment and Teacher Evaluation held in Baltimore, Maryland, on June 24 and 25, 2012.

http://www.youtube.com/watch?v=5oS81p23EFA

A presentation by Johanna Siebert, Director of Fine Arts, Webster Community School District, at the National Symposium on Music Assessment and Teacher Evaluation held in Baltimore, Maryland, on June 24 and 25, 2012.

Society for Music Teacher Education: Teacher Evaluation

http://smte.us/teacher-evaluation/

A site with the most current research and positions on the current status of teacher evaluation.

Norm-Referenced vs. Criterion-Referenced

http://www.edpsycinteractive.org/topics/measeval/crnmref.html

Easy table to help understand the differences between these two concepts.

Learning Domains

http://www.youtube.com/watch?v=NPBZQ4J46GI

Review of the three learning domains.

 ## CONNECT TO THE CLASSROOM

Prior to watching one of the teaching videos available on the website, familiarize yourself with the questions below. As you view the video, take notes on what you see and hear.

We suggest that you either download the video observation form from the text website or simply use a sheet of paper that has been divided into two columns. On the left side, list the events you see and hear taking place in the classroom. On the right side, make short notes about why you believe the teacher chose to use these events during the lesson. You may find it easiest to list all the events and then go back and make your notes on why the teacher chose those events as part of his or her instruction. After you watch the video, address the questions below.

1. How did this teacher help students establish musical independence?
2. Which national standards did this lesson address?
3. What evidence of a behavioral, cognitive, or constructivist approaches to student learning did you observe in this classroom? (Give examples of each, if possible.)
4. What motivational techniques did you observe in this classroom?
5. What forms of assessment did the teacher use in this lesson?
6. What assessment tools, if any, did he/she use? What other assessment tools could this teacher use in this lesson?
7. Would you say there was more (a) assessment of learning, (b) assessment for learning, or (c) assessment as learning? What evidence do you have to support this position?

EPILOGUE–REDISCOVERING WHO YOU ARE AS A DEVELOPING MUSIC TEACHER

INDIVIDUAL ACTIVITY

Revisiting Your Concept Map

Go back to the concept map you developed at the beginning of this text. Based on your experiences and understandings developed over your time with this text, examine your map for the following:

1. concepts that you believe are missing
2. concepts that are not completely formed or not represented accurately
3. concepts that are well-formed and complete
4. missing connections between concepts
5. connections that are not represented accurately, and
6. connections that are complete and accurate.

Based upon this examination, develop a new concept map that would more accurately represent your understanding of effective music teacher development. Once your new map is complete, compare it to your first map. What concepts do you understand differently than before you worked through this text? What concept understandings have been reinforced? What are new concepts that you may have not considered prior to this time?

Using the information in your concept map and the questions above, conduct a self-assessment. First, assess what you already know and can do that will help you become the professional music educator you desire to be. Second, assess what knowledge and skills you need to develop, and, finally, make a plan for how you are going to maintain your current knowledge and skills while developing the new knowledge and skills you need to acquire.

THE JOURNEY

As you read and worked through activities in this book (and in class) we hope you have taken some initial steps along your journey, moving from your role as *music student* to that of *music teacher.* These first steps are perhaps the most important in putting you on the path toward becoming the most effective professional music educator you are capable of becoming. By now, you are aware that the journey will likely never end. For those who are very goal-oriented, this realization may bring some feelings of trepidation about what you are doing. For others, you may be excited about the prospect of lifelong learning and growing in the profession; but you might be overwhelmed with the questions that have begun to surface. A look back at what you have experienced thus far on this journey may be helpful.

Throughout this book, we have asked you to examine your conscious and unconscious motivations for being a music teacher. In Part I, you began to explore your role as a prospective music teacher. You examined various roles that professional music educators adopt and compared the roles of *teachers as technicians* with *teachers as professionals.* You also noticed various qualities exhibited by excellent teachers and considered whether it was possible to develop these qualities in yourself. Through the use of metaphor, you began to examine both the expressed (explicit) and unexpressed (implicit) beliefs that guide your thinking and decision-making. You may be challenged as you continue to compare your expressed beliefs with the implicit beliefs you uncovered in this process. As you learned from exploring the work of Piaget, this kind of disequilibrium will bring you to a new understanding. Part I of the text concluded with an examination of the knowledge, skills, and dispositions you will need to develop as an effective music educator.

Moving into Part II you began to investigate the various teaching concerns you may encounter. You started by exploring the environments where music has been taught in the past, the various settings in which music is being taught currently, and developed ideas about the places that music may be taught in the future. You learned about the *four common places* (student, teacher, subject matter, and milieu) and noted their presence in every teaching/learning endeavor. You discussed how you can use the connections among the four common places to inform your teaching decisions. You noted the strengths and challenges of the American education system and how those issues might impact teaching music in today's and tomorrow's schools. You examined the *delivery skills* necessary for music teachers to present instruction in engaging ways. You debated the similarities and differences between acting and teaching, making note of skills related to effective use of your voice, body, and teaching space. Structure for music teaching including curriculum, long-range planning, and individual lesson planning were examined. Finally, you examined some methods and approaches used by music educators and compared the similarities among these to develop a list of music teaching concepts that could inform your teaching in the music classroom.

Part III moved your attention away from self-concerns and teaching concerns to student learning concerns. You acknowledged that, while you must be aware of your role as a music teacher and be able to design and present informed and effective instruction, you ultimately need to be aware of the impact you are having on your students. Starting with an honest exploration of student diversity, you looked at how you can both know about your students (i.e. group demographics) and how you can know your students as individuals. You also examined ways in which your students can come to know you as you develop an effective rapport as their music teacher. You considered what students should know and be able to do as musically educated individuals. You examined the *elements of music* and then, using the framework provided by the *National Standards for Music Education*, you noted how you might develop the various knowledge, skills, and dispositions necessary to facilitate musical independence among your students. Through the lenses of *behaviorism, cognitivism*, and *constructivism,* you discussed various views of how people learn and how this information can affect the ways you choose to help students become *self-regulated* learners. Finally, you made note of the various purposes, forms, types, and uses of assessment available to the music teacher. You examined various *assessment tools* that may be useful in assessing musical learning and how you can make use of assessment *of learning, for learning*, and *as learning* in your classrooms. There have been opportunities for many steps in your journey to become a professional music educator.

NEXT STEPS

Having taken some initial steps, you might be exhilarated at the prospect of entering such a dynamic and gratifying field. You are equally likely to be fearful about the gravity of taking on the responsibilities of being a professional music educator. Most likely, you are experiencing a combination of these emotions that flux with each question that enters your mind. Because there are so many questions, some prospective music teachers begin to have reservations about their suitability for the music teaching profession. We would like to state very clearly that having a wide array of questions concerning your professional development is very healthy and appropriate. It shows an honest respect for the career you are about to enter and that you are seriously considering what that process entails.

Most importantly, we believe that effective professional development will help you know what questions you need to ask so that you can meet the needs of your students. Many feel education should be concerned only with providing answers. This is likely the culture you have experienced most often in your own educational endeavors. Helping students find answers is an important part of education, but your professional education should also help you value important questions, perhaps even more than the answers, because the answers will vary. All of you are different people with diverse and unique backgrounds that influence the understandings you bring to your teaching. Moreover, each of you will be teaching in different settings with equally diverse student populations. Just considering these two factors, it is likely that answers to questions like "Who are my students?" "What should they learn?" and "How do they learn?" will be different for each of you. Rather than entering the profession armed with some 'pat' answers to a limited number of questions, you will be better served knowing what questions will allow you to acquire the answers *your* teaching environment will require. Therefore, your professional development should be focused, helping you develop the best questions to ask so you can find the right answers. **If you are currently contemplating all sorts of questions about teaching music, you are likely right where you need to be in your professional development as a music educator.**

As you embark on the remainder of your degree plan, we challenge you to be proactive in a couple of specific areas. Although a great deal of thought and expertise has impacted the design of your degree plan, no plan alone can provide what everyone needs in his or her professional development. Your first challenge is to look seriously at what you believe *you* need to know and be able to do as a professional music educator. Then consider what experiences you will have in your coursework that will help you develop the knowledge and skills *you* need. Enter your courses viewing them as opportunities to develop as a professional music educator and not simply as another class you must check off the degree plan to graduate. What you learn and how you retain it, as a result of this change of perspective, will be beneficial to your professional development. Remember, the goal is not just to get your degree (although that will feel very good), but to develop as a professional music educator who can positively impact students in your charge. As you broaden your perspective, you might consider that you are not simply learning for yourself, but you are learning for the benefit of all the students you will interact with in the not too distant future. They deserve to learn from a well-informed professional music educator and that can be you! You are the future of music education.

Your second challenge is to consider the knowledge and skills you need to develop that may not all be addressed in your degree plan. Once you identify these items, we suggest you locate the *more-knowledgeable-other(s)* who can help you develop the understandings and skills you need. University faculty members may fill this role, but you should also consider practicing music educators, local music merchants, and your collegiate colleagues as resources. Admittedly, it is risky venturing out on your own to find what you need. You will likely receive conflicting information and, at times, information that may even be detrimental to your development. You will need to consider all the information you acquire carefully. Many of the concepts developed in this text will help you weigh the benefits and risks of what you learn and experience in your explorations. Once you make decisions about what to try, and you learn from what does and does not work, you will 'own' the knowledge and skills you developed to a much greater degree than you would from reading it in a book. To be an effective professional music educator you need to take ownership of your teaching.

FINDING A BALANCE

As you consider the next steps in your professional development you should also look beyond your career path to take stock of your life goals. We believe these goals can easily include living a fulfilled life as a music educator. However, to do so, you must find a way to balance the personal and professional parts of your life. Hancock (2008) reports that 20 percent of music teachers leave the profession in the first three years and 40 percent to 50 percent leave by the fifth year. Many elements contribute to this attrition. "Significant predictors included young age (less than 30 years; 30–39 years), teaching in a secondary or private school, extracurricular hours, school wide concerns, limited support from administrators and parents, lower salary, and dissatisfaction with salary" (Hancock, 2008, p. 130). Throughout this text, we have examined the rigorous process of becoming a professional music educator and it likely comes as no surprise that effective music teachers often work long hours, spend time away from family, and do not have great monetary reward for their efforts. At times, music teachers do not enjoy great support from administrators, or from other teaching colleagues, and/or from parents or community members. These factors, and others, can have a detrimental effect on anyone's career, especially if that person is totally consumed by his or her job. Young teachers too often enter the profession with great excitement and anticipation only to find obstacles they had not considered. In the process of negotiating their way through these concerns, it is easy for these young teachers to focus entirely on the obstacles and lose sight of their original goals. This loss of focus can lead to stress and poor quality of life. Over time it can contribute to marital problems, abuse of students, and can even lead to criminal behavior (Rush & Lane, 2011).

To avoid the detrimental effects of the inevitable stresses that come with music teaching, it is essential that you begin working on the strategies you will use to manage your life. We believe that a healthy life as a music teacher must be balanced and that you should find ways to promote your financial health, your emotional health, and your physical health (Rush & Lane, 2011). It is unlikely that you decided to become a music educator because of the financial rewards that await you. However, you do need to meet your financial obligations. Many of you will leave college with student loan debt. Additionally, there will be initial needs that you have as a young professional, like obtaining a professional wardrobe. Perhaps replacing an aging car that was meant to just 'get me through school' is necessary. Some will move to new communities where you will need housing and all that goes with getting established in a new community. Any of these can put a financial strain on a young teacher. There are, however, ample resources to help young professionals with their financial planning. While we cannot recommend specific programs, we would encourage you to start early and have a plan to manage your finances. There will be surprises along the way, but the security of a plan will provide a foundation to work from when the unexpected happens. You likely will not become financially wealthy as a music educator, but with good money management you can have ample resources to live comfortably.

Emotional health requires that one attempts to avoid the 'roller coaster' of extreme highs and lows as much as possible. As teachers work with people, it is impossible to eliminate the natural ebb and flow of human emotion that comes with daily interactions. In fact, it would be unhealthy to close yourself off to these experiences and become emotionally untouched by the experiences in your professional life. There are two primary contributors to becoming overly emotionally invested in your career. First is the fact that most music teachers are very passionate about their work. Many of you were first attracted to music and music teaching because of the feelings you had about making music both alone and with others. When fueled with the prospect of working with children and enriching their lives with music, this passion can become all-consuming, leading to our second contributor: not being able to separate the job from 'real life' (Rush & Lane, 2011).

Young music teachers are particularly prone to allowing their jobs to consume all aspects of their lives (Hancock, 2009). To manage this, Rush and Lane (2011) offer several suggestions. All music teachers, particularly those who are single, should find activities they enjoy outside of school and perhaps even outside of music. This allows you to form a basis for relationships with others that is not job-related. They go on to suggest that music teachers with family plan to be home one day a week by 4:00 p.m., schedule playtime with young children, and have lunch with older children at school. They encourage music teachers to come home between the end of the school day and evening rehearsals or performances and plan to be home for a sit-down dinner at least twice a week.

Special efforts need to be made for spousal/partner relationships. Rush and Lane (2011) recommend that clear and continual lines of communication remain open. Regular 'date nights' should be scheduled for just the two of you where 'shop talk' is not allowed. On the job front, Rush and Lane (2011) suggest you schedule time to talk with your direct administrator about the demands of your position and keep him or her informed about your workload. Music teachers are notorious for taking on so much they become ineffective. We suggest you delegate parts of the job that can be done by someone other than you to parents and even students. They can take on many tasks that could otherwise consume much of your time. If you work on a staff, share the workload across staff members and pick up the slack for others when life events cause them (or you) to need the help. Rush and Lane (2011) go on to recommend you remind yourself often why you chose the profession. Surround yourself with great music you enjoy and recharge your batteries often through great professional development (e.g. state and national music conferences). It is important to remember that you can only give what you have.

Remaining physically healthy will require a number of strategies. First, be smart about general hygiene while you interact with large groups of people. It is not uncommon for a young teacher (even those in early field experience) to be ill by the third or fourth week of a new school year. Exposure to many children means exposure to many new germs. To avoid getting ill, wash your hands often or have hand sanitizer available. It is especially necessary to practice good common hygiene in brass and woodwind classes. Handle instruments carefully, and never play on a student's instrument without sanitizing it first. There are a number of commercial products available for just this purpose.

Maintaining a healthy voice is also critically important. This applies to all music teachers and not just those teaching in the vocal classroom. When you start to teach you will likely be using your voice for many more hours than you are normally accustomed. Vocal fatigue can be a real problem if you do not care for your voice properly. Avoid speaking at loud volumes for long periods of time. Drink plenty of water (coffee is not the same thing) to keep the vocal mechanism lubricated. If you begin to lose your voice or feel vocal strain, you need to limit the time you use your voice. If losing your voice begins to happen frequently, we advise seeing someone who specializes in vocal care, because some damage can be permanent.

Getting plenty of sleep is essential to being healthy as well. It is best for you to get regular sleep. Your body does not benefit from periods of no sleep followed by stretches of long sleep hours in an effort to 'catch up.' It is difficult, at times, to stop working on a project and go get some rest, especially in your first few years as a music teacher. As a college student you may have 'pulled an all-nighter' once in a while to get a project done or to prepare for an exam. Your day as a music teacher is much different than your day as a music student. You may have been able to operate minimally on very little sleep when your only responsibility was you and your needs. Being responsible to meet the needs of all your students is physically challenging even when you are well rested, and nearly impossible when you are sleep deprived. Adopting regular healthy sleep habits will require you to be a good time manager and to prioritize tasks effectively. For some, time management seems to be a natural part of their personalities; for others, time management can be a genuine challenge. If time management is an issue for you, we suggest you make use of all the resources available. A primary resource could be a mentor teacher who can help you establish efficient procedures for what you are doing. This mentor may not be another music teacher. Veteran teachers in all subject areas and grade levels have learned how to make effective use of their time. We recommend you avail yourself of all the input you can find concerning how to be an effective time manager.

Keeping physically fit is also beneficial for any music teacher. You may not have hours to go to the gym every day, but you can make efforts to be physically active. Simple things like taking the stairs instead of the elevator and walking or biking short distances rather than driving can help you stay active and may even provide a nice short respite from the stressors of your day. For those who want to engage in activity outside of music and meet others, most communities have walking, running, and/or biking clubs. These often include members at all ability levels, and they offer a great way to meet people from all different professions and have a support group to help you stay active at the same time. However you decide to be active, it will be a great help to keep you fresh and focused for your teaching.

A FINAL THOUGHT

A Japanese proverb states: "Better than a thousand days of diligent study is one day with a great teacher." We believe this ancient wisdom to be true today. You have chosen a noble profession that will repay your efforts by connecting you to the lives of people. You will enrich those lives by helping them understand themselves and their world more completely through music. With each person who is affected through his or her interactions with you, the world changes. We believe this change is for the better and that great music teachers make our world a better place in which to live. Your journey to the profession has just started. Take each step with purpose and the drive to be a world changer . . . one student at a time. Good luck and travel well.

REFERENCES

Abeles, H. F., Hoffer, C. R., & Klotman, R. H. (1996). *Foundations of music education* (2nd ed.). New York: Schirmer.

About The Midwest Clinic. (n.d.). *The Midwest clinic: An international band and orchestra conference*. Retrieved from http://www.midwestclinic.org/about_midwest.html

American Psychological Association. (2008). *Answers to your questions: For a better understanding about sexual orientation and homosexuality.* Washington, DC: Author. Retrieved from http://www.apa.org/topics/sexuality/sorientation.pdf

American Psychological Association. (2011). *Answers to your questions about transgender people, gender identity, and gender expression* (2nd ed.). Washington, DC: Author. Retrieved from http://www.apa.org/topics/sexuality/transgender.pdf

Asmus, E. (1999). Music assessment concepts. *Music Educators Journal 86*(2), 19–24. doi:10.2307/3399585

Atkinson, R. C., & Shiffrin, R. M. (1968). Human memory: A proposed system and its control processes. In Spence, K. W., & Spence, J. T. *The psychology of learning and motivation* (Vol 2, pp. 89–195). New York: Academic Press.

Aubusson, P. J., Harrison, A. G., & Ritchie, S. M. (2006). Metaphor and analogy: Serious thought in science education. In P. J. Aubusson, A. G. Harrision, & S. M. Ritchie (Eds.), *Metaphor and analogy in science education* (pp. 1–9). Dordrecht, The Netherlands: Springer.

Aud, S., Fox, M., & KewalRamani, A. (2010). *Status and Trends in the Education of Racial and Ethnic Groups* (NCES 2010–015). U.S. Department of Education, National Center for Education Statistics. Washington, DC: U.S. Government Printing Office.

Ausubel, D. A. (1960). The use of advanced organizers in the learning and retention of meaningful verbal material. *Journal of Educational Psychology, 51*, 267–271. doi:10.1037/h0046669

Azzara, C. D. (1999). An aural approach to improvisation: Music educators can teach improvisation even if they have not had extensive exposure to it themselves. Here are some basic strategies. *Music Educators Journal, 86*(3), 21–25. doi:10.2307/3399555

Azzara, C. D., & Grunow, R. F. (2006). *Developing musicianship through improvisation.* Chicago, IL: GIA

Bachelder, D. F., & Hunt, N. J. (2001). *Guide to teaching brass.* (6th ed.). Dubuque, IA: Wm. C. Brown.

Ball, D., Thames, M., & Phelps, G. (2008). Content knowledge for teaching: What makes it special? *Journal of Teacher Education, 59*(5), 389–407. doi:10.1177/0022487108324554

Bandura, A. (1986). *Social foundations of thought and action.* Englewood Cliffs, NJ: Prentice Hall.

Barrett, J. R. (2001). Interdisciplinary work and musical integrity. *Music Educators Journal, 87*(5), 27–31. doi:10.2307/3399705

Barrett, J. R. (2005). Planning for understanding: A reconeptualized view of the music curriculum. *Music Educators Journal, 91*(4), 21–25. doi:10.2307/3400154

Barrett, J. R., McCoy, C. W., & Veblen, K. K. (1997). *Sound ways of knowing: Music in the interdisciplinary curriculum.* New York: Schirmer.

Bauer, W. I., & Berg, M. H. (2001). Influences on instrumental music teaching. *Bulletin of the Council for Research in Music Education, 150,* 53–66.

Bean, J. C. (2011). *Engaging ideas.* San Francisco: Jossey-Bass.

Becker, B., & Luthar, S. (2002). Social-emotional factors affecting achievement outcomes among disadvantaged students: Closing the achievement gap. *Educational Psychologist, 37*(4), 197–214. doi:10.1207/S15326985EP3704_1

Bell, C. L. (2003). Beginning the dialogue: Teachers respond to the national standards. *Bulletin of the Council for Research in Music Education, 156,* 31–42.

Benedict, C. (2010). Curriculum. In H. Abeles & L. Custodero (Eds.), *Critical issues in music education* (pp. 143–166). New York: Oxford University Press.

Berg, M. H., & Mikzsa, P. (2010). An investigation of preservice music teacher development and concerns. *Journal of Music Teacher Education 20*(1), 39–55. doi:10.1177/1057083710363237

Bergonzi, L. (2009). Sexual orientation and music education: Continuing a tradition. *Music Educators Journal, 96*(2), 21–25. doi:10.1177/0027432109350929

Bettencourt, E., Gillett, M., & Hull, J. (1983). Effects of teacher enthusiasm training on student on-task behavior and achievement. *American Education Research Journal, 20*(3), 435–450. doi:10.3102/00028312020003435

Bierhoff, H.-W. (1989). *Person perception and attribution.* Berlin: Springer-Verlag.

Bjorklund, D. F., & Blasi, C. H. (2009). *Child and adolescent development: An integrated approach.* Belmont, CA: Wadsworth.

Blenkin, G., Edwards, G., & Kelly, A. (1992). *Change and the curriculum,* London: Paul Chapman.

Bloom, B. S. (1956). *Taxonomy of educational objectives, Handbook I: The cognitive domain.* New York: David McKay.

Boyer, R., & Rozmajzl, M. (2012). *Music fundamentals, methods, and materials for the elementary classroom teacher*. Boston, MA: Pearson.

Breed, G., & Colaiuta, V. (1974). Looking, blinking, and sitting: Nonverbal dynamics in the classroom. *Journal of Communication, 24*, 75–81. doi:10.1111/j.1460-2466.1974.tb00371.x

Brophy, J. (2004). *Motivating students to learn* (2nd ed.). Boston, MA: McGraw-Hill.

Brown, J.K. (2008). Student-centered instruction: Involving students in their own education. *Music Educators Journal, 94*(5), 30–35. doi:10.1177/00274321080940050108

Bruner, J.S. (1966). *Toward a theory of instruction.* New York: Norton.

Bruning, R.H., Schraw, G.J., & Ronning, R.R. (1999). *Cognitivie psychology and instruction* (3rd ed.). Columbus, OH: Merrill.

Burrack, F., & McKenzie, T. (2005). Enhanced student learning through cross-disciplinary projects. *Music Educators Journal, 91*(5), 45–50. doi:10.2307/3400142

Butler, R., & Neuman, O. (1995). Effects of task and ego-achievement goals on help-seeking behaviors and attitudes. *Journal of Educational Psychology, 87*, 261–271. doi:10.1037/0022-0663.87.2.261

Byo, S.J. (1999). Classroom teachers' and music specialists' perceived ability to implement the national standards for music education. *Journal of Research in Music Education, 47*(2), 111–123. doi:10.2307/3345717

Caldas S., & Bankston III, C. (1997). Effect of school population socioeconomic status on individual academic achievement. *Journal of Educational Research, 90*, 269–277. doi:10.1080/00220671.1997.10544583

Cameron, L. (2008). Metaphor in the construction of a learning envirnment. In E.A. Berendt (Ed.), *Metaphors for learning: Cross cultural perspectives* (pp. 159–176). Amsterdam: John Benjamins Publishing Co.

Campbell, M.R., & Thompson, L.K. (2007). Perceived concerns of preservice music education teachers: A cross-sectional study. *Journal of Research in Music Education, 55*(2), 162–176. doi: 10.1177/002242940705500206

Campbell, P.S. (2005). Deep listening to the musical world. *Music Educators Journal, 92*(1), 30–36. doi:10.2307/3400224

Carr-Saunders, A.M., & Wilson, P.A. (1933). *The professions.* Oxford, England: Clarendon Press.

Cass, V.C. (1979). Homosexual identity formation: A theoretical model. *Journal of Homosexuality, 4*(3), 219–235. doi: 10.1300/J082v04n03_01

Cassidy, J.W. (1990). Effect of intensity training on preservice teacher's instruction accuracy and delivery effectiveness. *Journal of Research in Music Education 38*(3), 164–74. doi: 10.2307/3345180

Catterall, J., Dumais, S., & Hampden-Thompson, G. (2012). *The arts and achievement in at-risk youth: Findings from four longitudinal studies.* Washington D.C.: The National Endowment for the Arts.

Cataldi, E., Laird, J., & Kewal Ramani, A. (2009). *High school dropout and completion rates in the United States: 2007.* National Center for Education Statistics, Washington, DC. Retrieved from http://nces.ed.gov/pubsearch/pubsinfo.asp?pubid = 2009064

Cavitt, M.E. (2005). Factors influencing participation in community bands. *Journal of Band Research, 41*(1), 42–59.

Chappell, J. (2010). Music in the moment, improvising part 1: Using melody as a starting point for spontaneous music making. *Intune, 8*(3), 25–28.

Chen, H., Wigand, R.T., & Nilan, M.S. (1999). Optimal experience of web activities. *Computers in Human Behavior, 15,* 585–608.

Cheng, M., Chan, K., Tang, S., & Chen, G. (2009). Pre-service teacher education students' epistemelogical beliefs and their conceptions of teaching. *Teaching and Teacher Education, 25*(2), 319–327. doi:10.1016/j.tate.2008.09.018

Chong, S., & Cheah, H. (2009). A value, skills and knowledge framework for initial teacher preparation programmes. *Australian Journal of Teacher Education 34*(3), article 1. Retrieved from http://ro.ecu.edu.au/ajte/vol34/iss3/1/

Choksy, L. (1999). *The Kodály method I: Comprehensive music education* (3rd ed.). Upper Saddle River, NJ: Prentice Hall.

Choksy, L., Abramson, R., Gillespie, A., Woods, D., & York, F. (2001). *Teaching music in the twenty-first century.* Upper Saddle River, NJ: Prentice Hall.

Christophel, D.M. (1990). The relationships among teacher immediacy behaviors, student motivation, and learning. *Communication Education, 39*(4), 323–340. doi: 10.1080/03634529009378813

Cienki, A. (2008). Why study metaphor and gesture? In A. Cienki & C. Muller (Eds.), *Metaphor and gesture* (pp. 5–25). Amsterdam: John Benjamins Publishing Co.

Cohen, M. (2012). Writing between rehearsals: A tool for assessment and building camaraderie. *Music Educators Journal, 98*(3), 43–48. doi:10.1177/0027432111434743

Combs, F.M. (2000). *Percussion manual.* Prospect Heights, IL: Waveland Press.

Common Core State Standards Initiative. (2012). *About the standards.* Retrieved from http://www.corestandards.org/about-the-standards

Consortium of National Arts Education Associations. (1994). *National standards for arts education: What every young person should know and be able to do in the arts.* Reston, VA: Music Educators National Conference.

Conway, C.M. (2002). Curriculum writing in music. *Music Educators Journal, 88*(6), 44–59. doi:10.2307/3399806

Conway, C. M. (2008). The implementation of the national standards in music education: Capturing the spirit of the standards: What were the national standards intended to accomplish? What are the challenges in implementing them? *Music Educators Journal, 94*(4), 34–39. doi: 10.1177/0027432108094004010404

Cooper, D. E. (1986). *Metaphor*. Oxford, England: Basil Blackwell.

Cooper, M. (1996). *Change your voice, change your life*. Chatsworth, CA: Wilshire Book Company.

Coopersmith, J. (2009). *Characteristics of public, private, and bureau of Indian education elementary and secondary school teachers in the United States: Results from the 2007–08 schools and staffing survey* (NCES 2009–324). National Center for Education Statistics, Institute of Education Sciences, U.S. Department of Education. Washington, DC.

Cormac, E. R. M. (1985). *A Cognitive theory of metaphor*. Cambridge, MA: MIT Press.

Covey, S. R. (2004). *The 7 habits of highly successful people: Powerful lessons in personal change*. New York: Free Press.

Csikszentmihalyi, M. (1990). *Flow: The psychology of optimal experience*. New York: Harper and Row.

Cunningham, D. J. (1992). Beyond educational psychology: Steps toward an educational semiotic. *Educational Psychology Review, 4*(2), 165–194. doi: 10.1007/BF01322343

Custodero, L. A. (2010). Meaning and experience: The musical learner. In H. F. Abeles & L. A. Custodero (Eds.). *Critical issues in music education: Contemporary theory and practice* (pp. 61–86). New York: Oxford University Press.

Dansereau, D. F. (1995). Derived structural schemas and the transfer of knowledge. In A. McKeough, J. Lupart, & A. Marini (Eds.), *Teaching for transfer: Fostering generalization in learning*. Mahwah, NJ: Earlbaum.

Darling-Hammond, L. (2012). *Creating a comprehensive system for evaluating and supporting effective teaching*. Stanford, CA: Stanford Center for Opportunity Policy in Education.

Daugherty, J., Custer, R., & Dixon, R. (2012). Mapping concepts for learning and assessment. *Technology and Engineering Teacher, 71*(8), 10–14.

Delzell, J. K., & Doerksen, P. F. (1998). Reconsidering the grade level for beginning instrumental music. *Update: Applications of Research in Music Education, 16*(2), 17–22.

Derry, J. S. (1996). Cognitive schema theory in the constructivist debate. *Educational Psychologist, 31*, 163–174. doi:10.1080/00461520.1996.9653264

Dobbins, B. (1980). Improvisation: An essential element of music proficiency. *Music Educators Journal, 66*(5), 36–41. doi:10.2307/3395774

Donaldson, M. L. (2010). No more valentines. *Educational Leadership, 67*(8), 54–58.

Dubos, R. (1974). *Beast or angel?* New York: Scribner.

Duke, R. A. (2005). *Intelligent music teaching: Essays on the core principles of effective instruction.* Austin, TX: Learning and Behavior Resources.

Duke, R. A., & Byo, J. L. (2009). *The habits of musicianship: A radical approach to beginning band.* Center for Music Learning at the University of Texas at Austin. Retrieved from http://cml.music.utexas.edu/online-resources/habits-of-musicianship/introduction/

East, K. (2009). Using Metaphors to uncover the selves in my practice. *Studying Teacher Education., 5*(1), 21–31. doi:10.1080/17425960902830377

Elliott, D. J. (1995). *Music matters.* New York: Oxford University Press.

Ellis A. K., & Fouts, J. T. (2001). Interdisciplinary curriculum: The research base. *Music Educators Journal, 87*(5), 22–26, 68. doi:10.2307/3399704

Ericsson, K. A., Charness, N., Hoffman, R. R., & Feltovich, P. J. (Eds). (2006). *The Cambridge handbook of expertise and expert performance.* New York: Cambridge University Press.

Erwin, J. H., Edwards, K. L., Kerchner, J. L., & Knight, J. W. (2003). *Prelude to music education.* Upper Saddle River, NJ: Prentice Hall.

Eureka Facts LLC. (2004). *MENC membership profile and segmentation report.* Rockville, MD: Author.

Fautley, M. (2010). *Assessment in music education.* Oxford, England: Oxford University Press.

Fink, L. D. (2004). Beyond small groups: Harnessing the extraordinary power of learning teams. In L. K. Michaelsen, A. B. Knight, & L. D. Fink (Eds.), *Team-based learning: A transformative use of small groups in college teaching* (pp. 3–26). Sterling, VA: Stylus.

Frego. D. (n.d.) *The approach of Emile Jaques-Dalcroze.* Retrieved from http://www.allianceamm.org/resources_elem_Dalcroze.html

Froehlich, H. C. (2007). *Sociology for music teachers: Perspective for practice.* Upper Saddle River, NJ: Pearson Education.

Fuller, F., & Bown, O. (1975). Becoming a teacher. In K. Ryan (Ed.), *Teacher education, Part II: The 74th yearbook of the National Society for the Study of Education* (pp. 25–52). Chicago: University of Chicago Press.

Gardner, H. (1993). *Frames of mind* (2nd ed.). New York: Basic Books.

Garrison, C., & Ehringhaus, M. (n.d.). *Formative and summative assessments in the classroom.* Retrieved from http://www.amle.org/Publications/WebExclusive/Assessment/tabid/1120/Default.aspx

Gay, G. (2000). *Culturally responsive teaching: Theory, research, and practice.* New York: Teachers College Press.

Ginocchio, J. (2003). Making composition work in your music program. *Music Educators Journal, 90*(1), 51–55. doi:10.2307/3399977

Ginott, H.G. (1972). *Teacher and child: A book for parents and teachers.* New York: Macmillan.

Godwin, G. (n.d.). BrainyQuote.com. Retrieved from BrainyQuote.com website: http://www.brainyquote.com/quotes/quotes/g/gailgodwin101424.html

Goldstein, J., & Noguera, P.A. (2006). A thoughtful approach to teacher evaluation. *Educational Leadership, 63*(6), 31–37.

Goldstein, S., Naglieri, J.A., S., & Williams, K.M. (2012). A national study of autistic symptoms in the general population of school-age children and those diagnosed with autism spectrum disorders. *Psychology in the Schools, 49*(10), 1001–1016. doi:10.1002/pits.21650

Gordon, E.E. (1998). *Introduction to research and the psychology of music.* Chicago: GIA Publications.

Gordon, E.E. (2002). *Rating scales and their uses for measuring and evaluating achievement in music performance.* Chicago: GIA Publications.

Gordon, E.E. (2007). *Learning sequences in music: A contemporary music learning theory.* Chicago: GIA Publications.

Green, L. (2001). *How popular musicians learn: A way ahead for music education.* Burlington, VT: Ashgate.

Green, L. (2005). The music curriculum as lived experience: Children's "natural" music-learning processes. *Music Educators Journal, 91*(4), 27–32. doi:10.2307/3400155

Grunow, R.F., & Gamble, D.K. (1989). Music learning sequence techniques in beginning instrumental music. In D.L. Walters and C.C. Taggart (Eds.), *Readings in music learning theory* (pp. 194–207). Chicago: GIA Publications.

Gump, P.V. (1987). School and classroom environments. In D. Stokols & I. Altman (Eds.), *Handbook of environmental psychology* (pp. 691–732). New York: Wiley.

Gusky, T., & Jung, L. (2013). *Answers to essential questions about standards, assessment, grading and reporting.* Thousand Oaks, CA: Corwin.

Hale, C., & Green, S. (2009). Six key principles for music assessment. *Music Educators Journal, (95)*7, 27–31. doi:10.1177/0027432109334772

Hall, E.T. (1966). *The Hidden Dimension.* New York: Doubleday.

Halliday, J. (1998). Technicism, reflective practice and authenticity in teacher education. *Teaching and Teacher Education, 14*(6), 597–605. doi:10.1016/S0742-051X(98)00010-9

Hamann D.L., Baker D.S., McAllister P.A., & Bauer W.I. (2000). Factors affecting university music students' perception of lesson quality and teaching effectiveness. *Journal of Research in Music Education, 48*, 102–113. doi:10.2307/3345569

Hamann, D. L., & Gillespie, R. (2004). *Strategies for teaching strings*. New York: Oxford University Press.

Hammer, E. (1994). *An evaluation of a microteaching model for training effective leaders of music ensembles in secondary schools*. (Doctoral dissertation). Retrieved from ProQuest Dissertations & Theses Full Text. (AAT 9509787).

Hancock, C. B. (2009). National estimates of retention, migration, and attrition. *Journal of Research in Music Education, 57*(2), 92–107. doi:10.1177/0022429409337299

Hanley, B., & Montgomery, J. (2005). Challenges to music education: Curriculum reconceptualized. *Music Educators Journal, 91*(4), 17–20. doi:10.2307/3400153

Hanna, W. (2007). The new Bloom's taxonomy: Implications for music education. *Arts Education Policy Review, 108*(4), 7–16. doi:10.3200/AEPR.108.4.7-16

Harrison, A. G., & Treagust, D. F. (2006). Teaching and learning with analogies: Friend or foe? In P. J. Aubusson, A. G. Harrision, & S. M. Ritchie (Eds.), *Metaphor and analogy in science education* (11–24). Dordrecht, The Netherlands: Springer.

Hastie, P. A. (1998). Effect of instructional context on teacher and student behaviors in physical education. *Journal of Classroom Interaction, 33*(2), 24–31.

Haston, W., & Leon-Guerrero, A. (2008). Sources of pedagogical content knowledge: Reports by preservice instrumental music teachers. *Journal of Music Teacher Education, 17*(2), 48–59. doi:10.1177/1057083708317644

Havnes, A., Smith, K., Dysthe, O., & Ludvigsen, K. (2012). Formative assessment and feedback: Making learning visible. *Studies in Educational Evaluation, 38*, 21–27.

Henderson, A. (2011). The new positivism: Research and education. *National Social Science Journal 3*5(2), 84–89.

Herbenick, D., Reece, M., Schick, V., Sanders, S. A., Dodge, B., & Fortenberry, J. D. (2010). Sexual behavior in the United States: Results from a national probability sample of men and women ages 14–94. *Journal of Sexual Medicine, 7*(Suppl. 5), 255–265. doi:10.1111/j.1743–6109.2010.02012.x

Herrnstein, R. J. (1977). The evolution of behvaiorism. *American Psychologist, 32*, 593–603. doi:10.1037/0003-066X.32.8.593

Hickey, M. (1997). Teaching ensembles to compose and improvise. *Music Educators Journal, 83*(6), 17–21. doi:10.2307/3399019

Hickey, M. (2003). *Why and how to teach music composition: A new horizon for music education*. Lanham, MD: Rowman and Littlefield.

Highet, G. (1989). *The art of teaching*. New York: Vintage Books.

Hintz, B. (1995). Helping students master improvisation. *Music Educators Journal, 82*(2), 32–36. doi:10.2307/3398867

Hodges, D.A., & Sebald, D.C. (2011). *Music in the human experience: An introduction to music psychology*. New York: Routledge.

Hogan, S., & Hudson, L. (1998). *Completely queer: The gay and lesbian encyclopedia*. New York: Henry Holt and Co.

Hopson, L., & Lee, E. (2011). Mitigating the effect of family poverty on academic and behavioral outcomes: The role of school climate in middle and high school. *Children and Youth Services Review, 33*(11), 2221–2229.

Humphrey, D.C., Koppich, J.E., Bland, J.A., & Bosetti, K.R. (2011). *Peer Review: Getting Serious About Teacher Evaluation*. Menlo Park, CA: SRI International.

Humphreys, J.T. (1992). Instrumental music in American education: In service of many masters. In M. Fonder (Ed.), *The Ithaca conference on American music education: Centennial profiles* (pp. 25–51). Ithaca NY: Ithaca College.

Ireson, J. (2008). *Learners, learning and educational activity*. New York: Routledge.

Isbell, D.S. (2012). Learning theories: Insights for music educators. *General Music Today, 25*(2), 19–23. doi:10.1177/1048371311425684

Jacob, B., & Lefgren, L. (2006). When principals rate teachers: The best—and the worst— stand out. *Education Next, 6*(2), 58–63.

Jacobson, T (Producer), & Hughes, J. (Director). (1986). *Ferris Bueller's day off* [Motion picture]. United States: Paramount Pictures.

Jagacinski, C.M., & Nicholls, J.G., (1987). Competence and affect in task involvement and ego involvement: The impact of social comparison information. *Journal of Educational Psychology, 79*(2), 107–114. doi: 10.1037/0022-0663.79.2.107

Jensen, J.K. (2000). Diversity in schools. In G. Olsen, J.R. Barrett, A.L. Barresi, N. Rasmussen, & J.K. Jensen (Eds.) *Looking in on music teaching*. New York: McGraw-Hill Primus.

Johnson, J.A., Dupuis, V.L., Musial, D., Hall, G.E., &Gollick, D.M. (2010). *Foundations of American education* (15th ed.). Allyn and Bacon: Boston, MA.

Jordan, J.M. (1989). Music learning theory applied to choral music performing groups. In D.L. Walters and C.C. Taggart (Eds.), *Readings in music learning theory* (pp. 168–182). Chicago: GIA Publications.

Jorgensen, E. (1988). The curriculum design process in music. *College Music Symposium, 28*, 94–105.

Juchniewicz J. (2010). The influence of social intelligence on effective music teaching. *Journal of Research in Music Education, 58*(3), 276–293. doi:10.1177/0022429410378368

Jung, E., & Rhodes, D. (2008). Revisiting disposition assessment in teacher education: Broadening the focus. *Assessment and Evaluation in Higher Education, 33*(6), 647–660. doi:10.1080/02602930701773059

Karelis, C. (2007). *The persistence of poverty: Why the economics of the well-off can help the poor.* New Haven, CT: Yale University Press.

Kaschub, M., & Smith, J.P. (2009). *Minds on music: Composition for creative and critical thinking.* Lanham, MD: Rowman and Littlefield.

Kaschub, M., & Smith, J.P. (Eds.) (2013). *Composing our future: Preparing music educators to teach composition.* New York: Oxford University Press.

Katzenmeyer, M., & Moller, G. (2009). *Awakening the sleeping giant: Helping teachers develop as leaders* (3rd ed.). Thousand Oaks, CA: Corwin.

Keene, J.A. (1987). *A history of music education in the United States* (2nd ed.). Hanover, NH: University Press of New England.

Keigher, A. (2009). *Characteristics of public, private, and bureau of Indian education elementary and secondary schools in the United States: Results from the 2007-08 schools and staffing survey* (NCES 2009-321). National Center for Education Statistics, Institute of Education Sciences, U.S. Department of Education. Washington, DC.

Kellaghan, T. (1971). The university and education. In University Staff Association (Ed.), *Contemporary developments in university education.* Dublin, University College.

Kelley, D.H., & Gorham, J. (1988). Effects of immediacy on recall of information. *Communication Education, 37*(3), 198–207. doi:10.1080/03634528809378719

Kelly, S.N. (2009). *Teaching music in American society: A social and cultural understanding of music education.* New York: Routledge.

Kids Count Data Center (n.d.). *Data across states.* Baltimore, MD: The Annie E. Casey Foundation. Retrieved from http://datacenter.kidscount.org/data#USA/2/2/3,4,5,6

Killian, J., Dye, K., & Wayman, J. (2013). Music student teachers: Pre-student teaching Concerns and post-student teaching perceptions over a 5-year period. *Journal of Research in Music Education, 61*(1), 63–79. doi:10.1177/0022429412474314

Klotman, R.H. (1996). *Teaching strings: Learning to teach through playing* (2nd ed.). New York: Schirmer.

Kolb, D.A. (1984) *Experiential learning: Experience as the source of learning and development.* Englewood Cliffs, NJ: Prentice Hall.

Korn, J.H. (2012). Writing and developing your philosophy of teaching. In W. Buskist & V.A. Benassi (Eds.), *Effective college and university teaching: Strategies and tactics for the new professoriate* (pp. 71–79). Thousand Oaks, CA: Sage.

Kratus, J. (1991). Growing with improvisation. *Music Educators Journal, 78*(4), 36–40. doi:10.2307/3398335

Kratus, J. (1995). A developmental approach to teaching music improvisation. *International Journal of Music Education, 26*(1), 27–38. doi:10.1177/025576149502600103

Labuta, J. A., & Smith, D. A. (1997). *Music education: Historical contexts and perspectives.* Upper Saddle River, NJ: Prentice Hall.

Landis, B., & Carder, P. (1972). *The eclectic curriculum in American music education: Contributions of Dalcroze, Kodaly, and Orff.* Washington, DC: Music Educators National Conference.

Landis, B., & Carder, P. (1990a). The Kodály approach. In P. Carder (Ed.), *The eclectic curriculum in American music education* (pp. 55–74). Reston, VA: Music Educators National Conference.

Landis, B., & Carder, P. (1990b). The Dalcroze approach. In P. Carder (Ed.), *The eclectic curriculum in American music education* (pp. 7–30). Reston, VA: Music Educators National Conference

Lakoff, G., & Johnson, M. (2003). *Metaphors we live by* (2nd ed.). Chicago: University of Chicago Press.

Laumann, E. O., Gagnon, J. H., Michael, R. T., & Michaels, S. (1994). *The social organization of sexuality: Sexual practices in the United States.* Chicago: University of Chicago Press.

Larson, M. S. (1977). *The rise of professionalism: A sociological analysis.* Berkeley: University of California Press.

Lave, J. (1991). Situated learning in communities of practice. In L. B. Resnick, J. M. Levine, & S. D. Teasley (Eds.). *Perspectives on socially shared cognition.* Washington, DC: American Psychological Association.

Lave J., & Wenger, E. (1991). *Situated learning: Legitimate peripheral participation.* Cambridge, England: Cambridge University Press.

Learn. (n.d.). In *Merriam-Webster's online dictionary.* Retrieved from http://www.merriam-webster.com/dictionary/learn

Lehrman, P. D. (2005). Do you hear what I hear? *Mix, 29*(7), 22–24, 148.

Leonhard C., & House, R. W. (1972). *Foundations and principles of music education* (2nd ed.). New York: McGraw-Hill.

LeVay, S., & Baldwin, J. (2012). *Human sexuality* (4th ed.). Sunderland, MA: Sinauer Associates.

Levine, D. W., O'Neal, E. C., Garwood, S. G., & McDonald, P. J. (1980). Classroom ecology: The effects of seating position on grades and participation. *Psychology Bulletin, 6,* 409–412.

Levinowitz, L. M. (1989). Informal music instruction as readiness for learning sequence activities. In D. L. Walters & C. C. Taggart (Eds.), *Readings in music learning theory* (pp. 74–83). Chicago: GIA Publications.

Linn, R., & Miller, D. (2005). *Measurement and assessment in teaching,* as cited in Mills, M. (2009). Capturing student progress via portfolios in the music classroom. *Music Educators Journal, 96*(2), 32–38. doi:10.1177/0027432109351463

Louk, D.P. (2002). *National standards for music education: General music teachers' attitudes and practices.* (Doctoral dissertation). Available from ProQuest Dissertation and Theses database (UMI No. 3042585).

MacLeod, R.B., & Napoles, J. (2012). Preservice teachers' perceptions of teaching effectiveness during teaching episodes with positive and negative feedback. *Journal of Music Teacher Education, 22*(1), 91–102. doi:10.1177/1057083711429851

Madsen, C.K., & Geringer, J.M. (1989). The relationship of teacher "on-task" to intensity and effective music teaching. *Canadian Music Educator, 30,* 87–94.

Madsen, C.K., Greer, R.D., & Madsen, C.H. (Eds.) (1975). *Research in music behavior: Modifying music behavior in the classroom.* New York: Teachers College Press.

Madsen, C. & Kaiser, K. (1999). Pre-internship fears of music therapists. *Journal of Music Therapy, 36*(1), 17–25.

Madsen, C.K., & Madsen, C.H. (1974). *Teaching/discipline: A positive approach for educational development* (2nd ed.). Boston: Allyn & Bacon.

Madsen, C.K., & Madsen, C.H. (1998). *Teaching/discipline: A positive approach* (4th ed.). Raleigh, NC: Contemporary Publishing Company.

Madsen, C.K., & Yarbrough, C. (1985). *Competency-based music education.* Raleigh, NC: Contemporary Publishing Company.

Madsen K. (2003). The effect of accuracy of instruction, teacher delivery, and student attentiveness on musicians' evaluation of teacher effectiveness. *Journal of Research in Music Education, 51*(1), 38–50. doi:10.2307/3345647

Magnusson, S., Krajcik, J., & Borko, H. (1999). Nature, sources and development of pedagogical content knowledge for science teaching. In J. Gess-Newsome & N.G. Lederman (Eds.), *Examining pedagogical content knowledge: The construct and its implications for science education* (pp. 95–132). Dordrecht, The Netherlands: Kluwer Academic.

Malecki, C., & Demaray, M. (2006). Social support as a buffer in the relationship between socioeconomic status and academic performance. *School Psychology Quarterly, 21*(4), 375–395. doi:10.1037/h0084129

Mark, M.L. (2008). *A concise history of American music education.* Lanham, MD: Rowman and Littlefield Education.

Mark, M.L., & Gary, C.L. (1992). *A history of American music education.* New York: Schirmer.

Marshall, H.D. (2004). Improvisation strategies and resources, Part 2. *General Music Today, 18*(1), 37–39. doi:10.1177/10483713040180010107

Marx, A., Fuhrer, U., & Hartig, T. (1999). Effects of classroom seating arrangements on children's question-asking. *Learning Environments Research, 2*(3), 249–263. doi:10.1023/A:1009901922191

McClaren, C.A. (2006). *The book of percussion pedagogy: The common elements approach for teachers and performers*. Greensboro, NC: C. Alan Publications.

McCombs, B.L., & Whisler, J.S. (1997). *The learner-centered classroom and school*. San Francisco, CA: Jossey-Bass.

McCrae, R.R., & Costa, P.T. (1987). Validation of the five-factor model of personality across instruments and observers. *Journal of Personality and Social Psychology, 52*(1), 81–90. doi:10.1037/0022-3514.52.1.81

McKoy, C.L. (2009). Cross-cultural competence of student teachers in music education. In S. Cooper (Ed.), *The Journal of the Desert Skies Symposium on Research in Music Education 2009 Proceedings* (pp. 128–144). Tucson, AZ: University of Arizona.

McPherson, G.E. (2005). From child to musician: Skill development during the beginning stages of learning an instrument. *Psychology of Music, 33*(1), 5–35. doi:10.1177/0305735605048012

Mead, V.H. (1994). *Dalcroze eurhythmics in today's music classroom*. New York: Schott.

Mehrabian, A. (1981). *Silent messages: Implicit communication of emotions and attitudes*. Belmont, CA: Wadsworth

Merriam, A.P. (1964). *The anthropology of music*. Evanston, IL: Northwestern University Press.

Miksza, P., Roeder, M., & Biggs, D. (2010). Surveying Colorado band directors' opinions of skills and characteristics important to successful music teaching. *Journal of Research in Music Education, 57*(4), 364–381. doi:10.1177/0022429409351655

Millard, R.J., & Stimpson, D.V. (1980). Enjoyment and productivity as a function of classroom seating location. *Perceptual and Motor Skills, 50*(2), 439–444. doi:10.2466/pms.1980.50.2.439

Miller, G.A. (1956). The magical number seven plus or minus two: Some limits on our capacity for processing information. *Psychological Review, 63*(2), 81–97. doi:10.1037/h0043158

Millican, J.S. (2008). A new framework for music education knowledge and skill. *Journal of Music Teacher Education, 18*(1), 67–78. doi:10.1177/1057083708323146

Millican, J.S. (2012). *Starting out right: Beginning band pedagogy*. Lanham, MD: Scarecrow Press.

Mills, M. (2009). Capturing student progress via portfolios in the music classroom. *Music Educators Journal, 96*(2), 32–38. doi:10.1177/0027432109351463

Montello, D. R. (1988). Classroom seating location and its effect on course achievement, participation, and attitudes. *Journal of Environmental Psychology, 8*(2), 149–157. doi:10.1016/S0272-4944(88)80005-7

Murray, T., & Arroyo, I. (2002). Toward measuring and maintaining the zone of proximal development in adaptive instructional systems. Proceedings of the 6th International Conference on Intelligent Tutoring Systems. In S.A. Cerri, G. Gouardères & F. Paraguaçu (Eds.), *Lecture notes in computer science 2363* (pp. 133–145). Berlin, Germany: Springer.

Nagel, J. (1994). Constructing ethnicity: Creating and recreating ethnic identify and culture. *Social Problems, 41*(1), 152–176. doi10.2307/3096847

National Arts Education Association. (2012). *National coalition for core arts standards.* Retrieved from http://www.arteducators.org/community/committees

National Association for Music Education (2011). *About.* Retrieved from http://musiced.nafme.org/about/

National Association for Music Education (2012). *National standards for music education.* Retrieved from http://musiced.nafme.org/resources/national-standards-for-music-education/

National Center for Educational Statistics (2012). *Students with disabilities.* Washington DC: U.S. Department of Education. Retrieved from http://nces.ed.gov/programs/digest/d12/tables/dt12_046.asp

National Council for Accreditation of Teacher Education. (2010). *NCATE Glossary.* Retrieved from http://www.ncate.org/standards/ncateunitstandards/ncateglossary/tabid/477/default.aspx

NBPTS (2002). *What teachers should know and be able to do.* National Board of Professional Teaching Standards. Retrieved from http://www.nbpts.org/five-core-propositions

New Teacher Project. (2009). *The widget effect.* New York: Author.

NGA Center—CCSSO (2010). *Common core state standards initiative.* Washington, DC: National Governors Association Center for Best Practices, Council of Chief State School Officers. Retrieved from http://www.corestandards.org/

Nichols, J. (2011). Rie's story, Ryan's journey: Music in the life of a transgendered student. *Bulletin of the Council for Research in Music Education, 188,* 42–43.

Oldfather, P. (1999). *Learning through children's eyes: Social constructivism and the desire to learn.* Washington, DC: American Psychological Association.

Orman, E. (2002). Comparison of the national standards for music education and elementary music specialists' use of class time. *Journal of Research in Music Education, 50*(2), 155– 164. doi:10.2307/3345819

Ormrod, J. E. (2004). *Human learning* (4th ed.). Upper Saddle River, NJ: Pearson.

Orzolek, D. (2008). Navigating the paradox of assessment in music education. In T. Brophy (Ed.). *Assessment in music education: Integrating curriculum, theory and practice.* (pp. 51–84). Chicago: GIA Music.

O'Toole, P. (2003). *Shaping sound musicians.* Chicago: GIA Music.

Pajares, M. F. (1992). Teachers' beliefs and educational research: Cleaning up a messy construct. *Review of Educational Research, 62*(3), 302–332. doi:10.3102/00346543062003307

Palmer, P. J. (2007). *The courage to teach: Exploring the inner landscape of a teacher's life* (2nd ed.). San Francisco: Jossey-Bass.

Parsad, B., & Spiegelman, M. (2011). *A snapshot of arts education in public elementary and secondary schools: 2009–10: First look.* Retreived from http://nces.ed.gov/pubs2011/2011078.pdf

Parsad, B., & Spiegelman, M. (2012). *Arts education in public elementary and secondary schools: 1999–2000 and 2009–10* (NCES 2012–014). National Center for Education Statistics, Institute of Education Sciences, U.S. Department of Education. Washington, DC.

Partnership for 21st Century Skills (n.d.). *A framework for 21st century learning.* Retrieved from http://www.p21.org/

Patrick, B.C., Hisley, J., & Kempler, T. (2000). "What's everybody so excited about?": The effects of teacher enthusiasm on student intrinsic motivation and vitality. *Journal of Experimental Education, 68*(3), 217–236. doi:10.1080/00220970009600093

Paul, S. J. (1994). Music education is a performance degree. *Yamaha's New Ways in Music Education, 9*(1), C2–C3.

Pavalko, R.M. (1988) *Sociology of occupations and professions* (2nd ed.). Itasca, IL: F.E. Peacock Publishers.

Payne, R. (2008). *Under-sources learners: 8 strategies to boost student achievement.* Highlands, TX: aha! Process Inc.

Perlmutter, A. (2010). Improv for everyone. *Teaching Music, 17*(6), 30–35.

Peterson, R.L., & Peterson, M.J. (1959). Short-term retention of individual verbal items. *Journal of Experimental Psychology, 58*(3), 193–198. doi:10.1037/h0049234

Pew Forum on Religious and Public Life, U.S. Religious Landscape Survey (2008). *Religious Affiliation: Diverse and Dynamic.* Retrieved from http://religions.pewforum.org/pdf/report-religious-landscape-study-full.pdf

Phillips, K. H. (1996). *Teaching kids to sing.* Belmont, CA: Wadsworth.

Piaget, J. (1954). *The construction of reality in the child.* New York: Basic Books.

Pintrich P.R., & Schunk, D.H. (2002). *Motivation in education: Theory, research and applications* (2nd ed.). Upper Saddle River, NJ: Pearson.

Pogonowski, L. (2001). A personal retrospective on the MCCP. *Music Educators Journal, 88*(1), 24–52. doi:10.2307/3399773

Pomerantz, E.M., & Saxon, J.L. (2001). Conceptions of ability as stable and self-evaluative processes: A longitudinal examination. *Child Development, 72*, 152–173. doi:10.1111/1467-8624.00271

Radocy, R., & Boyle, D. (1987). *Measurement and evaluation of musical experiences.* New York: Schirmer.

Raffini, J. (1988). *Student apathy: The protection of self-worth.* Washington, DC: National Education Association.

Raiber, M.A. (2011). Getting to the 'core' of the matter. *Oklahoma Music, 18*(1), 8,16.

Randle, I. (1997). The measure of success: Integrated thematic instruction. *The Clearinghouse: A Journal of Educational Strategies, Issues, and Ideas, 71*(2), 85–87. doi:10.1080/00098659709599331

Randolph-Gips, M., & Srinivasan, P. (2012). Modeling autism: A systems biology approach. *Journal of Clinical Bioinformatics, 2,* 1–17. doi: 10.1186/2043-9113-2-17

Regelski, T. (2002). On "Methodolartry' and music teaching as critical and reflective praxis. *Philosophy of Music Education Review 10*(2), 102–123. doi:10.1353/pme.2002.0021

Reimer, B. (2009). *Seeking the significance of music education: Essays and reflections.* Lanham, MD: Rowman and Littlefield.

Reimer, B (2012). Another perspective: Struggling toward wholeness in music education. *Music Educators Journal, 99*(2), 25–29. doi:10.1177/0027432112463856

Reynolds, A., & Hyun, K. (2004). Understanding music aptitude: Teachers' interpretations. *Research Studies in Music Education 23*(1), 18–31. doi:10.1177/1321103X040230010201

Richmond, J.W. (1997). Universal access for the universal language. *Arts Education Policy Review, 99*(2), 22–29. doi:10.1080/10632919709600767

Richmond, V.P., Gorham, J.S., & McCroskey, J.C. (1987). The relationship between selected immediacy behaviors and cognitive learning. In M. McLaughlin (Ed.), *Communication yearbook 10* (pp. 574–590). Beverly Hills, CA: Sage.

Riley, P.E. (2009). Pre-service music educators' perceptions of the national standards for music education. *Visions of Research in Music Education, 14.* Retrieved from http://www-usr.rider.edu/~vrme/

Robinson, M. (1995). Alternative assessment techniques for teachers: Are you at a loss for ways to assess your music students? *Music Educators Journal, 81*(5), 28–34. doi:10.2307/3398853

Rogoff, B. (1990). *Apprenticeship in thinking: Cognitive development in social context.* New York: Oxford University Press.

Rohwer, D., & Henry, W. (2004). University teachers' perceptions of requisite skills and characteristics of effective music teachers. *Journal of Music Teacher Education, 13*(2), 18–27. doi:10.1177/10570837040130020104

Rokeach, M. (1968). *Beliefs, attitudes, and values: A theory of organization and change.* San Francisco, CA: Jossey-Bass.

Ruitenberg, C. (2011). The trouble with dispositions: A critical examination of personal beliefs, professional commitments and actual conduct in teacher education. *Ethics and Education, 6*(1), 41–52. doi:10.1080/17449642.2011.587347

Runte, R. (1995). Is teaching a profession? In G. Taylor & R. Runte (Eds.), *Thinking about teaching: An introduction* (pp. 288–299). Toronto, Ontario, Canada: Harcourt Brace.

Rush, S., & Lane, J. (2011, November). *Quality of life issues for the modern band director.* Presentation at the North Carolina Music Educators Association In-Service Conference, Winston Salem, NC.

Russell, J. (2006). Building curriculum-based concerts. *Music Educators Journal, 92*(3), 34–39. doi:10.2307/3401138

Russell, J., & Austin, J. (2010). Assessment practices of secondary music teachers. *Journal of Research in Music Education 58*(1), 37–54. doi:10.1177/0022429409360062

Schleuter, S. L. (1997). *A sound approach to teaching instrumentalists: An application of content and learning sequences* (2nd ed.). New York: Schirmer.

Schmidt, W. (2000). Challenging the status quo in school performance classes: New approaches to band, choir, and orchestra suggested by the music standards. In B. Reimer, (Ed.), *Performing with understanding: The challenge of the national standards for music education* (pp. 45–58). Lanham, MD: Rowman and Littlefield.

Schug, M. (2003) Teacher-centered instruction: The Rodney Dangerfield of social studies. In L. Lemming, L. Ellington, & K. Porter-McGee (Eds.), *Where did social studies go wrong?* (pp. 94–110). http://www.edexcellencemedia.net/publications/2003/200308_wheredidsocialstudies/ContrariansFull.pdf

Schunk, D. H. (1987). Peer models and children's behavioral change. *Review of Educational Research, 57,* 149–174. doi:10.3102/00346543057002149

Schunk, D. H. (2008). *Learning theories: An educational perspective* (5th ed.). Boston: Allyn and Bacon.

Schussler, D., Stooksbury, L., & Bercaw, L. (2010). Understanding teacher candidate dispositions: Reflecting to build self-awareness. *Journal of Teacher Education, 61*(4), 350–63. doi:10.1177/0022487110371377

Schwab, J. J. (1959/1978). The practical: Translation into curriculum. In I. Westbury & N. Wilkof (Eds.) *Science, curriculum, and liberal education: Selected essays* (pp. 365–383). Chicago, IL: University of Chicago Press.

Schwab, J. J. (1983). The practical 4: Something for curriculum professors to do. *Curriculum Inquiry, 13*(3), 239–265.

Schwartz, B., & Reisberg, D. (1991). *Learning and memory*. New York: W. W. Norton.

Scott, J. K. (2007). Me? Teach improvisation to children? *General Music Today, 20*(2), 6–13. doi:10.1177/10483713070200020103

Scott, S. (2012). Rethinking the roles of assessment in music education. *Music Educators Journal, 98*(3), 31–35. doi:10.1177/0027432111434742

Scruggs, B. (2009). Constructivist practices to increase student engagement in the orchestra classroom. *Music Educators Journal, 95*(4), 53–59. doi:10.1177/0027432109335468

Shamrock, M. (n.d.). *The Orff-Schulwerk Approach.* Retrieved from http://www.allianceamm.org/resources_elem_Orff.html

Shepard, L. A. (2000). *The role of classroom assessment in teaching and learning.* California University, Los Angeles: CSE Technical Report.

Shiveley, J., & Misco, T. (2010). "But how about their attitudes and beliefs?": A four-step process for integrating and assessing dispositions in teacher education. *Clearing House, 83*(1), 9–14. doi:10.1080/00098650903267669

Shuler, S. (2011). Music assessment part 1: What and why. *Music Educators Journal 98*(2), 10–13. doi:10.1177/0027432111427651

Shulman, L. S. (1986). Those who understand: Knowledge growth in teaching. *Educational Researcher, 15*(2), 4–14. doi:10.3102/0013189X015002004

Shulman, L. S. (1987). Knowledge and teaching: Foundations of the new reform. *Harvard Educational Review, 57*(1), 1–21.

Shulman, L. S. (2004). *The wisdom of practice: Essays on teaching, learning, and learning to teach.* S. Wilson (Ed.). San Francisco, CA: Jossey-Bass.

Silver Burdett Making Music. (2008). Pearson Scott Foresman (www.pearson-school.com)

Skinner, B. F. (1938). *The behavior of organisms: An experimental analysis.* Englewood Cliffs, NJ: Prentice Hall.

Skinner, B. F. (1957). *Verbal behavior.* New York: Appleton-Century-Crofts.

Smith, M. K. (1996, 2000). Curriculum theory and practice. *The encyclopedia of informal education.* Retrieved from www.infed.org/biblio/b-curric.htm

Spaulding, C. (1992). *Motivation in the classroom.* New York: McGraw-Hill.

Spotlight on Music. (2011). McGraw Hill (https://www.mheonline.com/program/view/1/12/2239/003SM)

Standerfer, S., & Hunter, L. (2010). Square peg for a square hole: A standards- and repertoire-based curriculum model. *Music Educators Journal, 96*(3), 25–30. doi:10.1177/0027432109354976

Stantrock, J. W. (2008). *Educational psychology* (3rd ed.). New York: McGraw-Hill.

Stavrou, N. E. (2012). Fostering music creativity in pre-service teacher education: Challenges and possibilities. *International Journal of Music Education*. Advance online publication. doi10.1177/0255761411431391

Stelzer, T. (2003). *A critical analysis of the function of guidance counselor.* (Masters thesis, University of Wisconsin-Stout.) Retrieved from http://www2.uwstout.edu/content/lib/thesis/2003/2003stelzert.pdf

Sternberg, R. J., & Grigorenko, E. (Eds.) (1997). *Intelligence, heredity and environment.* Cambridge, England: Cambridge University Press.

Stipek, D. J. (2002). *Motivation to learn: From theory to practice* (4th ed.). Boston: Allyn & Bacon.

Stooksbury, L. M., Schussler, D. L., & Bercaw, L. A. (2009). Conceptualizing dispositions: Intellectual, cultural and moral domains of teaching. *Teachers and Teaching: Theory and Practice, 15*(6), 719–736. doi:10.1080/13540600903357041

Strand, K., & Newberry, E. (2007). Teachers share practical advice on classroom composing. *General Music Today, 20*(2), 14–19. doi:10.1177/10483713070200020104

Strauss, V. (2006). The rise of the testing culture. *Washington Post.* Retrieved from http://www.washingtonpost.com/wp-dyn/content/article/2006/10/09/AR2006100900925.html

Sumpter, T. L. (2008). *Professional status and the independent piano teaching occupation: A study and analysis of demographics, training, business policies, and studio practices.* (Doctoral dissertation.) Available from Proquest Dissertations and Theses database (UMI 3330315).

Tatto, M. T. (1998). The influence of teacher education on teachers beliefs about purposes of education, roles, and practice. *Journal of Teacher Education, 49*(1), 66–77. doi:10.1177/0022487198049001008

Tauber, R. T., & Mester, C. S. (2007). *Acting lessons for teachers: Using performance skills in the classroom* (2nd ed.). Westport, CT: Greenwood.

Taylor, M. W. (2010). *Replacing the "teacher-proof" curriculum with the "curriculum-proof" teacher: Toward a more systematic way for mathematics teachers to interact with their textbooks.* (Unpublished doctoral dissertation.) Stanford University, Stanford, CA.

Teach. (2010). In *Merriam-Webster online dictionary.* Retrieved from http://www.merriamwebster.com/dictionary/teach

Teach For America (n.d.). *Training and support.* Retrieved from http://www.teachforamerica.org/why-teach-for-america/training-and-support

Teachout, D. J. (1993). The importance of musical, environmental, performance, and referential factors on junior high band students' preferences for performance literature. *Contributions to Music Education, 20,* 25–31.

Teachout, D.J. (1997). Preservice and experienced teachers' opinions of skills and behaviors important to successful music teaching. *Journal of Research in Music Education, 45*(1), 41–50. doi:10.2307/3345464

Teachout, D.J. (2005). A call for action in music teacher education. *Journal of Music Teacher Education, 14*(2), 5–7. doi:10.1177/10570837050140020102

Teachout, D.J. (2007). Understanding the ties that bind and the possibilities for change. *Arts Education Policy Review 108*(6), 19–32.doi:10.3200/AEPR.108.6.19–32

Templeton, B. (2011). *Understanding poverty in the classroom: Changing perceptions for student success.* Lanham, MD: Rowman & Littlefield Education.

Thomas, G.P. (2006). Metaphor, students' conception of learning and teaching, and metacognition. In P.J. Aubusson, A.G. Harrison, & S.M. Ritchie (Eds.), *Metaphor and analogy in science education* (105–117). Dordrecht, The Netherlands: Springer.

Thompson, L.K. (2007). Considering beliefs in learning to teach music. *Music Educators Journal, 90*(3), 30–35. doi:10.1177/002743210709300317

Tomic, W. (1993). Behaviorism and cognitivism in education. *Psychology: A Journal of Human Behavior, 30*(3/4), 38–46.

Tyler, R. (1949). *Basic principles of curriculum and instruction.* Chicago: University of Chicago Press.

UBEATS (2011). *Universal biomusic education achievement tier in science: Curriculum downloads.* Retrieved from http://performingarts.uncg.edu/ubeats

U.S. Census Bureau. (2012). *Most children younger than age 1 are minorities, census bureau reports.* Washington, DC: Government Printing Office. Retrieved from http://www.census.gov/newsroom/releases/archives/population/cb12-90.html

U.S. Department of Health and Human Services. (2006). *Your rights under section 504 of the rehabilitation act.* Washington, DC: Office of Civil Rights. Retrieved from http://www.hhs.gov/ocr/civilrights/resources/factsheets/504.pdf

U.S. Department of Health and Human Services. (n.d.) *2013 Poverty guidelines.* Washington DC: Office of the Assistant Secretary for Planning and Evaluation. Retrieved from http://aspe.hhs.gov/poverty/13poverty.cfm

Valerio, W. (n.d.). *The Gordon approach: Music learning theory.* Retrieved from http://www.allianceamm.org/resources_elem_Gordon.html

Villegas, A.M. (2007). Dispositions in teacher education: A look at social justice. *Journal of Teacher Education, 58*(5), 370–380. doi:10.1177/0022487107308419

Volz, M.D. (2005). Improvisation begins with exploration. *Music Educators Journal, 92*(1), 50–53. doi:10.2307/3400227

Vrangalova Z., & Savin-Williams, R.C. (2012). Mostly heterosexual and mostly gay/lesbian: Evidence for new sexual orientation identities. *Archives of Sexual Behavior, 41*(1), 85–101. doi:10.1007/s10508-012-9921-y

Vygotsky, L.S. (1978). *Mind in society: The development of higher mental processes.* Cambridge, MA: Harvard University Press.

Wallin, N. L, Merker, B., & Brown, S. (2000). *The origins of music.* Cambridge, MA: Massachusetts Institute of Technology.

Wasicsko, M. (2007). The perceptual approach to teacher dispositions: The effective teacher as an effective person. In M. E. Diez & J. Raths (Eds.), *Dispositions in teacher education* (pp. 55–91). Charlotte, NC: Information Age Publishing.

Watson, B. (2009). What is education? The inhibiting effect of three agendas in schooling. *Journal of Beliefs and Values: Studies in Religion and Education, 30*(2), 133–144. doi:10.1080/13617670903175022

Watson, J.B. (1925). *Behaviorism.* New York: W.W. Norton.

Weiner, B. (1979). A theory of motivation for some classroom experiences. *Journal of Educational Psychology, 71*(1), 3–25. doi:10.1037/0022-0663.71.1.3

Weiner, B. (1984). Principles for a theory of student motivation and their application within an attributional framework. In R. Ames & C. Ames (Eds.), *Research on motivation in education: Student motivation* (Vol. 1. pp. 15–38). New York: Academic Press.

Weiner, B. (1986). *An attributional theory of motivation and emotion.* New York: Springer.

Welch, G. F., Purves, R., Hargreaves, D. J., & Marshall, N. (2010). Reflections on the "Teacher Identities in Music Education" [TIME] Project. *Action, Criticism, and Theory for Music Education, 9*(2), 11–32. Retrieved from http://act.maydaygroup.org/articles/Welch9_2.pdf

Wesolowski, B. (2012). Understanding and developing rubrics for music performance assessment. *Music Educators Journal, 98*(3), 36–42. doi:10.1177/0027432111432524

Westphal, F.W. (1989). *Guide to teaching woodwinds.* (5th ed.). Dubuque, IA: Wm. C. Brown.

Wiggins, J.H. (1989). Composition as a teaching tool. *Music Educators Journal, 75*(8), 35–38. doi:10.2307/3400295

Wiggins, J. (2001). *Teaching for musical understanding.* Boston: McGraw-Hill.

Williams, D.A. (2007). What are music educators doing and how well are we doing it? *Music Educators Journal, 94*(1), 18–23. doi:10.1177/002743210709400105

Winner, E. (1988). *The point of words: Children's understanding of metaphor and irony.* Cambridge, MA: Harvard University Press.

Wood, D.R., & Whitford, B.L., (2010). A look to the future. In B.L. Whitford & D.R. White (Eds.), *Teachers learning in community: Reaities and possibilities.* Albany, NY: SUNY Press.

Woodford, P.G. (2005). *Democracy and music education: Liberalism, ethics, and the politics of practice.* Bloomington, IN: Indiana University Press.

Woods, D. (1982). A model for curriculum construction in music. *Music Educators Journal, 68*(9), 42–44. doi:10.2307/3396000

Woodward, S.C. (2005). Critical matters in early childhood music education. In D. Elliot (Ed.), *Praxial music education: Reflections and dialogues* (pp. 249–266). New York: Oxford University Press.

Woody, R.H. (2012). Playing by ear: Foundation or frill? *Music Educators Journal, 99*(2), 82–88. doi:10.1177/0027432112459199

Woolfolk, A.E. (2012). *Educational psychology* (12th ed.). Upper Saddle River, NJ: Pearson Education, Inc.

Yarbrough, C. (1975). Effect of magnitude of conductor behavior on students in selected mixed choruses. *Journal of Research in Music Education, 23*(2), 134–146. doi:10.2307/3345286

Young, A.J. (1997). I think, therefore I'm motivated: The relations among cognitive strategy use, motivational orientation and classroom perceptions over time. *Learning and Individual Differences, 9*, 249–283. doi:10.1016/S1041-6080(97)90009-1

Zeichner, K.M., & Liston, D.P. (1987). Teaching student teachers to reflect. *Harvard Educational Review, 57*(1), 23–48.

INDEX

Page numbers in **bold** refer to figures, page numbers in *italic* refer to tables.